Exploring Langu Frameworks

Proceedings of the ALTE Kraków Conference, July 2011

Exploring Language Frameworks

Proceedings of the ALTE Kraków Conference, July 2011

Edited by
Evelina D Galaczi
Principal Research and Validation Manager, University of Cambridge ESOL Examinations
and
Cyril J Weir
Powdrill Professor in English Language Acquisition, University of Bedfordshire
Director of the Centre for Research in English Language Learning and Assessment

CAMBRIDGE UNIVERSITY PRESS
Cambridge, New York, Melbourne, Madrid, Cape Town,
Singapore, São Paulo, Delhi, Mexico City

Cambridge University Press
The Edinburgh Building, Cambridge CB2 8RU, UK

www.cambridge.org
Information on this title: www.cambridge.org/9781107677029

© UCLES 2013

First published 2013

Printed and bound in the United Kingdom by the MPG Books Group

A catalogue record for this publication is available from the British Library

Library of Congress Cataloging-in-Publication Data
ALTE Conference (4th : 2011 : Kraków, Poland)
Exploring Language Frameworks : proceedings of the ALTE Kraków Conference,
July 2011 / edited by Evelina D. Galaczi and Cyril J. Weir.
    p. cm. -- (Studies in language testing)
 Includes bibliographical references and index.
 ISBN 978-1-107-67702-9 (pbk.)
 1. Language and languages--Study and teaching--Europe--Evaluation--
Congresses. 2. Language and languages--Ability testing--Europe--Congresses. 3.
Second language acquisition--Ability testing--Europe--Congresses. I. Dimitrova-
Galaczi, Evelina, 1967- II. Weir, Cyril J. III. Title.

P118.75A482 2011
418.0028'7--dc23
2012040146

ISBN 978-1-107-67702-9 Paperback

CAMBRIDGE ENGLISH
Language Assessment
Part of the University of Cambridge

with compliments

Cambridge English Language Assessment 1 Hills Road, Cambridge, CB1 2EU United Kingdom

✆ t: +44 1223 553355 ✆ f: +44 1223 460278 ✉ helpdesk@cambridgeenglish.org ✳ www.cambridgeenglish.org

Contents

Statistical procedures

Acknowledgements

We would like to express our thanks to all the volume contributors for developing and writing up their original presentations given at the ALTE Kraków Conference in July 2011, and for their willingness to make subsequent revisions in line with our editorial suggestions.

The volume could not have reached publication without the professional, technological and administrative assistance of various staff members based at Cambridge ESOL including: John Savage, Sally Downes and Carrie Warren. Most of all, we would like to thank Martin Nuttall in the ALTE Secretariat, who went beyond the call of duty to respond to our queries. We are grateful to all of them for their support throughout the production process.

Finally, the publishers are grateful to the copyright holders for permission to use the copyright material reproduced in this book: Nick Saville for the use of his Figure 'Stages of the migrant's 'journey'', previously published in issue 6 of *Language Assessment Quarterly* (2009); Neil Jones for the use of the Figure 'ESLC test development process' from SurveyLang's *First European Survey on Language Competences: Technical Report* (2012); WIDA for the use of Figure 1 on page 109; *The Japan Times* for the use of the article in Figure 8 on page 148; Cambridge University Press for the use of the CEFR phonological grid from the *Common European Framework of Reference for Languages: Learning, Teaching and Assessment* (2001); the Interagency Language Roundtable for excerpts from the Skill Level Descriptions for Speaking and Oral Proficiency Interviews; and Cambridge Michigan Language Assessments (CAMLA) for excerpts from *Spaan Fellow Working Papers in Second or Foreign Language Assessment* Volume 2 (2004).

Series Editors' note

ALTE, the Association of Language Testers in Europe, includes many of the world's leading language assessment bodies among its 33 members. Together with over 50 affiliates, ALTE members represent the testing of 26 European languages. Founded in 1990 by the universities of Salamanca and Cambridge, ALTE has grown to become one of the most important bodies within the language assessment profession. ALTE celebrated 20 years of achievement with the ALTE 4th International Conference in Kraków, Poland in July 2011, providing a fitting finale to this important milestone for the association.

In its work to promote common standards and the transnational recognition of language skills certification, ALTE has done much to encourage quality and fairness in language testing. The development of ALTE's Code of Practice and Quality Management System are key highlights in the organisation's history, as are the previous ALTE conferences held in Cambridge, Berlin and Barcelona. ALTE Kraków 2011 provided an opportunity to review these and other achievements, and to look forward to future initiatives that will further support multilingualism and professional development.

ALTE Kraków 2011 was hosted by the Jagiellonian University and built upon the success of the three previous ALTE international conferences: the first, held in Barcelona in July 2001, hosted by the Generalitat de Catalunya, on the theme of 'European Language Testing in a Global Context' to celebrate the European Year of Languages; the second, held in Berlin in May 2005, hosted by the Goethe-Institut, on the theme of 'Language Assessment in a Multilingual Context' to support the 50th Anniversary of the European Cultural Convention; and the third, held in Cambridge in April 2008, hosted by University of Cambridge ESOL Examinations (Cambridge ESOL), which focused on the theme of 'The Social and Educational Impact of Language Assessment'. Edited proceedings from these events were published as Volumes 18, 27 and 31 in the now well-established and highly regarded *Studies in Language Testing* series.

The theme of the ALTE 4th International Conference – 'The Impact of Language Frameworks on Assessment, Learning and Teaching, viewed from the perspectives of Policies, Procedures and Challenges' – reflected the growing importance attached to the use of frameworks in language testing practice and policy making.

ALTE international conferences are among the largest multilingual events for the global language assessment community. The 2011 conference was no exception, with over 100 presenters, and plenary and keynote speakers representing some of the leading voices in the field, including Professor Lyle Bachman, Professor of Applied Linguistics at the University of California, and Professor Elana Shohamy, Chair of the Language Education Programme at the School of Education, Tel Aviv University.

Well over 300 delegates attended from over 50 countries and regions around the world. It was also a multilingual event, with presentations in five of the many different languages represented at the conference, and it provided an opportunity for participants to hear influential voices, discuss key issues and meet colleagues from a variety of different backgrounds.

One of the highlights of the conference was the LAMI (Language Assessment for Migration and Integration) Forum, held under the auspices of the Secretary General of the Council of Europe, Mr Thorbjørn Jagland. The theme of the forum – language testing and access – continued the discussions ALTE has been engaged in for a number of years relating to language testing in European migration policy but with a focus this time on the notion of access, in its literal and figurative meanings, and the implications for assessment. In recent years, increasing migration has led to more and more countries placing a greater emphasis on language ability for those wishing to apply for citizenship or as a requirement for obtaining a visa to first enter a country to study, work or for family reasons. These recent developments clearly have important ethical and political implications with concerns of possible unfair discrimination related to issues of access, and in this context the forum contributed to the ongoing discussions about the role of language assessment for migration purposes by bringing together key stakeholders including policy makers, language educators and language testers.

The ALTE conference marked another important stage in ALTE's development since it was originally founded with eight members in 1990, primarily to work on common levels of proficiency and common standards for the language testing process. Europe thrives on diversity and it is the need to respect and value this diversity while at the same time trying to find common ground that binds us together. The event in Kraków was a great opportunity for delegates to participate in a conference that reflects the diversity of Europe and the importance we all place in languages, language learning, the certification of language competence and the significance of the Common European Framework of Reference for languages in the development of plurilingualism and intercultural competences. But improving mutual understanding is equally important in the wider global context. The event in Kraków was a gathering of assessment professionals focusing not only on professional matters in our field but also engaging positively in debate on language in a social, economic and political context. If our voices are to be heard then we need to participate positively. We also need the capacity to see things from a number of perspectives and in organising this conference, one of the main aims was to allow for the divergence of views, opinions and perceptions in order to help this process of building mutual understanding.

ALTE provides a forum where assessment professionals can work together effectively and there are two particular projects where ALTE members have been working together successfully in recent years. The first is in relation to the survey of language competences in Europe. The survey was first mooted in March 2002, as part of a European Council strategy to 'improve the mastery of basic skills, in particular by teaching at least two foreign languages from a very early age'. Invitations to tender were issued in mid-2007 and SurveyLang, a consortium made up largely of ALTE members and led by Cambridge ESOL, was finally confirmed as the successful bidder in February 2008. The survey provides information on the general level of foreign language knowledge (in five languages: Italian, French, German, Spanish and English) of the pupils in 32 EU Member States and other partici-pating countries. It provides strategic information to policy makers, teachers and learners in all surveyed countries and it is anticipated that the collected data from the survey will help policy makers, teachers and practitioners to take decisions about how to improve foreign language teaching methods and thus the performance of pupils in foreign languages. This is an enormously challenging but also potentially extremely useful project.

ALTE members are also working increasingly with national minis-tries of education to help provide high-quality language assessment. The Lingua 2000 project in Italy was a highly successful example of this work some years ago when the Italian government made great use of international language certification to help in the learning and teaching of languages in Italian schools. More recently, ALTE members – the Cervantes Institute, the Goethe-Institut and Cambridge ESOL – have been working with the French Ministry of Education to provide language testing materials that meet inter-national standards and are linked to the CEFR.

While seeking opportunities for effective collaboration and conformity to standards of good practice, respecting and understanding our differences is a key aspect of ALTE's work. To advance these aims, ALTE has developed guidelines for the writing of test materials, ways of describing the content of examinations so that they can be compared more effectively, ALTE has built a framework of examinations that allows users to see how the different exams relate to each other and, importantly, members of ALTE have defined a multilingual glossary of language testing terms (developed and published in 10 languages in the late 1990s and now available in numerous additional languages). For instance, the latest edition was published in Basque in 2007, clearly demonstrating the sustainability of ALTE's work. Much of this work has been supported by funds provided by the European Commission through its Lingua programme, and much of it has been done in collabora-tion with the Council of Europe, which has played and continues to play such a significant role in language policy in Europe and now through the CEFR far beyond. All of this work is available on the ALTE website or from individual members of ALTE.

ALTE published its first international code of practice for language testing in 1994 and much work on refining this concept and documenting principles of good practice took place in the 1990s. Between 2000 and 2002 ALTE set up a Code of Practice Working Group which developed a Quality Management System leading to a Quality Auditing System that was piloted in 2005 and 2006 and introduced in 2007. ALTE has now audited most of its members on at least one of the examinations they provide. As a consequence of these developments, membership of ALTE is now based on demonstrating, through the Auditing System, that an organisation's examinations do conform to internationally recognised systems in a transparent and open way.

ALTE is in the process of developing web forums in English, French, German and Spanish in the first instance and we anticipate that the number of language forums will increase over the next few years. Within these, members will have access to the ALTE network, training materials, publications and training courses offered by ALTE throughout Europe on a relatively frequent basis.

One of ALTE's main aims is to share ideas and know-how, and events such as the ALTE 4th International Conference in Kraków provide an ideal opportunity for language teaching and testing professionals from around the world to meet and to pool expertise, and to consider together how best to resolve some of the important challenges facing society today. Not surprisingly, plans are already well in hand for ALTE's 5th International Conference to be held in Paris in April 2014.

As will be apparent, the conference papers presented here represent only a selection of the many excellent presentations made in Kraków which reflect a wide range of topics and concerns; they provide a flavour of the key themes addressed at the conference. The Introduction to this volume by Evelina Galaczi and Cyril Weir helps to highlight and summarise for readers the various strands that resonated throughout the conference, and points to important implications for the language testing community.

Cyril J Weir
Michael Milanovic

April 2012

Introduction

Evelina D Galaczi and Cyril J Weir

The term 'framework' and related synonyms such as 'guidelines' and 'standards' have acquired frequent usage in language testing debates in the last decade. We now often refer to the Common European Framework of Reference for languages (CEFR), the Interagency Language Roundtable (ILR) scale, the ACTFL Guidelines, to name but a few tools used in the description of language proficiency. We also talk about frameworks for test validation, for test fairness, for teaching, for accreditation, etc. With the increased influence of frameworks in the second/foreign language context it is important to take some time to consider their role in more detail. Thus the aim of this volume is to explore the role of language frameworks on assessment, learning and teaching. It does so through a collection of 21 edited papers based on presentations given at the 4th International Conference of the Association of Language Testers in Europe (ALTE) held in Kraków in July 2011. The 4th ALTE Conference came at a time when the role of language assessment in social and educational contexts is growing, its importance in national and local policies is increasing, and its role in helping to regulate international mobility and access to higher education and employment is expanding. The conference provided a valuable shared forum and a welcome opportunity to expand the discussion and debate about the role of language frameworks in a number of contexts. With its focus on the influence of frameworks in a range of contexts, this volume also continues the themes discussed in *Language Testing Matters* (volume 31 in the *Studies in Language Testing* series, edited by Taylor and Weir).

The selected papers represent a small subset of the many excellent presentations made at the ALTE conference. They have been chosen as representative of three core strands addressed during the conference. The papers have been grouped thematically, but it must be noted that the groupings are not mutually exclusive; indeed, we often saw in our editorial discussions that a number of alternative categories would also have been possible.

Section One deals with frameworks in *social contexts* and focuses on their role in migration and multilingual policy and practice. The two papers by Van Avermaet and Rocca and by Grego Bolli offer us useful insights into migration policy in a number of European countries and provide a valuable summary of the Language Assessment for Migration and Integration (LAMI) Forum organised by ALTE members and held at the ALTE 2011 conference under the auspices of the Secretary General of the Council of Europe, Mr Thorbjørn Jagland. **Piet Van Avermaet** and **Lorenzo Rocca**'s paper continues the discussions that ALTE has been engaged in for a number of years now, notably at previous forums in Berlin (2005 and 2009), Cambridge (2008), Rome (2010) and Munich (2011), which have considered the growing prominence and controversial role of language testing in European migration policy. The authors discuss the increase of migration in recent years, which has led to more and more countries placing a greater emphasis on using language tests for integration and citizenship purposes or as a requirement for obtaining a visa to first enter a country. They survey these recent developments from an ethical and political angle and argue that if language tests become a key discriminator in determining entry, it is crucial that any test used is fair and fit for purpose so that particular groups are not unfairly denied access at any stage in their journey as migrants. The LAMI forum was an opportunity to discuss some of the key questions involved both conceptually and through case studies in a number of countries: the United Kingdom, Belgium and Italy, and to explore how a framework could help in understanding the issues involved in language testing and access. **Giuliana Grego Bolli** builds upon Van Avermaet and Rocca's paper by discussing in more detail the latest migration policies in Italy and situating her discussion within the context of current and historical political, economic, social, cultural and educational issues. The author stresses that to deal with all of these issues effectively, we need a multidimensional approach which is supported by interdisciplinary expertise and coordinated actions, and argues that social sciences should play a fundamental role in proposing approaches and models functional to the management of migration processes. European institutions should consider the importance of introducing shared frameworks in the context of language and migration, as such frameworks could provide concrete and consistent guidelines to help institutions to deal with the different dimensions involved in a coherent and coordinated way.

The next set of papers in Section One shifts the focus to multilingual policies and projects initiated by the Council of Europe and the European Commission. In his opening paper **Waldemar Martyniuk** provides a detailed overview of the latest initiatives of the Council of Europe in support of an inclusive, plurilingual and intercultural approach to language education. The author reviews relevant policy documents and presents a range of tools already available or currently under development by the Language Policy Division and the European Centre for Modern Languages. He also discusses the rationale behind the next, fourth medium-term programme of the activities of the European Centre for Modern Languages (scheduled for 2012–15) which aims at facilitating European co-operation on the implementation of the new concept of language education. The next two papers deal with practical aspects of surveying multilingualism in different national contexts. **Paweł**

Poszytek's paper shows how a pan-European project – the Language Rich Europe project – is creating a framework for the investigation of the adherence of national multilingual policy and practice to European recommendations and resolutions. The paper focuses on the research tool used – the European Index of Multilingual Policies and Practices – and presents the background of this innovative research project which spans a broad spectrum of national policies and practices in formal education, and also in the business sector, the media and the public sphere. The paper also discusses the construct underlying the research tool and explores challenging issues regarding validity of the research. In the last paper in this section, **Michaela Perlmann-Balme** focuses on the European Survey on Language Competences, which is a major initiative by the European Commission to support the development of language learning policies across Europe. The purpose of the survey is to provide participating countries with comparable data on foreign language competence and knowledge about good practice in language learning. The author describes one of the fundamental stages of the project, which involved the development of language test tasks at four CEFR levels (A1 to B2), with the aim to create items that were as similar to each other and at the same time as true to their respective cultural and linguistic origin as possible. She further provides a useful discussion of the considerations which need to be taken into account when creating test tasks and items of identical difficulty across a range of languages without applying a method of mere translation.

  Section Two of the volume addresses the use of frameworks in *educational contexts*. In his opening paper **Neil Jones** provides a clear and thought-provoking overview of issues to be considered when conceptualising an inclusive framework for languages. The author takes us through key considerations in language learning (as first, second or foreign languages) which result in different profiles of language ability, but can be described through differing configurations of the same parameters: informal learning, formal language knowledge, social and academic contexts of use, and cognitive models. He argues that we need an inclusive theoretical framework to encompass all three kinds. The CEFR is an instance of a more general framework for foreign language learning, teaching and assessment. Jones argues that by adding parameters and illustrations it can be extended without challenging its validity for that original purpose. Doing so should enable language assessment to address many linguistically complex educational contexts, and contribute to improving educational outcomes for language learners of all kinds.

  In the next paper **Brian North** and **Elzbieta Jarosz** focus on the implementation of the CEFR in teacher-based assessment and outline a scheme for CEFR Certification recently introduced in EAQUALS (Evaluation and Accreditation of Quality in Language Services). The authors describe and discuss the 'EAQUALS Certificate of CEFR Achievement' scheme, which further develops procedures from the Council of Europe's *Manual* for relating examinations to the CEFR (2009), adapting them to the school context. They focus on specific elements of this accreditation and discuss the different stages of accreditation involved. In addition to explaining the rationale and procedures of the scheme, the authors also discuss some of the main problems inherent in school-based assessment of CEFR levels and the way in which the scheme is designed to address these issues.

The next paper shifts the focus beyond Europe to Japan and the CEFR-J – an adaptation of the original CEFR to language teaching, learning and assessment in Japanese contexts. **Masashi Negishi**, **Tomoko Takada** and **Yukio Tono** provide us with a progress report on the development of the CEFR-J. They discuss the CEFR's framework compatibility with English language teaching in Japan, and argue for the need for modifications in Japanese contexts. The authors present an interim report of the project and its stages: the compilation of the preliminary versions of the CEFR-J, the validation phase, and the pilot phase for using the revised CEFR-J at school. Their paper focuses predominantly on the first two stages of the project and also describes accompanying resources for implementing the CEFR-J into educational contexts in Japan, such as the CEFR-J wordlist and the Can Do descriptor database. The authors also provide a useful discussion of the potential impact of the CEFR-J on Japan's foreign language education policy.

In the next paper in this section, **Ursula Hehl** and **Nicole Kruczek** present an analysis of the impact of the CEFR on university language teaching practice, based on a comparison of two German university language centres and their application of the CEFR in course organisation, teaching and assessment. The authors outline general principles which need to be considered regarding course organisation and policies concerning placement and admittance to courses and the problems they pose, and address relevant questions such as how much course time students should be granted to take learners from one level to the next, and aspects of learner autonomy. The authors' discussion also focuses on teachers' knowledge about and implementation of the CEFR into their course practice and they argue that much remains to be done in terms of teacher training in order to ensure a more consistent understanding and application of the CEFR. The theme of developing assessment literacy and a more in-depth understanding of using frameworks is picked up in the final two papers in this section. In the first one, **Enrica Piccardo** focuses on the use of the CEFR by practitioners and argues that they often have only a partial knowledge of it and have difficulty integrating the CEFR into everyday practice. This is partially due, the author argues, to the lack of comprehensive training with regard to the principles and specifics of the CEFR. The paper overviews a four-year European project which aims to investigate the impact of the CEFR on the culture of evaluation in different contexts. The author discusses the data collected during the piloting phase of the project and explains how the project builds on these results in order to produce a tool to support teacher educators in building a more complex vision of language teaching, learning and assessment. Extending the concept of assessment literacy in the final paper in this section, **Marylin Kies** discusses the potential which frameworks such as the CEFR hold for facilitating communication, as they allow teachers, students, publishers, policy makers and examination boards to refer to common proficiency levels using a standard terminology. Kies discusses how institutional and professional test users may use frameworks as guidelines to decide which certification exams meet their requirements and focuses on three examples of frameworks: Weir's (2005) socio-cognitive validity framework which allows stakeholders to decide which exams are likely to provide trustworthy assessments, the Council of Europe's 2009 publication of their *Manual* relating language examinations to the CEFR, which allows users to judge the extent to which claims of linkage to the CEFR are substantiated, and the CEFR itself (Council of Europe 2001) or similar alternative proficiency frameworks which allow users to decide which exams assess the skills they require and which level of certification they should require.

Section Three of the volume focuses on the *practical issues* associated with the application of frameworks in test and scale development and validation. The section starts with a focus on rating scales and in the opening paper **David Horner** addresses the assessment of pronunciation, which, the author argues, has been inadequately dealt with by the CEFR. Horner examines the CEFR phonological control scale (2001:116) from the angle of intelligibility, accent and strain on the listener and proposes an alternative pronunciation scale which builds on the existing CEFR pronunciation scale, while addressing some of its shortcomings. He does so by developing a useful and comprehensive discussion of conceptual issues involved with the definition and assessment of pronunciation. In the next paper **Katrin Wisniewski** focuses on scales for assessing fluency and presents a detailed analysis of the CEFR A2 level fluency descriptors with the aim of finding empirical evidence for the usefulness and adequacy of the current descriptors. The author argues that the appearance of some aspects of the CEFR A2 fluency level description seems dependent on the task type and the target language, and also questions the construct underlying the CEFR fluency performance descriptors since there are concepts in the scale which relate not to fluency but to other aspects of second language competence. She presents valuable empirical evidence of key fluency variables which were found to play a role at this proficiency level in her research study and which could be used to guide the assessment of fluency. The next paper, by **Bart Deygers, Koen Van Gorp, Lucia Luyten** and **Sien Joos** addresses issues involved with rating scale design through a comparative study of two analytic rating scales. The authors focus their discussion on the Certificate of Dutch as a Foreign Language (Certificaat Nederlands als Vreemde Taal, CNaVT) and describe the development of a new polytomous rating scale which incorporates both CEFR guidance and content expert judgements. In the paper the authors provide a useful comparison of a dichotomous and a polytomous scale based on qualitative and quantitative data and provide interesting insights about the statistical robustness, authenticity and validity of the two scales. In the next paper, we move to the conceptual issue of the 'native speaker' as a criterion used in some frameworks and associated rating scales. **Rachel L Brooks** and **Beth Mackey** address the issue of the 'well educated native speaker' in the Interagency Language Roundtable (ILR) Skill Level Descriptions. The 'native speaker' concept, which has been called into question by second language acquisition and language testing practitioners, is an important consideration for scale developers and users. Following a discussion of the definition of a native speaker, the authors contextualise the issues surrounding the role and characteristics of the 'well-educated native speaker' within the ILR Skill Level Descriptions and discuss how the ILR scale, which is functional in nature, is used by the US Government to test native and non-native speakers of a language.

The next set of papers in this section provide useful insights into the role of frameworks in test development and validation. The first two papers address the use of translation and mediation tasks, a relatively under-researched area in language testing. **Ágnes Dévény** addresses the issue of whether foreign language mediation is an independent language skill and whether it can be considered a legitimate language examination subtest. She focuses on language examinations in Hungary, which often include a mediation task, and argues that foreign language mediation is an independent language skill which can be measured by specific criteria and which contributes to a more complex assessment of the test takers' language proficiency. In the next paper **Maria Brau** looks at the assessment of translation ability used by the United States Federal Bureau of Investigation. The author focuses on the ILR Translation Performance Skills Levels Descriptions which define the required tasks by characterising the source texts that an individual is required to deal successfully with at a given level. Based on these characterisations, the Federal Bureau of Investigation has developed testing instruments to assess translation performance. This paper discusses the development of the translation test and reviews the ensuing test validation investigations. The next paper, by **Marianne Nikolov** and **Gábor Szabó**, moves back to Hungary and to young language learners/test takers. The authors argue that it is necessary to shift from testing *of* learning to testing *for* learning, a key issue in the young learner classroom. Their paper presents the first results of a large-scale study involving learners aged 6–13 in Hungary, which aimed to develop, pilot, and validate new diagnostic tests for young learners in the four basic skills and to place the tests on a scale of difficulty corresponding to the A1 and A2 levels of the CEFR. The authors describe the data collection procedures and discuss the evidence which was gathered about the performance of the tests.

The final three papers are joined by the common theme of the role of statistical procedures in quality assurance. **Thomas Eckes**'s paper focuses on the investigation of differential item functioning (DIF), which plays a key role in frameworks on test fairness and test validity. In the paper the author describes an investigation in the context of the Reading and Listening sections of the Test of German as a Foreign Language (*Test Deutsch als Fremdsprache*, TestDaF) and through four different procedures for DIF analysis. He provides a useful discussion of the results in terms of theoretical and methodological issues. In the next paper **Gudrun Klein** focuses on the role of background variables and investigates their role in a language test for immigration in Germany, the Deutsch-Test für Zuwanderer (DTZ), which assesses immigrants' German language skills at CEFR Levels A2 and B1. The paper ends with an argument that in the spirit of test fairness, offering specific groups of individuals intensified support in exam preparation may be advisable. The final paper in this section, by **Vahid Aryadoust** and **Christine C M Goh** explores the relative merits of two scaling models (cognitive diagnostic models and confirmatory factor analysis), which have been developed originally for psychological studies and have now been adapted into language assessment. Their paper presents a discussion of the relative merits of the two scaling models, as applied to the listening test of the Michigan English Language Assessment Battery (MELAB) and provides recommendations for their use in modelling second language (L2) listening.

We hope that the insights provided in this volume regarding the influence of language frameworks in a variety of social and educational contexts will be a valuable resource for anyone seeking to understand the policies, procedures and challenges encountered in the application of language frameworks and the interplay of theoretical insights and practical considerations.

Evelina D Galaczi
Cyril J Weir

July 2012

Section One
Frameworks and social contexts

1 Language testing and access

Piet Van Avermaet
Centre for Diversity and Learning, University of Ghent, Belgium

Lorenzo Rocca
CVCL, University for Foreigners, Perugia, Italy

Abstract

This paper summarises the presentations, case studies and discussions of the Language Assessment for Migration and Integration (LAMI) Forum organised by Association of Language Testers in Europe (ALTE) members, held at the ALTE 4th International Conference in Kraków in July 2011 under the auspices of the Secretary General of the Council of Europe, Mr Thorbjørn Jagland.

The forum continued the discussions that ALTE has been engaged in for a number of years now, notably at previous forums in Berlin and Cambridge in 2005 and 2008, respectively, as well as at other events in Berlin (September 2009), Rome (May 2010) and Munich (March 2011) regarding the growing prominence of language testing in European migration policy. Having to demonstrate language proficiency as part of the process of entering a country to work or study is nothing new but in recent years, increasing migration has led to more and more countries placing a greater emphasis on using language tests for integration and citizenship purposes or as a requirement for obtaining a visa to first enter a country.

These recent developments clearly have important ethical and political implications with concerns of possible unfair discrimination related to issues of *access*. Although in terms of migration, access primarily means the opportunity to enter, or 'get into', a particular country, in reality, this also means access to many other aspects of everyday life such as education, increased job opportunities, health care, social welfare and human rights, and thus 'getting on' in life in the host country. Furthermore, there is also the danger that certain students may not be able to prepare adequately to take a test in the first place because they cannot access suitable tuition.

In general, educational assessment should be seen in a positive light since it helps structure learning, provides evidence of ability and gives a sense of achievement. However, if language tests become a key discriminator in determining entry, it is crucial that any test used is fair and fit for purpose so that particular groups are not unfairly denied access at any stage in their journey as migrants.

Given the ethical and political considerations now linked to language testing, as well as the social and political pressures to control migration and promote integration, it is essential that those bodies using language assessment in the context of migration fully understand the implications. The LAMI forum was an opportunity to discuss some of these issues and to explore how a framework could help in understanding the issues involved in language testing and access.

Such a framework will help tease apart the social, political and educational considerations and enable clearer thinking about the appropriate uses of language assessment. This may also lead to a better understanding of the ways in which different sorts of tests might be used effectively at different stages of the migrant's journey.

Part 1 Framing the context

The European perspective – the plurilingual and intercultural approach of the Council of Europe

The Council of Europe (CoE) is an intergovernmental organisation, set up in 1949 by 10 member states; it currently has 47 member states and is based in Strasbourg, France. The guiding principles of the CoE are democracy, human rights and the rule of law, and the issues of human rights and the legal status of migrants and refugees in Europe have been important challenges for the CoE for many years. This is clearly reflected in many of its conventions and recommendations, such as Article 8 of *The European Convention on Human Rights* (1953), the *European Convention on the Legal Status of Migrant Workers* (1977) and the *European Social Charter* (1996) which are central to the CoE's policy making *vis-à-vis* migration issues.

In 2008 the CoE organised the Conference of European Ministers responsible for Migration Affairs (held in Kiev) and in 2010 the Parliamentary Assembly of the Council of Europe (PACE) adopted *Recommendation 1917 on migrants and refugees: a continuing challenge for the Council of Europe* (2010b).

The CoE is also very clear in the way in which it defines the integration of migrants in host countries. In its Annual Report of 2008, the European Commission against Racism and Intolerance (ECRI) noted that 'successful integration is a two-way process, a process of mutual recognition, which bears no relation to assimilation' (2008:12). Similarly, in the *White Paper on Intercultural Dialogue "Living Together as Equals in Dignity"* integration is defined as 'a two-sided process and as the capacity of people to live together with full respect for the dignity of each individual' (Council of Europe 2008b:11).

In view of these comments, it is evident that the basic guiding principles for the CoE are respect for migrants' human rights and dignity, and the organisation has the following objectives in relation to migration:

- to facilitate the exchange of information and discussion on language policies for integration
- to examine how the principles contained in the Common European Framework of Reference for languages (CEFR) can best support the requirements of member states
- to offer guidance on ensuring quality in language training/testing and responding to needs.

For the CoE, languages are seen as pivotal to its policy. On the one hand, the CoE emphasises the importance of language competence since it provides the necessary basis for intercultural dialogue, social cohesion, democratic citizenship, and economic progress. On the other hand, in positioning languages so centrally in their policy, the CoE promotes and supports linguistic diversity in member states, the plurilingualism of citizens, and plurilingual and intercultural education. Plurilingualism is seen as the ability to develop skills in and use more than one language as a natural, innate potential of the human mind. The language repertoires of all people need support to develop fully since 'all are entitled to develop a degree of communicative ability in a number of languages over their lifetime in accordance with their needs'(Sheils 2008:257).

With regard to language, the CoE supports a clear set of inclusive principles for plurilingual and intercultural education:

- a good-quality education is a pre-requisite for social cohesion, democratic citizenship and intercultural dialogue
- well-developed language ability is a basis for and an outcome of good-quality education
- plurilingual and intercultural education aims to support the development of appropriate cultural and language competences as a necessary basis for full participation in educational processes
- to take into account and make use of all cultural and language competences available for the learners and to develop those required for their educational success
- a coherent approach to all languages present at school.

In order to put plurilingual policy and its underlying principles into practice, the CoE has developed a set of policy instruments, tools and initiatives (all these documents can be found on www.coe.int/lang):

- *Guide for the Development of Language Education Policies in Europe* (accompanied by Reference Studies) (2003)

- *Common European Framework of Reference for Languages: Learning Teaching and Assessment* (CEFR) (2001)
- *European Language Portfolio* (ELP)
- *Autobiography of Intercultural Encounters*
- *Language Education Policy Profiles*
- *Guide for the Development and Implementation of Curricula for Plurilingual and Intercultural Education* (2010a).

Furthermore, with a specific focus on adult migrants, the CoE (2008a) has written a concept paper on the role of languages in policies for the integration of adult migrants. Along with this paper a set of thematic studies have been developed:

- the CEFR and the development of policies for the integration of adult migrants
- quality assurance in the provision of language education and training for adult migrants – guidelines and options
- language tests for social cohesion and citizenship – an outline for policy makers (Association of Language Testers in Europe (ALTE) Authoring Group)
- language learning, teaching and assessment and the integration of adult migrants
- tailoring language provision and requirements to the needs and capacities of adult migrants.

In 2008 and 2010 the CoE conducted a survey (Extramiana and Van Avermaet 2010) in member states on language requirements for adult migrants. The objective was to get an overview of the main developments and trends concerning language requirements, including tests and language training. These surveys built on previous surveys that were conducted in co-operation with ALTE members in 2002 and 2007 (ibid), and a rapid increase in the number of integration courses and tests has been observed over the years.

However, although the differences between the 2008 and 2010 surveys are limited, a large variation between countries in terms of regulations and conditions, proficiency level required and sanctions can be seen. Although by 2010 language requirements had been established in slightly more countries than in 2008 and the required level of proficiency had increased in a few cases, for example from A2 to B1, a noticeable change was the fact that language requirements prior to entry are increasingly being applied and an interest in following this route is growing in other countries. Furthermore, in some countries it is still the case that no language courses are offered by the government and this implies that candidates have to go to the private sector for such courses and often have to pay for them.

The perspective of the testing community

In order to tease apart the social, political and educational considerations associated with the notion of access and its implications for language assessment, Saville (2009a) has proposed a frame of reference which can assist language test developers in addressing issues related to language assessment and migration more effectively.

Saville uses the metaphor of a 'migration journey' to define six key areas of migration. Saville's schematic diagram (see Figure 1) helps to clarify the stages of the 'journey', from pre-arrival and arrival in a country to application for citizenship which a potential migrant may go through, and provides six points of reference which can help test developers to focus with greater clarity on the use of assessments in relation to other important considerations *vis-à-vis* migrants.

The six stages that Saville distinguishes are: Pre-entry; Arrival and Entry; Extension of Stay; Settlement; Application for Naturalisation; and Granting of Citizenship. For each of these stages Saville describes the reasons for migration, the requirements, rights and responsibilities relevant to each stage of the process, and the consequences and impacts that may arise if the rules are breached.

Linguistic requirements may be set at each of the stages identified by Saville, so in each case the migrant is a potential test taker. It is essential then that the right test is developed. This means that the test has to be fit for the specific purpose for which it is intended and that it has to meet professional standards which take into account not only technical and practical concerns but also ethical concerns. In particular, the test developer has to ensure that the testing system is appropriate for the high-stakes decisions that will be made based on it, and that the test is suitable for the intended test taker groups in terms of content, level, mode of delivery, etc.

In order for this to be achieved, those involved in the development of assessment tools for migrants have to answer the following questions:

- **Who** is going to be tested (i.e. the candidate profiles)?
- What **features of the language** will be covered and what is the justification for this?
- What **proficiency level** (e.g. CEFR level) is realistic for different groups?
- **When** and **where** will the testing take place – the **venues and physical conditions**?
- How will the **administration** be conducted and how will the **integrity** of the test be assured?
- How will the **results** be issued and verified?
- How will the results be used and what **decisions** will rest on the outcomes?

- How will **data** be collected in order to validate the test (e.g. estimate its reliability)?
- How will the test's **impact** on individuals, and on society more generally, be evaluated?

The central shaded area in Figure 1 exemplifies the main transition stages where permissions are usually needed and where regulations have to be followed. The left-hand column represents those migrants who are already settled and who may have acquired the right to bring other family members to join them; and the right-hand column indicates the rights and responsibilities relevant to each stage of the migrant's journey and the sanctions that may be imposed if the rules are broken.

It goes without saying that every test has to be valid, and this is especially important when the stakes are high, as in the case of migrants. Passing or failing a language test can determine whether a migrant can stay in the host country or whether he or she can obtain or be denied citizenship.

Saville (2011) distinguishes two main issues of fairness: test integrity and test impact. The first focuses mainly on technical issues, e.g. to eliminate fraud. The issue of test impact emphasises the importance of finding out about effects and consequences. As an example of test integrity Saville (ibid) refers to parameter 6 of the ALTE minimum standards: 'All centres are selected to administer your examination according to clear, transparent, established procedures, and have access to regulations about how to do so.' Other examples of test integrity are that test providers have to put measures in place to minimise the risk of identity substitution and that measures have to be implemented concerning fraud prevention: e.g. test reports with an embedded photographic image of the candidate and online results verification and/or security features to prevent tampering and forgery of results.

With regard to test administration Saville (2011) argues that every test provider has to ask the following questions:

1. Is there a sufficient network of testing centres?
2. Are the test centres checked and regularly monitored?
3. Are the staff suitably vetted and trained?
4. Is there a high level of security and confidentiality throughout the whole process?
5. Are the physical conditions suitable (including arrangements for candidates with special requirements)?

If these questions are not properly addressed, the implications of ignoring quality assurance in the test administration system can be enormous. Among other issues, there is the predictability of test content; cheating, malpractice and impostors; inaccurate and non-verifiable results and biased, discriminatory tests. In essence this means that the test is then unfair to everyone.

Figure 1 Stages of the migrant's 'journey' (Saville 2009a)

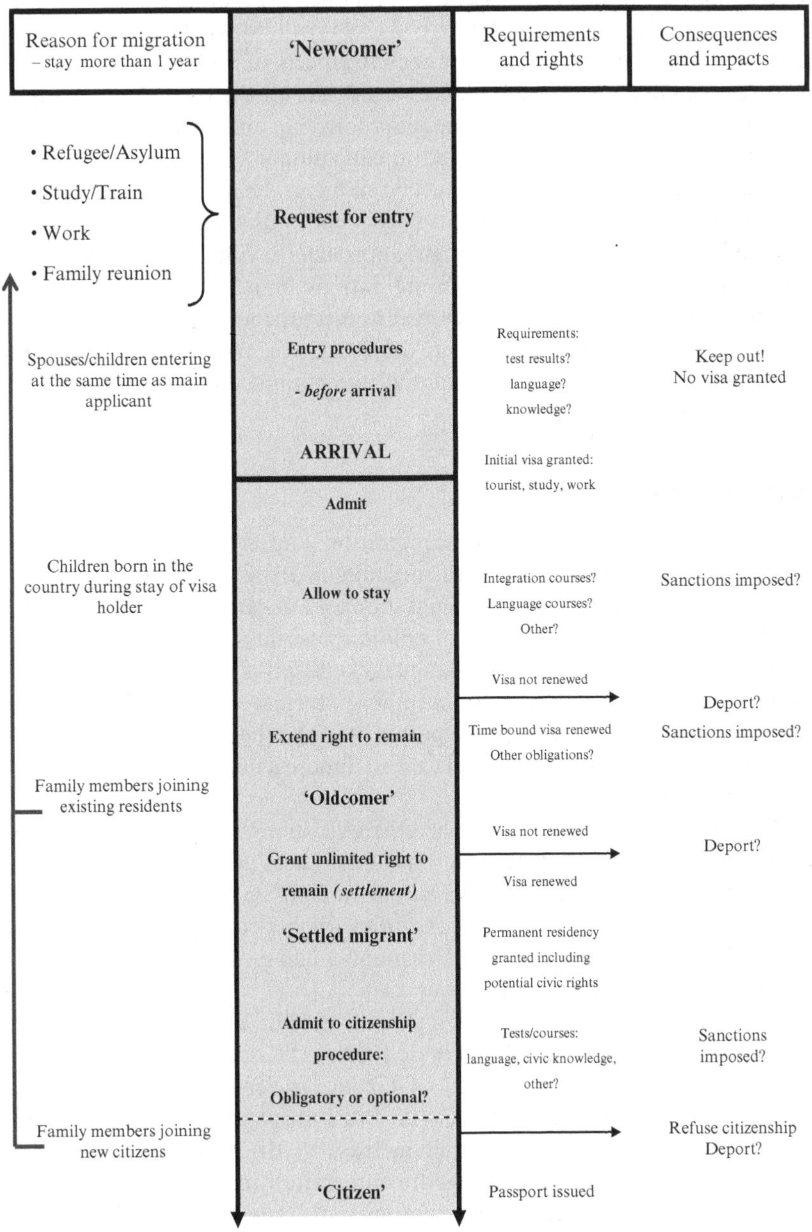

Reason for migration – stay more than 1 year	'Newcomer'	Requirements and rights	Consequences and impacts
• Refugee/Asylum • Study/Train • Work • Family reunion	**Request for entry**		
Spouses/children entering at the same time as main applicant	**Entry procedures** *- before* **arrival**	Requirements: test results? language? knowledge?	Keep out! No visa granted
	ARRIVAL	Initial visa granted: tourist, study, work	
	Admit		
Children born in the country during stay of visa holder	**Allow to stay**	Integration courses? Language courses? Other?	Sanctions imposed?
		Visa not renewed ⟶	Deport?
	Extend right to remain	Time bound visa renewed Other obligations?	Sanctions imposed?
Family members joining existing residents	**'Oldcomer'**		
		Visa not renewed ⟶	Deport?
	Grant unlimited right to remain *(settlement)*	Visa renewed	
	'Settled migrant'	Permanent residency granted including potential civic rights	
	Admit to citizenship procedure:	Tests/courses: language, civic knowledge, other?	Sanctions imposed?
	Obligatory or optional?		
Family members joining new citizens		⟶	Refuse citizenship Deport?
	'Citizen'	Passport issued	

Investigating impact is integral to validation and reviewing whether a test fits its specific purpose is an essential component in establishing the usefulness of an assessment system. This is consistent with Messick's views of validity (1989, 1996), especially 'consequential aspects of validity'. Impact also includes the effects and consequences a test has on the immediate learning context and on contexts beyond the classroom, e.g. on an individual's career or the life chances of migrants, and in educational systems and in society more generally. Impact research must be an integral part of a framework for developing and validating examination systems for use in migration contexts.

By adopting an 'impact by design' approach (Saville 2009b:269) and by using impact research to guide future actions, more effective assessment policies and practices can be developed to meet the needs of education and society. This will ensure that tests are designed to promote learning and help learners achieve their life goals, and that they are not used to deny access to certain groups of migrants.

A critical perspective

Building on Saville's diagram of the migration 'journey' above, we can identify potential hurdles to access for migrants in terms of language requirements during the process of their migration and integration. Whether it is a question of entering the country; of obtaining permanent residency, getting a job, entering school, accessing (language) education programmes, getting a house on the housing market; or becoming a formal or virtual citizen of the country (integration, social participation, social cohesion) – in all of these cases, language conditions are in place and impose a hurdle to finally becoming accepted as a 'moral citizen'.

As noted above, on the basis of different surveys over time, there has been a proliferation of integration tests and courses across Europe through policy emulation. While an ALTE survey in 2002 showed that four out of 14 countries (29%) had language conditions for citizenship, the 2007 ALTE survey showed that five years later this number had grown to 11 out of the 18 countries (61%) involved in the survey.

Similarly, the 2008 and 2010 surveys conducted by La délégation générale à la langue française et aux langues de France (DGLFLF) and the Centre for Diversity and Learning (SDL) of Ghent University, on behalf of the Language Policy Division of the Council of Europe (Extramiana and Van Avermaet 2010), revealed a further increase in the number of countries setting stricter language conditions for integration in the host country. A comparable percentage (75%) of countries in 2008 as in 2010 had linguistic requirements as part of integration regulations. In 2008, 19% of the countries involved had language requirements prior to entry to the host country whereas this was 26% in 2010. While in 2008 57% of the countries involved indicated that they had language requirements for permanent residency, this was 69% in 2010. Seventy-six per cent of the countries had language requirements for citizenship in 2008 but of the 23 countries in 2010 that said they had language requirements of one kind or another, almost all of them (96%) indicated that they had language conditions for citizenship.

This leads to the key question of why so many countries have such strict integration policies in which language always plays a central role. The official discourse is that this facilitates the process of integration; strengthens social cohesion and social participation; increases migrants' access to the labour market and further education; and is seen as a lever to become a 'virtual' citizen of the nation. Independent of the critical reflections one can make with regard to these policies, the question is whether they have any impact. Do pre-entry language tests serve an integration objective? Do language tests (and integration requirements in general) enhance access to the labour market, to further education? And do 'language for integration tests' contribute to the process of social participation and cohesion?

Given the relative lack of social impact studies, it is difficult to give a comprehensive answer to these questions. Most of the studies that claim to look at the impact of the policies in place only look at the number of migrants attending language courses, taking language tests, the dropout rates and the numbers of candidates that passed or failed the tests. Although these findings are very important, they do not tell us anything about the impact on integration processes or on social participation itself.

An interesting study on the social impact of integration policies was recently conducted by the Integration and Naturalisation Tests: the new way to European Citizenship (INTEC) Project (Strik, Böcker, Luiten and van Oers 2010). This was a comparative study in nine member states of the EU on the national policies concerning integration and naturalisation tests and their effects on integration. The countries involved were Austria, Belgium, Denmark, France, Germany, Hungary, Latvia, the Netherlands and the UK. The methodology used included both an analysis of policy documents and regulations, and some 329 interviews with immigrants, language schools/education centres, public officials and non-governmental organisations (NGOs).

The main outcome of this study was very clear:

> This research, however, did not find any reason to promote the connection of the integration requirements with the granting of a certain legal status (admission, permanent residence or citizenship). This connection is not necessary to motivate migrants, and it inevitably leads to the exclusion of certain groups from a secure legal status (Strik et al 2010).

The report went on to suggest that not only would this exclusion hamper the integration of such groups rather than promote it but would also negatively impact family life and conflict with the right to family reunion. It recommended that the policy should be reconsidered. The report also concluded that language and integration policy had a limited effect on the actual integration of migrants and that such policies should also take into account other factors such as a receptive society, equal opportunities in the labour market and efforts to fight discrimination. Van Avermaet (2012), in a small scale social impact study in Flanders, also found little evidence for the impact of integration policies in integration processes and social participation.

And yet we can observe that language requirements have become stricter and stricter in most countries. This can perhaps be explained by the fact that most EU countries feel a strong pressure to control migration flows, and to exclude potential immigrants with low educational and professional skills. Another explanation can be found in the monolingual ideologies that still strongly prevail in Europe. The official national language is seen as a powerful index of group belonging and its mastery as pivotal for the well-being of the national order. The actual integration policies (official language and the norms and values of the host country) are sold as common sense, as self-evident truths or doxas. Since the strong association between linguistic and cultural knowledge on the one hand and citizenship on the other is treated as a doxa, it is impervious to academic counter arguments or rational dissonance.

Nonetheless, it is noteworthy that in recent years critical voices are increasingly being heard in official quarters. In comments in February 2011 criticising the stricter conditions for family reunion that have been imposed in a number of European countries in recent years, and notably in the Netherlands, Thomas Hammarberg, the Commissioner for Human Rights of the Council of Europe, noted that even long-term residents and naturalised citizens are being deprived of the human right of family reunion as policies in host countries become more restrictive and selective. He stated unequivocally that: 'Applicants have to fulfil unreasonable requirements which create insurmountable obstacles to them living with their loved ones' (Hammarberg 2011).

The Dutch sociologist Schinkel (2008) calls the actual discourse and policies with regard to integration and language tests a form of 'social hypochondria'. Hypochondria can be defined as a preoccupation with the fear of having a serious disease based on the person's misinterpretation of bodily symptoms. Social hypochondria, then, can be defined as a preoccupation on the part of social agents with fears that a given social body (e.g. school, neighbourhood, workplace, country, nation, etc.) has a serious disease or disorder, based on the social agents' misinterpretation of the symptoms occurring in that social body.

Most important here are the preoccupations and complaints about perceived threats to 'social cohesion' and 'social integration'. Schinkel (2008) argues that the social body now feels constantly threatened by those who are considered not to belong, to be non-native. If empirical reality indicates that the feelings of threat to the health of a given social body on account of its ethnic composition, integration and social cohesion are not accurate, then these feelings should be considered a form of social hypochondria.

In view of the moves by governments to ever stricter language requirements for migrants, the language testing profession also has to take a broader socio-political and sociolinguistic perspective. This implies, among other things, carefully defining constructs like integration and social cohesion. The test developer has to reflect on the possible misuse and/or negative consequences of their tests. Test developers also have to interact with different stakeholders in society, including immigrants themselves, and should be concerned about whether taking a language test for integration enhances the processes of integration and social cohesion.

Shohamy (2001:146–149) distinguishes five perspectives for the language testing profession to act ethically:

1. **Ethical perspective**: professional morality as a (virtual) contract between test developer, test taker and society. Implication: societal consequences for the test developer in case of misuse is limited.
2. **Awareness raising perspective**: the responsibility of the test developer is to make the users aware of all aspects of a test (and its use).
3. **All consequences perspective**: test developer has to take the responsibility for all consequences of test use.
4. **Perspective of sanctioning**: in case of incorrect use of a test the test developer should be sanctioned.
5. **Perspective of shared responsibility and open communication**: shared responsibility of all people (including non-technicians, policy makers, etc.) involved in making, using, . . . a test through open communication.

While perspectives 1–4 do not change the balance of power between different stakeholders, perspective 5 changes the balance of power through communicative action and is not dominated by the institutions to which the actors belong.

The language testing profession should attempt to take perspective 5 as a point of departure for the development of language tests for integration and citizenship. This is particularly important in order to ensure that tests are fair to all test takers and that no groups of potential test takers are denied access in any of its interpretations at any stage of their migration journey. The development of a frame of reference such as the one described above will assist policymakers, academics and practitioners to work together to create a coherent and comprehensive approach to addressing issues related to language testing and access, such as the implications of using language testing at the pre-arrival and arrival stages of a migrant's journey and how to ensure tests are fair and fit for purpose.

Part 2   Case studies – UK, Belgium and Italy

To illustrate the migrant's journey described above in order to show the ways in which government policy acts together with social, economic and linguistic factors, this section of the paper reviews the three case studies presented at the Language and Migration (LAMI) forum in Kraków (2011). In recent years several European countries have introduced a requirement to provide evidence of language competence not only for those people wishing to apply for long-term residence permits, but also as a requirement for obtaining a visa to first enter a country to study, work or for family reasons, i.e. initial access to the country, and the three case studies present the current legislation with respect to these requirements in the United Kingdom, Belgium and Italy.

The UK case study offers an overall picture of the situation regarding language requirements and language assessment for migrants in the UK and draws attention to the complexity of the current situation: on the one hand, stakeholders' feedback is needed to avoid the risk of unfairness in language assessment, and on the other hand, cuts in funding are limiting the positive effects of language courses. The Belgian case study first relates the complexity of the national situation in terms of quite different realities and policies in Flanders and Wallonia and consequently of different integration policies in the two regions. Secondly, it reports the results of a study aimed at collecting feedback about stakeholders' perceptions of the national integration programme. The Italian case study offers a perspective on how some of the difficulties of language learning provision, in the context of migration, may be usefully solved. In fact, the purpose of this particular case study was to examine if and how a national project could represent a possible model to promote and foster:

- more communication, collaboration and co-ordination at national level in the field of migrants' language training and testing
- closer links between language training and testing through a common reference to the CEFR
- systematic feedback collection in order to better investigate the effects of the training and testing process on individuals, society and education.

The common denominator of the three case studies is the need to give migrants *access*, not only to the host country in the first instance, but also access to the job market, education, health care, and to human and civil rights. Thus, in the UK case study, the importance of campaigns such as *Right to a Voice* and *Action for ESOL* will be outlined, while impact studies that give insights into both education and society will be presented in the Belgian and Italian case studies. With regard to the area of impact studies, this paper puts forward the principle that impact studies are a way of ensuring that migrants' voices are heard and thus facilitate access. In fact, collecting feedback from stakeholders can be useful in order to look at the impact of assessment not only in the educational domain (Alderson and Wall 1993, Wall 2005) but also on society (Bachman 1990). Bachman and Palmer (1996) defined the concept of impact as the use of tests and test results in a societal context. 'Impact, therefore, ... operates at ... two levels ... i.e. at a micro level in terms of individuals who are affected by the particular test use and at a macro level in terms of the educational system or society' (Saville 2009b:25). Weiss (1998:8) described impact in terms of 'a synonym for outcome ... that ... may also refer to program effects for the larger community'. In the three research projects presented here, implementing systematic analysis of the effects that language courses and tests have *in primis* for migrants also means creating better conditions to collect migrants' feedback. Consequently, this kind of analysis implies providing real *access*, in terms of opportunities to give opinions and to let migrants feel more involved in the whole process, not only the language learning process, but, above all, the process of social inclusion, and thus, of linguistic integration.

More generally, the case studies give an overview of different kinds of professional contributions and approaches to this area, with the aim not only of offering a descriptive picture, but also to:

- outline critical aspects and limitations of language policies in the UK, Belgium and Italy
- provide future scenarios
- try to find solutions to some of the issues that arise.

The discussion also addresses more general issues, as specific components of a wider critical reflection on migration and language requirements, by trying to find a shared answer to these open questions:

- Should language tests in the migration context be used in isolation or should they be designed as part of a coherent language-training programme?
- Should expert teachers also collaborate in the testing process?
- Should CEFR descriptors be adapted to make them more suitable for the migration context?

The UK case study

Test for migrant purposes

Since November 2005, those applying for British citizenship have taken a compulsory language test. ESOL Entry level 3 (the equivalent level to B1 of the CEFR) was required, or alternatively, proof of progress through the levels towards it. Two years later, testing was also introduced for those requesting settlement in the UK. In 2008, five tiers were introduced to categorise migrants entering the UK, using a points-based system. Of those intending to settle in the country, highly skilled professionals (Tier 1) were required to obtain proof of C1 (CEFR) level ability and skilled workers (Tier 2) Level B2 (in all skills), with both needing to pass the *Life in the UK* test, a 35-item multiple-choice test assessing knowledge of British society and English reading skill at B1 level based on the accompanying *Life in the UK Handbook*.

As Saville (2009a:24) notes, 'one of the controversial aspects of this test is the nature of the citizenship construct itself which underpins it'. There is an ongoing discussion among experts concerning the correspondence between language test performance and language use in terms of the contents of the *Life in the UK* test. Since 2009, for students (Tier 4) entering the UK, the language requirements for undergraduates have been Level B2 and for those on a lower course, Level B1.

Tier 5 entrants include temporary workers and young people involved in cultural exchange schemes. Visas issued for 'family reunions' (spouses or partners of British citizens or settled individuals) require an A1 level in speaking and listening from an authorised test provider prior to entry.

Caps and cuts

Current UK policy has attempted to reduce migration and has made cuts in funding in response to the economic crisis. New caps on migration, in terms of annual limits, were set in April 2011, restricting the highly skilled (Tier 1) applicants to those of 'exceptional talent', often including entrepreneurs and investors. In 2008, 11% of all UK residents were born outside the country and in 2010, 41% of these held British nationality. London has the highest concentration of non-UK-born residents (28%). Thirteen per cent of those employed in the UK were born abroad, with native women having a 12% higher rate of employment than those born overseas, the lowest ratio being for women born in Pakistan and Bangladesh. Data indicates that between 2008 and 2010, the main reasons for migrants entering the UK changed. The numbers of those entering for work purposes decreased by 9%, while those for study increased by 13%. There has also been a slight increase in 'family reunions'. Applicants must provide evidence demonstrating the required level of English for their category or they will be refused a visa, access to the country, leave to remain indefinitely and any associated services. Those who fail the ESOL Entry level 3 and the *Life in the UK* test in Tiers 1 and 2 and family categories can retake the exam within a specified time.

In 2002, the UK Government introduced a national strategy to improve adult literacy and ESOL skills, and in 2004, the *Skills for Life* national qualifications were developed. The aim of this strategy is to improve the level of basic skills for 2.25 million adults, and at the same time to improve the quality of teaching and the standards of assessment. Until recently, *Skills for Life* courses were sponsored, but funding was reduced in 2007, with further cuts in 2011. Over the last two years, the number of ESOL courses available has dropped from 7,430 to 5,360. Those eligible for courses included people living or trying to settle in the UK whose first language is not English, refugees, asylum seekers, migrant workers, those from settled communities and the immediate family of those granted leave to remain in the UK for some years. In April 2011, the UK Border Agency (UKBA) published a new list of approved Secure English Language Tests, having radically changed the acceptance criteria.

Right to a Voice and Action for ESOL

Not all migrants have the same opportunities to *access* language courses or authorised test centres, and this creates unfairness. In order to counteract this unequal access, due not only to cuts in funding, but also to the discriminatory decisions of policymakers, many people expressed their views through campaigns such as *Right to a Voice* and *Action for ESOL*. In 2007, the UK Government withdrew the right of asylum seekers to attend English language courses for their first six months. Over 100 organisations joined the campaign *Right to a Voice*, with the aim of collecting voices from different stakeholders influenced by this policy decision: ESOL institutions, teachers and above all asylum seekers. To do so, the campaign created a 20-week programme of English learning activities to give users the chance to express their views, such as those summarised in the campaign leaflet: 'If I had to wait six months to learn English . . . I would have felt excluded and my motivation and ability to learn would have dropped' (National Institute for Adult Continuing Education 2008). While *Right to a Voice* focused on a particular kind of migrant (asylum seekers), *Action for ESOL* was a campaign launched to defend language courses in general. After the new cuts were announced, *Action for ESOL* started to ask for better ESOL provision, in order to guarantee migrants greater *access*. With this aim, 20,000 people signed a petition to support the point stated in the Briefing Paper of the campaign that 'sustained funding of ESOL is not a luxury, it is an essential public service' (Action for ESOL 2011).

The Belgian case study

Belgium: complex state, complicated citizenship

The situation in Belgium is complex, regarding both citizenship and the state itself, given that there are six different governments and three different

Figure 2 Governments and languages in Belgium

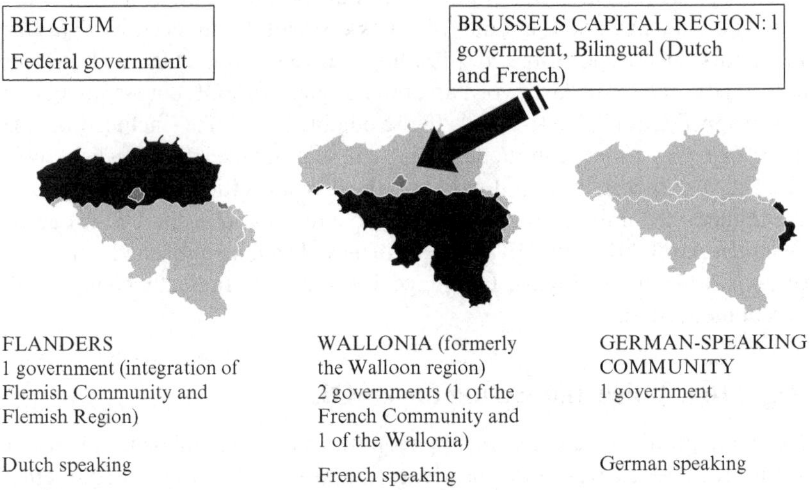

| BELGIUM | BRUSSELS CAPITAL REGION: 1 |
| Federal government | government, Bilingual (Dutch and French) |

FLANDERS
1 government (integration of
Flemish Community and
Flemish Region)

Dutch speaking

WALLONIA (formerly
the Walloon region)
2 governments (1 of the
French Community and
1 of the Wallonia)

French speaking

GERMAN-SPEAKING
COMMUNITY
1 government

German speaking

languages. Figure 2 shows that in Flanders, Dutch is spoken, in the south (Wallonia), French is the recognised language, and finally there is a smaller German-speaking community in the east.

Specific powers concerning migration are attributed to each level of decision-making. Policy at federal level deals with formal citizenship, including migration policy, voting rights for foreigners, permanent residency and obtaining Belgian nationality. The regional level of government in Belgium is not responsible for any formal stage in the migrant's journey. However, Flanders does have an 'integration policy'. Newcomers and some oldcomers have to take a language course as part of an integration programme. This Flemish policy has no formal benefits for migrants who are successful on an integration programme. Such a policy focuses more on the moral aspect of citizenship. Therefore, in contrast with other countries, in Belgium there is a very strong link between formal and moral citizenship, as migrants are expected to integrate into the society they live in without implications for their formal status in the regions of Belgium.

Differences in policy: Flanders and Wallonia

The autonomy of the different regions has led to very different policies on integration. In Flanders, for example, where right-wing parties have had more success, integration is a political issue. In 2010, the Flemish Minister for Integration underlined the importance of a common language, insisting that proficiency in the Dutch language was a key to education and employment. Speaking of identity and autonomy, the Flemish 'Minister-President' suggested there was a need for a 'Copernican' revolution, where the centre of gravity would no longer be the federal state. Each region would act as a nation-state and determine its own policy and agenda. Wallonia, on the other hand, with no extreme-right-wing parties, is more attached to the idea of a federal state, but shows signs of moving towards regional awareness. The area has been renamed 'Wallonia' as opposed to Walloon Region, and a new motto has been established – *Wallonie, terre d'accueil*, meaning 'a welcoming land'. As a consequence of the contrasting political situations in Flanders and Wallonia, the policy framework for integration of the two regions differs; Flanders is more interventionist, though at the same time oscillating between multiculturalism and assimilation, while Wallonia is more *laissez-faire*, encouraging multiculturalism, although this is unstated.

Concrete steps taken by the government in Flanders for integration (moral citizenship) include creating a special minister with responsibility for civic integration, introducing compulsory civic integration courses for certain categories of newcomers, making 'willingness to learn' the Dutch language a requirement for some social benefits, and having parents sign a 'declaration of involvement' when enrolling their child in school.

The Flemish policy programme on civic integration states that 'old and new Flemings have to have access to the necessary instruments to play an active role in our society' (Bourgeois 2009). However, the N-VA (Nieuw-Vlaamse Alliantie, the party of the Minister for Civic Integration) proposes a compulsory, but fair, civic integration programme for newcomers in Flanders who wish to obtain Flemish citizenship. Candidates do not have to take a language test. N-VA would like civic integration to start in the country of origin, as a kind of *pre-access*. Policies introduced in the 1990s, such as recognition and funding of migrant organisations, are also to be continued to encourage multiculturalism. In Wallonia, issues of integration and citizenship are not seen as such a problem, consequently there are no specific ministerial responsibilities regarding civic integration and no civic integration policy for newcomers.

Impact study in Flanders

A two-phase study was carried out in Flanders between 2008 and 2009 to look at the social impact of the integration policy in Flanders (Van Avermaet 2012). Forty informants were interviewed using a semi-structured questionnaire, to ascertain the views of the three main stakeholder groups: teachers, immigrants and members of the 'majority group', i.e. employers, employment agencies and lay people in the street.

Teachers

For most teachers, the fact that there is no central standard language assessment was not a problem. This can be explained by the fact that Flanders has no culture and tradition in its educational systems of centralised testing. Tests are the sole responsibility of teachers. The general opinion was that a language test is a central part of getting an integration certificate. However, some felt that other aspects, such as participation and commitment within the course, were just as important as the test itself.

Immigrants

Immigrants enrolled on a course at the time felt it would increase their future job prospects. However, those who had completed a course and not found employment were quite negative about the value of the certificate, and others thought that the language they had acquired was not useful for their work situation. On the other hand, several older immigrants regretted not having taken the opportunity of doing a language course at an early stage.

Members of the 'majority group'

All employers said that language is the crucial criterion for obtaining a job, although most do not ask for evidence of a Dutch language or an integration certificate, preferring to assess the person themselves at the interview. Employment agencies held similar views, considering certification to be of limited value. The 'majority group' was equally divided between those convinced that a centrally developed language test is necessary and those who trust teachers to devise their own.

Critical considerations

Although Belgium continues to have one of the most lenient policies for obtaining nationality, Flanders and Wallonia have very different stances on the issue of 'moral' citizenship, and the 'integration policy' in Flanders has been accused of holding on to old and obsolete values, effectively leading to the exclusion of some migrant groups.

The Italian case study

New language requirements

Until 2010, there were no language requirements for migrants in Italy for the purpose of obtaining a long-term residency permit or citizenship. However, since then, new legislation has been introduced for newcomers and for migrants already settled in Italy (see Grego Bolli, this volume), and for both groups, a formal test has been provided to assess knowledge of Italian and, in the case of the newcomers, the Integration Agreement requires the migrant to also pass a Knowledge of Society test.

Test for migrants: CVCL's approach and the ILN project

CVCL's (Centro per la Valutazione e le Certificazioni Linguistiche dell'Università per Stranieri di Perugia) approach to assessment in the migration context has always been to establish a link between language teaching/learning and assessment. The language certificates produced by CVCL in this context are the concrete representation of this approach. They have been developed and produced by CVCL experts jointly with a group of teachers working in state schools called CTP (Centri Territoriali Permanenti per l'Educazione degli Adulti), who are involved in the teaching of Italian to migrants. This collaboration between the two different areas of expertise also led to the production of specific syllabuses to prepare students for the exams. The syllabuses are based on the linguistic exponents found in *Profilo della lingua italiana* (Spinelli and Parizzi 2010).

This 'holistic approach' to the area of learning/teaching and assessment was the main reason why CVCL was involved in a national project in 2010 called ILN – *Italiano, lingua nostra* ('Italian, our language') – commissioned by the Italian Ministry of Interior and supported by European funding. The project was undertaken by CVCL, in collaboration with a network of centres involved in language tuition for adult migrants.

ILN: aims

The ILN project represented a learning opportunity for a limited number of migrants (N=2,843). They were self-selected, but had to reflect a specific profile of users, as not everyone was able to benefit from the European Fund for Integration (EFI). Those who were not entitled to benefit from the EFI included EU citizens, non-documented migrants, migrants under 16 or over 65 years old, refugees, prisoners and migrants who have lived in Italy for more than five years. As a result, only 16.4% of the overall migrant population are potential beneficiaries of the EFI: that is about 918,000 out of more than 5 million. Consequently, the 645 migrant respondents may be considered only a small sample of the 918,000 migrants who could be involved in A2 language courses.

Despite the limited number of migrants, the ILN project was a unique experiment in the Italian context, representing an opportunity to reflect on the deficiencies of the existing system. In fact, in order to complete the project, it was necessary to overcome weaknesses of this system (see Grego Bolli, this volume), such as:

- poor co-ordination in language training, in terms of objectives and contents of language courses: teaching materials, manuals, etc.

- high percentage of drop-outs
- lack of correspondence between language training and assessment.

ILN managed to guarantee more uniformity in the training process through central coordination as far as syllabus definition and teaching materials are concerned. The focus of the training process was not only on the classroom, but also on the outside world to support the social inclusion. The 149 language courses spread across 10 regions provided 50 hours of lessons in the classroom, plus 20 hours of outside activities involving communication in real-life situations.

A better knowledge of society was also supported through teaching materials: in particular, a *Knowledge of Society* book was jointly produced for the A2 learners by the CTPs and CVCL. It was subdivided by subject: health education, civics, safety at work, advertisements, history and geography outlines, the constitution. In ILN, different channels had the aim of guaranteeing central coordination and of improving the monitoring phase. During the project, ILN provided newsletters, online chats, a blog and a forum to improve communication among stakeholders.

The purpose of this case study is to examine to what extent this national project could provide a possible model for similar work, including as it does, high levels of collaboration between stakeholders through an integrated approach. The analysis of the data will give more insights about the impact of the combination of language training and language certification on teachers' daily work and on migrants' learning, social and personal experiences (see Grego Bolli, this volume).

ILN: data

Data was collected at the end of the ILN project through the administration of two questionnaires, one for students (SQ) and one for teachers (TQ), which look at the impact of the project in three different areas: social, personal and educational.

The two questionnaires had been pretested and validated for this purpose, and were administered anonymously to the A2-level learners and their teachers after the final exam. They were presented in closed questions, where users had to mark 1 to 5, depending on how much they agree with the closed statements (not much = 1; a lot = 5).

The SQ questionnaire was divided into seven sections, representing seven different key areas, and in order to concentrate on the migrants' needs, the research questions focused on the migrants' relationship with Italian society, the Italian language, the ILN A2 language and Knowledge of Society course, the CELI A2 exam, the training process and also – in the last section – the new law that introduced language requirements for the first time in Italy. Graphs showing the results of the data are included in the Appendix.

ILN: migrants involved

ILN collected 645 SQs and 63 TQs, and 74 nationalities were represented. It is interesting to show the relationship between the two different sets of data: the occurrence of the top four nationalities in the total non-EU population in Italy and their occurrence in the ILN sample (Figure 3 in the Appendix). Although it is possible to notice some similarities, there are also a number of relevant differences.

As far as the similarities are concerned, Moroccans are the second largest group in Italy and the largest in ILN. Historically they represent the main group of CTP users; according to the United Nations Educational, Scientific and Cultural Organization (UNESCO) world map of illiteracy, Morocco is the nearest country to Italy with the percentage of illiterate people higher than 50%. With regard to differences, it was noted that although Albanians are the biggest migrant group in Italy, they are only the sixth largest among groups represented in the project. A possible reason for this is that in many cases they are already well integrated into Italian society: they have been resident for a long time and the Italian language no longer represents an obstacle for them. However in the case of Chinese migrants, it can be noted that although they represent the third largest migrant group in Italy, they rank only eighth in terms of the number of participants in the ILN project. This may be related to the view expressed by the CoE that 'Integration is a dynamic, two-way process of mutual interaction, requiring not only efforts by national, regional and local authorities but also a greater commitment by the host community and immigrants' (2009).

Some items in the questionnaire may suggest that respondents from the Chinese community are not as engaged with the target culture as other communities. For example, in the section, 'The Italian language at home', while 13.8% of the total SQ respondents answered '*I never speak Italian at home*', the percentage rises to 100% when only the Chinese answers are considered.

Migrants involved and level of literacy

Another relevant topic relates to the years spent at school and the level of literacy (Figure 4 in the Appendix). According to the SQs, 18.3% of respondents had spent fewer than five years at school and the percentage goes up further to 50% when only the data taken from the TQs is considered. This is because teachers responding to this question only took into account the migrants in their traditional classes, not in ILN. The percentage of students who have spent fewer than five years at school rises to 88% when those involved in traditional language courses administered by private centres are included.

The number of Moroccans involved in ILN who spent fewer than five years at school totalled 84%. The UNESCO world map on illiteracy, as well as Adami (2009), stress the fundamental link between poor levels of literacy and social inclusion. In addition, high percentages like the ones mentioned above (50% with little schooling in the state schools and 88% in private centres), clearly represent a strong reason to reflect critically on what could be done to fill the gap in the CEFR below A1 level and to create frameworks for adult illiteracy. This work should become a priority for teachers and language testers involved in the migration context.

Literacy and writing

The wide gap between oral interaction and writing is inversely proportional to literacy and the CEFR levels. As a consequence, the SQ data shows that the test tasks found to be most useful, both during the course and in the final examination, are those tasks which go some way to bridging the gap between writing and other language skills. It is very interesting to look at the feedback in relation to writing in two different contexts: in ILN, nothing (including writing components) was compulsory. Migrants opted to take writing items because they wanted to improve their weakest skill. In the new Italian legislation (Decree 4 June 2010), the A2 test is compulsory in order to obtain the long-term residence permit. In some interviews given to the media after the administration of the first test, migrants said, 'Let me speak, but don't ask me to write!' (*Oggi*, 9 March 2001).

Language competence for social inclusion

In the second section of the SQ, the focus is on the role of the Italian language for social inclusion. The results indicated that the Italian language is obviously an important tool for communication, but also (as shown in Figure 5 in the Appendix) it is essential in order to gain respect in society. In other words, the language offers a kind of social key for better access, with more rights – a social key which we hope will open 'closed gates'. The vast majority give the response that language is useful to communicate better (left side of Figure 5) and to be more respected (right side of Figure 5).

ILN: users' feedback

Taking into account the whole training process, the feedback is generally very positive: students and teachers consider ILN as an opportunity, something useful. However, a negative aspect that emerges concerns the stress due to very busy timetables, the effort required and the anxiety caused because of deadlines which are often too close.

Feedback about the lessons

The feedback about the lessons seems very positive in the SQ. Looking in more detail at the question of the time spent outside the classroom, it is interesting to note that these hours seem to facilitate *access* not only to the local community, but also to classmates by creating a better 'community for learning' and for practising the language with a peer group. In fact, as far as the statement '*the hours outside helped me to know my classmates better and make friends with them*' is concerned, there is a large degree of agreement with regard to the positive options that describe how these hours consolidate relationships, above all helping the older students to get to know other people better. In fact, older students, as was also confirmed in the TQs, often have more difficulties in establishing relationships, sharing experiences, and opening their minds to the outside world. In this respect, *access* should not only be discussed in relation to professional, cultural and religious features, but also in relation to age. In a similar vein, when reviewing the responses to another question in the SQ regarding what respondents do not like about Italy, older students responded above all that '*we don't have Italian friends*'.

Feedback about the teaching material

The SQ gives information on the students' feedback about teaching materials. In particular, Figures 6 and 7 in the Appendix show that the *Knowledge of Society* book was greatly appreciated because it provided useful information to get to know Italian society better, to help users in their daily life and to help them in preparing the final exam.

ILN: correspondence between language training and assessment

The TQ investigated in more detail the feedback concerning the actions of central coordination, in terms of lesson planning, asking if teachers agreed or disagreed with the statement '*knowing the course ended with the final exam helped me with lesson planning and to make the best use of time*', or other statements, such as '*gave me a clear direction, with clearer outlines*'. Also in the case of lesson planning, the number of positive answers is very high, as Figure 8 in the Appendix shows.

Similarly, Figure 9 shows that quite a high concentration of respondents selected the option '*I do not agree much*' with the statement '*knowing the course ended with the final exam led to a sort of standardisation of the format, not positive in terms of less creativity*'. Therefore, teachers seem not to have suffered too much because of the time spent on exam preparation. Coming back to the introduction, these TQ answers seem to confirm the necessity of promoting and consolidating the link between language training and testing.

Another key question was: '*Can students and teachers consider ILN as a starting point?*' From Figure 10 in the Appendix, it can be seen that the majority of students answered, '*yes, it is a starting point, because I still have to improve*'.

Confirmation of this view is clearly underlined by Figure 11 in the Appendix: the majority of teachers answered, '*yes, it is only a starting point because this kind of project should:*

- *provide more hours of lessons (not less than 100)*
- *be extended also to the upper levels of the CEFR (in particular to B1)*
- *become compulsory (and always without any charge)*
- *become part of a more systematic and structured action.'*

This last bullet point strongly confirms how all the stakeholders, particularly teachers, need coordination at the national level.

Feedback about the exam

Another issue concerns the final exam. Matching the SQs and the TQs, the consensus is very high *vis-à-vis* the statements regarding what the final exam represented:

- in the SQ, *'a goal that I wanted to reach'* and, above all, *'an added reason to attend the course'*, and
- in the TQ, *'something that meant students attended more regularly'*, guaranteeing teaching with more continuity.

Two different perspectives shown in Figure 12 in the Appendix confirm the same fundamental point: this was definitely a success for ILN in terms of a high attendance rate and a low drop-out rate (15.8% versus the national average of 33.4%). In addition, the attendance rate supports the positive effects of the link between training and assessment, which has been postulated, in particular in the context of migration.

Feedback about the continuum (training course plus final exam)

It is very useful to underline two different points of view that emerged from the SQ and the TQ with regard to the same question, *'Are 70 hours of instruction sufficient to move from A1 (after common entry test) and approach an A2 exam?'* (Figure 13 in the Appendix.)

Students generally answered in the affirmative and this was also confirmed by the high percentage of students who passed the final exam, thus obtaining the A2 certification. On the other hand, the perception of teachers seems to be the opposite: it is possible that many Italian teachers are still accustomed to comparing the language competence of their students to a subjective and theoretical concept of 'perfect knowledge', a knowledge not scaled in progressive levels, often mainly grammar-oriented, that can be 'good' or 'bad'; hence, from this perspective, 70 hours to reach a 'good' competence is clearly not enough.

CEFR levels in the migration context

The last question in the TQ was an open question, *'Using your experience, do you think the profiles of the CEFR are applicable for training courses in the context of migration?'*

These are the five recurring answers:

1. '*Absolutely*' *(23%)*.
2. '*Yes, we have to use the profiles because they represent guidelines that are fundamental to giving coherence and criteria to observe the can do statements*' *(9%)*.
3. '*Yes, but it is necessary to integrate and adapt the descriptors after a specific needs analysis of the users*' *(51%)*.
4. '*Yes, but it is necessary to complete the gap before A1: the Framework does not help teachers in describing sub levels of illiteracy, so present in a context of migration*' *(41%)*.
5. '*Yes, but it is important for a syllabus not to link a language course to a unique level of the CEFR; this is because, especially in that context, the learners often don't have an homogeneous profile, with a big distance between oral interaction and writing*' *(37%)*.

Again, it is possible to notice two recurrent aspects in the migration context: the priority to create frameworks, which contain descriptors for those who are illiterate, and the need to adapt the CEFR descriptors to make them more suitable for the different kinds of user, especially in the lower proficiency range.

Language policy and migrants feedback

The last closed question in the SQ was, '*In Italy a law (Decree 4 June 2010) will soon introduce the requirement to pass a language test in order to obtain the long term residency permit*'. There was a near-unanimous response from students, irrespective of gender, age or nationality, showing a high degree of agreement with the statement, '*I think that it is right for the Italian state to ask for a compulsory certificate of language competence*'. However, it must be noted that the ILN students were privileged students who had just completed a course, taken the final exam, and had benefited from an opportunity to study and take an exam free of charge. In addition, all the students also endorsed the other option, '*I think that asking for a compulsory certificate of language competence is right, but the State must give me the chance to learn Italian. I can't manage on my own: I need to attend a course*'. In other words, it is possible to conclude that migrants feel the State should not require assessment without providing training; final exams, in the migration context, should not be isolated but rather intended as part of a coherent training programme. This confirms the first additional consideration of this paper: language tests for migration purposes should be designed as an inclusive part of a process.

Limitations and critical considerations

Working on the intersection between second language learning and language for social inclusion, the need to combine these two concepts through the close relationship between teaching and assessment emerges clearly. In this sense, ILN could be considered as an example of good practice in sharing, monitoring and conducting an impact study. Unfortunately, however, it is not part of a systematic action plan. ILN, in fact, was only for a minority of migrants: CVCL was only able to involve fewer than 3,000 migrants out of an overall presence in Italy of more than 5 million. What is needed is a more structured approach that should be agreed after consultation with relevant experts and national institutions. However, state funding for social integration in Italy has already been reduced from 2.52 billion Euros in 2008 to 349 million Euros in the most recent legislation. Both the restrictive profile required by law for European Fund for Integration benefits and the cut in funding are limiting the migrants' *access* to the process of linguistic integration and social inclusion.

Conclusions

Some final considerations emerge from these case studies: first of all a warning about the consequences of the reductions in state funding within the context of migration. In the UK *Skills for Life* saw a 27% reduction in terms of the number of courses administered and, in Italy, the funds for social integration were reduced by 76.3%. As a direct consequence of these cuts, there has already been a shift from language training to language assessment.

The second consideration concerns the need for more systematic communication and an effective exchange of information at European level. There has been a long debate within the language testing community in relation to the socio-political use of language tests. ALTE, as a professional association, and LAMI, as a specific working group of experts in this area, have worked hard to address these issues and disseminate an understanding of the legislation in European countries in relation to migration policies. Nevertheless, there is still a further need for more sharing of information and concrete experiences.

Thirdly, there is a need for more systematic study and research in terms of migration policies, language requirements and their impact on migrant communities, education, and society. By reporting on the migration policies of the UK, Belgium and Italy, and by underlining the importance of a continuous monitoring process, through specific impact studies to look at the stakeholders' feedback on language requirements, this paper has contributed to this important issue.

Given that assessment processes with respect to social inclusion involve professional ethics and extend to the political repercussions of test results, it is clear that ensuring that standard procedures are met when preparing language certification is still fundamental, but it is no longer enough; for best practice, it is essential to consider the social impact that tests have. The common denominator of the three case studies presented above is the aim of demonstrating the link between impact and *access*: only through an analysis of the consequences that language policies, courses and tests have is it possible to let the migrants' voice be heard.

A fourth consideration concerns the need to provide a more structured approach and systematic action at European level that incorporates the above-mentioned impact study. This should have two related and positive effects, namely to involve a larger number of migrants in the training process and to improve communication, collaboration and coordination between all the stakeholders, in order to develop a closer training–testing link.

The three case studies presented in this paper have highlighted the function of *Skills for life* in the UK, the N-VA programme in Belgium and ILN in Italy in representing three examples of a *continuum* between teaching and assessment, between the status of *student* and the status of *candidate*. This continuum represents the *conditio sine qua non* in order not to isolate evaluation for migration purposes, but to relate it to a specific training programme. In future, more can be done in terms of adapting the CEFR descriptors to take into account users' needs, as well as involving appropriately experienced teachers and introducing different types of assessment, which are fit for the purpose for which they are intended.

Acknowledgements

The authors are grateful to Professor Giuliana Grego Bolli, Dr Nick Saville and Michael Corrigan for their comments on the earlier versions of this paper and to Martin Nuttall for his assistance in editing the paper.

References

Action for ESOL (2011) *Briefing paper*, available online: actionforesol.org/wp-content/uploads/2010/06/ESOLBriefing2011

Adami, H (2009) *The Role of Literacy in the Acculturation Process of Migrants*, Strasbourg: Council of Europe, available online: www.coe.int/t/dg4/linguistic/Source/Adami_Migrants_EN.rtf

Alderson, J C and Wall, D (Eds) (1993) Does washback exist? *Applied Linguistics* 14, 115–129.

ALTE Authoring Group (2008) *Language Tests for Social Cohesion and Citizenship – an Outline for Policymakers*, Council of Europe Thematic Studies, Strasbourg: Council of Europe.

ALTE Code of Practice (COP) Working Group (2004) *ALTE Minimum Standards*, available online: www.alte.org/attachments/files/minimum_standards.pdf

Bachman, L F (1990) *Fundamental Considerations in Language Learning*, Oxford: Oxford University Press.

Bachman, L and Palmer, A (1996) *Language Testing in Practice*, Oxford: Oxford University Press.

Bourgeois, G (2009) *Policy Paper 2009–2014 (Civic) Integration*, available online: www.vlaanderen.be/sites/default/files/documents/engelstalige_beleidsnota_inburgering_en_integratie.pdf

Caritas di Roma (2010) *Immigrazione. Dossier statistico*, Roma: Anterem.

Consiglio d'Europa (2002) *Quadro Comune Europeo di Riferimento*, Firenze: La Nuova Italia.

Council of Europe (1953) *Convention for the Protection of Human Rights and Fundamental Freedoms*, available online: human-rights-convention.org

Council of Europe (1977) *European Convention on the Legal Status of Migrant Workers*, available online: conventions.coe.int/Treaty/en/Treaties/Html/093.htm

Council of Europe (1996) *European Social Charter*, available online: www.conventions.coe.int/Treaty/EN/Treaties/Html/163.htm

Council of Europe (2008a) *The role of languages in policies for the integration of adult migrants*, concept paper prepared for the seminar The Linguistic Integration of Adult Migrants, Strasbourg: June 2008, available online: www.coe.int/t/dg4/linguistic/Source/Migrants_ConceptPaper_EN.doc

Council of Europe (2008b) *White Paper on Intercultural Dialogue "Living Together As Equals in Dignity"*, available online: www.coe.int/t/dg4/intercultural/Source/White%20Paper_final_revised_EN.pdf

Council of Europe (2009) *Stockholm Programme*, Brussels, available online: register.consilium.europa.eu/pdf/en/09/st17/st17024.en09.pdf

Council of Europe (2010a) *Guide for the Development and Implementation of Curricula for Plurilingual and Intercultural Education*, available online: www.coe.int/t/dg4/linguistic/Source/Source2010_ForumGeneva/GuideEPI2010_EN.pdf

Council of Europe (2010b) *Recommendation 1917 on migrants and refugees: a continuing challenge for the Council of Europe*, available online: www.coe.int/t/dg4/linguistic/migrants2_EN.asp#P359_45858

European Commission against Racism and Intolerance (2008) *Annual Report on ECRI's Activities*, available online: www.coe.int/t/dghl/monitoring/ecri/activities/Annual_Reports/Annual%20report%202008.pdf

Extramiana, C and Van Avermaet, P (2010) *Language requirements for adult migrants in Council of Europe member states: report on a survey*, available online: www.coe.int/t/dg4/linguistic/Source/Mig-ReportSurvey2011_EN.pdf

Flemish Government (2009) *The Flemish Government 2009–2014. A vigorous Flanders in decisive times*, available online: www.vlaanderen.be/nl/publicaties/detail/the-flemish-government-2009-2014-a-vigorous-flanders-in-decisive-times-for-an-innovative-sustainable-and-warm-society

Grego Bolli, G and Rocca, L (2010) *Test linguistici per la coesione sociale e la cittadinanza. Linee guida per politici e istituzioni. Versione in italiano*, available online: www.cvcl.it/mediacenter/FE/articoli/nuove-pubblicazioni.html

Hammarberg, T (2011) *Restrictive laws prevent families from reuniting*, available online: commissioner.cws.coe.int/tiki-view_blog_post.php?postId=113

Hawkey, R (2006) *Impact Theory and Practice: Studies of the IELTS Test and Progetto Lingue 2000*, Studies in Language Testing volume 24, Cambridge: UCLES/Cambridge University Press.

Home Office (2010) *Control of immigration: quarterly statistical summary*, available online: www.homeoffice.gov.uk

Home Office (2011) *Family migration: evidence and analysis*, 2nd edn., available online: www.homeoffice.gov.uk

Messick, S (1989) *Validity*, in Linn, R L (Ed.) *Educational Measurement*, 3rd edn., New York: Macmillan, 13–103.

Messick, S (1996) Validity and washback in language testing, *Language Testing* 13 (3), 241–256.

Minuz, F (2005) *Italiano L2 e alfabetizzazione in età adulta*, Roma: Carocci.

National Institute for Adult Continuing Education (2008) *A Right To A Voice*, available online: www.niace.org.uk/sites/default/files/RTV-leaflet.pdf

Rocca, L (2008) *Percorsi di certificazione linguistica in contesti di immigrazione*, Perugia: Guerra.

Saville, N (2009a) Language assessment in the management of international migration: a framework for considering the issues, *Language Assessment Quarterly* 6 (1), Routledge, 17–29.

Saville, N (2009b) *Developing a model for investigating the impact of language assessment within educational contexts by a public examination provider*, unpublished thesis, University of Bedfordshire.

Saville, N (2011) *Language Testing and Access – a Framework for Considering the Issues*, paper presented at the LAMI Forum, ALTE 4th International Conference, Kraków, July 2011.

Saville, N and Van Avermaet, P (2008) Language testing for migration and citizenship, in Taylor, L and Weir, C (Eds) *Multilingualism and Assessment*: *Proceedings of the ALTE Berlin Conference May 2005*, Studies in Language Testing volume 27, Cambridge: UCLES/Cambridge University Press, 265–275.

Schinkel, W (2008) *De gedroomde samenleving*, Kampen: uitgeverij Klement.

Sheils, J (2008) Language assessment and citizenship: European policy perspective, in Taylor, L and Weir, C (Eds) *Multilingualism and Assessment*. *Proceedings of the ALTE Berlin Conference May 2005*, Studies in Language Testing volume 27, Cambridge: UCLES/Cambridge University Press, 255–264.

Shohamy, E, (2001) *The Power of Tests – A Critical Perspective on the Uses of Language Tests*, Harlow, Essex: Pearson.

Spinelli, B and Parizzi, F (2010) *Profilo della lingua italiana*, Firenze: La Nuova Italia.

Strik, T, Böcker, A, Luiten, M, and van Oers, R (2010) *The INTEC Project: Synthesis Report*, Nijmegen: Radboud University.

Susi, F (1993) *I bisogni formativi e culturali degli immigrati stranieri*, Milano: Franco Angeli.

Van Avermaet, P (2012) L'intégration linguistique en Europe. Quelques observations critique, in Adami, H and Leclercq, V (Eds) *Les migrants face aux langues des pays d'accueil*, Villeneuve d'Ascq: Septentrion, 153–171.

Wall, D (2005) *The Impact of High-Stakes Testing on Classroom Teaching: A Case Study Using Insights from Testing and Innovation Theory*, Studies in Language Testing volume 22, Cambridge: UCLES/Cambridge University Press.

Weiss, C H (1988) *Evaluation: Methods for Studying Programs & Policies*, Upper Saddle River, NJ: Prentice Hall.

Appendix

Figure 3 Occurrence of the top four nationalities in the total non-EU population

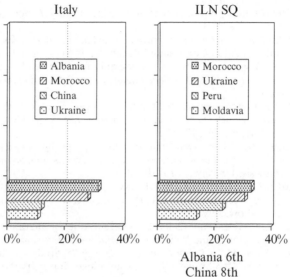

Albania 6th
China 8th

Figure 4 Years spent at school

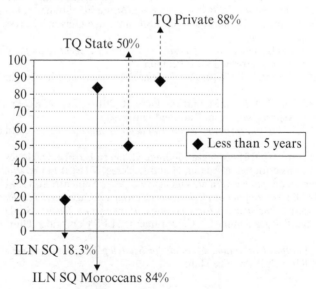

Figure 5 The role of the Italian language for social inclusion
(1 = Not important 5 = Very important)

To communicate more   To be more respected

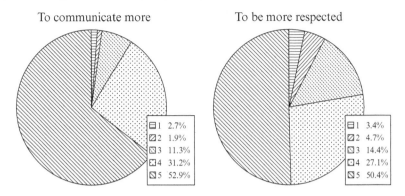

⊟1	2.7%
☑2	1.9%
⊠3	11.3%
☒4	31.2%
◩5	52.9%

⊟1	3.4%
☑2	4.7%
⊠3	14.4%
☒4	27.1%
◩5	50.4%

Figure 6 *Knowledge of Society* book as an instrument to collect useful information for daily life
(1 = Do not agree 5 = Agree)

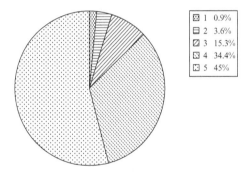

⊠ 1	0.9%
⊟ 2	3.6%
☑ 3	15.3%
⊠ 4	34.4%
◪ 5	45%

Figure 7 Knowledge of Society book as an instrument to better prepare students for the final exam
(1 = Do not agree 5 = Agree)

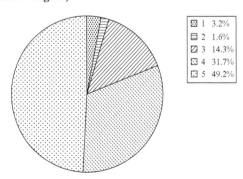

⊠ 1	3.2%
⊟ 2	1.6%
☑ 3	14.3%
⊠ 4	31.7%
◪ 5	49.2%

Figure 8 Positive influence of the final exam in lesson planning
(1 = Do not agree 5 = Agree)

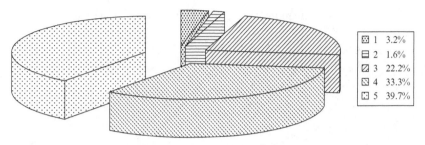

⊠	1	3.2%
⊟	2	1.6%
⧄	3	22.2%
⬚	4	33.3%
⬚	5	39.7%

Figure 9 How teachers perceive the risk of standardisation in terms of the
impact on their daily teaching
(1 = Do not agree 5 = Agree)

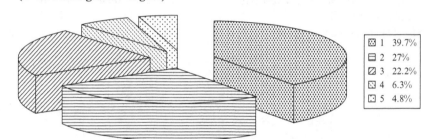

⊠	1	39.7%
⊟	2	27%
⧄	3	22.2%
⬚	4	6.3%
⬚	5	4.8%

Figure 10 Do students consider ILN as only a starting point in their learning
process?
(1 = Do not agree 5 = Agree)

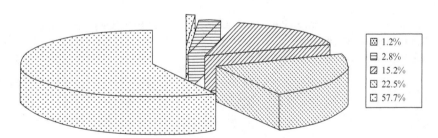

⊠	1.2%
⊟	2.8%
⧄	15.2%
⬚	22.5%
⬚	57.7%

Figure 11 Why teachers consider ILN as only a starting point

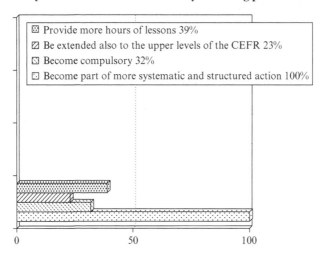

☒ Provide more hours of lessons 39%
☑ Be extended also to the upper levels of the CEFR 23%
☒ Become compulsory 32%
☐ Become part of more systematic and structured action 100%

Figure 12 What the final exam represented
(1 = Do not agree 5 = Agree)

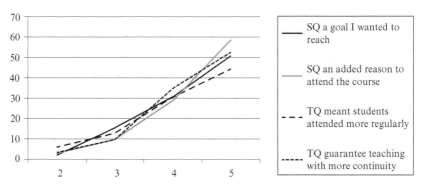

SQ a goal I wanted to reach

SQ an added reason to attend the course

TQ meant students attended more regularly

TQ guarantee teaching with more continuity

Figure 13 Adequate course time?
(1 = Do not agree 5 = Agree)

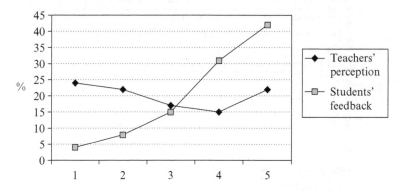

2 Migration policies in Italy in relation to language requirements. The project *Italiano, lingua nostra*: impact and limitations

Giuliana Grego Bolli

Centro per la Valutazione e le Certificazioni linguistiche
Università per Stranieri di Perugia, Italy

Abstract

This paper relates migration policies and language testing to migration as a global, cyclical phenomenon, a major component of the history of humanity since the early beginnings of civilisation. Compared to its origins, modern migration involves a number of political, economic, social, cultural and educational issues. This paper will argue that to deal with all of these effectively, we need a multidimensional approach, a variety of expertise and coordinated actions. For this reason, social sciences should play a fundamental role in proposing approaches and models functional to the management of migration processes, in different contexts and situations. From an educational point of view, knowledge of the host country's language has become, in recent years, one of the key educational issues treated and discussed by experts and policymakers. As a consequence, language requirements, and, in particular, the assessment of these requirements, have recently been introduced and presented by the majority of European governments as necessary tools to foster migrants' social inclusion. However, such policy inevitably leads to exclusion of some. This paper will propose some critical considerations in relation to this point, looking in particular at the latest migration policies in Italy.

Migration policies and language requirements vary from one country to another across Europe, and, in spite of quite similar official pronouncements, European institutions should consider the importance of introducing shared frameworks in this context. Frameworks are important and potentially very useful tools, not only in the educational domain. Migration, and related issues, could also benefit from shared frameworks or specific 'guidelines', consistently applied at the European level, in order to deal with the different dimensions (political, economic, social, cultural and educational) involved in a coherent and coordinated way. An addition to the title of this contribution could be: "The need for shared frameworks".

Introduction

This paper is divided into four interrelated parts, each addressing key topics and issues. The first part is a brief overview of different aspects of migration that have involved both Europe and Italy in the ancient past, as well as in more recent times; the second is about how contemporary European society seems to deal with immigration, inclusion, integration, language requirements and language assessment. The third one focuses on the Italian context and the way Italy is dealing with immigration, language training and language requirements nationally. The last part turns to a national project titled *Italiano, lingua nostra* (ILN) promoted by the Italian Ministry of Interior and realised by Centro per la Valutazione e le Certificazioni linguistiche (CVCL) in 2010 jointly with public and private institutions. The paper will also present the feedback received so far through questionnaires and videoed interviews with both students and teachers involved in the project. The ILN project, according to the results and the feedback collected so far, could constitute a possible model to establish a closer and consistent link between language training and language assessment, as well as a closer collaboration between languages teachers and language testers. The ILN, with its aims, the collaborations established at national level, and the feedback provided, contributes to reassigning the appropriate functions of promoting knowledge and providing useful insights to education and society about language assessment.

Introductory considerations

Migration has been part of the origins and history of humanity over the centuries, and is certainly not related only to the present time. Looking for the exact meaning in the dictionary, the following definition of the verb 'migrate' is reported: 'to move from one country, place or locality to another' (Merriam-Webster 2012). A second definition gives more insights about motivation, which is still partially valid: 'to pass usually periodically from one region or climate to another for feeding or breeding' (Merriam-Webster 2012). *Migration* is a general term widely used nowadays; *emigration* and *immigration* are closely linked, both terms deriving from migration, but are more specific: when we say that people emigrate we do not only say that people leave their country, region or place, but we also affirm their intention to live in another country, region or place permanently or for a limited period of time. Immigration (internal and external) is the flip-side of emigration: it indicates the perspective of the hosting country. This is why migration, particularly mass migration, historically involves both the migrants' country and society of origin and the new country, not only in terms of internal political, social, demographic and economic consequences, but also of reciprocal involvement and responsibilities.

Aspects of migration in Europe and in Italy: a historical perspective

The following brief overview of both European and Italian emigration has two aims:

- firstly, to stress the importance of keeping records of the past and making useful comparisons between the past and the present times, between the huge overseas European emigration flows across the last two centuries and the more recent immigration flows particularly in the last 30 years (Pugliese 2006:81), obviously taking into account that contexts, conditions and the motivations can vary over centuries and years
- secondly, to remember that the migrants should not be characterised as the *others*, as we are often used to considering them, but on the contrary, that migration is a major component of our own history and can definitely be positive both for the sending and receiving countries.

In Europe

Europe has experienced both mass immigration and mass emigration. In the ancient past, mass migrations frequently became invasions because they were aimed at conquering countries and cities by force. Several invasions can be cited as very influential on the history of Europe: the Huns' invasion (4th century); the Arab invasions (7th–8th century); the Mongol invasions (13th century), and the invasions of the Ottoman Turks (15th–16th century). They have caused long periods of war, devastations and great political, social and cultural changes in Europe.

The great European emigration

More recently, over the last two centuries, Europe has also been a land of mass emigration considering that 'about 52 million people were recorded as having left European countries for overseas destinations between 1815 and 1930' (Baines 1991:1). The level of migration reached in this period, particularly in relation to the population at that time, is higher compared to the contemporary migration flows (Hatton and Williamson 1998:3). The main destinations of this emigration flow were the United States, Argentina, Canada, Brazil and Australia. The European countries most affected were (the order is based on number of emigrants): Britain, Italy, Ireland, Austria-Hungary, Germany (including Prussian Poland), Spain, Russia (including Russian Poland) Portugal, Sweden, Norway, Finland, France, Denmark, Switzerland, Netherlands, and Belgium (Baines 1991:3).

Such a huge population transfer could not fail to have profound effects on the global distribution of population, income and wealth, becoming a part of both a long-run equilibrium adjustment within an evolving new global labour market, as Hatton and Williamson (1992) highlighted, and the development of a new, international economy (Baines 1991, Taylor 1971). Even if European emigration has been characterised by considerable diversity in terms of destinations, the composition of the flow of migrants and their motivations, it is interesting to look at possible generic causes of this mass emigration. Hatton and Williamson (1992), drawing on the contributions of Easterlin (1961), Tomaske (1971), Massey (1988) and Baines (1991), provide well documented explanations for the European emigration experience from 1850 to 1913, coming to the conclusion that 'emigration responded systematically to real wages gaps between home and abroad, but that this response depended strongly on direct demographic influences and weakly on the level of industrialization at home' (1992:3). For example, in the case of a fertility boom and infant mortality decline, the result would be a gap between the labour-abundant Old World and the labour-scarce New World about 20 or 30 years later. Despite the fact that there are several possible variables causing mass emigration: poverty, climate, famine, pogrom, political, social and economic conditions, demographic growth, differences in labour market opportunities between the sending and the receiving countries, and that their combination or predominance, as well as internal dynamics, can vary or be differently interrelated, it is probably reasonable to conclude that they have remained basically the same over the centuries.

In Italy

Italy can be considered as an archetype of migration, in terms of invasions in the ancient past, emigration, both external and internal from the 19th to the 20th century, and immigration: non-natives arriving in Italy since the second half of the 1970s to settle there permanently. Because of this, the Italian experience can be considered as a useful reference point for more general considerations that can instructively illuminate other contexts.

The ancient past

The fall, or more correctly, the progressive implosion of the Western Roman Empire was, to some extent, accelerated by the pressure of the barbarian invasions: Ostrogoths, Visigoths, Franks, Angles, Saxons, etc; even if the historians generally agree that the fall did not depend entirely on invasions, but rather on a general, social, moral, political, economic and military collapse of Rome and its civilizations. As Morghen notes (1962:22): 'The Empire fell, chiefly, under the weight of its own vastness and because of the fading of its core values, on which its complex structure had been supported for centuries' (trans. Grego Bolli).

A more religious and spiritual perspective is proposed by Reale (2003:147), speaking about the European roots and the contemporary European *mission*: dealing with different outside cultures, trying to mediate among them without losing its own identity and its cultural and religious traditions. In conclusion, both Morghen and Reale give quite similar interpretations of the Western Roman Empire's collapse, which can be easily linked to the risk Europe is running nowadays if it is not able to manage the mass immigration it is facing, through coherent, co-ordinated and concrete actions.

The Italian diaspora

Still the most influential aspect of migration, as far as Italy is concerned, is the so-called Italian diaspora, which is the mass external emigration of around 25 million Italians from the Italian Unification in 1861 to the so-called Italian economic miracle in the early 1960s. As Pugliese (2006:19) notes: 'Italy has experienced two significant migratory experiences abroad: the transoceanic one during the years bridging the 19th and 20th centuries – the Great Emigration – and that of the period after World War II towards (other) European countries' (trans. Grego Bolli). During this long period, Italians migrated mainly to North and South America, Australia and to Europe. Nowadays, around 74 million Italian descendants live in North America (19 million), South America (more than 48 million), Australia (about 1 million) and Europe (6 million) (Vedovelli 2011). Italy has a long tradition of internal temporary emigration as well. In the early 1890s, around 1 million people worked outside their region for at least two months each year (Smith 1959: 373). From 1955 to 1975, 2,344,839 people emigrated from the southern regions to the central and northern ones (Pugliese 2006:42–44).

Extreme poverty, particularly in the rural areas, unemployment, and overpopulation were the main reasons for the Italian diaspora. It is also interesting to mention the purely commercial factors, such as the shipping companies' great profits from the emigrants' transportation, which contributed to the Italian emigration flow. The shipping companies, in fact, started to publicise the great and unique opportunities that could be found in the New World in order to attract more passengers and increase profits (Fondazione Migrantes 2011:463–465, Smith 1959:373–378).

The impact and the consequences both in Italy and in the receiving countries of the Italian diaspora have been important. The Italians, like all the emigrants from Europe and outside Europe, contributed enormously to the economic growth of the New World, and also in Italy:

> Emigration represents the social phenomenon which has perhaps con-
> tributed more than any other social change to modernisation that has
> taken place in Italy . . . since the post-war period. In addition to remov-
> ing traditional rural poverty . . . the relief of demographic pressure on
> the land improved the income conditions . . . of peasants who remained,
> whilst the flow of remittances raised the overall level of income . . .,
> stimulating the overall demand for goods and thus also representing an
> indirect stimulus to the economic development of the industrial areas
> throughout the country (Pugliese 2006:41) (trans. Grego Bolli).

Italy: from the past to the present times, from external and internal emigration to international immigration

It is important to make clear from the outset that the numbers of immigrants coming into modern-day Italy are small in comparison to the numbers of migrants who left Italy to live elsewhere. Currently, migrants in Italy are around 8% of the population, a percentage which is a little higher compared to the rest of Europe, around 6.5%. The number of immigrants in Italy more than doubled between 2000 and 2010. The Government implemented different policies to control and limit the number of migrants entering the country. According to a recent report provided by the Ministry of Labour, the internal labour market's demand for foreign workers is estimated around 100,000 per year for the period 2011 to 2015, and should increase to 260,000 during the period 2016 to 2020 (Ministry of Labour, *Immigration Report* 2011). Nevertheless, the demand could easily become higher compared to the number of migrants allowed to enter the country each year on the basis of these estimates. This is also true of Europe:

> The number of extra-EU immigrants are still rising despite the efforts to
> control and limit them. This immigration does still seem to be fulfilling a
> structural demand for migrants, driven by the demographic demand of
> declining childbirth and aging population, and the economic restructur-
> ing of European national welfare state economies into a global service
> economy (Favell 2009:176).

Despite the experience of migration acquired from the past, which could potentially contribute to a more objective understanding of the immigration flows, Italy was (and probably still is) unprepared to manage relatively high numbers of immigrants who are very different in terms of culture, traditions, and language. Other European countries started dealing with immigration decades ago, particularly from their former colonies, in very different ways, although not always, and not completely, successfully. Coherent, compre-hensive and common immigration policies are still lacking in Europe, yet they are necessary to have more common and co-ordinated approaches to deal with the different migration issues. In this respect, Favell (2009:175) notes that 'nearly every European nation-state has formulated, in recent years, a policy on "integration" of immigrants that reflects mainly nation-building concerns about imparting national cultures and values to newcomers, and very little of the kind of post-national responses to immigration that would be the consequences of a thorough Europeanization of the issues involved'.

Contemporary society and immigration flows

As we learn from history and previous experiences, it is almost impossible to stop immigration flows and it is very difficult to limit and control them, particularly when they are prompted by dramatic endemic, demographic, economic contrasts between countries of origin and countries of destination and when they are caused by profound and parallel political and social crises. Nevertheless, immigration flows need to be managed. This means that contemporary society in Europe, in Italy and all over the world, must find a positive, constructive way to deal with migration. It is of course a very complex, multidisciplinary process, and not the sole responsibility of linguists or language testers to take decisions; nevertheless as citizens, as researchers, as experts in language assessment we can in all likelihood contribute with social and intellectual pressure, in the course of assuming our own professional responsibilities.

Probably only a long-term educational process, based on dialogue and involving both the immigrant and host communities, could lead to reciprocal knowledge and respect, which is the only basis for real inclusion and, in the long run, for a possible integration of immigrants. This concept of intercultural dialogue has been elaborated by the German political philosopher Dallmayr (2010) drawing on the insights of other famous and influential philosophers such as Gadamer, Heidegger, and Merleau-Ponty. Dallmayr (2010:108) reports Gadamer's definition of dialogue:

> Dialogue is a mode of 'experimental testing' . . . or inquiry; its fruit is not the triumph of one opinion over another but rather a mutual learning process during which the partners gain a better understanding of both the subject matter and themselves. [The intercultural dialogue, in this perspective, implies that] participants in cross cultural encounter are expected neither to erase themselves nor to appropriate or subjugate the other's differences; rather, the point is to achieve a . . . recognition of differences (Dallmayr 2010:115).

What Dallmayr proposes is a kind of reciprocal, transformative and humanising learning experience based on the mutual respect of liberal and democratic values. Migration policies in Europe and their application more often appear to pull in the opposite direction to the positive concept of intercultural dialogue elaborated by Dallmayr. Furthermore, what can be noticed is quite a contrast between theory and practice, between what is written and declared and what is effectively done.

All the European Charters are based on fundamental concepts such as equality, respect of diversity, non-discrimination, mutual understanding, tolerance, humanity and fraternity. Several important, fundamental documents have been produced by the European Commission (e.g. European Commission 2008) and by the Council of Europe (e.g. Council of Europe 2008) in recent years, and a lot of programmes and initiatives have been launched by these two organisations. Many similar public declarations have been made also by policy makers around Europe and in Italy. However, in practice, there is neither a common policy nor central coordination at the European level; basically every country decides on its own. In addition, the current world economic crisis is producing serious consequences at political and social levels, letting national identities develop and impose themselves, often identifying immigrants as a national threat (Bonifazi 2007:179–180). In this increasingly complex scenario, where sentiments of national identity are often used by political parties to increase their support, politicians are becoming increasingly wary over making political decisions which may be unpopular. Language requirements recently introduced almost all over Europe seem to allow decisions, and therefore responsibility, to be avoided in connection with these decisions, with the result of excluding part of the population of migrants, usually the most vulnerable, the illiterate, or near-illiterate, the isolated (usually women), the unemployed, and the least informed.

Currently, knowledge of the language of the new country, and ability to use it, is improperly presented as the main tool for integration and the certification of an adequate level language of knowledge is required to obtain fundamental rights such as long-term residency permits, citizenship, and naturalization depending on each country's legislation (see Van Avermaet and Rocca, this volume). As McNamara (2008), Saville and Van Avermaet (2008), and Van Avermaet (2009) have stressed, this becomes clearly a sociopolitical use of language assessment that requires not only professional or technical consideration, but also careful ethical consideration. It is indisputable that the ability to use the language is an important tool in order to support social inclusion and that language assessment could contribute to raise awareness of this; nevertheless, language assessment results should not replace political decisions in terms of migrants' exclusion. This is not the function of language assessment nor is it the purpose of using language tests.

The Italian context

The Italian context, in terms of recently introduced laws, seems to display the same contradictions mentioned above, in common with most other European countries. Before presenting the new Italian legislation concerning language requirements for immigrants, a brief introduction to the Italian context in terms of language training systems offered by the government to migrants, the institutions involved, the migrants' effective involvement in language training and related issues, will be provided.

Immigrants' language training

Both public and private institutions are involved in immigrants' language tuition in Italy. In 1997, a network of public schools was set up in order to provide continuing education to adults. These schools, called Centri Territoriali Permanenti (CTPs), have also been charged with providing language tuition for immigrants. This tuition is not compulsory and is free of charge. There are 540 CTPs in 398 cities across the Italian territory and more than 4,000 teachers are involved in immigrants' language tuition. In addition, there are several Charity Organisations (e.g. Sant'Egidio, Caritas, Scuole Migranti) deeply involved in migrants' language training and support. As there is no official data at national level, it's very difficult to find out the number of volunteer teachers involved in these organisations. Nevertheless, this number is very unlikely to be higher than 4,000, taking into account the number of volunteer teachers in regions with the highest rate of immigation such as Lazio (562) or Piemonte (447). Therefore, the overall number of teachers involved in immigrants' language training in the Italian territory is far below the actual need.

Strengths and weaknesses of the system overall

The strengths of the system include, among others, the language training which is free of charge, the availability of courses across the Italian territory, and the needs analysis that is conducted in the state schools at the beginning of the courses in order to plan a programme with suitable methods and content. There is also particular attention to flexibility (e.g. courses in the evening, exams on Sunday), in order to benefit the maximum number of immigrants. In addition, teachers, particularly in state schools, are generally trained to teach in this context, and are regularly provided with further relevant training.

There are also weaknesses in the system, including, in terms of courses attendance, a high percentage of course drop-outs (33%). That a high level of drop-outs should be counted as a weakness is based on a supposition, as no data regarding the reasons for dropping out exists. A further weakness is the lack of co-ordination and monitoring at national level and, consequently, that no evidence is collected at a national level that could contribute to understanding the migrants' learning process, their difficulties, their needs in educational terms, or the teaching process. The major weakness is, however, that only a really small percentage of the overall immigrant population is involved in the training process (only 10.1% of adult immigrants, according to the data provided by the Ministry of Education for 2008/ 2009). This could depend on lack of interest (it is possible to learn how to speak a language just by speaking with natives), or more likely, on poor provision of information about training opportunities. The lack of a monitoring process at national level and consequently of empirical data does not allow a real analysis, but even more worryingly it is suggestive of a difficulty in passing information on to immigrants and in getting them involved. This could have even more serious consequences in terms of access to work opportunities and more generally to social inclusion. This picture highlights the isolation of immigrants that contrasts with the declared general aim of social inclusion.

Despite the fact that there are around 5 million legal immigrants in Italy, the training system has not collapsed due to the low immigrant involvement. In fact, both state and private institutions together would not be able to satisfy a larger demand for language tuition. Only a small percentage of immigrants could therefore benefit from the training opportunities offered at national level. In addition, state funding for social integration dropped by 76.3% as compared to 2008. As a consequence, the main resources available in this area are represented by European funds. This is why it should be recommended that all the projects realised through European funds should first take into account the reality and the needs facing immigrants and secondly, they should respond to a common European framework to better plan concrete and coordinated actions.

The new legislation in Italy and the language requirements consequently introduced

In the current scenario in Italy, which is, to some extent, very contradictory and dominated by a severe reduction in state funding, the new legislation, in terms of language requirements, seems to be very demanding for immigrants, more restrictive compared to the past and potentially very *exclusion oriented*. The new legislation distinguishes newcomers (coming from non-EU countries: 'Third Country Nationals', as they are called) from migrants already settled in Italy. For the newcomers, a specific Integration Agreement was issued by President Napolitano on 14 September 2011 (Decreto del Presidente della Repubblica (DPR) 179). For immigrants already in Italy, a decree was issued by the Ministry of Interior jointly with the Ministry of Education on 4 June 2010 (Decreto Interministeriale (DM) 4 June 2010). A law proposal regarding citizenship has still to be discussed by parliament, and there are no language requirements at the moment.

Newcomers

Nowadays, all immigrants arriving in Italy (referred to as 'newcomers'), from non-EU countries who are above 16 years old, are obliged to sign the Integration Agreement when they apply for a residence permit upon their arrival. Knowledge of the language and of some elements of civics are fundamental components of the Agreement. The immigrants obtain a residence permit depending on a complex credits system. According to the system, all immigrants are given 16 credits after signing the Agreement. They keep all the credits only if they attend a training session (from 5 to 10 hours) on basic elements of civics (basic knowledge of the Italian Constitution, of the organisation of state institutions and of the welfare system) organised specifically and without any charge by the government, otherwise the 16 credits will be reduced to 1. The materials for the training are translated into the migrant's mother tongue.

After two years residing in Italy, immigrants are required to have gained 30 credits overall and, in addition, they have to pass an A2 test (that can be limited only to speaking) and a Knowledge of Society test in order to obtain a residence permit. If they do not succeed, they have one further year before being deported. In order to get the credits, theoretically the newcomers have various options: to get a prescribed language certificate, to attend one or more language courses, to present other kinds of educational or professional titles, or other documentation specified in the Agreement. An annex of the Agreement defines how many credits are assigned in each case.

As far as language Certificates are concerned, they can be awarded by the four Italian institutions currently recognised for this specific function by the Italian government (Università per Stranieri di Perugia, Università per Stranieri di Siena, Università Roma Tre, Società Dante Alighieri). According to the Agreement, the CTPs can also award their language certificates in this area. It is not yet clear which organisations will assess the knowledge of elements of civics. What is definitely clear is that in Italy language and Knowledge of Society certificates, as in other European States (Van Avermaet 2009), are likely to be the quickest and most economical option, in terms of time and resources, for the great majority of newcomers.

Immigrants already settled in Italy

A decree for immigrants already settled in Italy was issued on 4 June 2010. The immigrants involved are: those who are not EU citizens, those who are not refugees and those over 14 and under 65 years old. According to the law, the immigrants have two options in order to obtain the long-term residency permit: pass an A2 CEFR level language test, or submit other kinds of educational certificates prescribed in the law, such as: an attendance certificate for a language course with an exam at the end; an attendance certificate for a university course or a postgraduate course; language certificates awarded by the four Italian institutions already mentioned: Università per Stranieri di Perugia, Università per Stranieri di Siena, Università Roma Tre, Società Dante Alighieri; or secondary school diplomas obtained within the education system.

The CTPs A2 test: issues

The CTPs A2 language test was introduced by law, and is a formal assessment aimed at testing reading, listening and writing using traditional test techniques such as multiple choice, matching, gap filling, short answers; speaking is not currently assessed. According to a specific agreement signed in November 2010 by the Ministry of Interior and the Ministry of Education, the test is produced, administered and marked approximately every two months by around 380 CTPs selected by the Ministry of Education, who also provide the results. General specifications and guidelines have been produced by the four Italian institutions traditionally involved in language certification, not only for Level A2, but also A1 and B1. These guidelines have already been partially modified by the Ministry of Education (Ministero dell'Istruzione, dell' Universitàe della Ricera 2010).

According to the data provided by the Ministry of Education, from February 2011 to the end of June 2011 38,712 tests were administered, mostly in the northern and central parts of Italy (Milan, Rome, Brescia, Florence and Venice were the cities with the higher number of candidates). 4,227 (11.2%) candidates did not pass the test. Because these tests are high stakes and will have a great impact on Italian society, a number of issues will be discussed in relation to them. The issues relate to different areas: the test production process, administration and marking, co-ordination and monitoring of the whole process at national level, impact and consequences, school teachers' preparation in terms of formal, summative assessment and candidates' preparation for the test. None of these critical areas seem to be addressed properly by the system at the moment: the lack of any kind of national co-ordination implies that each CTP or network of CTPs produces its own test without any kind of piloting, pretesting or post-test analysis, and therefore the difficulty of the test can vary significantly from one CTP to another. The whole test production process is not going to be monitored at national level, so even specifications and guidelines provided by the four Italian institutions already mentioned can be easily disregarded. Despite the inevitable impact of the test, the Italian government seems uninterested in promoting research studies on the impact of the test on the stakeholders. In addition, Italian teachers' competence in producing high-stakes proficiency tests is very limited.

Candidates are not required to attend preparatory courses. This implies that immigrants who do not follow a specific language course have to familiarise themselves with the test specifications alone, not being completely sure that test specifications will remain the same either across test administrations or within the national territory. Due to the poor schooling of around 38% of immigrants registered in the CTPs (Ministero dell'Istruzione, dell' Universitàe della Ricera 2009), a further issue is about the impact of the traditional test methods used, which generally require quite a high level of schooling and test familiarisation in order to elicit responses representative of candidate abilities.

In conclusion, the introduction of the new language requirements presents the same problems and contradictions mentioned at European level. Formal assessment and tests are not really imposed by the new regulations, theoretically there seem to be other possible options, but in practice, tests will become the quickest and most economical option for the majority of the immigrants in order to obtain fundamental rights. Moreover, taking into account the current difficult national economic situation, and the consequent state funding reduction in this area, it is not possible to increase the offer of language and professional training for immigrants, hence every initiative or project is basically realised through European funds. A final, worrying, consideration about the lack of co-ordination and monitoring at national level of all these assessment initiatives is that this can really compromise fundamental criteria such as fairness and comparability of the assessments across the national territory and through different test administrations. Mere reference to the CEFR levels or to specifications and guidelines does not currently guarantee either any fairness or any real comparability.

The project *Italiano, lingua nostra* (ILN)

ILN is a national project, realised in 2010 (lasting from the end of February to the middle of June) at the Università per Stranieri di Perugia, by CVCL in collaboration with state and private institutions and charity organisations and was promoted and funded by the Italian Ministry of Interior using European funds. According to the objectives of the European fund for the Integration of Third-Country Nationals who supported the project, it aimed to:

- offer a training opportunity in order to promote the immigrants' social inclusion
- improve immigrants' knowledge of Italian
- improve immigrants' knowledge of Italian society and civics
- offer immigrants the opportunity of getting language certificates that could be used also for work purposes (at that time, language or civics certificates were not mandatory).

The project was the first systematic experiment at national level in terms of collaboration, coordination and communication between teaching and assessment, among all the different stakeholders involved in the project, something which is currently totally lacking in Italy within the migration context. The success of the project, according to the feedback collected so far, through the questionnaires administered (Van Avermaet and Rocca, this volume) may suggest the project as a possible model for further similar initiatives to be developed in this area, taking into account the aspects already mentioned:

collaboration, coordination, communication, constant monitoring applied to the training and testing process, feedback systematically collected through questionnaires and video interviews from both students and teachers, and a study on the impact of the actions realised during the project on education and society.

Salient features

In addition to continual collaboration between teachers and testing experts in order to share competences and experiences, there was also effective and systematic coordination organised by CVCL at national level, in terms of syllabus definition, and selection of teaching and testing materials. Continual monitoring of all the training and testing processes was conducted through phone calls, email, weekly web chats with teachers and CTP managers, forms completed by teachers, and newsletters published on the project's website. Additionally, to involve immigrants and improve communication, several forms of communication were made available by CVCL through the project's website: a blog, a forum, and email.

After courses and exams had concluded, separate questionnaires were administered to both students and teachers, together with interviews which were video recorded. Both provide interesting feedback which highlights strengths and weaknesses of the project, and also insights about the impact of the project on both education and society. Van Avermaet and Rocca (this volume) describe this in detail.

Outcomes

149 language courses at A1 and A2 levels, with some elements of civics, were provided in 10 Italian regions, and in 51 cities. 44 schools and CTPs, 30 charity organisations, and 175 teachers were involved. 2,843 students were registered at the beginning of the courses and 2,390 completed the training, with only a 15.8% drop-out rate. During the courses, some "meeting the society" activities were organised and students, accompanied by cultural mediators, visited public institutions such as hospitals, police stations, train stations, banks, post offices, museums, and libraries, in order to allow immigrants to meet people working in these places and learn how to interact with the organisations. Some class lessons and some "meeting the society" activities were video recorded and will be part of a DVD on the project. After the completion of courses, 1,957 Certificato di Conoscenza della Lingua Italiana (CELI) exams at Level A1 and A2 were administered and 88% of the candidates passed the exams and obtained a certificate. Of the questionnaires produced for students and teachers, 645 were administered to students and 63 to teachers. Both were statistically analysed. In addition to this, the interviews of 232 students and 60 teachers were recorded and analysed.

Some critical considerations

The responses received from the questionnaires have provided useful insights into the strengths and the weaknesses of the project. From the students' point of view, the project was a great opportunity in terms of a free language course, final exam and books. They also considered the project a very useful experience in terms of knowledge of society, self confidence and social inclusion. The final exam was particularly positively judged as a reward for their efforts. From the teachers' perspective, internal coordination, the clear, common objectives, well-defined priorities, and support for planning were positively regarded. As far as the final exam is concerned, teachers did not like spending too much time in preparing students for it (in terms of method and procedures), even if they considered the exam important in increasing students' motivation and consequently, class attendance (van Avermaet and Rocca, this volume).

This project, like others, was a good opportunity for only a small number of immigrants (compared to the overall immigrant population). They were probably the best informed ones who were willing to search for opportunities offered by the government to improve their condition. The problem of informing and involving the others remains completely unresolved by such isolated projects. The final consideration refers to those immigrants with poor literacy: the training offered by the project was insufficient for them, as the final exam was unachievable. Assisting immigrants with low levels of literacy is another major problem which needs attention, and must involve coordination, collaboration and monitoring.

Concluding remarks

Two emblematic pictures (www.google.com/images) conclude this contribution. 'From Genova's harbour to Lampedusa's coasts' would be a fitting caption for both. They refer to Italian emigration and immigration flows that are affecting Italy nowadays, but they could be useful for more general considerations. In the view of this contributor they remind us of three things:

- that migration is part of our own history, and we should keep a record of it, learning from our own history how to better deal with migration in the present times
- that migration will probably change our society, as happened in the past
- that the nature of this change depends on how we manage it.

Migration flows combined with the global economic crisis represent one of the crucial issues that contemporary society has to deal with. They should definitely be addressed through a global and multidisciplinary approach. Language requirements, recently introduced all over Europe, have very little to do with it; they are quick, functional answers to various national situations, and internal political and social debates. Nevertheless they can be quite powerful tools, more oriented to the exclusion of migrants than to their social inclusion, if not properly supported. Professionals in the area of language assessment should have more official involvement with European institutions in this area, to seek more effective collaboration, common choices and decisions at European level. In relation to this, shared frameworks defining concrete actions, with specific guidelines applied to the frameworks, could be very useful for dealing with the different aspects involved in language assessment in this context in a more responsible, coherent and coordinated way.

References

Baines, D (1991) *Emigration from Europe 1815–1930*, Cambridge: Cambridge University Press.

Bonifazi, C (2007) *L'immigrazione straniera in Italia*, Bologna: il Mulino.

Council of Europe (2008) *White Paper on Intercultural Dialogue: "Living together as equals in dignity"*, available online: www.coe.int/dialogue

Dallmayr, F (2010) *Integral Pluralism. Beyond Culture Wars*, Lexington: The University Press of Kentucky.

DM (Decreto Interministeriale) (2010) available online: www.interno.it// sites//0954_2010_06_16_DM_04062010.html

DPR (Decreto del Presidente della Repubblica) 179 (2011) available online: www. cgil.it/DBLEGISLATIVO/179.pdf

Easterlin, R A (1961) Influences in European overseas emigration before World War I, in *Economic Development and Cultural Change*, Chicago: The University of Chicago Press, 331–351.

European Commission (2008) *Green Paper "Migration & Mobility: challenges and opportunity for EU education systems"*, Brussels: Commission of the European Communities.

Favell, A (2009) Immigration, migration, and free movement in the making of Europe, in Checkel, J T and Katzenstein, P J (Eds) *European Identity*, Cambridge: Cambridge University Press, 167–189.

Fondazione Migrantes (2011) *Rapporto Italiani nel mondo 2011*, Roma: Idos Edizioni.

Gadamer, H G (1989) *Truth and Method*, 2nd edn., New York: Crossroad Publishing.

Hatton, T J and Williamson, J G (1992) What drove the mass migrations from Europe in the late nineteenth century? in *Harvard Institute of Economic Research Working Papers 1614*, Harvard: Institute of Economic Research.

Hatton, T J and Williamson, J G (1998) *The Age of Mass Migration. Causes and Economic Impact*, Oxford: Oxford University Press.

Heidegger, M (1957) *Identität und Differenz*, 4th edn., Pfullingen: Neske.

Massey, D S (1988) Economic development and international migration in comparative perspective, *Population and Development Review* 14 (3), 383–413.

McNamara, T (2008) The social-political and power dimensions of tests, in Shohamy, E and Hornberger, N H (Eds), *Encyclopedia of Language and Education Vol. 7: Language Testing and Assessment*, 2nd edn., Dordrecht, The Netherlands: Springer, 415–427.

Merleau-Ponty, M (1973) Dialogue and the perception of the Other, in Lefort, C (Ed.) *The Prose of the World*, Evanston Ill: Northwestern University Press, 139–140.

Merriam-Webster (2012) *Merriam-Webster Online Dictionary*, available online: www.merriam-webster.com

Ministero dell'Istruzione, dell'Università e della Ricera (2009) *Rapporto di sintesi monitoraggio dell'Istruzione degli Adulti a.s. 2007/08*, available online: www.indire.it/ida/content/index.php?action=lettura&id_m=8254&id_cnt=8444

Ministero dell'Istruzione, dell'Università e della Ricera (2010) *Vademecum*, available online: ebookbrowse.com/2010-12-miur-vademecum-test-italiano-pdf-d326041238

Morghen, R (1962) *Il Medioevo cristiano*, 3rd edn., Bari: Laterza.

Pugliese, E (2006) *L'Italia tra migrazioni internazionali e migrazione interne*, 2nd edn., Bologna: il Mulino.

Reale, G (2003) *Radici culturali e spirituali dell'Europa*, Milano: Raffaello Cortina Editore.

Saville, N and Van Avermaet, P (2008) Language testing for migration and citizenship, in Taylor, L and Weir, C J (Eds) *Multilingualism and Assessment. Proceedings of the ALTE Berlin Conference, May 2005*, Studies in Language Testing volume 27, Cambridge: UCLES/Cambridge University Press, 265–275.

Smith, D M (1959) *Storia d'Italia. Dal 1861 al 1958*, Bari: Laterza.

Taylor, M (1971) *The Distant Magnet. European Emigration to the USA*, London: Eyre & Spottiswoode.

Tomaske, J A (1971) The determinants of intercountry differences in European Emigration: 1881–1900, in *Journal of Economic History Volume 31*, 840–853.

Van Avermaet, P (2009) Fortress Europe? Language policy regimes for immigration and citizenship, in Hogan-Brun, G, Mar-Molinero, C and Stevenson, P (Eds) *Testing Regimes: Cross-national Perspectives on Language, Migration and Citizenship. Discourse Approaches to Politics, Society and Culture Series*, Amsterdam: Benjamins, 15–43.

Vedovelli, M (Ed.) (2011) *Storia linguistica dell'emigrazione italiana nel mondo*, Roma Carocci editore.

3 The inclusive, plurilingual and intercultural approach of the Council of Europe and its implications for evaluation and assessment in language education

Waldemar Martyniuk

Council of Europe
European Centre for Modern Languages, Graz, Austria

Abstract

This article features the latest initiatives of the Council of Europe in support of an inclusive, plurilingual and intercultural approach to language education, reviewing relevant policy documents, and presenting the range of tools already made available and those currently under development by the Language Policy Division (LPD) and the European Centre for Modern Languages (ECML). It also presents the rationale behind the next, fourth medium-term programme of the ECML activities (2012–15) that aims at facilitating European cooperation on the implementation of the new concept of language education.

Introduction

The Council of Europe aims at maintaining and enhancing linguistic and cultural diversity in Europe and promoting learning and use of languages as a means to support intercultural dialogue, social cohesion and democratic citizenship, and as an important economic asset in a modern knowledge-based society. The Council of Europe's efforts in this respect are well illustrated by the development of such reference documents and tools as the Common European Framework of Reference for languages (CEFR) (Council of Europe 2001a) and the *European Language Portfolio* (ELP) (Council of Europe 2001b), conventions such as the *European Charter for Regional or Minority Languages* (Council of Europe 1992), and policy documents such as the *White Paper on Intercultural Dialogue* (Council of Europe 2008b), *From*

Linguistic Diversity to Plurilingual Education: Guide for the Development of Language Education Policies in Europe (Council of Europe 2007), the quite recent *Recommendation No. R (2008) 7 of the Committee of Ministers on the Use of the CEFR and the Promotion of Plurilingualism* (Council of Europe 2008a), and the most recent report of the Group of Eminent Persons of the Council of Europe *Living Together: Combining Diversity and Freedom in 21st-century Europe* (Council of Europe 2011b).

The European Union shares these aims and its support for linguistic diversity in Europe is reflected in such policy documents as *Multilingualism: An Asset for Europe and a Shared Commitment* (European Commission 2008) and the *Council Resolution on a European Strategy for Multilingualism* (European Union 2008).

The Council of Europe promotes strongly the notion of plurilingualism – an individual ability to develop competences in and use more than one language – as an important human value. In the Council's work, adequate development of language competences is viewed as a pre-requisite for unrestricted and fair access to good-quality education, which, in turn, constitutes the necessary basis for ensuring social cohesion, promoting democratic citizenship, fostering intercultural dialogue and managing migration – priorities specified by the Warsaw Summit 2005 aimed at building a more humane and inclusive Europe. This is reflected in the documents and tools included on the online *Platform of Resources and References for Plurilingual and Intercultural Education* developed and launched recently by the Language Policy Division (LPD) in consultation with all 47 member states.

Within its upcoming fourth medium-term programme of activities (2012–15) the European Centre for Modern Languages (ECML) in Graz aims at facilitating European cooperation on the implementation of the new concept of inclusive, plurilingual and intercultural education initiated by the Language Policy Division. In the crucial stage of testing, awareness raising, adapting and implementing this educational policy in practice, the ECML can act as a laboratory for targeted policy application and innovative practice. The cooperation the ECML initiated in 2010 with the major International Non-Government Organisations – stakeholders in the areas of language education and research, including the Association of Language Testers in Europe (ALTE) – will become an important dimension of this work.

Council of Europe's *Platform of Resources and References for Plurilingual and Intercultural Education*

Recently, the LPD launched a *Platform of Resources and References for Plurilingual and Intercultural Education*, expanding the scope of consideration beyond the domain of foreign modern languages and including classical languages and languages of schooling: learning, teaching and assessment of languages taught as school subjects (the majority language such as Swedish in Sweden, Polish in Poland, etc.) and language competences required for other school subjects – language across curriculum. The *Platform* offers a new, open and dynamic framework of reference, with a system of definitions, descriptions and descriptors, studies and good practices which member states are invited to consult and use in support of their policy to promote equal access to quality education. Accompanying the *Platform* is the *Guide for the Development and Implementation of Curricula for Plurilingual and Intercultural Education* (Council of Europe 2010). With this new instrument the Council consequently draws attention to the needs of the individual learner, underlining that access to education and success at school heavily depend on language competences. Some learners may be disadvantaged at school because their competences do not match the school's expectations: children from socially disadvantaged backgrounds, children from migrant families, or children whose first language is a regional language. An adequate command of the language(s) of schooling is crucial to success at school and social advancement. A major challenge for today's education systems is to support learners in acquiring adequate language and intercultural competences which will enable them to develop as strong individuals and operate effectively and successfully as citizens. The *Guide* is intended to facilitate improved implementation of the values and principles of plurilingual and intercultural education in the teaching of all languages – foreign, regional or minority, classical, and languages of schooling. It provides a general picture of the issues and principles involved in designing and/or improving curricula, and of pedagogical and didactic approaches which open the way to fuller realisation of the general aim of plurilingual and intercultural education.

Inclusive, plurilingual and intercultural approach – evaluation and assessment issues

The Language Policy Division of the Council of Europe has developed and is offering for public use a number of tools related specifically to language testing and assessment. The following instruments and materials have been made available so far:

- *Relating Language Examinations to the Common European Framework of Reference for Languages: Learning, Teaching, Assessment (CEFR). A Manual* (Council of Europe 2009b)
- *Further Material on Maintaining Standards across Languages, Contexts and Administrations by Exploiting Teacher Judgment and IRT Scaling* (North and Jones 2009)
- *Reference Supplement to the Manual for Relating Examinations to the CEFR* (Council of Europe 2009c)

- illustrations of the CEFR levels of language proficiency
- content analysis grids for speaking, writing, listening and reading materials.

Two publications offering related research perspectives and case studies supplement the toolkit (Figueras and Noijons 2009, Martyniuk 2010). Most recently, a *Manual for Language Test Development and Examining for Use with the CEFR* was produced by ALTE on behalf of the Language Policy Division (Council of Europe 2011a).

Accompanying the *Platform* of resources and references for plurilingual and intercultural education is a series of studies discussing specific aspects of the new approach, among them evaluation and assessment issues. Lengyel (2010), in a study on continuous assessment procedures as accompaniment to individualised learning and teaching gives an overview over different approaches to language diagnostics examining their suitability for multilingual settings. The author gives several examples of diagnostic tools and procedures such as questionnaires and interviews, analytical approaches (profile analysis), observation tools, self-assessment and documentation practices, offering possible strategies for their implementation in multilingual classrooms, and concluding that no 'one size fits all' approach is possible.

Discussing the new role for portfolio approaches in dealing with evaluation and assessment under the extended plurilingual and intercultural approach, Fleming and Little (2010) examine the need for further development of two Council of Europe instruments: the English Language Portfolio and *Autobiography of Intercultural Encounters* (Council of Europe 2009a) for use in primary and secondary education. For primary education, they see a need for a new generation of portfolios that include but also go beyond the English Language Portfolio and include descriptors for pupils' first language (L1) literacy development. On post-primary and secondary level they suggest developing specific portfolio approaches for language and non-language subjects, or, alternatively, integrating language as subject and language in other subjects by genres or types of language use, and revising the English Language Portfolio's standard adult passport to track development of learners' plurilingual repertoires. The authors conclude by offering key questions defining the new role for portfolio approaches, namely how can a portfolio approach:

- encourage appropriate meta-awareness and reflection on language to support learning?
- provide a rich record of achievement in the development of competence in all aspects of language?
- help raise subject teachers' awareness of how language is integral to learning the subject?
- raise learners' critical awareness of their developing plurilingual profile and intercultural capacity?

- include a social/communal element that prompts learners to see themselves in relation to others in their developing language profile?

Lenz and Berthele (2010) identify selected competences particularly relevant to plurilingual and intercultural education such as:

- mediation
- polyglot dialogue
- intercomprehension in reading
- intercultural competence.

Using the Assessment Use Argument approach (Bachman and Palmer 2010), they examine the relevance, the intended consequences and decisions based on assessment, the construct to be assessed and interpretations, and the assessments and assessment records with regard to each of these competences. Their findings are that many possible assessments of these competences are well suited for formative purposes but there are only limited possibilities for standardised, high-stakes assessment and more actual practice is needed in this respect.

The contribution of the ECML to the implementation of inclusive, plurilingual and intercultural approaches to education

The ECML, a Council of Europe Partial Agreement based in Graz, Austria, has been serving the community of language education professionals in its 34 member states for over 15 years. The Centre's successful programmes of activities, such as the Languages for Social Cohesion programme (2004–07), have comprised more than 50 projects coordinated by international teams of experts and directly involved over 6,000 language professionals in Europe and beyond, with the impact reaching as far afield as Canada, Japan and countries in Africa. Empowering language professionals is the overarching objective of the current, third programme of ECML activities to be concluded by the end of 2011. At the time of writing (September 2011), 23 international project teams established by the Centre are finalising their work on developing practical approaches and tools for language education, which also support the application of language policy instruments developed by the Council's Language Policy Division and the implementation of recommendations related to the European Charter for Regional or Minority Languages. The programme includes activities which are intended to help teachers to cope with current challenges, enhance their skills and have a greater impact on their professional environment. The projects are divided into four thematic areas: evaluation and assessment, continuity across educational stages, content and language integrated learning (CLIL), and approaches to plurilingual education. Within the evaluation and assessment strand, eight international project teams set out to answer questions such as:

- How can learners and teachers (and other stakeholders) know that learning has been successful?
- What evaluation strategies can they adopt?
- How can evaluation and assessment facilitate the planning of future learning?
- How can school examinations be linked to European standards?
- How should teachers react to the shift towards more centralised evaluation?

With its next, fourth medium-term programme of activities *Learning Through Languages: Promoting inclusive, plurilingual and intercultural education 2012–2015*, the Centre responds to national priorities as, for example, reflected in the recommendations included in the national Language Education Policy Profiles conducted by the LPD at the request of national governments. It aims at facilitating European cooperation on the implementation of the new concept of plurilingual and intercultural education initiated by the LPD and formally supported by the member states of the Council of Europe within the programme *Language policies and the right to education for social inclusion (2010–2014)*, adopted by the Steering Committee for Education and the Steering Committee for Higher Education and Research. In the crucial stage of testing, awareness raising, adapting and implementing this educational policy in practice the ECML can act as a laboratory for targeted policy application and innovative practice.

The ECML's 2012–15 programme seeks to draw attention to the fact that access for all to good-quality education represents a precondition for democratic developments in European societies. Against this backdrop the ECML programme will focus on the key agent, the 'motor' or promoter of positive and productive multilingual societies: the learner. Within societies and in cooperation between societies developments at all levels, be it social, economic or political, heavily draw upon successful learning taking place at all stages of life and reaching out to all people living in the society. Thus, the learner is not only a child or adolescent between the ages of 7 to 16, which marks the period of obligatory schooling in most European countries. Rather, every human being at all stages in life is a learner within a lifelong learning process.

In the context of increasing diversification of students in classrooms and continued compartmentalisation of learning provision in educational institutions, the ECML programme seeks to point at the crucial, integrative role of languages in all subjects and beyond, in informal learning settings. Quality education as a prerequisite for successful schooling and for a lifelong learning career needs to incorporate inclusive, plurilingual and intercultural pedagogic approaches – which do not replace the teaching and learning of particular languages but rather complement and broaden their scope:

- in the foreign language classroom
- in the majority language classroom
- in subjects other than languages (notwithstanding the fact that languages play a key role in all subjects)
- in provision and preparation for informal and non-formal learning.

The ECML's long-term vision on language education is building upon the philosophy of the CEFR emphasising that human beings do 'not keep . . . languages and cultures in strictly separated mental compartments, but rather build . . . up a communicative competence to which all knowledge and experience of language contributes and in which languages interrelate and interact' (Council of Europe 2001a:4). Under the new programme, the perspective expands from a comparatively narrow focus on foreign language learning to learning in all educational contexts and domains always incorporating language learning in the mother tongue of the learner or in an additional language of the learner's repertoire. In the lifelong learning perspective the transversal aspect of language education becomes even more relevant because the subject areas listed above are not maintained as strictly as they are during the schooling process. Indeed, interdisciplinary courses are far more frequently offered for adult education than at schools and this can be an asset in implementing inclusive, plurilingual and intercultural pedagogy.

The growing linguistic and cultural diversity in today's European societies makes it evident that in order to cater adequately for each learner's needs – supporting the development of each learner's linguistic and intercultural capacities required for their personal well-being and success and for the benefit of the society they are a part of – provision needs to build on *inclusive, plurilingual* and *intercultural* pedagogic approaches.

Inclusive education evolved from Special Needs Education and its philosophy is to counteract exclusion and discrimination of children with disabilities. In a broader context, this discussion was brought forward under the label 'integration', targeting other disadvantaged learner groups like migrants, cultural and linguistic minorities, children or adults of low economic or social status, etc. The discussions about necessary reform and change of education in order to achieve quality education for all have made clear that the challenge of diversity cannot be met by integration efforts on the side of the marginalised group only. Rather, all have to pursue and work towards the common goal of taking a holistic approach ensuring equal opportunities and rights for all. In this context, inclusive approaches are being promoted as a way to provide learning environments that allow for democratic, effective and sustainable learning processes, and outcomes and output for the benefit of all. Following this ideal, the ECML programme intends to further elaborate the obvious link between linguistic and intercultural competences and inclusion to identify approaches for practical implementation in the classroom.

Plurilingual education and resulting pedagogic approaches aim at respecting and developing each learner's language repertoire, enabling the speaker to use languages with different degrees of proficiency and adapted to different contexts (home, school, public, private, professional, etc.). The concept of plurilingualism was first elaborated in the CEFR (Council of Europe 2001a). It was pointed out that the implementation of plurilingual education would have a profound impact on language education by moving away from the ideal of 'mastering' a foreign language to the perspective of developing the learner's unique individual linguistic abilities and competences. In the context of the discussion on quality education for all it is the social aspect of plurilingual education that has been stressed. Awareness-raising activities targeting languages present in classrooms but usually not considered as learning objects are being considered as powerful means to develop peer learning built on tolerance, respect for and knowledge about each other. In view of this dimension, plurilingual education ideally complements the inclusive and intercultural components of the envisaged pedagogic approaches.

The need for European citizens to develop *intercultural competences* has been widely acknowledged by educational authorities and teaching professionals. In the Council of Europe's *White Paper on Intercultural Dialogue* (Council of Europe 2008b) it is pointed out that attitudes, behaviour, knowledge and skills relevant in intercultural contexts are not acquired as a side-effect of developing language competences but need to be explicitly placed on the educational agenda in order to be taught, learned, practised, elaborated and adapted to individual needs and social contexts. There is a clear link between intercultural education and language (specifically foreign language) education. But in view of the role of intercultural dialogue in the context of democratic citizenship and human rights education it became clear that intercultural education needs to become a constituent part of formal education and a nurtured element of the informal/non-formal learning context in good-quality education in Europe.

Taking such a coherent and holistic view on education presents an important developmental step in the work of the ECML and its envisaged impact on education for the benefit of European societies. Europe wide, the ECML is in a unique position to bring together all educational strands, relevant institutions, associations and interest groups beyond the inner circle of the language education community.

References

Bachman, L and Palmer, A (2010) *Language Assessment in Practice*, Oxford; New York: Oxford University Press.

Council of Europe (1992) *European Charter for Regional or Minority Languages*, available online: conventions.coe.int/treaty/en/Treaties/Html/148.htm

Council of Europe (2001a) *Common European Framework of Reference for Languages: Learning, Teaching, Assessment*, Cambridge: Cambridge University Press.

Council of Europe (2001b) *The European Language Portfolio*, available online: www.coe.int/portfolio

Council of Europe (2007) *From Linguistic Diversity to Plurilingual Education: Guide for the Development of Language Education Policies in Europe*, Strasbourg: Council of Europe.

Council of Europe (2008a) *Recommendation No. R (2008) 7 of the Committee of Ministers on the Use of the CEFR and the Promotion of Plurilingualism*, Strasbourg: Council of Europe.

Council of Europe (2008b) *White Paper on Intercultural Dialogue*, Strasbourg: Council of Europe.

Council of Europe (2009a) *Autobiography of Intercultural Encounters*, available online: www.coe.int/t/dg4/autobiography/AutobiographyTool_en.asp

Council of Europe (2009b) *Relating Language Examinations to the Common European Framework of Reference for Languages: Learning, Teaching, Assessment (CEFR). A Manual*, Strasbourg: Council of Europe.

Council of Europe (2009c) *Reference Supplement to the Manual for Relating Examinations to the CEFR*, Strasbourg: Council of Europe.

Council of Europe (2010) *Guide for the Development and Implementation of Curricula for Plurilingual and Intercultural Education*, Strasbourg: Council of Europe.

Council of Europe (2011a) *Manual for Language Test Development and Examining for Use with the CEFR*, Strasbourg: Council of Europe.

Council of Europe (2011b) *Living Together: Combining Diversity and Freedom in 21st-century Europe*, Strasbourg: Council of Europe.

European Commission (2008) *Multilingualism: An Asset for Europe and a Shared Commitment*, Brussels: European Commission.

European Union (2008) *Council Resolution on a European Strategy for Multilingualism*, Brussels: Council of the European Union.

Figueras, N and Noijons, J (Eds) (2009) *Linking to the CEFR Levels: Research Perspectives*, Arnhem: Cito, EALTA.

Fleming, M and Little, D (2010) *Languages in and for Education: a Role for Portfolio Approaches?*, Strasbourg: Council of Europe.

Lengyel, D (2010) *Language Diagnostics in Multilingual Settings with Respect to Continuous Assessment Procedures as Accompaniment of Individualized Learning and Teaching*, Strasbourg: Council of Europe.

Lenz, P and Berthele, R (2010) *Assessment in Plurilingual and Intercultural Education*, Strasbourg: Council of Europe.

Martyniuk, W (Ed.) (2010) *Aligning Tests with the CEFR: Reflections On Using the Council of Europe's Draft Manual*, Studies in Languages Testing volume 33, Cambridge: UCLES/Cambridge University Press.

North, B and Jones, N (2009) *Further Material on Maintaining Standards across Languages, Contexts and Administrations by Exploiting Teacher Judgment and IRT Scaling*, Strasbourg: Council of Europe.

Useful websites

An updated list of relevant Council of Europe documents such as guides, policy papers, conference documents, case studies, as well as web links can be found on the following websites:

Council of Europe:	http://www.coe.int
Language Policy Division:	http://www.coe.int/lang
European Language Portfolio:	http://www.coe.int/portfolio
European Centre for Modern Languages:	http://www.ecml.at
European Day of Languages:	http://www.coe.int/EDL
The United Nations Educational, Scientific and Cultural Organization (UNESCO)	http://www.unesco.org

4 European Index of Multilingual Policies and Practices

Paweł Poszytek
Fundacja Sztuka Uczenia, Poland

Abstract

This article shows how the Language Rich Europe project is creating a framework for comparative analysis called the European Index of Multilingual Policies and Practices. It presents the background of this innovative research as well as the construct of the research tool, namely the standards which form the matrix for the analysis, the domains measured, how they are measured, and how the data is disseminated and presented. The article also explores challenging issues regarding the validity of the research and problems with the creation of composite indices. These are fundamental considerations since the research area is very broad, ranging from official, national policies through practices in formal education to how language issues are approached in the business sector, media and public spheres. The article also depicts the results of a pilot study in one of the participating countries. Finally, future steps and cycles of the project are described.

Background

The Language Rich Europe (LRE) Index is the main research tool of a pan-European project, Language Rich Europe. The LRE project is carried out by a consortium of over 30 acknowledged institutions in Europe under the leadership of the British Council. This initiative is co-financed by the European Commission.

The project, with its Index as a pioneering new tool for monitoring the level of adherence of national multilingual policies and practices to European recommendations and resolutions, seeks to capture the attention of leaders in government, business and society across Europe in order to: (1) illustrate the current situation, highlighting good policy and practice in order to enable informed policy choices; (2) inspire a new language focus among decision makers by demonstrating the importance of languages in stable and prosperous societies; and (3) motivate more learners and users of languages. Accordingly, on a more practical level the objectives of the project are the following:

- better understanding of good practices in language teaching and learning for social inclusion and competitiveness
- enhanced cooperation and commitment to improving language policies and practices
- increased awareness of European recommendations and how countries perform against them
- creation of a sustainable European benchmarking tool to evaluate policies and practices (Hope 2011:5).

In addition, it must be stressed at this point that European recommendations and resolutions are understood here very broadly with reference to main policy documents released both by the Council of Europe (CoE) and the European Union (EU) institutions mainly over the last decade. Although Mackiewicz's claim still holds true that there is not one single document that sums up what might be called 'European language policy' (Mackiewicz 2004:174), both the CoE's and the EU's documents form the matrix which may be treated as the reference for what might be called European language policy. Among many others, it includes milestone documents such as *European Charter for Regional or Minority Languages* (Council of Europe 1992) and *Action Plan for 2004–2006: Promoting Language Learning and Linguistic Diversity* (European Commission 2004), *A New Framework Strategy for Multilingualism* (European Commission 2005), *Final Report of High Level Group on Multilingualism* (European Commission 2007), *Multilingualism: an Asset for Europe and a Shared Commitment* (European Commission 2008), *Resolution on a European Strategy for Multilingualism* (Council of the European Union 2008), *A Rewarding Challenge: How the Multiplicity of Languages Could Strengthen Europe* (Maalouf 2008) and *Languages Mean Business. Companies Work Better with Languages* (Davignon 2008). The full list and comments referring to these and other relevant documents can be found in Extra and Yagmur (2011:7–9, 23–26) and Poszytek (2011:26–27). Accordingly, the main aim of the LRE project is to monitor national language policies against European language policy in reference to national, foreign, regional and minority languages, as well as to compare the state of affairs in the participating 20 countries and four regions across Europe.

Finally, the question must be raised if there is a need for such monitoring and comparison. Although much has been done for languages on European, national and regional levels, evidence shows that the take-up of European guidance in the field of languages has been uneven across Europe. Additionally, policy cooperation on different levels has always proved challenging and the knowledge gained from this process has not been shared systematically (Hope 2011:4). Consequently, before carrying the process of implementing policies even further, it seems necessary to reflect on what has been achieved so far and learn some lessons from it. Nardo, Saisana, Saltelli,

Tarantola, Hoffman and Giovannini (2005:8) stress that composite indicators, and the LRE Index is one of these, are more and more recognised as tools in policy analysis and public communication.

Construct of the LRE Index

The main distinctive feature of the LRE Index is that it is a descriptive tool for awareness raising at both the public and the political macro-level, which presents descriptive indices per strand and per country or region in order to reflect the degree of adherence to European benchmarks in terms of European guidelines or recommendations. These recommendations, derived from the documents listed in the Background section of this paper, set the standards in the following areas of language learning, teaching and use:

- provisions for teaching and learning of regional, ethnic and migrant languages
- mastering two foreign languages and a mother tongue during the period of formal education – the so-called 2+1 standard
- promoting language diversity and the idea of multilingualism
- establishing clear aims of language education at all stages
- providing smooth transition in learning languages between the end of one learning stage and the beginning of another one
- promoting the idea of Content and Language Integrated Learning (CLIL) through defining the standards of teacher training and creation of didactic materials
- establishing a transparent system of language certification on the basis of the Common European Framework of Reference for languages (CEFR) (Council of Europe 2001) for languages developed by the CoE
- introduction of mentoring system to support young teachers
- acknowledgement of teacher qualifications across Europe
- promoting languages in media
- promoting languages in business – taking care of language development of employees, making use of apprenticeship opportunities abroad and communication channels via different languages
- promoting languages in the context of lifelong learning and the labour market
- promoting the contribution of multilingualism to creativity through enhancing the access to other ways of thinking and interpreting
- promoting European languages outside Europe.

Accordingly, the Index refers to all these issues and it is structured along the following lines:

- official documents and databases on language diversity – strand 1
- languages in pre-primary and primary education – strand 2
- languages in secondary education – strand 3
- languages in vocational and university education – strand 4
- languages in the media – strand 5
- languages in public services and spaces – strand 6
- languages in business – strand 7.

The questionnaire, which is used to collect the data for the Index, includes over 200 questions across all the strands. Depending on the strand, the data is collected differently. For the first meta-strand, as well as for strands 2 and 3, the data is collected from experts in the field (usually two experts in each participating country provide the answers to the questions). As regards strands 4, 5 and 6, the data is collected in the two biggest cities in the country and in a third one which is located in the area where the biggest regional language is used in this country. For strand 4, the data is collected with the use of interviews with principals of three vocational schools and three universities per city; for strands 5 and 6 as many interviews are carried out as necessary with owners of bookshops, newsagents and heads of relevant municipal institutions, such as city councils, hospitals, police stations, libraries, etc. In addition, data collectors check data by themselves, for example, the use of languages in transportation services. The primary data for strand 7 is collected in the same way as for strands 4–6. In each participating country or region 24 companies located in the cities characterised above are interviewed. The number of companies results from the categorisation based on three main parameters: (1) the size of the company: small, medium, large; (2) the type of the company: supermarket, building/construction company, hotel, bank; (3) the scope of the company: local/regional, national, multinational/ international.

This tri-city-oriented approach to collect primary data for strands 4–7 derives from the following assumptions:

- multilingualism is most prevalent in urban settings
- cities are primary spaces where urban planners create local policies on multilingualism
- cities reinforce translocal and transnational dynamics in dealing with diversity

(Extra and Yagmur 2011:18).

All Index questions are designed in a way which enables the retrieval of rateable data. This data, in return, is then weighed according to a specified algorithm. The procedure leads to obtaining a country profile. A score of 100 would mean 100% adherence to the European standards mentioned above.

Challenging issues and quality assurance measures

As mentioned above, the LRE Index takes the form of a composite indicator. This has different implications for the validity of the research. On the one hand, composite indicators by their nature:

- can summarise complex or multi-dimensional issues in view of supporting decision-makers
- are easier to interpret than trying to find a trend in many separate indicators
- facilitate the task of ranking countries on complex issues in a benchmarking exercise
- can assess progress of countries over time on complex issues
- reduce the size of a set of indicators or include more information within the existing size limit
- place issues of country performance and progress at the centre of the policy arena
- facilitate communication with general public (i.e. citizens, media, etc.) and promote accountability

(Nardo et al 2005:8).

All these features closely reflect the main aims of the LRE project. However, Nardo et al also enumerate problematic issues connected with the use of composite indicators such as: creating misleading policy messages and simplistic policy conclusions, disguising serious failings and leading to inappropriate policies, misuse, and political influence (Nardo et al 2005:8).

In order to avoid the threats mentioned above, Nardo et al (2005:9–10) propose a set of factors to be considered while constructing indices to guarantee quality and soundness of the research, namely the *theoretical framework* chosen, *data selection, multivariate analysis, missing data, normalisation of data, weighting and aggregation, robustness and sensitivity* and *links to other variables*.

These factors are reflected in the LRE Index in the following ways: a *theoretically formulated construct* underlies the LRE Index, as seen in the design of the questionnaire, which closely reflects European recommendations and guidelines. In the initial phase of the project the questions for the questionnaire were developed by a team of researchers, policy makers and officials from the Netherlands, UK, Hungary, Germany and Poland, including the author of this article. This team was subsequently transformed into a steering group of the whole project. Finally, a Tilburg University team from Babylon Centre assumed responsibility for the research part of the project, and a steering group including a representative of the CoE and the panel of internationally acknowledged experts formed during the later phase of the project advised on and approved the development of the Index. In the beginning of 2011 the Index questionnare was trialled in Poland, Spain and Catalonia by national teams working closely with the Tilburg research team and the steering committee of the project. The pilot in Poland was carried out by the author of this paper and the detailed issues which emerged out of this excercise are discussed later in this paper. Regardless of the country or region where the pilot excercise took place, similar problems arose around four areas: (i) translation problems and the issues connected with interpretation of the questions (this is a common problem of all pan-European projects resulting from diversity of linguistic and cultural contexts); (ii) different educational systems; (iii) logistic problems with collecting the data, which sometimes resulted in lack of available data for certain questions or reluctance on the part of interviewees to provide the data, especially for the business strand; (iv) the gaps in reference to all European benchmarks.

The amendment of the LRE Index questionniare in light of the pilot phase contributed to its external validity and direct links to European benchmarks. However, this approach poses a lot of challenges in relation to internal validity since some of these recommendations are very general and difficult to interpret. For example, one of the EU standards in teaching foreign languages is to start early but it is not clear from EU documents how early this start should be and what conditions of such teaching should be guaranteed, especially since experts are divided in their opinion on whether an early language start is beneficial to the learner. Consequently, a country would score higher in the LRE Index if it provides evidence that an early language start is guaranteed in the official educational system, even as early as at pre-primary level regardless of the exact age of learners. Additional variables such as the cut-off age for best cognitive development of a learner are not taken into consideration since the aim of the Index questionnaire is not to improve the matrix it refers to, but to reflect it as fully as possible. Again, it must be stressed that the Index measures the level of adherence to the European matrix of recommendations, regardless of how valid they are by their own nature. Additionally, apart from permanent points of interest in language policy, European recommendations fluctuate according to short-term overarching policies and priorities, not to mention the fact that this whole matrix of individual recommendations has gaps in relation to certain aspects of language learning and teaching. For instance, the issue of languages for competitiveness and working life prevails, whereas the issue of the contribution of language learning to personal development and benefits is treated marginally. Besides, there is a general tendency for European documents to target provisions for language learning, teaching and use and to stress the importance of languages in the context of the labour market instead of exploring content issues. In consequence this means, for example, that the Index does not measure what methodology is used for teaching languages in individual countries. On the other hand, it includes a separate strand devoted to vocational education and the position of languages in it. And again, as explained above, the Index does not introduce variables which are not derived from exact European recommendations. Otherwise the Index could not claim external validity in the context of European benchmarks.

As regards *data selection*, the country coverage aspect in the form of collecting meta-data, general data and tri-city formula has already been discussed in the Background section of this paper. In addition, it must be added that in this respect the following prerequisites underlie the construction of the LRE Index: (1) the Index questions should deliver rateable data for each of the seven strands; (2) rateable data should be weighed (see below for details); (3) yes/no questions where one of the two answers would predictably lead to 100% scores should be avoided; (4) the Index should be robust enough for repeated measurement over time (see also below) (Extra and Yagmur 2011:21).

Multivariate analysis, such as the structure of indicators, suitability of data and selected methodological challenges, including validity issues, has already been discussed earlier. Due to the extensive and complex area of language learning, teaching and use to be covered, a reasonable compromise had to be reached in choosing measurable parameters which define the Index reflecting European recommendations, and are at the same time meaningful to the the research end-users, who are mainly policy makers in this case.

Missing data in the main study did not pose a substantial problem because, as was mentioned above, the pilot excercise highlighted potential issues and precautions were undertaken to collect all the necessary data in the respective countries. Extremely rare cases were reported by data collectors about difficulty in data retrieving. For example, in cases where this problem was connected with data concerning the number of book translations in libraries, instead of retrieving it from the electronic library system, estimates were provided via interviews with library employees.

Normalisation of data is manifested by creating a country profile depicted above in the form of a spidergraph. Although it allows the ranking of countries, which is the simplest normalisation technique, first of all it enables us to see the distance of a given country towards a common reference point, i.e. European standards. It also makes it possible to see the distance to the best European score and to the average. However, it must be mentioned at this point that spidergraphs were used in the pilot study and they will probably be replaced by bar charts in the main study since the latter possibility does not allow the direct ranking of countries.

Weighting and aggregation have been the subject of thorough analysis on the part of the panel of international experts involved. The final weighting procedure for individual answers for subsequent questions was developed in the light of the experience from the pilot phase of the project. In addition, not only the score for individual strands is aggregated but also the score for substrands. For example, the strand for adult education is split into language education in vocational schools and universities. However, it is not the aim of the project to derive one overall score per country.

As concerns *robustness and sensitivity*, individual sub-indicators underwent thorough scrutiny. This meant mapping all individual sub-indicators onto the European matrix of recommendations to check if all recommendations are represented and manifested in the questionnaire. In order to achieve this and having in mind that there is no single European document for reference but plenty of different types of materials both from the EU and the CoE, the census of European recommendations was created to double check if all of them are included in the Index questions. The census was prepared by a separate team of experts. The mapping exercise was followed by experts' discussion on the meaningfulness of each sub-indicator. The discussion led to the creation of a complete Index. However, this, in turn, resulted in problems with scoring of some of the sub-indicators or questions. In rare cases which posed difficulties, the score also depends on individual decisions sanctioned by prior discussions of the experts. It was also decided that such cases may be explained and discussed in the accompanying country essays written by national experts in order to complete the picture derived from the data. This gives the research an additional dimension and diminishes the effect of putting different countries with different contexts into one unified framework which might overlook certain aspects specific for individual countries.

As regards *links to other variables*, relating and aligning the LRE Index to European recommendations and guidelines have already been extensively discussed earlier in this paper. In practical terms this means that if one of the European recommendations for companies is to send their employees for apprenticeship abroad, the questionnaire asks the interviewees from companies if they are aware that EU programmes facilitate such mobility and if they use it. It must be also mentioned at this stage that in subsequent cycles of the project, which aim to focus on changes in national policies, the inclusion of data from other research projects is also planned. For example, the LRE Index does not provide information on real language proficiency of pupils and students at schools and universities. However, the measurement of pupils' language proficiency at the end of International Standard Classification of Education (ISCED) 2 level according to the Organisation for Economic Cooperation and Development (OECD) classification is going to be carried out across Europe by another project financed by the EU. It would be plausible to incorporate these results into the LRE Index in future.

As mentioned above, the decisions on the *visualisation* of the Index have been made taking into consideration political sensitiveness and the fact that some of the countries and the CoE itself do not accept a ranking approach in showing the data. Yet, efforts are being made so that the way the Index is visualised could both foster international debate and exchange of good practice, which in practice imposes some form of ranking, and at the same time would be acceptable for those who do not want to be ranked. Accordingly, the countries' results will be mainly presented with the use of bar charts in the official project publication) whereas mapping of individual countries' results onto each other for comparison will only be possible through specially developed engines and applications on the project web page, which in turn would allow users to access relevant publically available information.

The possibility of decomposing the Index and *going back to the detail* does not pose a problem in the LRE study, either. This is guaranteed by two main factors: (1) each strand consists of sub-components; (2) the analysis of country performance is extended by accompanying country essays/reports, which provide contextual analysis.

Additional quality assurance measures

Despite following acknowledged scientific models providing guidelines for index construction, there may still be room for scepticism on the part of some policy makers and experts. The former may undermine the value of the Index because of political implications such as negative perception of their country in the light of the Index's findings, especially in cases when some of these policy makers are highly dependent on their own governments and when their countries' scores are low or infavourable compared to other countries' scores. The latter may question the feasibility of such an undertaking due to its extremely high level of complexity and multidimensionality caused not only by the fact that different sorts of parameters are measured with the same tool but also by the fact that sometimes totally different national contexts have to be taken into consideration with the use of one standard model framework. This scepticism may also result from concerns that an indicator such as the LRE Index comprises research areas/strands of a different nature, which in consequence leads to different validity issues and the fact that the level of validity of the tool may differ from strand to strand. However, these are issues which permanently accompany constructions of composite indicators – that is their nature and their embedded characteristic. However, it must be noted that the level of validity of the research will grow even higher over future cycles of the research. Periodic repetition of the research and data collection as well as insights from national and European debates will help to refine and fine-tune the research tool. By analogy, the same process of increasing the validity of the tool takes place in testing language proficiency.

Yet, in order to guarantee the fairness of the Index to the fullest possible extent, additional quality assurance measures were undertaken while designing and constructing the LRE Index. First of all, the LRE Index is based on an already developed, tested and used methodology, namely: the Migrant Integration Policy Index (MIPEX) methodology (Huddleston and Niessen

2011). Besides, at all stages of development of the Index, peer reviews were used across Europe, an expert panel was established, data collectors were trained and the whole process was permanently monitored by the steering committee. All these were followed by a pilot exercise in the beginning of 2011 in Poland, Spain and Catalonia resulting in many improvements and shedding light on various potential areas of threats to the validity of the research. Finally, after publishing the results (scheduled for mid-2012), familiarisation activities are being planned with policy makers and researchers across Europe for further debate and refinement of the Index during the forthcoming cycles of the research.

Pilot study results from Poland and its implications

The pilot study in Poland was carried out according to the designed procedures without major obstacles although the following problems were identified:

- ambiguity of some of the questions
- vagueness of some of the questions resulting from the national context
- difficulty in selecting vocational insitutions since in the Polish education system different sorts of vocational schools exist being classified by OECD under ISCED 3, ISCED 4 and even ISCED 5 level, which means that the age range between them is quite substantial
- reluctance on the part of companies to provide data.

The pilot study results in Poland are the following:

The preliminary findings about Poland show that it has the strongest multilingual profile in strand 6 – languages in media (76.9%), strand 3 – languages in secondary education (65.5%) and strand 1 – documents and databases on language diversity (63.4%). Strand 7, in this case, representing languages in public services and spaces, and strand 5 meaning languages in business, deliver weaker multilingual profiles. Within strand 1, documents and databases on language diversity, the country scored quite high for the language documents sub-strand (70%) and much lower for the sub-strand, language databases (44.4%). Please note that the sequence of strands in the pilot study differs from the sequence in the main study. Multilingual policies and practices in secondary schools (strand 3) (65.5%) turned out to be stronger compared to those in primary schools (strand 2) (37.8%), whereas the score for adult language education (strand 4) is somewhere in between (43.4%). Nevertheless, there are considerable differences between the proportions of multilingualism found among teachers on the one hand and in the organisation of education on the other. The low scores in the Polish context are mostly due to a lower representation of immigrant and regional languages in primary and secondary schools (Extra and Yagmur 2011:35).

As a result of the pilot exercise carried out in Poland, Spain and Catalonia, the following amendements to the LRE Index have been introduced:

- Ambiguous or complex questions have been made clearer.
- The strand for adult language education has been renamed as the strand for adult vocational training and university education.
- The types of vocational schools and universities to be included in the data collection process have been made more precise. For example, for a more meaningful comparison only general education universities have been included and specialist ones, such as medical, technical or art universities have been excluded.
- The number of companies to be interviewed per country has been decreased from the initially proposed 50 to 24, in the interest of feasibility. The minimum requirement of 24 companies interviewed per country still guarantees that the sample size is statistically acceptable.
- The exact typology of companies has been introduced based on their size: local, regional, national and multinational and on their profile: banks, supermarkets, construction companies and hotels.
- The sequence of strands has been changed putting languages in business at the end as strand 7 since the data collection in this strand is based on primary data only.
- Questions have been added for better reflection of European recommendations as discussed above in this paper.
- The final manuals for weighting and scoring have been produced.
- The way the Index is visualised and presented has been changed from spidergraphs to bar charts due to the reasons explained above in the paper.

Final remarks

The current stage of this research project is as follows: the data for the main study has been collected in all participating countries and regions and it is being processed. Final research results are planned to be published in mid-2012 and disseminated afterwards. Dissemination activities will also include one launching event and two national workshops in each participating country or region across Europe aiming at producing national language policies. These policies are meant to be well informed by LRE research, elaborated together with national policy makers, accepted by national authorities and possibly implemented nationally. On the one hand, national authorities will be equipped with the necessary knowledge to implement changes in their policy seeing the strengths and weaknesses of current solutions in reference to European recommendations. On the other hand if they wish they could see how their country performs against other countries, which might potentially lead to closer international cooperation and exchange of good practice. Moreover, the publication of the final project and the dedicated web page will offer the possibility to explore the data and generate different sorts of comparisons across countries, strands and sub-strands, and will provide those interested with valid data for their purposes. The end of the first cycle of the project is scheduled for early 2013. The continuation of the project will be previewed within subsequent cycles, which will additionally enable the tracking of changes and trends in policy implementation over time.

References

British Council (2011) *Towards a Language Rich Europe. Multilingual Essays on Language Policies and Practices*, Berlin: British Council.

Council of Europe (1992) *European Charter for Regional or Minority Languages*, European Treaty Series – No 148, Strasbourg: Council of Europe.

Council of Europe (2001) *Common European Framework of Reference for Languages: Learning, Teaching, Assessment*, Cambridge: Cambridge University Press.

Council of the European Union (2008) *Resolution on a European strategy for multilingualism*, available online: www.consilium.europa.eu/ueDocs/cms_Data/docs/pressData/en/educ/104230.pdf

Davignon, V E (2008) *Languages Mean Business. Companies Work Better with Languages*, Brussels: European Commission.

European Commission (2004) *Action Plan for 2004 – 2006: Promoting Language Learning and Linguistic Diversity*, Luxembourg: Office for Official Publications of the European Communities.

European Commission (2005) *A new framework strategy for multilingualism*, communication from the Commission to the Council, the European Parliament, the European Economic and Social Committee and the Committee of the Regions, Brussels, November 2005.

European Commission (2007) *Final Report of High Level Group on Multilingualism*, Luxembourg: Office for Official Publications of the European Communities.

European Commission (2008) *Multilingualism: an asset for Europe and a shared commitment*, communication from the Commission to the Council, the European Parliament, the European Economic and Social Committee and the Committee of the Regions, Brussels, November 2008.

Extra, G and Yagmur, K (2011) *Language Rich Europe Field Manual on Multilingual Policies and Practices in Europe*, Tilburg: Babylon Centre for Studies of the Multicultural Societies.

Hope, M (2011) Introduction, in British Council (2011) *Towards a Language Rich Europe. Multilingual Essays on Language Policies and Practices*, Berlin: British Council, 4–9.

Huddleston, T and Niessen, J (2011) *Migrant Integration Policy. Index III*, Brussels: British Council and Migration Policy Group.

Maalouf, A (Ed.) (2008) *A Rewarding Challenge: How the Multiplicity of*

Languages Could Strengthen Europe, Luxembourg: Office for Official Publications of the European Communities.

Mackiewicz, W (2004) Higher education and language policy in the European Union, in Milanovic, M and Weir, C (Eds) *European Language Testing in a Global Context – Proceedings of the ALTE Barcelona Conference July 2001*, Studies in Language Testing volume 18, Cambridge: UCLES/Cambridge University Press, 173–186.

Nardo, M, Saisana, M, Saltelli, A, Tarantola, S, Hoffman, A and Giovannini E (2005) *Handbook on Constructing Composite Indicators: Methodology and User Guide*, available online: composite-indicators.jrc.ec.europa.eu/Document/ Handbook%20on%20CIs.pdf

OECD (2005) *OECD Statistics Working Papers 2005/03*, available online: www. oecd-ilibrary.org/economics/oecd-statistics-working-papers_18152031

Poszytek, P (2011) Language policy in the educational system in Poland, in British Council *Towards a Language Rich Europe. Multilingual Essays on Language Policies and Practices*, Berlin: British Council, 23–27.

5 European Survey on Language Competences – comparability of A1 level competences across five languages

Michaela Perlmann-Balme
Goethe-Institut, München, Germany

Abstract

This paper presents some insights into the European Survey on Language Competences (ESLC) by looking at the phases of language test development, production, pretesting and benchmarking, as well as different perceptions in respect to, for example, content, grammar and lexis. The European Survey on Language Competences is a major initiative by the European Commission to support the development of language learning policies across Europe. The purpose of this survey is to provide participating countries with comparable data on foreign language competence and knowledge about good practice in language learning. The survey tests the two most widely taught European languages (out of English, French, German, Italian and Spanish) in each country from a representative sample of pupils in their final year of lower secondary education. Five language partners worked together to create language test tasks on four levels of the Common European Framework of Reference for languages (CEFR) – A1, A2, B1 and B2. The aim was to create items that were as similar to each other and at the same time as true to their respective cultural and linguistic origins as possible. In the context of this close collaboration of five language partners, it has become possible to observe to what extent test tasks and items of identical difficulty can be created without applying a method of mere translation.

Introduction

> 'Without data, you are just another person with an opinion!'
> Andreas Schleicher, 2011, PISA
> (Ripley 2011)

This paper explores the value of the Common European Framework of Reference for languages (CEFR) to language testers and language policy makers. It will illustrate how the CEFR constitutes a basis for collecting and delivering information – i.e. data – on the foreign language competences of young learners across countries of the European Union (EU).

In 2001, when the CEFR was published, many countries already had their own examination level system in place but these systems were not comparable. Nationwide school-leaving exams had only internal value. For example, what the German school-leaving exam 'Abitur' meant in comparison with the school-leaving A-level in languages in the British system was unknown, at least in detail. The CEFR for the first time provided a common reference tool that made such levels transparent and comparable across systems. It became used in policy documents of EU member states such as in the *Progetto Lingue 2000* in Italy (Hawkey 2006). However, the CEFR is still not used for teaching at the school level, which among other reasons is due to the fact that it is not reader friendly. The CEFR, although mostly used by test developers, is most of all a source of language learners' abilities. It is, however, not an assessment tool in itself, as it is solely a description of *what* learners should be able to do and *how well* they can do this on the different levels. It does not provide rating scales for young learners, for example, but rather a basis on which such scales can be developed.

In a similar way to the PISA (Programme for International Student Assessment) studies which assess school performance in the fields of reading, mathematics and science with 15-year-olds in the Organisation for Economic Co-operation and Development (OECD) countries, the European Survey on Language Competences (ESLC) allows a comparison of levels of competence between different countries. ESLC collects data on competences in the first and second foreign language taught at schools. In its first iteration of 2011, those languages were English, French, German, Spanish and Italian. PISA collects data on reading, mathematics and science. Both surveys are thus about comparing the success of national school systems in teaching and learning. Both measure the achievement of groups and not of individuals. The information the ESLC gives will be useful for making decisions about the way in which teaching of foreign languages in the European Community should be developed in the future.

The ESLC focuses on four levels from A1 to B2. This paper will focus on one of them – the level A1. In the 1990s, when the Council of Europe initiated the discussion of language proficiency levels, the A1 level, which then was also called *Breakthrough* level (Trim 2009), was neglected by a considerable number of language testers. In the area of international certification it seemed useless to test a level where learners have so little to show and which had so little use for the job market. Thus, the first framework created in the 1990s by the Association of Language Testers in Europe (ALTE) started at A2 level (CEFR, 2001: 249). For lesser taught languages, however, which had formed the FINGS group (Finnish, Irish, Norwegian, Greek and Swedish) in

ALTE, the Breakthrough level had some importance at the time. For languages such as English, Spanish, French and German it was felt that there was almost 'nothing' worth assessing. This attitude changed in the course of the first decade of this century as a consequence of a growing demand for language testing for the purpose of migration and integration and with the demand for language testing growing in national school systems. In contrast to the neglect in the 1990s described above, the CEFR included this low level when it was first published in 2001 (Council of Europe 2001). For a survey of pupils' competences in schools, the A1 level is of high relevance especially for the second foreign language. In fact, in a lot of cases it can be expected that even this first level is a challenge for many schools where fewer and fewer hours are devoted to foreign languages in the curriculum.

This paper will look at cross-language comparability. While PISA used the same translated tasks in all countries, it was a decision of the European Commission to create parallel but not identical tests in the five languages for ESLC. Comparability is therefore crucial for accepting the results of this survey. In this paper the issue of comparability will be explored from three dimensions:

1. How different can tasks be without shifting the level and making it unfair for learners of one foreign language, e.g. of English, in comparison to another, e.g. German?
2. How can tests in these different languages be made as similar as possible, in view of the different structures of different languages?
3. How can equal difficulty be guaranteed across languages?

The aim is to show to what extent comparability is possible, and to explore what else can be done in addition to just introducing common task types. This paper tries to describe some results of this project. (At the time of writing, the final report had not been published. The Executive Summary and the Final and Technical Reports from the First European Survey on Language Competences were released on 21 June 2012 by the European Commission. For a comprehensive report of the project, the reader is directed to those reports, which can be found on www.surveylang.org/de/ and www.survey-lang.org/de/Project-news-and-resources/Project-news-and-resources.html).

The European Survey on Language Competences

This section will give a brief overview of the ESLC project as a whole. In the second part it will concentrate on the question of comparability.

The initiative to carry out this project came from the member states of the EU. In the course of the so-called Barcelona Process, launched in 1995, they decided in 2002 that each European citizen should master their mother tongue plus two European languages. For the purpose of better policy making, the

Table 1 Number of students allocated in Main Study test

Country	English	German	French	Spanish	Italian	Grand total
Belgium (French)	x	x				
Belgium (German)	x		x			
Belgium (Flemish)	x		x			
Bulgaria	x	x				
Croatia	x	x				
Estonia	x	x				
France	x			x		
Greece	x		x			
Malta	x				x	
Netherlands	x	x				
Poland	x	x				
Portugal	x		x			
Slovenia	x	x				
Spain	x		x			
Sweden	x			x		
United Kingdom		x	x			
Grand total	29,075	11,592	9,727	3,584	1,381	55,359

European Commission called for a survey under the name *European Indicator of Language Competence*. The ESLC was carried out in 2011. After this first iteration, this survey is planned to be carried out every three years.

The age of the target group was set at school-leaving age, which in general is 15 or 16 in European countries. In some cases, this was extended to 17. All European countries were invited to participate including countries which had applied for EU member status such as Croatia. However, only 14 out of 26 countries took part in this first iteration. The reason why only approximately half of all member states took part is mainly due to the financial crisis that hit Europe at the time of this study. The financial obligations of the partici-pating countries which had to establish and support a National Research Coordinator for the project were substantial. Another reason was that similar surveys were carried out almost at the same time in individual countries such as Germany. It was felt it would be too much of a strain on participating schools. The total numbers of participants shown in Table 1 do not include those of the United Kingdom, which had asked for a separate time slot for the Main Study. Table 1 shows the countries that took part in the main 2011 study and the total number of the participating students. For comparison, in the PISA study conducted in 2000, 32 out of the 34 OECD member states participated.

As for the number of participants per country, the target of 1,500 was reached everywhere. Table 1 also shows which languages the participating countries opted for. The total of 55,359 sampled students in 2,000 schools in 14 countries were tested in their first or second foreign language. The skills tested were reading, listening and writing, and testing took place on levels A1–A2, A2–B1 or B1–B2.

Table 2 Members of the SurveyLang consortium

Country	Institution	Responsibilities
England	Cambridge ESOL	Project management and test items in English
France	Centre International d´Éducation et Pédagogie (CIEP), Sèvres	Test items in French
Germany	Goethe-Institut, Munich	Test items in German
Italy	Università per Stranieri di Perugia	Test items in Italian
Spain	Universidad de Salamanca and Instituto Cervantes	Test items in Spanish
Netherlands	CITO, National Institute for Educational Measurement, Arnhem	Questionnaires and data analysis for Main Study
Belgium/Hungary	GALLUP Europe	Sampling and testing tool

The choice of the languages tested in this survey lay in the hands of the member states. After the member states had been asked to name the first and second most taught foreign languages in their school systems, English, German, French, Spanish and Italian were chosen for the first iteration of the ESLC. The distribution of the five languages as seen in Table 1 is not unexpected. In all participating countries except the United Kingdom, English was tested as the first and most widely taught foreign language. German was taught in eight of the 14 countries as the second most taught language after English, French in six, and Spanish in two. Italian was tested only in Malta as the second most taught language. Thus, Italian had a special place in the study. It was tested only on three instead of four levels because there were no Maltese participants for Level A1 to be expected. However, the Italian experts contributed to all items on A1 level. The question of which second foreign language was to be tested was in some cases controversial. In France, for example, there was a competition between German and Spanish.

In May 2007, a group of ALTE members founded a European Economic Interest Grouping under the name SurveyLang and took part in the tender process initiated by the EU. Table 2 specifies the consortium. The members come from eight European countries.

The five testing institutions mentioned above are providers of language tests in their own language. They have developed and currently deliver tests for young learners. CITO had taken part as project partner responsible for the questionnaires in the PISA studies. In contrast to regular language tests, this survey links the competence in the foreign language to the socio-economic background of the students as found through questionnaires. Questions such as how many books were in the household of the student were taken as indices for educational background.

While the language testing group was responsible for the development of the testing items, CITO was responsible for the questionnaires. It was decided that the background variables for the living and learning conditions of the participating students should be closely related to or be the same as the ones used in PISA. GALLUP was responsible for providing a tool for authoring test items and for rendering tests as computer-based or paper-based versions, as well as for the sampling of the schools and students.

There were four main stages where a common quality control system was applied in order to prove the appropriateness of the test items:

- Proof of Concept Trial
- Prestesting
- Field Trial
- Main Study.

The Proof of Concept Trial aimed at the selection of tasks mainly on the basis of content and comparability. Pretesting aimed at gathering statistical information on the performance of language test items, mainly difficulty and discrimination. The number of test items was reduced after this stage by 33%. The Field Trial focused on the practicality of using USB sticks in computer-based testing. Due to the high complexity of delivering computer-based language tests in schools in 14 countries with different technical standards, a field trial seemed necessary in order to try out the technical aspects – especially loss of data. Secondly, the delivery of listening tasks in the computer tool had to be subjected to a practice test. The unexpected and unsatisfactory completion of writing tasks by the participants was an issue that was revealed by the Field Trial as well. After the Field Trial, the number of test items was reduced again by 33%. The Main Study was the actual survey. It involved the administration of the language test and the questionnaires in life conditions. On the Levels A1 and A2 test items were the same in all five languages, with the exception of Italian, which was not tested on A1 level. The surviving third of the test items were rendered in both computer-based or alternatively in paper and pencil format.

With respect to the questions of how tests in these different languages can be made as similar as possible and how different tasks can be in order not to shift the level and make it unfair for learners, there were a number of practical outcomes. Common test specifications were produced, and thereby a high degree of similarity guaranteed in the task concerning test focus, text types and length, item types, numbers of items. The *Item Writer Guidelines* also gave practical descriptions of what to include and what to avoid when writing an item. On the basis of these documents, a parallel test item production in five languages commenced.

Guaranteeing cross-language comparability also involved a cross-language quality control system concerning procedures. Applying the procedures in the five language testing institutions mentioned in Table 2 meant a transfer of know-how across institutions. This transfer comprised documents such as specifications, guidelines, results in the form of optical mark recognition (OMR) and vetting sheets. It also comprised the procedure itself such as the item analysis.

The materials were commissioned by each language partner. Item writers were commissioned to create test items in the three skills – reading, listening and writing. Speaking was not included at this stage because it was deemed to be technically too demanding to administer in a decentralised computer-based system. Before starting, item writers had to be familiarised with the level system of the CEFR. The language partners were responsible for the editing of the materials. They selected the centres for pretesting. Pretesting institutions and places were chosen depending on their accessibility. For the Field Trial, it was partly done in countries outside of Europe such as Belarus or Mali. A common optically readable mark sheet was used for all pretesting. The item analysis for the pretesting was done centrally by the University of Cambridge ESOL Examinations team. A review of the results of the pretesting was done across the five languages so that common standards were applied for the removal of 'bad' items. The pretest construction, as well as the question paper construction, was done centrally by the use of an item bank. The routine test production process, from commissioning test material to placing the items into a bank for use in tests as shown in Figure 1, was expanded by two stages noted as 'Cross-language vet (tasks)'. Instead of the vetting by language specialists within a language, there was cross-language vetting of the ESLC test items which had been produced, as shown in Figure 1.

The quality of all items produced in the five languages was thus controlled by all partners. Vetters had to be competent in at least two of the five languages of the survey. Shared vetting forms were used in order to standardise the cross-language vetting procedure and operationalise the received feedback forms were used. Figure 2 shows an excerpt from a vetting sheet, completed with comments by a vetter.

The CEFR as a descriptive apparatus

The most decisive influence the CEFR had on the ESLC is that it provided a model of language use which views language through a social as well as a cognitive dimension. The CEFR language model defines languages on the basis of domains of use, functions and activities rather than on the basis of knowledge of grammar and structure. The target learners for whom the CEFR defines these language activities are adult and educated. The ESLC, on the contrary, collects information on young learners of all educational backgrounds. The communicative, action-based approach of the tasks had to be adapted to the age group of 15–17-year-olds. The focus of the study was: 'What do 15-year-old students need the foreign language for in real life?' rather than 'What grammar and how many words do 15-year-old students need to know in the foreign language?' Applied to the skill of writing, for

Figure 1   ESLC test development process (Jones, Ashton, Maris, Schouwstra, Verhelst, Partchev, Koops, Robinson, Chattopadhyay, Hideg and Ryssevik 2012:35)

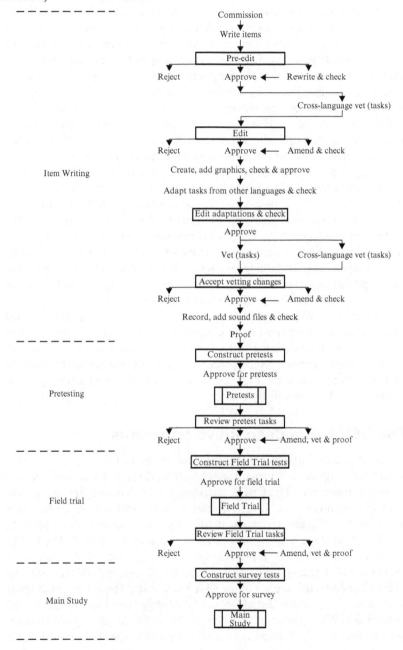

Figure 2 Vetting sheet for cross-language vetting (excerpt)

Task ID: | E | L | 2 | 3 | 1 | Task Name: | Missing (ski trip) |

Vetter's name: | Name | Vetter's first language: | German |

Please see Guidance notes for completion of this form.

Recommended action
(Please tick the appropriate box after working through 1–3 below.)
No amendments required
Some amendments required   [x]
Task not suitable; replacement recommended

1. Task specification
Does the task meet the specification in terms of:

	Y/N		Y/N		Y/N
Input (text type):	y	Task type:	y		
Text length:	y	Number of items:	n	Number of options:	y

Comments (related to the task specification):
It should be 6 items for B1 (one is missing which should not be a dialogue)

instance, this means: 'When do 15-year-old students need to write in a foreign language? What do they write about?' The occasions and reasons for writing emails among young learners do not differ between young French and young German students, for example. As a conclusion, it was decided that A1 and A2 writing tasks and items should be identical across all languages and at all levels in order to provide a firm linking between the languages.

In order to supplement the missing descriptors in the CEFR the *Bergen 'Can do' Project* (Hasselgreen 2005) has provided lists of Can Do descriptors for students and thus expanded the CEFR. With respect to A1 level, the descriptors used were the following:

- Reading: I can understand familiar names, words and very simple sentences, for example, on notices and posters or in catalogues.
- Listening: I can understand questions and instructions if people speak carefully and slowly, and I can follow short, simple directions.
- Writing: I can write a few words and phrases that relate to myself, my family, where I live, my school.

Table 3 shows which testing focuses and item types were chosen for the skill of reading.

The definition of domains relevant for the target group of 15-year-old students was an important common basis for item writing. The three domains which were chosen were 'real world', 'school world' and 'personal world'. The 'real world' domain, for example, comprised activities such as 'using public transport', e.g. buying a ticket from a ticket machine in a country

Table 3 ESLC testing focus for reading according to the ESLC Item Writer Guidelines (SurveyLang 2012:9–10; adapted)

Ability/subskill	Task type and format
1 Reading a simple postcard or email, identifying factual information relating to personal and familiar themes.	**R-Text Multiple-Choice Question-G** Short personal text (email, postcard), with graphic support
2 Understanding word-level topic-specific notions from personal and familiar domains.	**R-Matching-Table** A list of vocabulary from 3 named thematic areas
3 Understanding general notions (existential, spatial, relational) as used to describe pictures or graphically displayed information.	**R-Graphic-Matching or R-Graphic-Multiple-Choice Question** A picture or some graphically displayed information, with a set of statements describing it.

where the language is spoken. The 'school world' comprised topics like 'my teacher', 'my favourite subjects', 'my new class mate' or 'foreign exchange students'. The domain 'personal world' included topics such as 'my room', 'my day', 'my relations to my parents and siblings'.

When choosing the testing focus for A1 tasks, the language partners could draw on an extensive list of descriptors and item formats which has been used in language exams they had already developed for their language. Cambridge ESOL contributed experience from *ASSET languages*, CIEP drew on the *Diplôme d'études en langue française* (DELF) as well as on the work on the *Bildungsstandards* (educational standards) for French in Germany which were developed by the Standing Conference of the Ministers of Education and Cultural Affairs of the Länder in the Federal Republic of Germany. The Goethe-Institut contributed materials from the young learners' exam *Fit in Deutsch 1* (Gerbes and Perlmann-Balme 2003); the university of Salamanca from *DELE Nivel inicial* (Instituto Cervantes 2006); the Italian partner had *CELI impatto* (Spinelli and Parizzi 2010). A short list of 10 task types which were shared was drawn up: four for reading, four for listening and two for writing.

The concern amongst the language partners that the English tests would be taken as models for all languages and that therefore there was not enough cultural pluralism was overcome by some internal research about adaptation carried out as part of the preliminaries of the project. The research question was: Can test items be translated or adapted from one language into the other without changing in level? In an exercise, five A1 reading tasks were translated from one into one or two other languages. A Spanish reading task was translated into English and German and a German task translated into English. As a result of this exercise it became clear that only the cloze-test-task was not appropriate for translation because the demands of grammar are too diverse for the different languages. It became apparent that in other tasks (like matching or multiple choice), where the focus is on comprehension of content points, the differences of language structure do not play a vital role (as, for instance, the three genders and four cases in the German language). All other tasks delivered comparable results when translated in different languages. On the evidence of this exercise, it was concluded that adaption of materials from one language into another was possible for the members of the language testing group.

Besides the issue of grammar or structure, lexis was a second challenge for the comparability of the A1 language tests. When the test development took place, it was only for German and Spanish that the test developers could draw on a word list on A1 level, which was adjusted to the needs of young learners. These word lists were part of inventories for the different languages. The first of these inventories was *Profile Deutsch* (Glaboniat, Müller, Rusch, Schmitz and Wertenschlag 2005), followed by the Spanish *Plan Curricular Del Instituto Cervantes* (Instituto Cervantes 2006). For Italian, the *Profilo Della Lingua Italiana Livelli Di Riferimento Del QCER A1 A2 B1 B2* (Spinelli and Parizzi 2010) was published during the development process. The consequence of this situation was occasional diversity concerning the use of words across the different languages. The choice of the musical instruments, for instance, differed between the languages, because in German and Spanish only 'piano' and 'guitar' were allowed as adequate to A1. The same situation occurred with respect to the subjects learned at school or the sites visited on a school trip. While in Italian the visit to a 'museum' was seen as appropriate, in German this was a visit to a 'swimming pool'. These differences were confined to a distractor in a multiple-choice item. This experience made it clear that expert judgement on the word lists across the languages is needed for future iterations of the ESLC.

After interesting discussions on language differences in lexis and grammar in some reading and listening items, the language testing team decided which of the test items to choose for the Main Study on the basis of their statistical characteristics. For the Level A1, the Main Study contained A1 items based on all five languages; the remaining reading items were based on French, Italian and German originals, adapted for the other languages; the listening items were based on Spanish, English and Italian originals, the writing items were based on French and English originals. The scope of the A1 item writing was calculated on the assumption that at least one third of the items could be eliminated after pretesting and analysis. The total number of items commissioned was 830 in 188 tasks. Per language that worked out on the level A1 as 40 reading items in eight tasks, 35 listening items in eight tasks and 25 writing items in eight tasks.

Marking

The skill of writing is of particular interest for the issue of comparability because it adds two more dimensions: not just comparability of the task and the marking criteria, but also a common marking method of ranking and training to be applied in the participating countries.

With a view of comparability of the writing tasks, they were defined with CEFR levels in mind. Therefore, very basic messages were chosen for A1 level. The result of the application of the task-based approach was that only emails, very short letters, and postcards were offered as text types. Emails as a modern form of communication were considered especially appropriate. However, no specific knowledge of electronic forms was expected as necessary for this text type. The language testing group found it important to choose and define in the task realistic reasons for writing in a foreign language. On A1 level, for example, there is an invitation to a party of a friend who is a native speaker of the target language. On B2, there is a formal letter as an application of an exchange student formulated in the target language. The expected language functions, i.e. invitations, apologies, reports, as well as the recipient are indicated in the task. The length of the expected response is indicated by the number of the words expected, which for A1 was 20 to 30. However there were no penalties for longer texts. A typical A1 task was to

Table 4 ESLC A1 writing task (European Commission 2012:102–103)

	English – Holiday photo
	You are on holiday. Send an email to an English friend with this photo of your holiday. Tell your friend about: • the hotel • the weather • what the people are doing. Write 20–30 words.

French – Photo de vacances	**German – Urlaubsfoto**
Tu es en vacances. Tu envoies un email à un ami avec cette photo de tes vacances. Tu utilises la photo pour parler de : • l'hôtel • le temps • les activités. Tu écris 20–30 mots.	Du hast Ferien. Schreib deiner deutschen Freundin eine E-Mail mit diesem Urlaubsfoto. Schreib deiner Freundin über: • das Hotel • das Wetter • was die Leute machen. Schreib 20–30 Wörter.

Spanish – Foto de vacaciones	**Italian – A1 level not tested**
Estás de vacaciones. Envía un e-mail a un amigo español con esta foto de tus vacaciones. Escribe sobre: • el hotel • el tiempo • qué hace la gente. Escribe 20–30 palabras.	

write greetings from holidays, describing everyday things like the hotel, the weather and what people were doing on the basis of a photo, which was provided. An example of an email task can be seen in Table 4.

Similar to the writing tasks, it was felt that *common marking criteria* for writing were necessary and that it was possible to attain them. Comparability was not an issue among the partners of the language testing group. The marking criteria were based on descriptors of the CEFR relevant to writing: writing samples were marked for communication and language. The criterion 'communication' comprised the answers to the questions:

- How completely does the response address the task?
- How well are the points expanded?
- How well have style and register been applied?

The criterion 'language' comprised descriptors from Table 3 of the CEFR (2001:28–29): Range, Accuracy and Coherence.

As for the common marking method, it was perceived as not possible to take for granted that markers in all 14 countries had an identical interpretation of the CEFR levels. Moreover, it was deemed impossible to give all markers involved in 14 countries a coherent familiarisation and training in the CEFR as part of the project. This condition of the project had to be taken into account when deciding on the method of marking. The ESLC does not ask markers to decide if a script is at A1 level but whether a script is better or not as good as an exemplar. This means that a student's script is compared with an exemplar which has been selected, marked, and commented on by the language testing partner in advance. The comparison between a script to be marked and the exemplar takes place for each criterion. So, if there are two criteria, for example for A1 and A2 level, each script is compared for these two criteria. The decision for this ranking method was made by the project team. The crucial point was seen in the training of the markers. It was felt that in a large-scale survey such as this one it is not possible to train markers to the same degree as is done in the language institutions represented by the language partners. Since the writing production of students was mainly marked in the country of origin by trained local markers, it was necessary to ensure that these markers apply the criteria in the same way. The marked exemplar is a script that represented middle marks, i.e. 2 out of 3. When compared with scripts of the students, their text can be marked as either stronger, i.e. 3, or weaker, i.e. 1 than the exemplar. Table 5 provides four A1 exemplars in English, French, Spanish and German for the task of sending greetings from holidays.

An important part of the training materials was the commentaries which accompanied the exemplar, an element to which the language partners paid special attention. These commentaries were used for marker training. Their

Table 5 ESLC A1 exemplars on task 'Holiday card' (European Commission 2012: 106–111)

English	German
Hi! I living in Hotel Bellevue and this is nice, We have swimming pool and a nice resturant. The weather is very good, its sunny and very hot. And the people play vollyball and they are nice. Good bye!	Hallo Sonja, Wie gehst-du? Was machst-du in dein Urlaub? Ich bin in Hawaï. Ich schlafe in dem „Hotel Bellevue". Das Wetter ist super. Der Son ist immer das! Ich habe viele Freunde und wir spielen oft Volley. Ich bin glücklich. Bye bye Jan Kowalski

French	Spanish
Bounjour Anna. Ça va ? Je suis en vacances avec ma famille. C'est très bien ici ! L'hôtel est supèr, le mange est bon, . . . ! Le temps ici est genial. Tous les jours, il fait du soleil. Je trouve des amis, est nous nageons dans la mer où nous jouons au foot, volleyball, . . . ! À prochaine samedi. Jeanne	Hola, estoy en Hotel Bellevue en Español. Es un Hotel muy grande y bien. Tienes un piscina, un plan de voleybol y más guapo chicas. Hace sol y calor, tengo 30 grados. Español es un país muy impresionante. ¡Ciao! Alejandro

function was to make sure that the markers had the same concept of what should be called an 'error' and what quality these errors had. The intention was only to focus on successful communication, which is the philosophy of the CEFR. Formal errors like spelling mistakes ('Son' instead of 'Sonne', 'wie gehst-du' instead of 'wie geht es dir' in the German examplar), missing gender and case endings in German were considered not to impede communication. The language partners had to guarantee comparability in their marking by training and comparing their marking practices first by judging and commenting on the same scripts across languages. They ranked a number of scripts in the common language, English, and compared the results. They also compared the formulation of the commentaries to the exemplars. In the criteria of 'language', not only errors were pointed out and assessed, but also, examples of effective use of language were listed in the commentaries. It was after this discussion that the language partners felt that it was possible for the seminars dealing with the five languages to apply the common criteria in the same way.

To ensure that all ESLC markers in the 14 countries were using the marking criteria in the same way to rate learners' performances, the language partners conducted two training seminars. These were conducted with identical sets of materials and procedures. The first one was held in 2010 as preparation for the Field Trial, the second one in 2011 as preparation for the

Main Study. Both took place in Sèvres near Paris and were hosted by CIEP. The trainers were either the project leaders of French, German, Spanish and Italian or specialists, as was the case for English. Participants were delegates from the member states who themselves carried out the training of markers in their own country. These representatives were expected to conduct the same seminar for the local markers in their respective countries. The content of this training was the application of the method on all levels.

Intended to guarantee a high degree of comparability, the training of markers was one of the key stages of the project. The purpose of the training of markers was to train them in the method of ranking and of using exemplars. The markers were selected by the NRCs in the participating countries. They were trained in the countries by trainers, normally also the NRCs, who had been trained centrally in all the languages. The markers did not necessarily have to be practising school teachers. In the case of the Netherlands for instance, they were students trained by a member of CITO who acted as National Research Coordinator. As a means of checking the reliability of the local marking and of detecting by-country effects, there was double marking and central marking of a representative proportion of all scripts. Central marking was done in the institution representing the language, for example, in the case of German by the Goethe-Institut in Munich. After the seminar in 2010 in Sèvres and the local training in the countries, the marking of the scripts from the Field Trials took place and yielded some results which were relevant for the issue of comparability. It was possible to compare the behaviour of the markers in the different countries with that of the central markers (normally three persons). Figure 3

Figure 3 Behaviour of markers marking an A1/A2 task, Field Trial

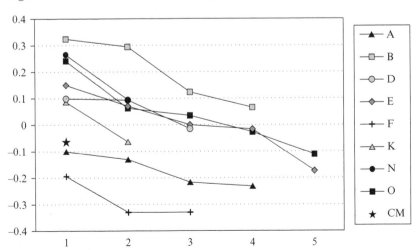

shows Field Trial data for German on the marking of writing A1/A2 for the criterion 'language'. These results were very similar to the other languages involved.

The graph presents the results for eight participating countries from A to O. The x axis shows the number of raters within one country involved in the marking, the y axis shows the degree of harshness or leniency of these raters. The star is the result for the central marking at the Goethe-Institut, Munich. It is slightly off centre '0' and therefore slightly lenient. The curves far away from zero deviate more considerably from the central marking than those nearby. Each of the dots per line represents several markers. The curves on different levels illustrate differences in leniency/harshness between countries in the marking. The relatively flat curve for country A shows consistent marking within this country in this study whereas the decreasing curve in country K reveals some considerable difference between markers in that country. Another possible interpretation for the consistency which is shown by a flat curve is the following: in country A the training of the markers was probably more successful than in country K because in country A, rating was more consistent. Therefore, a question for further research is: are the differences based on the markers involved or are they based on the criteria involved? The language testing team saw the criteria as the most important and relatively easy feature to manipulate. The field trial made it possible to detect and counteract by-country effects. As a consequence of these results, the four criteria on the B1 and B2 levels were reduced to two. The training programme for the second trainer seminar was changed and the concept of scaling was considered. For future iterations of ESLC, the question of the numbers and the complexity of criteria has to be revisited. With centralisation of marking, the issue of consistency could be changed. Consequently, for a future iteration the question of central marking of writing has to be addressed.

Conclusion

This paper has given a description of some major steps in the development of a common language test across five European languages. It has overviewed and discussed some major steps in the development of a common language test across five European languages. It has put a number of project materials in the public domain for the first time. There are a number of lessons to be learned from this process. The project demonstrated that comparability of tests across languages is the result of careful planning and a matter of having the appropriate procedures in place, such as cross-language vetting and marking. In a multilingual survey, these procedures need multilingual experts that have foreign language competences in at least two languages. It is true to say that these procedures in ESLC have led to some considerable know-how transfer among the experts involved. Secondly, it can be concluded that the CEFR helps to achieve comparability by providing a common ground of levels, approaches to and definitions of language learning, teaching and testing. The CEFR is, however, not a replacement for language-specific tools like word lists, grammar inventories etc. The English Profile Programme will be a milestone in this respect. The CEFR is not a ready-made assessment tool that only has to be applied. This became apparent especially for the skill of writing. In the marking of writing, there were a number of lessons to be learned. As the Field Trial results revealed significant by country effects, the issue of central versus decentralized marking should be revisited when the next iteration is planned. The ESLC made the language partners realise that testing the productive skills is particularly challenging for yielding convincing results. However, that does not mean that productive skills should not be included in a survey. On the contrary, in the next iteration of the ESLC, speaking should be included as well. Because productive skills have high face validity, they inform language policy makers of the true abilities of the tested students. The results described in this paper are so encouraging that for a new iteration of the ESLC, it seems possible to be able to go one step further with the aim for comparability. It should be possible to adapt tasks on all levels of the survey, i.e. on B1 and B2 as well.

References

Council of Europe (2001) *Common European Framework of Reference for Languages: Learning, Teaching, Assessment.* Cambridge: Cambridge University Press.

European Commission (2012) *First European Survey on Language Competences: Final Report*, Brussels: European Commission.

Gerbes, J and Perlmann-Balme, M (2003) *Fit in Deutsch. Prüfungsziele, Testbeschreibung*, München: Goethe-Institut.

Glaboniat, M, Müller, M, Rusch, P, Schmitz, H and Wertenschlag, L (2005) *Profile Deutsch. Gemeinsamer europäischer Referenzrahmen. Lernzielbestimmungen, Kannbeschreibungen, Kommunikative Mittel, Niveau A1–A2, B1– B2, C1–C2*, Berlin, München: Langenscheidt.

Hasselgreen, A (2005) *Bergen 'Can Do' project*, Strasbourg: Council of Europe Publishing.

Hawkey, R (2006) *Impact Theory and Practice: Studies of the IELTS test and Progetto Lingue*, Studies in Language Testing volume 24, Cambridge: UCLES/Cambridge University Press.

Instituto Cervantes (2006) *Plan curricular del Instituto Cervantes: Niveles de Referencia par el Espanol.* 3 Volumes: *A1/A2, B1/B2, C1/C2 de VV.AA*, Madrid: Biblioteca Nueva.

Jones, N, Ashton, K, Maris, G, Schouwstra, S, Verhelst, N, Partchev, I, Koops, J, Robinson, M, Chattopadhyay, M, Hideg, G and Ryssevik, J (2012) *First European Survey on Language Competences: Technical Report*, Brussels: European Commission.

Ripley, A (2011) The World's Schoolmaster: How the German Scientist is using test data to revolutionize global learning, *The Atlantic* 7 (8), 109–110.

Spinelli, B and Parizzi, F (2010) *Profilo della lingua italiana. Livelli di riferimento del QCER A1, A2, B1, B2* , Firenze: La Nuova Italia.

SurveyLang (2012) *First European Survey on Language Competences: Item Writer Guidelines Reading.*

Trim, J L M (2009) *Breakthrough*, unpublished manuscript, available online: www.englishprofile.org/index.php?option=com_content&view=article&id=119&Itemid=92

University of Cambridge ESOL Examinations (2011) *English Profile – Introducing the CEFR for English*, available online: www.englishprofile.org/images/pdf/theenglishprofilebooklet.pdf

Section Two
Frameworks and educational contexts

6 Defining an inclusive framework for languages

Neil Jones
University of Cambridge ESOL Examinations,
United Kingdom

Abstract

Languages are learned differently, as first, second or foreign languages. Such different experiences result in different profiles of language ability, but these can be described through differing configurations of the same parameters: informal learning, formal language knowledge, social and academic contexts of use, and cognitive stage. We need an inclusive theoretical framework to encompass all three kinds of learning because these learners co-exist and intersect within educational settings which direct their learning, and qualifications frameworks which compare and judge them. The Common European Framework of Reference for languages (CEFR) is an instance of a more general framework, parameterised and illustrated for the case of foreign languages. By adding parameters and illustrations we can extend it without challenging its validity for that original purpose. Doing so should enable language assessment to deal elegantly with many linguistically complex educational contexts, and contribute to improving educational outcomes for language learners of all kinds.

The need for an inclusive framework

Languages are learned differently, as first, second or foreign languages. Such different experiences result in different profiles of language ability, but these can be described in terms of differing configurations of a rather small number of parameters: kinds of competence or knowledge (informally and intuitively acquired, or formally taught); contexts of language use (social or academic); and cognitive stage. This paper argues the need for a single, inclusive theoretical framework to encompass all aspects of language learning because language learners co-exist and intersect within educational settings which direct their learning, and qualifications frameworks which compare and judge them.

I will present the Common European Framework of Reference for languages (CEFR) as one instance of a more general, inclusive framework, parameterised and illustrated for the specific case of foreign languages. As a mode of exposition I will show how by adding parameters and illustrations we can extend it without challenging its validity for that original purpose. Doing so should enable language assessment to deal elegantly with many linguistically complex educational contexts, and contribute to improving educational outcomes for language learners of all kinds.

Let us begin by considering some of the complex contexts of language learning which exam boards like University of Cambridge ESOL Examinations (Cambridge ESOL) find themselves engaging with. The following examples may seem unusual or even contrived, but they all refer to actual contexts with which I am familiar:

1. A system of pathfinder schools is being set up in an Arabic-speaking country, where from age 4 to 18 children will be taught through the medium of English, in all subjects except religion.
2. In a country where English is the primary medium of education, the mother-tongue languages are effectively becoming second languages. They are still seen as culturally valuable, and exam results are important in determining progression through secondary education.
3. American community colleges offer access to higher education for many students not having English as a first language: recent immigrants, as well as 'generation 1.5' students. These two groups have different English language needs.
4. An exam board offering qualifications in English as a first language and English as a second language wishes to relate these to each other in a single framework.

In addressing the conference theme of the impact of language frameworks on assessment, learning and teaching, this paper will argue that, as the above cases illustrate, contexts of learning and teaching may be linguistically complex. All stakeholders (not only exam boards) need a framework which encompasses the complexity. And, of course, the impact of exams reflects what our frameworks neglect, as much as what they include.

The CEFR

It seems hard to avoid taking the CEFR as a starting point, given its very prominent role in language education policy and in assessment. Thus I will develop my argument from a critical evaluation of the CEFR in terms of its limited stated purpose: to provide a framework for foreign language (FL) learning, teaching and assessment. Considering how to extend the CEFR to deal better with this narrower purpose will help us begin to see the more general framework of which it is an instance. I intend this as a constructive exercise.

We should consider the functions which frameworks serve. Firstly, there is the conceptual, or descriptive, function. This includes *scoping* – defining which contexts are included or excluded, and comparison – identifying commonalities and differences between contexts within the framework.

Description then informs action: goal setting, organisation of syllabus and teaching, monitoring and assessment of progress towards objectives, and evaluation of the efficacy of the system. Finally, it may be that a framework takes on a regulatory function, standardising procedures, or assuming authority to accredit learning outcomes.

The scope of the CEFR is explicitly stated to be FL learning. In my view it should be seen primarily as a *conceptual* framework, identifying how contexts of FL learning differ, and laying out the range of options with respect to objectives, content, and methodology. At the same time it claims that *despite* these differences, contexts can be usefully compared in terms of a rather general and inclusive notion of functional language ability. It is as a framework of *levels* that the CEFR has proved so influential.

The CEFR levels framework is illustrated by a number of descriptor scales. Given the status that these scales have been generally accorded it is important to consider them in some detail. In the intention of the authors, the descriptor scales are context free but context relevant (Council of Europe 2001:21). That is, they should be general enough to apply to all contexts, but specific enough to interpret, and perhaps translate into specific learning objectives. However, there is inevitably a tension between the generality of the levels and the specificity of the descriptors. What is undoubtedly a great strength of the CEFR illustrative descriptor scales is that they are derived from empirical research: they are not mere armchair conjectures about what proficiency looks like (although, as has been pointed out, they might be seen to reflect the perceptions of teachers more than determined facts about observed abilities (Alderson 2007, Hulstijn 2007)). But this strength is simultaneously their weakness: they reflect the specific contexts in which the research was conducted, and this limits their generality.

We should consider the intended and effective status of the descriptors. They are proposed as illustrations of CEFR levels, but the scales seem to function as *definitions* of the reference levels, for example in the way they are selected from to compile the global Common Reference Levels tables (Table 1: Global scales, Table 2: Self-assessment grid (Council of Europe 2001:24–29)) or in section 3.6: *Content coherence in Common Reference Levels*, where each level is epitomised by identifying the salient features of selected descriptors (Council of Europe 2001:33). While there is no doubting the pragmatic usefulness of these compilations, they seem to an extent to undermine the stress placed elsewhere in the CEFR on using the range of descriptor scales selectively, in order to *profile* contexts and learners – that is, to point up what makes them different. The argument developed in this paper is consistent with the notion of profiling.

Their position in the body of the text, which represents a change from the draft text of the CEFR, has given the descriptor scales unintended prominence. As that draft said:

> The establishment of a set of common reference points in no way limits how different sectors in different pedagogic cultures may choose to organise or describe their system of levels and modules. *It is also to be expected that the precise formulation of the set of common reference points, the wording of the descriptors, will develop over time* as the experience of member states and of institutions with related expertise is incorporated into the description (Council of Europe 1998:131; emphasis added).

I have discussed the status of the illustrative descriptors at length because words are important. They colour understanding of what the CEFR is. People are reluctant to challenge them, or use their own words, as I will illustrate below. Such obedience to words militates in the direction of making the CEFR into a closed system, even if, of course, this is not the intention of its authors, who state at the outset: 'we have not set out to tell people what to do or how to do it' (Council of Europe 2001:1).

We should probably not take depictions of the CEFR as being 'manipulated unthinkingly by juggernaut-like centralizing institutions' (Davies 2008:438) too seriously. Certainly, we should treat the publication *Relating Language Examinations to the Common European Framework of Reference for Languages: Learning, Teaching, Assessment. A Manual* (Council of Europe 2009) as a useful guide, rather than a necessary and sufficient prescription of good practice. We should politely decline offers to police the correct application of the CEFR (Alderson 2007). But above all, if we do perceive a danger of the CEFR becoming a bureaucratic instrument of standardisation then the best defence is to insist on its open nature. A key principle that we should advocate with respect to its use is that each context of learning must be related to the CEFR on its own terms – it is not a case of applying the CEFR prescriptively to every context.

The CEFR as an instance of a more general framework

We should see the CEFR as an instance of a more general framework, parameterised and illustrated for a particular FL learning context. Even for this specific purpose it is somewhat narrowly defined. Considering how to extend the CEFR for its FL learning purpose will help us to see the more general framework of which it is an instance.

There are two FL learning contexts which are not best treated by the CEFR:

- young learners, because there is no explicit treatment of cognitive stage
- CLIL (Content and Language Integrated Learning) because language for learning is not clearly distinguished from language for social use.

These two contexts are related: CLIL may involve young learners learning school subjects through the medium of a foreign language. This is in fact the case for a wide variety of second language (L2) learning contexts.

To take these two factors into account it is necessary to expand our familiar proficiency dimension by two additional dimensions – age and academic content area. The result is a three-dimensional matrix where each cell distinguishes a learner at a specific proficiency level, at a specific age, studying a specific subject. This is exactly what is provided by the WIDA consortium's *English Language Proficiency Standards for English Language Learners in Kindergarten through Grade 12* (WIDA 2012).

Figure 1 Example of a WIDA consortium English Language Proficiency Standard

WIDA consortium example:
English Language Proficiency Standard 3: *English language learners communicate information, ideas, and concepts necessary for academic success in the content area of* **Mathematics**.
(Grade cluster 1–2)

Example topics	Level 1 Entering	Level 2 Beginning	Level 3 Developing
Graphs Interpretation of data	Shade or color graphs according to oral commands modeled by a teacher (e.g., "Here is a graph. Color this bar red.")	Identify data in graphs from oral commands modeled by a teacher (e.g., "Which bar shows the most?")	Locate information on graphs based on oral statements (e.g., "Which bar shows that most people like ice cream?")
Number sense	Provide comparative data on graphs from oral descriptions (e.g., "Fill in the graph. Most children are wearing red, some are wearing blue, and the fewest are wearing green.")	Provide identifying information that involves real-world numbers (e.g., age, address, or telephone number) to a peer	Give examples of things with realworld numbers (e.g., room numbers, bus numbers, or calendars) to a peer

In many contexts it is vital to distinguish the use of language for social interaction from its use as the medium of learning. This is the well-known distinction made by Cummins between basic interpersonal communication skills (BICS) and cognitive academic language proficiency (CALP) (Cummins 1979, 1984). BICS are the 'surface' skills of listening and speaking which are typically acquired quickly by many students, particularly by those who spend a lot of their school time interacting with native speakers. CALP is the basis for children's ability to cope with the academic demands placed upon them in the various subjects. Cummins found that many children develop native speaker fluency (i.e. BICS) within two years of immersion in the target language, but that it takes between five to seven years for a child to be working on a level with native speakers as far as academic language is concerned.

In a CLIL or L2 setting CALP requires specific attention from an early age and possibly from a low proficiency level. This is not reflected in the descriptor scales of the CEFR. Rather, these reflect the customary progression in a language school, where it is only at the C levels that 'academic' use of language is envisaged. The problem here is one of under-representation of important constructs. It would be solved by clearly distinguishing these two aspects of proficiency. And yet one finds an apparent reluctance to challenge the CEFR descriptors. For example, consider the following passage from the *Guide for the development and implementation of curricula for plurilingual and intercultural education* (Council of Europe 2010: 29):

> The pre-B2 phases in studying the language of schooling as a subject coincide with a stage in young people's general development (physical, cognitive, etc.) when they are using it, not only for social purposes outside school, but also in studying other subjects. Use of the CEFR descriptors to organise their progression may be harder here, although experience shows that those descriptors can – when supplemented and/or adapted to match the curriculum – be usefully and effectively applied to certain groups.

In this passage the distinction between academic and social language use is clearly made, and the difficulty of using the CEFR descriptors is recognised. But the response is to propose *ad hoc* adaptation of the descriptors, rather than an explicit model for treating each of these distinct aspects separately. The reader may feel that I am paying too much attention to forms of words, but my intention is to stress the importance of clear description as a prerequisite of motivated action. In this case such action might involve developing new descriptor scales for the academic aspects of competence, assessing children on both aspects, providing specific training in academic use if this is found necessary, and so on.

The paradox of the native speaker

I will use the paradoxical treatment of the native speaker in the text of the CEFR to identify another important parameter that we would need to include in an extended framework. According to the CEFR: 'Level C2, whilst it has been termed "Mastery", is not intended to imply native-speaker or near native-speaker competence. What is intended is to characterise the degree of precision, appropriateness and ease with the language which typifies the speech of those who represent highly successful learners' (Council of Europe 2001:36). According to this statement native speakers have a higher level than C2. And yet there are C2 descriptors which clearly describe competences that many native speakers do not have, such as the following examples from the CEFR's Common Reference Levels self-assessment grid (Council of Europe 2001:26–29):

- *Reading*: I can read with ease virtually all forms of the written language, including abstract, structurally or linguistically complex texts such as manuals, specialised articles and literary works.
- *Spoken production*: I can present a clear, smoothly flowing description or argument in a style appropriate to the context and with an effective logical structure which helps the recipient to notice and remember significant points.
- *Writing*: I can write clear, smoothly flowing text in an appropriate style. I can write complex letters, reports or articles which present a case with an effective logical structure which helps the recipient to notice and remember significant points. I can write summaries and reviews of professional or literary works.

Clearly, there are educated competences described here which very successful FL learners may acquire, but which many native speakers never do. At the same time, there is much that native speakers naturally acquire which remains beyond the reach of all but a few FL learners. Naturally, these are not described in the CEFR because they are not relevant to the FL learning context. Mother tongue language (MTL) is characterised by the linguistic reflexes of a developed socio-cultural competence (culture in the 'broad' sense): a shared grasp of idiom, cultural allusion, folk wisdoms, and so on.

Bernstein (1971) addressed the question of why English working-class students did relatively badly in language-based subjects. He identified two linguistic codes, *restricted* and *elaborated* codes. Restricted code is used with insiders who share assumptions and understanding on the topic. It creates a feeling of belonging to a certain group. Elaborated code is more explicit, detailed, and does not require the listener to read between the lines. Bernstein (1971:135) does not elevate one code above the other: 'One code is not better than another; each possesses its own aesthetic, its own possibilities. Society, however, may place different values on the orders of experience elicited, maintained and progressively strengthened through the different coding systems'. But the extended code has similarities to Cummins' cognitive academic proficiency, and not acquiring it represents the same disadvantage for the native speaker as it does for the L2 learner. (For a related discussion of the native speaker in the assessment scales, see Brooks and Mackey, this volume.)

Aspects of language development and learning

In considering how to extend the CEFR to deal better with different FL or L2 learning contexts, and in exploring a little the status of the native speaker, I have introduced the major parameters necessary for a more general framework capable of accommodating such complexity. These are illustrated in Figure 2.

Figure 2 Aspects of language development and learning

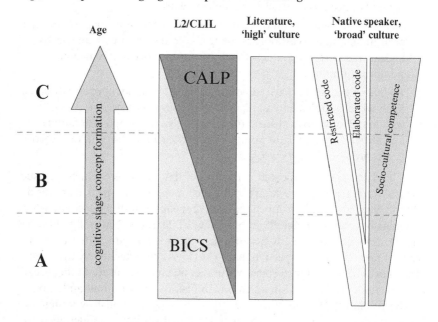

Age, and the age-determined process of cognitive development, is a factor which conditions all the others. It should be represented as a separate dimension, except that other things being equal, increasing age brings increasing proficiency.

CALP and BICS are shown not as in the CEFR, stacked one on top of the other, but as two distinct but parallel processes. Literary studies, or 'high' culture, are shown alongside the MTL speaker's array of competences – 'broad' culture.

The figure sketches in A, B and C levels. What these might mean in such a heterogeneous framework is something I will return to below.

At this point the reader might look again at the four examples of linguistically complex learning or assessment contexts presented at the outset, and consider how the additional aspects of language development proposed here could be brought to bear on describing these contexts and formulating an appropriate approach to each.

Language education: the individual perspective

I will now make a dramatic shift in focus, from the macro level of large educational projects to the level of the individual learner, and consider the fundamental role which language plays in the individual's development. For all of the aspects identified so far are (or could be) part of the experience of every language user: everyone is a native speaker; everyone learns through language; everyone can benefit from learning new languages and be enriched by the experiences and opportunities which languages afford. A general framework could connect all these aspects, enabling a coherent approach to language education. What is the relevance of this to the Association of Language Testers in Europe (ALTE)? It suggests that to define our business as 'language proficiency' may be to define it too narrowly. 'Language education' may cover it better.

Clearly the role of assessment expertise in learning is up for review and rethinking, and we can identify two general trends: one which looks to implement more sophisticated models of competence, supported by ever more powerful statistical methods, and another which envisages the emergence of a more complementary relationship between standardised psychometric testing and other more heterogeneous, classroom-based, formative approaches (Jones 2012). It is the latter route which I find more promising and which I will explore here.

As the Council of Europe Language Policy Division has recently reminded us, we should not neglect that other Council of Europe project: the *Platform of resources and references for plurilingual and intercultural education* (also called the Languages of Schooling project). The reminder comes in a foreword to the new ALTE test construction manual by Joe Shiels, who has since retired as Director of the Language Policy Division. While thanking ALTE for its contribution, he goes on to say:

> The Council of Europe's initiatives to promote plurilingual and intercultural education, and a global approach to all languages in and for education, present new challenges for curriculum development, teaching and assessment, not least that of assessing learners' proficiency in using their plurilingual and intercultural repertoire. We look forward to the essential contribution of professional associations such as ALTE in our efforts to promote the values of the Council of Europe in the field of language education (ALTE 2011:5).

In this he echoes the *Guide for the development and implementation of curricula for plurilingual and intercultural education* (Council of Europe 2010), which points to an 'obvious imbalance in implementation of the CEFR's provisions' which 'chiefly affects plurilingual and intercultural education, although this is one of the CEFR's main emphases' (2010:5). Lussier (2011) presented work on testing plurilingual and intercultural competence, and confirmed the findings of the above guide, that 'evaluation of plurilingual and intercultural competence will essentially be formative', and will be unlikely to engage the energies of certificate-awarding bodies, given that 'no-one has decided what can in fact be evaluated, and formal qualifications are, as yet, little in demand' (2010:40).

This discussion makes clear that if we extend our assessment remit beyond the familiar concept of proficiency, to engage with the objectives of language education more widely construed, then our current toolkit of summative testing procedures will not suffice. The above-mentioned guide is surely correct in pointing to the interconnectedness of and potential synergies between aspects of language education in schools. Its assertion that 'language teaching in schools must go beyond the communication competences specified on the various levels of the CEFR' (Council of Europe 2010:29) is one which many of us could agree with.

Language education implies more than achieving some level of proficiency in a language. It comprises a range of learning skills and learning objectives that are critical to becoming competent learners not just in one language, but more importantly, given that the languages we need in later life are probably not those we learned at school, of languages generally. It is what Hawkins (1999) wrote of as an 'apprenticeship in languages': 'We will no longer measure effectiveness of the apprenticeship in languages by mere ability to "survive" in a series of situations, but by how the foreign language experience contributes to learning how to learn through language, and to confidence as a (mathetic) language user' (1999:138). By *mathetic* Hawkins intends: serving discovery, understanding, learning. It relates as much to one's mother tongue as to foreign languages.

At the ALTE conference in Vilnius (2007) I used the term 'can-dos for the classroom' to encompass the wider range of skills and objectives included in the language education programme. These included knowledge about language (KAL), the bundle of objectives familiar under the name *assessment for learning*, learning how to learn (LHTL), language awareness, i.e. the objectives associated above all with the work of Hawkins (1999), and inter-cultural competence.

Learning-oriented assessment

Learning-oriented assessment (LOA) is the area of research Cambridge ESOL is developing to explore possible relationships between different levels of assessment. Assessment as a formal process has familiar roles at several stages within education: determining curricular aims, diagnostic profiling of students at entry, monitoring progress against targets, and final evaluation of learning outcomes. Assessment in the sense of those cognitive processes involved when teachers or students provide or react to correction and feedback, self-monitor, reflect or evaluate, is an inseparable element of learning interaction, and of any model of learning. LOA explores the functional relationship between these different levels of assessment, encompassing both the macro level of framing educational goals and evaluating outcomes, and the micro level of individual learning interactions which take place in the classroom or outside it. A practical model will define strongly complementary roles for assessment and teaching expertise.

Levels in a general framework

I am suggesting that the general framework which we need in order to engage with the language education programme requires going beyond our current proficiency testing paradigm to exploit a heterogeneous toolkit of procedures for observation, measurement and evaluation. It is characteristic that the Languages of Schooling group has largely avoided reference to a framework, or to levels, preferring to speak of values. I have wondered whether this does not reflect a classical philosophical opposition between Anglo-Saxon analysis and empiricism (the CEFR) and continental idealism (the Languages of Schooling). Certainly our accustomed language proficiency focus leads us to see progression in language learning as a scalable phenomenon, with the CEFR levels offering the possibility of measuring and making qualified comparisons across contexts.

But how much progression in language learning is natural, how much conventional? That is, to what extent are our proficiency dimensions also achievement dimensions? How many of the dimensions of language learning outlined here can be usefully treated in terms either of a natural or a conventional progression? And given the heterogeneous nature of the dimensions in an inclusive languages framework, how can levels be defined?

Regarding the last question, I believe that the CEFR shows us how. The lowest identified level is the first point at which there is any significant competence to describe, where 'significant' reflects a social judgement. In 1913 for English this lowest significant level was the Cambridge Certificate of Proficiency in English, now associated with CEFR Level C2. Over the years it has been progressively revised downwards so that today it stands at CEFR

Level A1, and as other conference presentations attested, there are contexts where pre-A1 levels have been found necessary as initial learning targets.

The highest identified level is the last one worth describing because it is observed sufficiently frequently in the relevant population. Thus in a few countries highly successful in teaching English language the view may be expressed that *Cambridge Proficiency English (CPE)* is below the Level C2. A reasonable response to this is: if C2 were more difficult than *CPE* it would not exist as a level, because there would be too few learners to make it worth having. This is an essentially normative view, but it confirms the saying that behind any criterion-referenced test you will find norm-referenced assumptions – that is, standards exist in the range where they are possible, useful and observable. In this line of thinking there is no need for a D level, unless perhaps to recognise virtuoso levels of competence that fall outside the range of the normal target population – simultaneous interpreters, for example, might fall in this category.

In summary

We should be aware of the whole educational enterprise because impact reflects what we neglect as much as what we address. The CEFR is an open, developing system, and it is important that it should be viewed as extensible and flexible, not as a straitjacket. A few more categories – cognitive stage, CALP, BICS, the native speaker – enable better analysis of the FL learning context, and also enable us to transcend that context. Our inclusive framework for language education impacts high-level planning and development, but also offers a way of conceptualising and shaping the language education of the individual learner. Thus it takes in language across the curriculum, learning-oriented classroom interaction, and a range of general learning skills – can-dos for the classroom. Our current measurement approaches will take us a certain distance in working with the inclusive framework, but will require supplementing with a range of other procedures for teaching, observation, monitoring and evaluation.

References

Alderson, J C (2007) The CEFR and the need for more research, *The Modern Language Journal* 91 (4), 659–663.

Association of Language Testers in Europe (2011) *Manual For Language Test Development and Examining*, Strasbourg: Council of Europe Languages Policy Division.

Bernstein, B (1971) *Class, Codes and Control,* Volume 1, London: Routledge & Kegan Paul.

Council of Europe (1998) *Modern Languages: Learning, Teaching, Assessment. A Common European Framework of Reference*, Strasbourg: Language Policy Division.

Council of Europe (2001) *Common European Framework of Reference for Languages: Learning, Teaching, Assessment*, Cambridge: Cambridge University Press.

Council of Europe (2009) *Relating Language Examinations to the Common European Framework of Reference for Languages: Learning, Teaching, Assessment (CEFR). A Manual*, Strasbourg, France: Council of Europe.

Council of Europe (2010) *Guide for the Development and Implementation of Curricula for Plurilingual and Intercultural Education*, Strasbourg, France: Council of Europe.

Cummins, J (1979) Cognitive/academic language proficiency, linguistic interdependence, the optimum age question and some other matters, *Working Papers on Bilingualism* 19, 121–129.

Cummins, J (1984) *Bilingualism and Special Education: Issues in Assessment and Pedagogy*, Clevedon, England: Multilingual Matters.

Davies, A (2008) Ethics and professionalism, in Shohamy, E (Ed.) *Language Testing and Assessment*, Encyclopedia of Language and Education volume 7, New York: Springer, 429–443.

Hawkins, E W (1999) Foreign language study and language awareness, *Language Awareness* 8, 124–142.

Hulstijn, J H (2007) The shaky ground beneath the CEFR: quantitative and qualitative dimensions of language proficiency, *The Modern Language Journal* 91 (4), 663–667.

Jones, N (2012) Reliability and dependability, in Fulcher, D and Davidson, F (Eds) *The Routledge Handbook of Language Testing*, London and New York: Routledge, 350–362.

Lussier, D (2011) *Planning curriculum and testing in intercultural communicative competence*, paper presented at the 4th International Conference of the Association of Language Testers in Europe (ALTE), Kraków, July 2011.

WIDA (2012) *English Language Proficiency Standards for English Language Learners in Kindergarten through Grade 12*, available online from: www.wida.us/standards/elp.aspx

7 Implementing the CEFR in teacher-based assessment: approaches and challenges

Brian North and Elzbieta Jarosz
Evaluation and Accreditation of Quality in Language
Services (EAQUALS), Switzerland

Abstract

This paper outlines a scheme for Common European Framework of Reference for languages (CEFR) Certification recently introduced in EAQUALS (Evaluation and Accreditation of Quality in Language Services). The EAQUALS Certificate of CEFR Achievement scheme further develops procedures from the Council of Europe's *Manual* (2009) for relating examinations to the CEFR, adapting them to the school context. To issue Certificates of CEFR Achievement, EAQUALS accredited members join a supplementary accreditation scheme. This extra CEFR accreditation entails a detailed investigation by the EAQUALS Assessment Panel of the institution's approach to CEFR curriculum linkage, to specification of teaching and assessment content and tasks, standardisation training, the development and benchmarking of local reference samples, assessment practices themselves – and moderation techniques. Provisional accreditation is granted after this investigation and confirmed through an inspection of the assessment in practice in the institution in question. The further operation of the scheme is then routinely checked during the regular EAQUALS inspections of the institution.

In addition to explaining the rationale and procedures of the scheme, the paper points out some of the main problems inherent in school-based assessment of CEFR level, which inevitably focuses on teacher assessment. It outlines the way in which the scheme is designed to address these issues, and discusses the experience of schools that have applied for the scheme – and of the Assessment Panel. It summarises the way in which the scheme has changed from a simple accreditation scheme to a developmental pathway. Finally, the current work of the EAQUALS Curriculum and Assessment SIP (Special Interest Project) in further developing the CEFR–based scenario concept, introduced in the *British Council- EAQUALS Core Inventory for General English* (North, Ortega and Sheehan 2010) in order to develop assessment task templates, is outlined.

An introduction to EAQUALS

EAQUALS was founded in 1991 in Trieste as the European Association for Quality Language Services and, in recognition of the fact that its mission has now spread outside Europe, recently changed its name to *Evaluation and Accreditation of Quality in Language Services*. EAQUALS' core role is to offer international accreditation for providers of language learning programmes and services who wish to go beyond the minimum standards defined by national registration authorities and accreditation schemes. EAQUALS currently has just over 100 accredited members plus 20 or so Associate Members, the majority of whom are cultural institutes (e.g. The British Council), national language teaching quality associations (e.g. Polish Association of Schools of English (PASE)) or examining boards (e.g. Cambridge ESOL). At the EAQUALS 2011 Annual General Meeting in Prague, a scheme for individual membership was also launched.

EAQUALS, like the Association of Language Testers in Europe (ALTE) and the Eurocentres Foundation, is a non-governmental organisation (NGO) in the field of language learning to the Council of Europe, with participatory status. EAQUALS and ALTE collaborated to produce one of the earliest versions of the European Language Portfolio in 2000 and to create the very first electronic Portfolio in 2005 (see www.eelp.org). EAQUALS is indeed closely associated with CEFR-related language teaching and learning in the way that ALTE is closely associated with CEFR-related language testing. The EAQUALS website contains quite a range of CEFR–related resources, the most recent of which is the *British Council- EAQUALS Core Inventory for General English* (North, Ortega and Sheehan 2010), the product of a joint project with the British Council. This publication identifies a common, best practice interpretation of appropriate language content at the different CEFR levels. The project also produced a concept of *CEFR-based scenarios* to demonstrate archetypical top-down and bottom-up linking of linguistic content to real-world contexts, tasks and purposes. This concept is being further developed for assessment in the work of a current EAQUALS Special Interest Project, as reported later in the paper.

EAQUALS' original purpose in 1991 was to provide a scheme like that of the British Council's scheme in the UK to language providers who taught other languages and/or who had schools outside the UK. Unlike many schemes that have just codes of practice and possibly examination of documents, the EAQUALS scheme involves a thorough inspection with three points of emphasis, each of which has had a strong influence on the form taken by the scheme for the assessment and certification of CEFR achievement that is the subject of this paper. Firstly, in the spirit of the British Council scheme which helped to inspire it, the EAQUALS scheme focuses on evidence of excellence in *operational practice*. Secondly the scheme has a *developmental nature*. At the end of an inspection, recommendations are issued as well as, in some cases, requirements. Schools have a short period in which to provide evidence that they have now met the requirements of the EAQUALS standard in order to become (re)-accredited, and this may involve a re-inspection. However, they are encouraged to take the recommendations equally seriously and there is an expectation that at the following inspection, four years later, there will be evidence that recommendations have been followed up in practice. In this way, the standard of quality in accredited programmes naturally develops further over time. Finally EAQUALS maintains a *context-independent common standard.* Inspections are always carried out by two inspectors and at least one of those inspectors will be from a different pedagogic culture. It would, for example, be inconceivable for a school offering intensive short-stay programmes for French in France to be inspected by two other providers of such programmes.

The EAQUALS standards are grouped under 12 areas as follows:

1. Teaching.
2. Academic management – Curriculum and syllabus.
3. Academic management – Progress assessment & certification.
4. Academic management – Quality assurance.
5. Academic resources.
6. Other services to course participants.
7. Staff contracts, terms and conditions.
8. Qualifications, experience and training.
9. Communications.
10. Information.
11. Premises.
12. Management and administration.

It is the second and third areas that concern the EAQUALS Curriculum and Assessment Special Interest Group, which currently has two SIPs (Special Interest Projects): a CEFR Certification SIP and a CEFR Assessment Tasks SIP. Summarising somewhat, the main requirements of the EAQUALS scheme in this area are as follows:

- A coherent level system based on the CEFR levels, expanded into sub-levels as appropriate to context.
- A valid and reliable placement procedure including one or more tests, which will normally include an oral.
- A credible system by which teachers can monitor progress and provide feedback. (This concerns assessment for learning and does not necessarily require a CEFR element or use of descriptors.)
- A valid and reliable procedure for assessing individual attainment at the end of a course.

- A valid and reliable system of certificating this attainment. (Though this does not necessarily involve internal certification of the CEFR level reached.)

The EAQUALS CEFR certification scheme

At the end of 2008, EAQUALS decided to develop a scheme for CEFR certification. Preparation for the scheme involved the development of self-help training guides and resources that are available to members on the EAQUALS website, the production of a secure website to create the certificates, which each have a unique number and can be printed in several languages, and above all the establishment of a set of accreditation procedures. The latter are in effect an optional 'bolt on' to the main EAQUALS scheme. The first phase, which leads to provisional accreditation, is the evaluation at a distance of the programme provider's interpretation of the CEFR levels, the implementation of them in the curriculum, teacher training, assessment procedures and assessment instruments, plus the adequacy of the moderation techniques that have been put in place. The implementation in daily practice of the system is then checked at all subsequent EAQUALS inspections. A member of the EAQUALS Assessment Panel, a sub-committee of the main EAQUALS Accreditation Panel, is often one of the inspectors at the first inspection after the introduction of the certification scheme to the programme.

North (2004) had pointed out that the broad sets of procedures recommended in the publication *Relating Language Examinations to the Common European Framework of Reference for Languages: Learning, teaching, assessment (CEFR): A Manual* (Council of Europe 2009) were applicable to schools as well as tests. Indeed one of the reasons for adopting the fundamental scheme in the *Manual* (Specification, Standardisation/Standard-setting and Validation) was that it corresponds to the classic plan-do-check Quality Management cycle.

Naturally there are big differences between the two contexts – school assessment and standardised tests – and language educators will probably not wish or need to go to the same lengths as examining bodies should, especially with regard to validation. Schools will also tend to have assessment approaches based on teacher assessment unless external standardised tests are provided. Space does not permit detailed treatment of the debate over the advantages and disadvantages of standardised tests as opposed to teacher assessment – which is a particularly live issue in Switzerland at the moment. In discussing the CEFR illustrative descriptor scales, Milanovic points out (2011:9) that the 'risk of using the scales in a prescriptive way is that this might imply a "one size fits all" approach to measuring language ability'. Yet this danger is even greater when standardised tests, rather than teacher interpretation of common scales, are prescribed for contexts as variable as those within the EAQUALS membership. If standardised tests are implemented, then there is also the issue of teachers just rehearsing the tests rather than meeting learners' needs, a development that is generally acknowledged to have become a serious problem in England. Finally there is the problem of standard-setting for standardised tests. At the European Association of Language Testing and Assessment/International Association of Teachers of English as Foreign Language Testing Evaluation and Assessment Special Interest Group seminar in Barcelona in September 2010, John De Jong contrasted the variability of the pass standard in 1970s Dutch school tests with the stability over the same years of the pass standard operationalised by teachers. The teachers passed a steady percentage of candidates each year whilst the tests passed high percentages one year and low percentages the next due to faulty standard-setting. This, he said, was a major reason he stopped teaching and became a tester. Bad, amateurish standard-setting is worse than no standard-setting or indeed no tests.

However, teacher assessment has serious problems too. De Jong's point cited above concerns the consistency of teachers' normative referencing over years; it does not actually prove that the assessments of the teachers concerned were correct. Teachers in general are capable of internalising a standard accurately as he suggests, provided they are trained in that standard. A staffroom of teachers working with a fully CEFR-based curriculum will in practice have pretty much the same interpretation of the levels, since learners, classes and materials are all referred to in terms of them. Provided that this interpretation was based on an engagement with the CEFR and a reflection on current practice, guided by the resources available for that purpose, as opposed to being merely a convenient relabelling of pre-existing course organisation, then the teachers' common interpretation of the CEFR levels will be sufficiently accurate. After all, the CEFR descriptor scales were created on the basis of the way teachers in different contexts interpreted the wording of the descriptors when using them to assess the learners in their classes, and there was negligible DIF (differential item functioning; variability) across educational sectors, target languages or language regions (North 2000).

The intractable problem comes when teachers implement that internalised standard in their assessments. Here all of the classic rater errors will come into play, for example: ignorance of the constructs and criteria, stubborn use of personal constructs and criteria rather than the intended ones, unconscious excessive focus on one criterion (e.g. linguistic accuracy), excessive strictness or lenience, central tendency and especially a refusal to give the top grade, and finally overall intra-rater inconsistency. In addition, there are problems unique to the context of teachers and classes. As Lenz and Berthele (2010) point out in discussing the issue, *reference group error* (prejudice in the literal meaning of the word: you are Albanian, Albanians are like this, therefore you are like this) is a very real problem with teacher assessment.

It is a problem not confined to mainstream education. Language teachers with international classes can erroneously assume that learners of certain nationalities (e.g. Japanese) cannot speak, simply because the learners give themselves a little longer to get started, defer to others or tolerate silence, and the teachers do not set up properly structured tasks that require everyone to speak. The second major rater error with teachers assessing classes is what North (2000:323) called *excessive norm-referencing*. Teachers often tend to want to reward their good students and show differences which they can see between the performances of the learners in the class. This is essentially a problem of focus: the class teacher sees the level – and its sublevels – in close-up. It then can appear 'unfair' to them that several learners get the same results when they themselves can see noticeable differences. Therefore they may exaggerate the achievement of the best learners and underestimate that of the weaker learners and manipulate the assessment instrument to do this.

In the context of a certification scheme for educational institutions, rater error in teacher assessment is a particularly serious problem, even after it has been identified. Whereas a testing body can stop using a particular person acting as a rater, a school cannot easily prevent a teacher acting as an assessor. All one can do is introduce systematic moderation and quality control.

Therefore, although the EAQUALS scheme is based on very similar principles to the CEFR examination *Manual*, there is a much higher emphasis on moderation. Moderation is in fact only mentioned in passing in the section of the *Manual* on standardisation training in terms of the 'planning of continuous verification and on-going monitoring, dissemination and follow-up actions' (Council of Europe 2009:39).

The main elements of the EAQUALS certification scheme are therefore:

- curriculum coherence with the CEFR (= specification)
- familiarisation and standardisation training
- assessment procedures
- moderation techniques.

Curriculum coherence with the CEFR

The wording of the standard EAQUALS requirements listed at the end of the section above in conjunction with the fact that EAQUALS schools all have CEFR-based curricula might suggest that the introduction of a scheme for certification of the CEFR level attained at the end of the course would be a simple matter. However, the degree of CEFR implementation that is expected by EAQUALS is considerably greater if a school wishes to issue certificates. In an EAQUALS inspection, three grades are given: Grade 1 (Point of Excellence); Grade 2 (Meets EAQUALS Requirement) and Grade 3 (Does not meet EAQUALS Requirement).

In terms of CEFR curriculum implementation, there is quite a difference between meeting the normal EAQUALS Requirement and demonstrating the excellence that is required for the certification scheme. As can be seen from Table 1, which summarises the respective requirements, a far more detailed engagement with the CEFR and with CEFR-based Can Do descriptors is demanded from institutions issuing certificates. This is necessary if teachers are to be thoroughly familiar with the levels, and hence able to assess learner achievement in relation to them. Conversely, none of the points on teaching or on self-assessment that would be regarded as criteria of excellence for the main EAQUALS scheme are actually minimum requirements to issue CEFR certificates. Most schools that have engaged with the CEFR as far as to issue certificates probably would integrate descriptors more into teaching self-assessment, but it is perfectly possible to report a CEFR outcome without doing this. Nor is it necessary to report the CEFR level at arrival (placement testing) in order to assess it accurately at the end.

Familiarisation and standardisation training

Familiarisation with the CEFR levels through training and awareness-raising exercises is always necessary as people tend to think they know the levels without consulting the descriptors or official illustrative samples. Instead they often associate the CEFR levels with levels they previously used. Familiarisation exercises normally involve descriptor sorting tasks, but the most useful, initial form of familiarisation is to see the levels in action – in video sequences such as those available online for English, French, Spanish, German and Italian on: www.ciep.fr/en/publi_evalcert/dvd-productions-orales-cecrl/index.php

Standardisation involves firstly training in such a standard interpretation of the levels, using the illustrative samples provided for that purpose, and secondly the transfer of that standardised interpretation to the benchmarking of local reference samples. This second step is important for a number of reasons, which is why the EAQUALS certification scheme requires the school to send a DVD or audio cassette with locally benchmarked samples. These samples demonstrate that the school has understood the levels, provided examples of assessment tasks in operation, given a positive task for the school to transfer their understanding of the levels, and – most importantly – provided more locally relevant illustrative samples for future training.

It is, however, very important that one does not confuse standardisation training and benchmarking in such a context. In standardisation, participants are trainees being introduced to or reminded of the level, the criteria, the administration procedures etc. It is a formal process with external authority represented by the workshop leader, the CEFR-related criteria, the calibrated samples and their documentation linking the performances to the

Table 1 The CEFR and EAQUALS standards

	Grade 2 EAQUALS Requirement	Grade 1 Criteria of Excellence	Certificate Requirement
Levels			
Levels referenced to the CEFR global descriptors of CEFR levels	X	X	X
Using CEFR-calibrated exams as benchmarks	X	X	X
Familiarising teachers with CEFR overviews and descriptors		X	X
Standardisation training (DVDs and/or scripts)		X	X
Benchmarking local samples (DVDs or audio)		X	X
Curriculum & Syllabus			
Curriculum and levels referenced meaningfully to CEFR	X	X	X
CEFR Can Do global objective for each of the four skills for each level	X	X	X
Schemes of work specifying what the course participants will achieve (Can Do, functions, vocab, grammar), with corresponding checklists for planning	X	X	X
Coherent reference to CEFR both in planning and implementation so as to have a real influence on setting clear learning objectives		X	X
Checklists of Can Do learning aims, adapted to the institution, for planning specific objectives		X	X
Materials cross-referenced to CEFR-based descriptors		X	
Teaching			
The principles of the CEFR – learner-centred and action-oriented – are clearly applied, with effective use of Can Dos		X	
Can Dos in learning aims for week or for lessons		X	
Can Dos in learning aims for lesson (e.g. 'Aims Box')		X	
Activities and lesson stages linked to Can Dos		X	
Intercultural training		X	

Table 1 continued

	Grade 2 EAQUALS Requirement	Grade 1 Criteria of Excellence	Certificate Requirement
Assessment			
Placement test/interview reports a CEFR level (or sublevel)		X	
Individualised, not just based on the general level of the class		X	X
Continuous assessment includes checklists of Can Dos		X	X
Assessment tasks for both spoken interaction and for spoken production, related to CEFR descriptors		X	X
CEFR-based assessment criteria – related to CEFR descriptors		X	X
Supporting teacher assessment with tests		X	X
Collective assessment: double marking of at least a sample		X	X
Progress records with CEFR levels/sublevels		X	X
Systematic checking by the Academic Manager of the CEFR grades awarded by teachers		X	
Effective use of self-assessment		X	
Self-assessment with CEFR-based Can Dos		X	
Self-assessment with (EAQUALS/ALTE) Portfolio		X	

descriptors in CEFR Table 3 (Council of Europe 2001:28–9). Standardisation training is not an exercise in democracy: the school is implementing an interpretation of the CEFR levels that they wish to correspond to the common, international interpretation shared with other members of EAQUALS and the institutions and experts who provide the documented, illustrative samples. The right answer to the question 'What level is this learner?' is not necessarily an arithmetic average of the opinions of those present in a particular staffroom, in a particular country, all accustomed to the same exam and the same course books. Their interpretation may be over-influenced by short cuts taken by the national institutions who labelled those books and exams – or even by their own relabelling of their existing courses.

In benchmarking, on the other hand, participants are valued, trained experts (although very possibly the same people who did the standardisation training in the morning!). Here it is important to record individual judgements before they are swayed by over-dominant members of the group in discussion. It is, of course, also important to get the permission of the learners who are recorded.

Assessment procedures

The scheme focuses on the assessment of speaking. In addition to teacher 'continuous assessment' in relation to CEFR-based descriptors, supported by the results of progress tests that may not be fully validated, there must be a formal assessment of speaking in a specific assessment activity, applying CEFR-based criteria. This decision was taken for a number of reasons. Firstly, speaking is regarded by clients as the core skill. Secondly, the standardisation and moderation of the assessment of speaking is close to procedures that already happen in good language programmes (e.g. communicative group work; systematic observation). Thirdly, the process is very visible and conducive to discussion and the spread of good practice. Finally, many schools do not have the expertise or resources to develop and validate listening and reading tests, a point returned to later in the third section of this paper. In addition, progress tests of language usage tend in practice to focus on sentence-level language usage and to remain unvalidated. Where such items have been incorporated into a validated, calibrated item bank referenced to CEFR levels, as is the case in Eurocentres, such tests can also report a CEFR level for the areas concerned. But although unvalidated tests of language usage can support a teacher by giving an indication of the extent to which a learner has mastered the language points associated with a level, they cannot in themselves report a level in the way that a test with a validated cut score can or a properly conducted assessment of speaking can. Since standard-setting to validate test cut scores is a complex issue, the focus was put on speaking.

There was some discussion in the early phases of the project as to whether it should be compulsory for the criteria used in speaking assessments to be specifically related to CEFR descriptors (CEFR Table 3: Council of Europe 2001: 28–9; subscales from CEFR Chapter 5: Council of Europe 2001:101–30; writing grid from the *Manual*: Council of Europe 2009:187). It was decided that, although an assessment grid might include some non-CEFR categories and descriptors, the style of all descriptors should be concrete and positive, like that of the CEFR descriptors. The assessment instrument might be one single grid of categories and levels like CEFR Table 3, especially for a programme in which teachers teach classes at different levels (e.g. Eurocentres). On the other hand, there might be a series of grids that each focus only on the target level, with one descriptor per chosen category. The latter approach has been taken by most schools in the scheme. There are several advantages to this approach. Firstly, it is easier to explain the criteria to learners. Thus, the teacher can highlight the competences that the learners must acquire for communicative success, rather than just focusing on lists of things they 'can do'. Secondly, when criteria are presented in what is in effect a short checklist, a rating scale (usually 1 to 5) can be applied to each descriptor. In this way the teachers are given the opportunity to differentiate between excellent and adequate performance, rather than just making a Yes/No decision for each criterion for the level concerned.

Moderation

Even after standardisation training has been implemented, moderation will always be necessary. Some assessors can be quite resistant to training and the effects of the standardisation also start to wear off immediately after the training anyway. In addition, the kind of rater errors discussed earlier will continue. Some assessors will still use personal concepts rather than the official criteria as their reference. Many will continue to be over-influenced by one criterion (e.g. accuracy or pronunciation), and many will still refuse to give a top or bottom grade (= error of central tendency). The sad fact of the matter is that training may not always change 'hard cases'.

Moderation techniques can be divided into collective assessment techniques and quality control techniques. Collective techniques involve some form of double marking, perhaps of a structured sample of candidates (e.g. every fifth consecutive candidate), or – after rank ordering – the top, middle and bottom learners in a class. Administrative quality control techniques will involve studying collateral information on the learners on the one hand, and/or developing progress norms: what range of progress do people at this level normally make? Such norms can then be used to identify classes whose grades differ significantly from the norm, for further investigation. These grades might genuinely be due to an unusually good or bad teacher or to an unusually strong or weak class – but it is worth following up. In addition, scores from a standardised test may be used to smooth the results from teacher assessment in a form of statistical moderation, as in Eurocentres.

The application

To summarise, the scheme requires the institution to provide evidence that CEFR principles and levels are fully implemented in the curriculum and syllabuses so that learning objectives are derived from CEFR, that the assessment specifications and criteria are CEFR-based, that sufficient standardisation training has been done using the materials made available so that the interpretation of the levels is sensible, and finally that adequate moderation techniques (e.g. double-marking) and other quality control mechanisms have been implemented. In order to provide that evidence, the institution is asked to send the following materials for inspection by the EAQUALS Assessment Panel:

- curriculum and syllabus documents with learning objectives derived from the CEFR
- a coherent description of the assessment system
- written guidelines for teachers
- CEFR-based continuous assessment instruments
- sample CEFR-based assessment tasks, tests, guidelines
- CEFR-based criteria grids
- a set of locally recorded, CEFR-rated samples to be double checked by the EAQUALS expert panel
- samples of individual progress records
- content and schedule of staff CEFR standardisation training
- details of moderation techniques employed.

Difficulties encountered and action taken

In implementing the scheme, two main types of problems have occurred: procedural issues and substantive issues. As regards the latter, the two points that institutions find most difficult are producing the DVDs with oral samples and implementing adequate moderation techniques. These are things that schools would not normally do. However, checking that the members of the scheme have achieved an accurate interpretation of the CEFR levels and are capable of ensuring proper application of that interpretation is at the core of a scheme based on teacher assessments. There was considerable debate, especially in the EAQUALS Executive Committee and Board, as to whether keeping the requirement to benchmark local samples was necessary. But now that the scheme is starting to take off, one can see that the DVD recordings are the single most important source of information. In addition, the Assessment Panel has decided to embark on a collaborative effort with the institutions in the scheme in order to provide proper documentation of the bank of samples. This documentation will be based on the model provided by the CEFR illustrative DVDs for English (Eurocentres and Migros Club Schools 2004) and French (CIEP and Eurocentres 2005).

The most time-consuming problems have been procedural ones. The linguistic complications are not to be underestimated. A school in Croatia usually has its documentation in Croatian. This is the kind of issue EAQUALS is used to dealing with, but it is still complicated. Very clear instructions are needed regarding the organisation of the documentation to be sent in and there has to be a clear procedure to cope with the (not infrequent) cases when it is sent differently or in incomplete form. Lines of communication between the institution and Assessment Panel are complex, especially with follow-up procedures to deal with Requirements set in the initial verdict by the panel.

The action taken has been to streamline various processes, overhaul the instructions and documents and to institute a formal support pathway. This pathway provides each applicant institution with help in the preparation of their systems and application. This mechanism is shown in Figure 1.

Figure 1 Support pathway for applicants

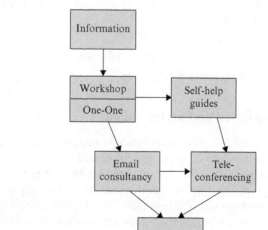

Current development: scenarios for assessment tasks

Meanwhile, while applicants have been joining the Certification Scheme, a new Special Interest Project has been set up. As mentioned at the beginning of this paper, one of the outcomes of the *Core Inventory for General English* was a CEFR-based scenario concept (Ortega 2010:72). The motivation behind this was a perceived need, when publishing lists of possible content, to counteract the unfortunately common misconception that descriptors form some kind of teaching menu, that they are in some way discrete items that should be taught and assessed one after another. Any real-world or any classroom activity will almost certainly involve tasks and competences represented by clusters of descriptors. The scenarios in this model have two pages; a first page specifies the objectives for a learning module or an assessment. Global real-world aspects such as the domain, the context, the real-world tasks and the language activities involved are defined, as well as relevant CEFR-based descriptors both for language activities (selected or adapted from CEFR Chapter 4: Language use and the language user/learner) and for criteria (from CEFR Chapter 5: The competences of the user/learner). These more macro objectives are then supplemented by a list of enabling objectives, the relevant competences (strategic, pragmatic, and linguistic), including grammar points and vocabulary areas. These points are drawn from the content of the *Core Inventory*.

This type of scenario is not a test specification because nothing is defined as regards concrete assessment tasks, expected responses or assessment conditions. Much of the time, a teacher will not want to go into such detail, preferring instead to focus on identifying the steps necessary for the acquisition of the competences concerned and their integration into a pedagogic sequence. The sequencing of such pedagogic steps is in fact the subject of the second page of the scenarios in the model referred to. However, developing the scenario concept further into task templates for formal classroom assessment is the subject of the current EAQUALS Special Interest Project in the Curriculum and Assessment area.

The aims of the project are to develop sets of ideas for assessment tasks at CEFR levels to a standard format (= 'task collections'), to elaborate some of those into full scenarios for each level, which in effect become templates for assessments, and then to provide for each scenario illustrative assessment materials for English and French. The initial focus has been on reading and listening, since these are the areas that schools have reported as being most problematic for them. If listening and reading are included in progress tests, the material tends to come from course books, which is inappropriate.

The intention is to expand the task collection by conducting brainstorming workshops in certain schools, validate the assessment materials so

Table 2 Assessment task idea for B1 listening

CEFR descriptor(s)	I can catch the main points in TV programmes on familiar topics when the delivery is relatively slow and clear. I can follow a lecture or talk within my own field, provided the subject matter is familiar and the presentation straightforward and clearly structured.
Micro-activities	• Distinguish main points from specific details • Understand an explicitly signalled line of narrative/ argument • Understand specific details
Text features	• TV programme with short report/guide and interview(s) • Topics; familiar and regularly encountered in a school, work or leisure context • Presentation: straightforward and clearly structured • Delivery: clear, standard, relatively slow
Task features	• Could hear twice/three times • Recognising new sections (relevant to topics of questions) • Identifying essential information
Example with item types	Follow a TV guided commentary on a place (e.g. Tour of Hampton Court, Versailles; extract from travel programme/tourism promotion) • T/F/NS • Matching or Information transfer (table or diagram) • Open-ended questions
Feedback	I can follow a TV lecture, talk or guided tour and understand specific details if: • the subject matter is familiar • the presentation is clearly structured • the narrative is explicitly signalled • the language is clear and relatively slow • I can watch the video twice

produced through peer review and then empirically trial them. One idea in the task collection for listening at B1 is shown in Table 2.

In the fully worked scenario, the enabling objectives (strategic, pragmatic and linguistic) are detailed as before, but the second page now gives a template for tasks associated with the text. In the example given above, this template is completed with an illustrative example: a video tour of Hampton Court. This text has three tasks attached: True/False, Matching and Open questions. Table 3 gives the template for the first task (True/False) as an example.

This particular assessment has been pre-trialled once so far, with an English class of Swiss 14-year-olds. The class scored 60% on the True/False and 85% on the Matching but only 40% on the Open questions. The teacher's comment was that they found it very interesting and wanted to know more, but that 'it was difficult for them to write about it instantly in English as they

Table 3 Template for listening assessment (Task 1)

General description		Follow short introduction to a TV guided commentary on Hampton Court, answering 5 True/False/Not Stated questions while listening
Source		*The Tudors: Behind Hampton Court*: http://www.youtube.com/ watch?v=mX7ABmAlcAE Natalie Dormer of The Tudors celebrates the 500th anniversary of Henry VIII's coronation by touring the Hampton Court Palace
Text features	Authenticity	Authentic
	Length	Total 10 minutes
	Visual support	Yes – commentary should match unfolding film
Item type/number		Introduction: True/False/Not stated: (5 questions)
Task rubric		Follow this introduction to a TV guided commentary on a historic place of interest, Hampton Court Palace, near London. Answer the 5 questions. Mark 'T' if the statement is True, 'F' if it is false and 'NS' if the information is Not Stated in the commentary.
Time		While playing
Mark scheme		5×1 mark = 5 marks

are not used to doing so without a dictionary and they do not have much general knowledge about Tudor times anyway'. This underlies the importance of proper specification and trialling of even low-stakes assessment items in order to check that (a) the desired construct is being tested and (b) that necessary support is given.

Conclusion

The Assessment Tasks group has had five two-day workshops at the time of writing, in November 2010 (London), February 2011 (Lausanne), April 2011 (Brighton), October 2011 (London) and March 2012 (London again). We have now completed the task collections with, for English, at least one fully developed scenario for each level for listening and reading, illustrated with example assessment tasks. For French there has been a concentration on Level A2, with some 10 scenarios at that level illustrated with tasks. An interesting aspect of the work has been the development of micro-activities, text features and task features from CEFR descriptors, as well as the identification of suitable text-genres implied by them. The next step is systematic piloting of the materials, which is planned for autumn 2012.

Meanwhile, the Certification group has embarked on standardised documentation for the video samples collected. The intention for 2013 is to merge the work from the two sub-groups and focus on scenarios and task materials for the assessment of speaking and integrated skills.

References

CIEP and Eurocentres (2005) *DVD de productions orales ilustrant pour le français, les niveaux du Cadre européen commun de réference pour les langues du Conseil de l'Europe*, Paris: CIEP/Didier.

Council of Europe (2001) *Common European Framework of Reference for Languages: Learning, Teaching, Assessment*. Cambridge, Cambridge University Press.

Council of Europe (2009) *Relating Language Examinations to the Common European Framework of Reference for Languages: Learning, teaching, assessment (CEFR). A Manual*, Strasbourg: Council of Europe.

Eurocentres and Migros Club Schools (2004) *CEFR Illustrative Samples: For Relating Language Examinations to the Common European Framework of Reference for Languages: Learning, Teaching, Assessment. English-Swiss Adult Learners*, Strasbourg: Council of Europe.

Lenz, P and Berthele, R (2010) *Assessment in Plurilingual and Intercultural Education, Satellite Study No 2, Guide for the Development and Implementation of Curricula for Plurilingual and Intercultural Education*, document prepared for the Policy Forum 'The Right of Learners to Quality and Equity in Education – The Role of Linguistic and Intercultural Competence', Geneva, Switzerland, 2–4 November 2010.

Milanovic, M (2011) Introduction, in ALTE (2011) *Manual for Language Test Development and Examining – for use with the CEFR*, Cambridge: ALTE, 6–9.

North, B (2000) *The Development of a Common Framework Scale of Language Proficiency*, New York: Peter Lang.

North, B (2004) Relating assessments, examinations and courses to the CEF, in Morrow, K (Ed.) *Insights from the Common European Framework*, Oxford: Oxford University Press, 77–90.

North, B, Ortega Calvo, Á and Sheehan, S (2010) *British Council–EAQUALS Core Inventory for General English*, London: British Council/EAQUALS.

Ortega Calvo, Á (2010) Qué son en realidad los niveles C? Desarrollo de sus descriptores en el MCER y el PEL, in Ortega Calvo (Ed.) *Niveles C: Currículos, Programación, Enseñanza y Certificación*, Madrid: IFIIE – Ministerio de Educación, 21–85.

8 A progress report on the development of the CEFR-J

Masashi Negishi
Tokyo University of Foreign Studies, Japan

Tomoko Takada
Meikai University, Japan

Yukio Tono
Tokyo University of Foreign Studies, Japan

Abstract

The Common European Framework of Reference for languages (CEFR) (Council of Europe 2001) is becoming increasingly influential not only in Europe but also in other parts of the world. Although this framework has been shown to be compatible with English language teaching in Japan in many respects, it seems that the CEFR needs some modifications. In this paper, we present an interim report on the development of the CEFR-J, a modified version of the original CEFR to Japanese contexts. This project consists of the following stages: (a) the compilation of the preliminary versions of the CEFR-J, (b) the validation phase of the CEFR-J, and (c) the pilot for using the revised CEFR-J at school. The present paper reports mainly on the first two stages. After the compilation of the alpha version of the CEFR-J, based upon the original CEFR, as well as other resources on illustrative descriptors developed inside and outside Japan, the consistency of the wordings against three dimensions of illustrative descriptors (performance, criteria and condition) was checked and all the descriptors were translated into English. Then a revision was made on the first version based upon feedback from several CEFR specialists, which resulted in the beta version of the CEFR-J. At the validation phase, a number of projects are in progress at the time of writing this paper. Our validation is based on the analysis of responses from Japanese teachers and learners, which include self-assessment data and performance tests in five skills. This paper also describes some accompanying resources for implementing the CEFR-J into educational contexts in Japan, such as the CEFR-J wordlist as well as the Can Do descriptor database. A brief overview of these ongoing projects is presented, followed by a discussion on the potential impact of the CEFR-J on Japan's foreign language education policy.

The background to English language teaching in Japan

English is a core subject in the school curriculum from primary to tertiary education in Japan. In 2011, a new subject called Foreign Language Activities started at primary schools in Japan. For this subject, most schools teach mainly English, although the name of the subject is Foreign Language Activities. Lower secondary school education (12–15 years) is compulsory in Japan, and English is a compulsory subject there. Although upper secondary school education (15–18 years) is not compulsory, approximately 98% of lower secondary school students go on to upper secondary schools, and most of them study English. English classes are also being offered at most universities and many companies.

For English language education in primary and secondary schools, we have something called the Courses of Study, or national curricula, but we do not have their equivalent for university education or other adult education programmes. The Courses of Study for English have been compiled by English language teaching specialists in Japan, based on their expertise and teaching experience, and are publicly notified by the Ministry of Education to the public. Despite the existence of the Courses of Study, we do not have a shared comprehensive picture of life-long English language education. This is partly because of the separation of the Courses of Study for primary and secondary schools, and the lack of curricula for tertiary and adult education. Furthermore, although the Courses of Study include teaching objectives and a list of things to teach, we have not had any agreed attainment targets in language teaching so far. Nor do we have any consensus as to how to attain those targets or how to assess the attainment. Therefore, we have an urgent need for a common language framework to discuss English language teaching, learning, and assessment in Japan.

The background to the CEFR-J

A quest for a common language framework

After considering a number of language frameworks available to us, such as the American Council for the Teaching of Foreign Languages (ACTFL) Proficiency Guidelines and the Canadian Language Benchmarks, we decided to adopt the Common European Framework of Reference for languages (CEFR), partly because its influence is spreading across Europe and beyond, and partly because it is comprehensive in terms of skills and range of language proficiency. With the CEFR, we believe that policy makers in Japan could draw a bigger picture of English language teaching and learning, and that we could relate our target and attainment to world standards, since, according to North, Ortega and Sheehan, the CEFR 'is now accepted as *the* international standard for language teaching and learning' (2010:6). Although the CEFR was originally developed in Europe, we assumed that we could use this framework for English language teaching in Japan as well, since it is a language-independent framework, in which an action-oriented approach is adopted.

The applicability of the CEFR to Japanese learners of English

Of relevance here are two surveys carried out by Negishi in order to investigate if the CEFR is applicable to Japanese learners of English as it is (reported in Nakajima and Nagata 2006). The instrument used was the CEFR Can Do questionnaire extracted from DIALANG self-assessment statements (Council of Europe 2001:231–237), and it was translated into Japanese. Three hundred and sixty Japanese university students participated in this survey. The answer to each questionnaire item was treated as a response to a test item. The answers were Can Do or Can't Do dichotomous data, and the item difficulties were calculated by XCALIBRE.

The items for each skill were ordered along a −3 to +3 scale, as shown in Figures 1 to 3. As can be seen from these Figures, most of the items were put in the order of the CEFR levels. Therefore, it can be assumed that the order of difficulty of the CEFR descriptors, which were created in Europe, is more or less the same with Japanese English as a Foreign Language (EFL) learners.

Figure 1 CEFR Can Do questionnaire survey (1): results for Writing

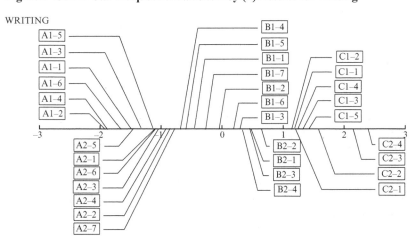

Figure 2 CEFR Can Do questionnaire survey (1): results for Listening

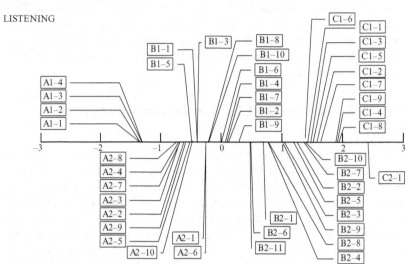

Figure 3 CEFR Can Do questionnaire survey (1): results for Reading

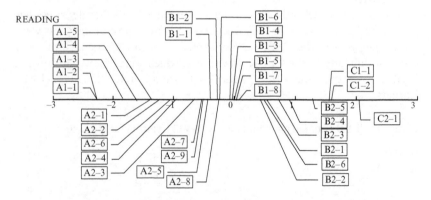

However, it is worth noting that there were some 'outliers' that did not belong to the cluster of the descriptors in the corresponding CEFR level. One of the interesting Reading outliers was A2-8 *I can understand simple instructions on equipment encountered in everyday life – such as a public telephone.* This descriptor was originally an A2 item, but it turned out to be at B1. The participants might have been unfamiliar with 'instructions on equipment' written in English, and considered it to be more difficult. (In passing, this descriptor seems to be a little outdated because of the reference to 'a public telephone', so the 10-year-old CEFR itself might need some adjustment.)

Another interesting example was A1-5: *I can understand short, simple messages, e.g. on postcards.* This A1 item turned out to be more difficult than A2-1: *I can understand short, simple texts containing the most common words, including some shared international words.* This might be because Japanese postcards tend to contain much more information than their European counterparts, and therefore the Japanese EFL learners considered it to be more difficult than it was originally assumed in the CEFR. In summary, the CEFR Can Do descriptors were ordered more or less the same with Japanese learners. However, the tasks which they had little experience of in real life or in the classroom were judged to be more difficult than the levels they were originally assigned to, whereas the tasks they had experienced were judged to be easier.

This study was followed up by the next research project, in which Negishi (2006) investigated whether we might be able to adjust the difficulties of the outlier Can Do descriptors by providing examples. The methodology adopted for this research was basically the same as for the previous study, except for the fact that the outlier items were administered with examples. The responses were based on a Likert scale, and item difficulties were calculated with FACETS (Linacre 1989). The participants were 727 Japanese upper secondary school and university students. The results showed that it was possible to adjust outlier CEFR Can Do descriptors by providing examples. However, the written scripts for listening descriptors made the items more difficult. Hence the need for real examples for unfamiliar Can Do questionnaire items.

From these surveys, we can conclude that it is possible to use the CEFR descriptors for English language teaching in Japan, but that they need some adaptation. This is acceptable under the guidelines of the Council of Europe, which states that 'the framework should be open and flexible, so that it can be applied, with such adaptations as prove necessary, to particular situations' (2001:7). In order to use the CEFR descriptors for English language teaching in Japan, it will be necessary for us to identify which parts need modification, with further evidence.

The distribution of Japanese EFL learners' CEFR levels

At the next stage, we considered the appropriateness of the branching of the CEFR levels for Japanese EFL learners. In so doing, we first attempted to identify Japanese EFL learners' CEFR levels. However, it is extremely difficult to get a representative sample of an entire nation, based on exam results, and to align them to the CEFR levels.

Eventually, we obtained the results of two interesting surveys, which seemed to be both appropriate and relevant. The English proficiency level of Japanese secondary school students was investigated in the first survey. This data is unique in that all the students of a particular prefecture in Japan

Figure 4 Results of the Japanese lower secondary school students (age 15)

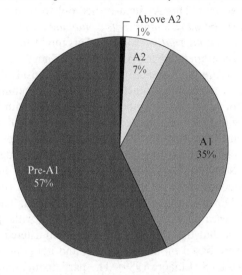

Figure 5 Results of the Japanese upper secondary school students (age 17)

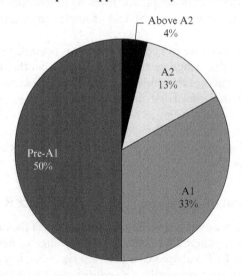

took an English proficiency test which can be aligned to the CEFR levels. According to this survey (see Figure 4), at the end of three years' learning of English, 57% of the students had not reached A1, 35% were at A1, and 7% were at A2. At the end of five years (see Figure 5), 50% had not reached A1, 33% were at A1, 13% at A2, and 4% above A2.

In the other survey, the English proficiency level of all the employees of an electronics manufacturer in Japan was investigated. This manufacturer is listed in the first section of the Tokyo Stock Exchange, and has 7,171 employees. The CEFR level distribution of the employees is as follows. As can be seen from Figure 6 and Table 1, more than 80% of the employees are at A levels, whereas very few people are at C levels. For example, in Table 1 0.01% of the employees are at C2 in Speaking. That is, only one person has succeeded in reaching this level; C level is surprisingly high for Japanese EFL learners. To Japanese people's credit, they are not incompetent in learning all the foreign languages. In fact, according to Otani (2007), Japanese people far exceed other first language (L1) learners in learning Korean and Chinese. This is basically a matter of so-called linguistic and cultural distance.

As can be seen in Table 1 and Figure 6, more than 80% of Japanese EFL learners are Non/Basic Users (A1 and A2), less than 20% are Independent

Table 1 The distribution of Japanese EFL learners' CEFR levels: company employees

	Listening	Reading	Writing	Speaking
C2	0.11%	0.08%	0.11%	0.01%
C1	1.13%	0.20%	0.32%	0.01%
B2	1.94%	5.69%	4.66%	1.70%
B1	12.06%	7.67%	12.49%	6.39%
A2	32.65%	31.98%	40.97%	37.04%
A1	52.11%	54.39%	41.44%	54.85%

Figure 6 The distribution of Japanese EFL learners' CEFR levels: company employees

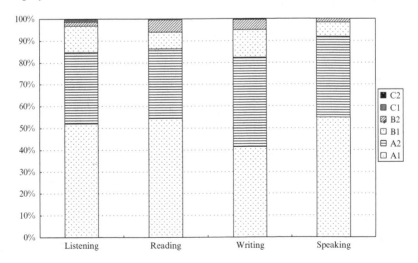

Users (B1 and B2), and Proficient Users (C1 and C2) are almost nil. The EFL learner population in Japan can be assumed to be heavily skewed towards lower levels.

The development of the CEFR-J

The results of the surveys suggest that there is a need to subdivide the lower CEFR levels and also to add a lower stage before A1. As for the validity of the introduction of pre-A1, different ideas have been voiced so far. However, the Council of Europe (2001:31) clearly states:

> Level A1 (Breakthrough) is probably the lowest 'level' of generative language proficiency which can be identified. Before this stage is reached, however, there may be a range of specific tasks which learners can perform effectively using a very restricted range of language and which are relevant to the needs of the learners concerned . . . In certain contexts, for example with young learners, it may be appropriate to elaborate such a 'milestone'.

So we decided to include pre-A1, because Japanese learners are not sufficiently familiar with the English alphabet, and also because a great number of Japanese learners do not reach A1, as defined by some test alignment tables.

The fact that the population of Japanese EFL learners skews towards the lower levels suggests the need for the branching of the A1–B2 levels. Regarding this issue, the Council of Europe (2001:32) states:

> The advantage of a branching approach is that a common set of levels and/or descriptors can be 'cut' into practical local levels at different points by different users to suit local needs and yet still relate back to a common system. The numbering allows further subdivisions to be made without losing the reference to the main objective being referred to.

All of the relevant surveys suggest the need to develop a modified version of the original CEFR for English language teaching in Japan, which we refer to as the CEFR-J. Hereafter, we will present a progress report on the development of the CEFR-J. The development of the CEFR-J was initiated by a group funded by the Grant-in-Aid for Scientific Research by the Ministry of Education, led by Ikuo Koike, in 2004, and it was subsequently taken over by the group headed by Yukio Tono in 2008. 2011 was the final year of the project. This group consisted of 18 members.

The established principles of the development of the CEFR-J were:

1. Add Pre-A1.
2. Divide A1 into three levels: A1.1, A1.2, A1.3.
3. Divide A2 into two levels: A2.1, A2.2.
4. Divide B1 into two levels: B1.1, B1.2.
5. Divide B2 into two levels: B2.1, B2.2.
6. No change for C1 and C2.
7. Adapt Can Do descriptors to the Japanese context.

We collected descriptors available in Japan: some were from English proficiency tests and others from schools. We also collected the descriptors found in the CEFR and the European Language Portfolio (ELP), and compiled them in an Excel file, so that relevant descriptors could be searched electronically.

The descriptors in the initial version of the CEFR-J included a number of inconsistencies in their wording. A CEFR specialist from the UK (Dr Anthony Green) was invited as consultant about the development of Can Do descriptors. In his workshop, he advised us to break down the descriptors. Each descriptor was broken down into three categories: The descriptors for productive skills were broken down into (1) performance, (2) criteria, and (3) condition, whereas those for receptive skills were broken down into (1) task,

Table 2 An example of a broken-down CEFR-J Spoken Interaction Can Do descriptor

A1.3 Spoken Interaction	Performance	Criteria (Quality)	Condition
I can ask and answer simple questions about very familiar topics (e.g. hobbies, sports, club activities), provided that people speak slowly and clearly with some repetition and rephrasing.	I can ask and answer . . . questions about . . . topics (e.g. hobbies, sports, club activities)	simple very familiar	provided that people speak slowly and clearly with some repetition and rephrasing.

Table 3 An example of a broken-down CEFR-J Listening Can Do descriptor

B2.1 Listening	Task	Text	Condition
I can follow extended speech and complex lines of argument provided the topic is reasonably familiar.	I can follow	extended speech and complex lines of argument	provided the topic is reasonably familiar.

(2) text, and (3) condition. Tables 2 and 3 provide examples of the broken-down Can Do descriptors.

The descriptors were randomly checked, vertically and horizontally, for consistencies, and the wording was changed where necessary. The broken-down Can Do descriptors were then reassembled.

As we finalised the beta version of the CEFR-J, we had feedback from a number of CEFR specialists in the UK. Anthony Green in particular gave us very detailed comments on the wording of the descriptors, and we revised them accordingly. Thus, we have completed the beta version of the CEFR-J. Dr Green posed a question: are we aiming to make a Japanese version of the self-assessment grid as in the CEFR or a Japanese version of the ELP (European Language Portfolio)? Dr Neil Jones, reviewing the entire CEFR-J, stated that the present set of descriptors was 'primarily directed at the teacher' (personal communication), and therefore we would need another set of descriptors for younger learners. According to Dr Jones, it is essential, at first, 'to orient the teachers in the notion of proficiency levels and give them a starting point for organizing their teaching and interpreting learners' progress', and then to get the young learners 'to understand the goals of language learning in these action-oriented terms, and develop their capacity to reflect on their current level and to direct their efforts to move forward'. He echoed Dr Green in posing a question about what the purpose of the development of the CEFR-J was.

Figure 7 CEFR-J project: overview

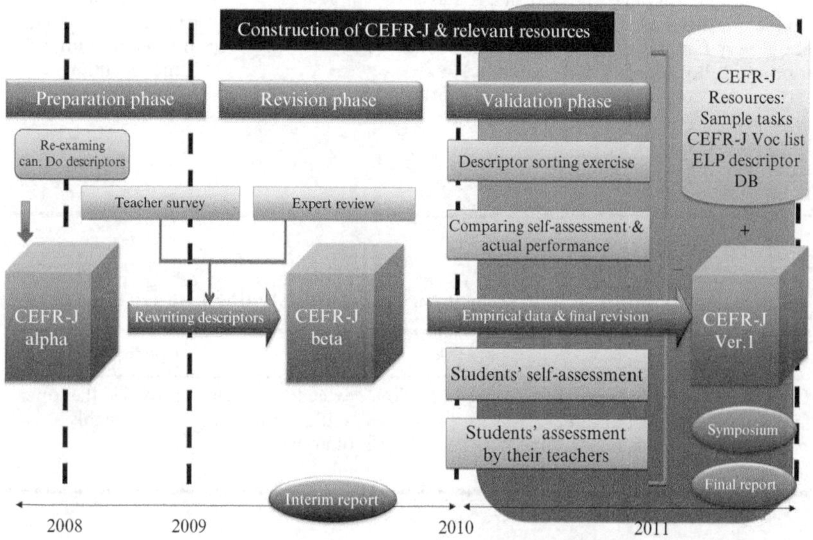

Figure 7 illustrates the overview of our CEFR-J project. As of February 2012, we are in the validation phase, working on a 'Descriptor Sorting Exercise', 'Comparing Self-assessment and Actual Performance', 'Students' Self-assessment', and 'Students' Assessment by their Teachers'. The validation started with the analysis of responses from Japanese teachers and learners. We asked Japanese teachers to put the Can Do descriptors in order of difficulty, and asked for their comments on the descriptors. As for learners, we are collecting their self-assessment data through online Can Do questionnaires, and also carrying out performance tests based on the descriptors for listening, reading, spoken interaction, spoken production, and writing in order to analyse the relationship between their self-assessment and their actual performance.

Some issues on the interpretations of CEFR-J descriptors

Pitfalls and benefits of using the CEFR-J

This section reports some problems that came up as we worked on one of the four validation studies: 'Comparing Self-assessment and Actual Performances'. This validation study required us to develop tasks that correspond to selective Can Do descriptors. We hoped that these tasks would serve a dual purpose: (a) test instruments for the validation study, and (b) benchmark performance or sample texts for CEFR-J descriptors. The focus in this paper is on (a). During the process of the development of tasks, some problems surfaced, which eventually turned out to be a beneficial use of the CEFR-J.

One major problem was that the interpretations of CEFR-J descriptors sometimes differed among us to the extent where the differences could not be ignored. In the case of developing reading tasks, for example, we sometimes did not agree on the text types and levels of the tasks that we created. We read our own assumptions of language teaching and learning into descriptors. Since variability exists among us, the CEFR-J authors, we can easily predict further variability among potential CEFR-J users. This is why we thought this problem was worth consideration.

Thus, one of the pitfalls of using the CEFR-J is that the framework can allow more leeway than we expect. At the same time, however, our efforts to adjust the differences in our interpretations yielded a desired by-product. As we discussed discrepancies, we thoroughly examined the meanings of descriptors, and critically reflected on our pedagogical practice that may have affected our interpretations of CEFR-J descriptors. It turned out that adjusting the differences stimulated discussion and helped us deepen our insight into language teaching. Thus, our struggle inadvertently revealed both pitfalls and benefits of the use of the CEFR-J, which led us to think that reporting the problems we faced and how we handled them would be of significance.

Development of tasks for CEFR-J reading descriptors

Our research group conducted the validation study by assigning each of the five skills, that is, listening, reading, spoken interaction, spoken production, and writing, to five subgroups. The present paper focuses on the reading skill, for which Tomoko Takada is responsible. The reading subgroup consisted of four members, each of whom wrote a few tasks for one of the four levels: A1.3, A2.1, A2.2, and B1.1. Next, we asked two CEFR specialists to review them, to predict the item difficulty of each item, and to provide any comments and suggestions. Both of the CEFR specialists were staff members of the Society for Testing English Proficiency (Eiken), which is a Tokyo-based testing body. One was a native speaker who has been engaged in the standard setting of Eiken test items on the CEFR. The other was a Japanese who was a project member of the Eiken Can Do list. Based on their feedback, we modified some tasks and replaced others with new ones.

Disagreement in our interpretations of some reading descriptors

We did not agree on the representativeness of three tasks for reading descriptors. Two of them had a problem with text types, while the other one raised a problem of appropriateness of adding footnotes to the text. Each task will be discussed below.

The first one was written for one of the A1.3 descriptors: *I can understand narratives written in simple words, supported by illustrations and pictures.* The 130-word passage, which was accompanied by an illustration, started with 'please look at the picture', and described what the people in it were doing. The passage was followed by seven true–false questions. One argument went that the text was a picture description instead of a narrative, enabling test takers to answer most of the true–false questions without reading the text. On the other hand, there was an argument that any type of combination of a narrative and illustrations applies to this descriptor. After some discussion, we eventually discarded this task on the grounds that the text was not representative of the concept stated in the descriptor.

The second task that posed a problem corresponded to one of the A2.1 descriptors: *I can understand the main points of texts dealing with everyday topics (e.g. life, hobbies, sports) and obtain the information I need.* The task consisted of a 210-word conversation script with five sentences deleted, and five options from which test takers were asked to choose an appropriate sentence for each blank. The conversation dealt with an everyday topic, in which a girl suggested that a boy should join a jazz band. The problem with this task was that the text was originally spoken language. It is true that we read written forms of spoken language such as captions on television screens and dialogues in novels, but they do not represent a reading text. For this reason, we discarded this task.

Of 10 reading tasks we wrote for the validation study, two were scripts of spoken language. The mismatch between the text type intended by the CEFR-J descriptor and the text type actually selected for the task may have been induced by the teaching and testing practice in Japan. The texts in junior high school textbooks authorized by the Ministry of Education are mostly dialogues instead of reading passages. Also, dialogue completion tasks in a written form are common in major English tests administered in Japan. One example is the University Testing Center Examination, a unified entrance examination for universities taken by approximately 550,000 applicants annually. Another example is the Eiken test, which is taken by 2.3 million people annually. We are accustomed to this test type to such a degree that completing a script of spoken language is perceived as a reading test.

The lesson we learned from these two examples is that the CEFR-J descriptors can be interpreted in various ways, depending on factors such as the users' teaching background. When the CEFR-J is completed and publicized in the near future, users may write language tasks which they claim to be based on its descriptors. However, there is a possibility that the tasks do not exactly reflect the constructs embedded in the descriptors. We are worried that this is very likely to happen in Japan, where the action-based approach is a relatively new idea on a practical level although it has become gradually known on a conceptual level. Unlike in Europe, where communicative language teaching (CLT) originated, the implementation of CLT in Japan is still in its infancy.

The third example is a text chosen for B1.1: *I can understand the main points of English newspaper and magazine articles adapted for educational purposes*. The text, which is cited in Figure 8, was a 300-word article excerpted from *The Student Times*, a newspaper published for learners of English in Japan. It comes with an introduction written in Japanese, and a number of words in it are listed with their Japanese equivalents in footnotes.

Figure 8 A text chosen for a B1.1 reading task

> John Lennon fans celebrate in Central Park
> Fans of the late John Lennon, the former member of the Beatles, commemorated the 30th anniversary of his death on December 8, in Central Park in New York. (This part was originally written in Japanese.)

1. John Lennon's fans celebrated his life Dec. 8 by visiting Strawberry Fields, the Central Park garden dedicated in his honor, while a newly released interview he gave shortly before his death showed he was optimistic about his future.
2. On the 30th anniversary of Lennon's murder outside his Manhattan apartment building, admirers played his music nearby at Strawberry Fields and placed flowers on a mosaic named for his song Imagine.
3. The steady stream of visitors represented the range of people who love Lennon, from those who watched his career unfold as it happened to those who know only his music.
4. Father-daughter pair Paul DeLuca, 50, and Marissa Deluca, 17, came from Boston to mark the day.
5. "I grew up with his voice," said Marissa Deluca. "The Beatles are the soundtrack to my childhood," she said. "His voice is just kind of like home."
6. Her father said, "Nothing is timeless like the stuff John and Paul (McCartney) wrote."
7. In Liverpool, where Lennon was from, hundreds gathered for a vigil Dec. 8 around the Peace and Harmony sculpture, recently unveiled by Lennon's first wife, Cynthia, and their son Julian in Chavasse Park.
8. In the newly released interview, conducted by Rolling Stone magazine just three days before he was gunned down, John Lennon complained about his critics – saying they were just interested in "dead heroes" and mused that he had "plenty of time" to accomplish his goals.
9. At 40, he was also reflective of what he had accomplished, and remained committed to his goal of peace and love on Earth.
10. "I'm not claiming divinity. I've never claimed purity of soul. I've never claimed to have the answers to life. I only put out songs and answer questions as honestly as I can. But I still believe in peace, love and understanding."

1. dedicated 〜にささげられている。　optimistic 楽観的な。
2. admirers ファン。　mosaic モザイク。
3. steady stream of 〜　絶え間なく続く〜。　unfold 開花する。
6. timeless 永遠の。
7. vigil 夜通しの祈り。
8. was gunned down 射殺された。　critics 批評家。　mused じっと考えた。
   accomplish 成し遂げる。
9. (was) reflective of 〜　〜について考えていた。　10. divinity 神の力。

Source: The Student Times, December 17 2010.

Literally speaking, this text is an English newspaper article 'adapted for educational purposes' as the descriptor states, but things were not that simple. We did not agree on how much L1 support was adequate on the B1 level. Fourteen footnotes were provided for this 300-word article, which means that 1 out of 21 words were footnoted. One argument went that we should keep everything intact including the 14 footnotes because the text is exactly an article 'adapted for educational purposes'. The other argument went that the text for a reading test should not provide more than sufficient footnotes and that we should eliminate some of them.

Since this problem was pointed out by the two CEFR specialists we consulted, we tried to understand what 'an English newspaper article adapted for educational purposes' entails. Therefore, we turned to other newspapers adapted for educational purposes to find their common textual features. We realised that they come in a variety of forms. An article adapted for educational purposes can be:

- an article that is linguistically controlled
- an article with reading tasks for learners
- an article with lesson plans for teachers
- an article with L1 support (footnotes, L1 introduction, etc.)
- a combination of any of the above.

The B1.1 descriptor in question is written in general terms as is the case with other CEFR-J descriptors, not specifying which type of text we should use. It is the users that select texts appropriate for this proficiency level.

For our validation study, we decided to use an article linguistically controlled with some L1 support but not as much as the original text provides. For this decision, we took two things into consideration. First, our CEFR-J assumes that learners are in the classroom situation, so L1 support reflects the local context. Second, providing more than enough footnotes, when the descriptor in question calls for the understanding of main points, may send readers a false message that they are expected to pay attention to every single word. For these reasons, we removed nine out of 14 footnotes, after confirming that the nine words were labelled as a high school level on a corpus-based vocabulary list published in Japan.

The lesson we learned from this process is that we need to thoroughly understand the constructs embedded in reading descriptors to select texts suitable for them. Also, we must look critically at the texts to examine if they really reflect the given constructs. As we have seen, all the 'newspaper articles adapted for educational purposes' do not necessarily fit in this descriptor, because there are newspapers that place emphasis on linguistic knowledge and sub-skills other than fluent reading. For instance, the one we cited emphasises vocabulary building with substantial L1 support.

It does not mean that articles with L1 support should be excluded from B1.1. In fact, learners should be exposed to authentic materials at B1, or the threshold level. The framework is not prescriptive, and framework users should be open to a range of newspaper articles. What is important, though, is that we must have valid reasons for the selection of texts.

Implications of the process of task design

As stated above, interpretations of CEFR-J descriptors can vary among individual users. Although this is a problematic area of the application of the CEFR-J that we must be prepared for, it may be possible to turn this negative outcome into a positive one. As we struggled to bridge the differences between our interpretations, we critically examined our views and practice of language teaching and testing. We had a much closer look at the descriptors from different perspectives, and we critically reviewed the relation between the descriptors and the tasks we designed based on them. Through this process, we reflected on our current pedagogical approaches and the needs of the learners we are responsible for. This was an unexpected positive spin-off of the validation study.

The CEFR is 'intended to overcome the barriers to communication among professionals working in the field of modern languages arising from the *different* educational systems in Europe' (Council of Europe 2001:1, emphasis added). Barriers do exist among EFL professionals in the *same* educational system in Japan. We believe that CEFR-J has the potential to help language-related professionals in Japan to overcome the barriers to communication.

Accompanying resources for implementing the CEFR-J

Support materials for using the CEFR-J

We developed the beta version of the CEFR-J, modelled on the self-assessment grid in the original CEFR, and based on the empirical data we have collected, we are now in the process of revising and finalising Version 1 of the CEFR-J (see the Appendix), which was released in March 2012. In addition, we are also developing a Japanese version of the English Language Portfolio, based on the CEFR-J descriptors, teaching materials, assessment tools, etc. At the same time, we plan to prepare an inventory of language-specific linguistic features related to the CEFR levels, since we use this non-language specific framework for English.

It is especially important for a framework to be presented with concrete materials, when it is disseminated in countries like Japan. As for the use of the CEFR for English language teaching, there are two intriguing developments in Europe. One is the publication of *A Core Inventory for General English* (North et al 2010), and the other is the English Profile Programme (see Green 2012, Hawkins and Filipović 2012). Both have presented us with very interesting insights into English language teaching and learning, and we have decided to follow some of their approaches for developing accompanying materials for CEFR-J.

In order to implement the CEFR-J in school settings in Japan, we are preparing accompanying materials to promote easy access to the CEFR-J and its use. Three major projects are now underway: (1) a CEFR-J wordlist, (2) a database of Can Do descriptors, and (3) a database of grammar and phrases for each CEFR level. This is closely related to the 'Reference Level Descriptions' (Alderson 2007). We will elaborate on the first two below.

The CEFR-J wordlist

The CEFR-J wordlist is based on the analysis of major English textbooks used in China, Korea and Taiwan. These regions/countries are similar to Japan in the sense that they are all in EFL contexts, but they are different from Japan because English has been introduced from primary school for some time already. We examined the English textbooks used in those regions/ countries in order to examine what was taught at primary school level and how the progression of the course contents was achieved across different grades. We divided the textbooks into the following five sub-categories based on the levels of the CEFR and an additional Pre-A1 level for our purpose, roughly assigned on the basis of the evaluation of textbook contents and their courses of study:

Pre-A1 corpus:	Primary school	Grade 3–6
A1 corpus:	Lower secondary school	Grade 1
A2 corpus:	Lower secondary school	Grade 2–3
B1 corpus:	Upper secondary school	Grade 1–2
B2 corpus:	Upper secondary school	Grade 3

We then processed the vocabulary lists of subcorpora classified into those five levels, in order to decide the CEFR level of vocabulary. For example, by extracting words that commonly appear at Pre-A1 level onwards, i.e. Pre-A1 through B2, across all three regions, we can safely say that those words are basic enough to be classified into the Pre-A1 level vocabulary. By limiting the vocabulary to only those which appeared at a given CEFR level and across all the subsequent, higher levels at the same time, we avoided including words which might have appeared in textbooks incidentally. It also helped to prevent us from expanding the wordlist too much and to make our wordlist within a reasonably adequate size. Table 4 shows the number of words that actually occurred in each sub-corpus. Altogether, there were 5,639 words covering Pre-A1 to B2 levels. Now we are preparing the wordlist in such a way that we present each unit of the wordlist by 1,000-word range for the sake of convenience, and present 1,000 words for the first three levels (Pre-A1, A1 and A2) and additional sets of 2,000 words for B1 and B2 respectively, totalling 6,000 words.

These numbers are a realistic goal for average learners of English at each level as we mentioned earlier. The reality is, however, that teaching 1,000 words by the end of the first year of lower secondary school would be very difficult unless we seriously think about introducing English as one of the core subjects at primary school level. It should be noted that all three countries/regions – China, Korea, and Taiwan – have started English instructions at Grade 3 or 4 in primary school, 2 to 3 hours a week. This wordlist actually implies that in the current situation in Japan, learners are supposed to attain A1 level by the end of lower secondary school. We also recommend that the first 2,000 words, covered by Pre-A1 through A2 levels, should be used primarily as productive vocabulary, while the other 4,000 could be first learned as receptive vocabulary and gradually shifted toward productive knowledge.

The CEFR-J wordlist has additional features, such as the information of general vs. specific notions to each word. This information is originally developed in van Ek and Trim (1991) and in the subsequent T-series. Words and phrases were selected to represent certain functions and notions, then sub-classified into 'general' vs. 'specific' notions. In our CEFR-J wordlist, most of the nouns are labelled and tagged in the database, with these general/specific notions, based on the *Core Inventory* developed by the British Council (North et al 2010) and the T-series. Table 5 illustrates the search results of the Pre-A1 level vocabulary with part-of-speech (POS) information and notion tags.

The Can Do descriptor database

The Can Do descriptor database is based on analysis of Can Do descriptors collected from various versions of the European Language Portfolio. Altogether, more than 2,800 Can Do descriptors were examined. Duplications were removed and very similar descriptors were merged into one. Finally, we had a list of 647 descriptors which were then translated into Japanese. This list will help curriculum or syllabus designers to have more

Table 4 The breakdown of the CEFR-J wordlist

CEFR level	Pre-A1/A1	A2	B1	B2	Total
Textbook analysis	976	1,057	1,884	1,722	5,639
Our target vocabulary size	1,000	1,000	2,000	2,000	6,000

Table 5 Examples of the CEFR-J wordlist (Pre-A1 level vocabulary with POS and notion tags)

Lemma	CEFR	POS	Specific Notion Category 1	Specific Notion Category 2
activity	Pre-A1	n	Leisure activities	
actor	Pre-A1	n	Work and jobs	Film
afternoon	Pre-A1	n		
age	Pre-A1	n	Personal information	
airplane	Pre-A1	n	Ways of travelling	
airport	Pre-A1	n	Travel and services vocab	Things in the town, shops and shopping
animal	Pre-A1	n		
answer	Pre-A1	n		
apple	Pre-A1	n	Food and drink	
apron	Pre-A1	n	Objects and rooms	
arm	Pre-A1	n	Personal information	
art	Pre-A1	n	Hobbies and pastimes	Education
aunt	Pre-A1	n	Family life	
baby	Pre-A1	n	Family life	
back	Pre-A1	n		
bag	Pre-A1	n	Shopping	Clothes
ball	Pre-A1	n	Hobbies and pastimes	
banana	Pre-A1	n	Food and drink	
bank	Pre-A1	n	Things in the town, shops and shopping	

specific images about what learners at each CEFR level Can Do. There is no such list available so far in Japan, and this would be a very useful resource for the smooth implementation of our framework into our educational system.

Table 6 shows a snapshot of the database. We can extract Can Do statements with Japanese translations in a very flexible manner, limiting the search to either CEFR levels or skill categories or both. For A1 and A2 level descriptors, two versions of translations are provided: one for general users and the other for younger learners. This aims to support teachers and syllabus/materials developers who intend to apply our framework to primary education and teaching English to kids.

General conclusion

As shown in one of our surveys, EFL learners may need examples for unfamiliar Can Do descriptors. Language teaching researchers came up with different ideas for Can Do descriptors, probably because they have their own learning and teaching experiences, and we can assume the discrepancies in ideas for the Can Do descriptors will be even greater among teaching practitioners throughout Japan. Therefore, we need to provide concrete tasks and texts in order to disseminate the CEFR-J in Japan. In this respect, the resources we are now preparing for the CEFR-J are absolutely essential.

Table 6 Extracted descriptors with Japanese translations from the Can Do descriptor database

Level	Category/ Code	ELP descriptors	Translations in Japanese	Translations for younger learners
A1	IS1-A1	I can say who I am, ask someone's name and introduce someone.	自分が誰であるか言うことができ、相手の名前を尋ねたり、相手のことを紹介することができる	自分の名前を言ったり、相手の名前を聞いたり、相手の紹介ができる
A1	IS1-A1-1	I can ask and answer simple questions, initiate and respond to simple statements in areas of immediate need or on very familiar topics.	簡単な質問をしたり、簡単な質問に答えることができる。また必要性の高いことや身近な話題について発言したり、反応することができる	簡単な質問をしたり、簡単な質問に答えることができる。また身近なことについて話したり、質問に答えることができる
A1	IS1-A1-1	I can make myself understood in a simple way but I am dependent on my partner being prepared to repeat more slowly and rephrase what I say and to help me to say what I want.	簡易な方法であれば通じるが、ゆっくり繰り返してくれたり、自分が言った事を言い直してくれたり、自分が言いたいことが言えるよう助けてくれるような相手に依存している	相手がゆっくり話したり、自分が言ったことを確認してくれるなど、やさしい人だったら自分の簡単な英語は通じる
A1	IS2-A1	I can understand simple questions about myself and my family when people speak slowly and clearly (e.g. 'What's your name?' 'How old are you?' 'How are you?' etc.).	相手がゆっくりはっきり話してくれれば、「名前は？」「歳は？」「調子はどう？」などの自分や家族についての簡単な質問を理解することができる	相手がゆっくりはっきり話してくれれば、自分や家族についての簡単な質問が分かる
A1	IS2-A1	I can understand simple words and phrases, like 'excuse me', 'sorry', 'thank you', etc.	「すみません」「ごめんなさい」「ありがとう」といった簡単な語句を理解することができる	「すみません」「ごめんなさい」「ありがとう」といった簡単な語句が分かる
A1	IS2-A1	I can understand simple greetings, like 'hello', 'good bye', 'good morning', etc.	「やあ」「さようなら」「おはよう」といった簡単な挨拶を理解することができる	「やあ」「さようなら」「おはよう」といった簡単な挨拶が分かる

The impact of the CEFR-J is yet to be seen, because we have not completed the project yet. However, the Japanese Ministry of Education Committee has just announced proposals for improving Japanese people's foreign language ability. These proposals include the development of Can Do descriptors at national and local level, and a drastic reform of university entrance examinations in English. When we complete this project, we will be able to provide policy makers, researchers, and practitioners in Japan with a shared, comprehensive, and coherent picture of English language teaching and learning. We hope our experience of the development of the CEFR-J will give you some practical assistance about what to do when you try to adapt the CEFR to your local context.

Acknowledgments

The authors would like to acknowledge the contribution of Anthony Green, Neil Jones, Cyril Weir, Nick Saville and Szilvia Papp for the development of the CEFR-J.

References

Alderson, C (2007) The CEFR and the need for more research, *Modern Language Journal* 91 (4), 659–663.

Council of Europe (2001) *Common European Framework of Reference for Languages: Learning, Teaching, Assessment*. Cambridge: Cambridge University Press.

Green, A (2012) *Language Functions Revisited: Theoretical and Empirical Bases for Language Construct Definition Across the Ability Range*, English Profile Studies volume 2, Cambridge: UCLES/Cambridge University Press.

Green, T (2011) Conflicting purposes in the use of can-do statements in language education, in Schmidt, M G, Naganuma, N, O'Dwyer, F, Imig, A and Sakai, K (Eds), *Can-do Statements in Language Education in Japan and Beyond*, Tokyo: Asahi Press, 35–48.

Hawkins, J A and Buttery, P (2010) Criterial features in learner corpora: theory and illustrations, *English Profile Journal* 1, 1–23.

Hawkins, J A and Filipović, L (2012) *Criterial Features in L2 English: Specifying the Reference Levels of the Common European Framework*, English Profile Studies volume 1, Cambridge: UCLES/Cambridge University Press.

Linacre, J M (1989) *Multi-faceted Measurement*, Chicago: MESA Press.

Nakajima, M and Nagata, M (2006) CEFR no nihonjin gaikokugo gakusyusya heno tekioukanousei [The applicability of the CEFR to Japanese learners of foreign languages], *JAFLE Bulletin* 9, 5–24.

Negishi, M (2006) CEFR no nihonjin gaikokugo gakushusha heno tekiyoukanousei no koujouni mukete [Towards the improvement of the applicability of the CEFR to Japanese learners of foreign languages], in Negishi, M, Umino, T and Yoshitomi, A (Eds) *Gengo Johogaku Kenkyu Houkoku 14: Dainigengo Syutokuriron ni Motoduku Gengokyoiku to Hyoka Moderu [The Report on Linguistic Informatics Reseach 14: Language Pedagogy and Assessment Model Based on Second Language Acquisition Theory]*, 79–101.

North, B, Ortega Calvo, Á and Sheehan, S (2010) *British Council–EAQUALS Core Inventory for General English*, London: British Council/EAQUALS.

Otani, Y (2007) *Nihonjin nitotte eigotoha nanika (What is English for Japanese People?)*, Tokyo: Taishukanshoten.

Van Ek, J A and Trim, J L M (1991) *Threshold Level 1990*, Strasbourg: Council of Europe.

Appendix

CEFR-J (English)

Skills		Pre-A1	A1.1	A1.2	A1.3	A2.1	A2.2
U N D E R S T A N D I N G	Listening	I can catch everyday, familiar words, provided they are delivered clearly and slowly.	I can understand short, simple instructions such as "Stand up." "Sit down." "Stop." etc., provided they are delivered face-to-face, slowly and clearly.	I can understand short conversations about familiar topics (e.g. hobbies, sports, club activities), provided they are delivered in slow and clear speech.	I can understand phrases and expressions related to matters of immediate relevance to me or my family, school, neighborhood etc, provided they are delivered slowly and clearly.	I can understand short, simple announcements e.g. on public transport or in stations or airports, provided they are delivered slowly and clearly.	I can understand and follow a series of instructions for sports, cooking, etc. provided they are delivered slowly and clearly.
		I can recognise the letters of the English alphabet, when they are pronounced.	I can catch key information necessary for everyday life such as numbers, prices, dates, days of the week, provided they are delivered slowly and clearly.	I can catch concrete information (e.g. places and times) on familiar topics encountered in everyday life, provided it is delivered in slow and clear speech.	I can understand instructions and explanations necessary for simple transactions (e.g. shopping and eating out), provided they are delivered slowly and clearly.	I can understand the main points of straightforward factual messages (e.g. a school assignment, a travel itinerary), provided speech is clearly articulated in a familiar accent.	I can understand instructions about procedures (e.g. cooking, handicrafts), with visual aids, provided they are delivered in slow and clear speech involving rephrasing and repetition.
	Reading	I can recognise words in a picture book that are already familiar through oral activities.	I can read and understand very short, simple, directions used in everyday life such as "No parking", "No food or drink" etc.	I can understand very short, simple, everyday texts, such as simple posters and invitation cards.	I can understand texts of personal interest (e.g. articles about sports, music, travel, etc.) written with simple words supported by illustrations and pictures.	I can understand explanatory texts describing people, places, everyday life, and culture, etc., written in simple words.	I can find the information I need, from practical, concrete, predictable texts (e.g. travel guidebooks, recipes), provided they are written in simple English.

CEFR-J (English)

B1.1	B1.2	B2.1	B2.2	C1	C2
I can understand the gist of explanations of cultural practices and customs that are unfamiliar to me, provided they are delivered in slow and clear speech involving rephrasing and repetition.	I can understand the majority of the concrete information content of recorded or broadcast audio material on topics of personal interest spoken at normal speed.	I can understand the main points of a conversation between native speakers in television programmes and in films, provided they are delivered at normal speed and in standard English.	I can follow a variety of conver-sations between native speakers, in television programmes and in films, which make no linguistic adjustments for non-native speakers.	I can under-stand extended speech even when it is not clearly structured and when relation-ships are only implied and not signalled explicitly. I can understand television prog-rammes and films without too much effort.	I have no difficulty in understanding any kind of spoken language, whether live or broadcast, even when delivered at fast native speed, provided I have some time to get familiar with the accent.
I can understand the main points of extended discussions around me, provided speech is clearly articulated and in a familiar accent.	I can understand the main points of short radio news items about familiar topics if they are delivered in a clear, familiar accent.	I can follow extended speech and complex lines of argument provided the topic is reasonably familiar.	I can understand the speaker's point of view about topics of current common interest and in specialised fields, provided it is delivered at a natural speed and articulated in standard English.		
I can understand the main points of English newspaper and magazine articles adapted for educational purposes.	I can search the internet or reference books, and obtain school- or work-related information, paying attention to its structure. Given the occasional use of a dictionary, I can under-stand it, relating it to any accom-panying figures or tables.	I can read texts dealing with topics of general interest, such as current affairs, without consulting a dictionary, and can compare differences and similarities between multiple points of view.	I can scan through rather complex texts e.g. articles and reports, and can identify key passages. I can adapt my reading speed and style, and read accurately, when I decide closer study is worthwhile.	I can under-stand long and complex factual and literary texts, appreciating distinctions of style. I can understand specialised articles and longer technical instructions, even when they do not relate to my field.	I can read with ease virtually all forms of the written lang-uage, including abstract, structurally or linguis-tically complex texts such as manuals, specialised articles and literary works.

157

Skills		Pre-A1	A1.1	A1.2	A1.3	A2.1	A2.2
U N D E R S T A N D I N G	Reading	I can recognise upper- and lower-case letters printed in block type.	I can understand a fast-food restaurant menu that has pictures or photos, and choose the food and drink in the menu.	I can understand very short reports of recent events such as text messages from friends or relatives, describing travel memories, etc.	I can understand short narratives with illustrations and pictures written in simple words.	I can understand short narratives and biographies written in simple words.	I can understand the main points of texts dealing with everyday topics (e.g. life, hobbies, sports) and obtain the information I need.
S P E A K I N G	Spoken inter-action	I can express my wishes and make requests in areas of immediate need such as "*Help!*" and "*I want ~*", using basic phrases. I can express what I want by pointing at it, if necessary.	I can ask and answer questions about times, dates, and places, using familiar, formulaic expressions.	I can respond simply in basic, everyday interactions such as talking about what I can/cannot do or describing colour, using a limited repertoire of expressions.	I can ask and answer simple questions about familiar topics such as hobbies, club activities, provided people speak clearly.	I can give simple directions from place to place, using basic expressions such as "turn right" and "go straight" along with sequencers such as first, then, and next.	I can exchange opinions and feelings, express agreement and disagreement, and compare things and people using simple English.
		I can use common, formulaic, daily and seasonal greetings, and respond to those greetings.	I can ask and answer about personal topics (e.g. family, daily routines, hobby), using mostly familiar expressions and some basic sentences (although these are not necessarily accurate).	I can exchange simple opinions about very familiar topics such as likes and dislikes for sports, foods, etc., using a limited repertoire of expressions, provided that people speak clearly.	I can make, accept and decline offers, using simple words and a limited range of expressions.	I can get across basic information and exchange simple opinions, using pictures or objects to help me.	I can interact in predictable everyday situations (e.g., a post office, a station, a shop), using a wide range of words and expressions.

B1.1	B1.2	B2.1	B2.2	C1	C2
I can understand clearly written instructions (e.g. for playing games, for filling in a form, for assembling things).	I can understand the plot of longer narratives written in plain English.	I can understand in detail specifications, instruction manuals, or reports written for my own field of work, provided I can reread difficult sections.	I can extract necessary information and the points of the argument from articles and reference materials in my specialised field without consulting a dictionary.		
I can express opinions and exchange information about familiar topics (e.g. school, hobbies, hopes for the future), using a wide range of simple English.	I can explain in detail and with confidence a problem which has arisen in places such as hospitals or city halls. I can get the right treatment by providing relevant, detailed information.	I can discuss the main points of news stories I have read about in the newspapers/ on the internet or watched on TV, provided the topic is reasonably familiar to me.	I can actively engage in conversations on a wide range of topics from the general to more specialised cultural and academic fields and express my ideas accurately and fluently.	I can express myself fluently and sponta-neously without much obvious searching for expressions. I can use language flexibly and effectively for social and professional purposes. I can formulate ideas and opinions with precision and relate my contribution skilfully to those of other speakers.	I can take part effortlessly in any conver-sation or discussion and have a good familiarity with idiomatic expressions and colloquialisms. I can express myself fluently and convey finer shades of meaning precisely. If I do have a problem I can backtrack and restructure around the difficulty so smoothly that other people are hardly aware of it.
I can maintain a social conversation about concrete topics of personal interest, using a wide range of simple English.	I can explain with confidence a problem which has arisen in fami-liar places such as a station or a shop (e.g. purchasing the wrong ticket) and obtain the right product or service by requesting politely and expressing gratitude (assuming that the provider of the service is cooperative).	I can discuss abstract topics, provided they are within my terms of knowledge, my interests, and my experience, although I sometimes cannot contribute to discussions between native speakers.	I can exchange opinions about magazine articles using a wide range of colloquial expressions.		

Exploring Language Frameworks

Skills		Pre-A1	A1.1	A1.2	A1.3	A2.1	A2.2
S P E A K I N G	Spoken production	I can convey very limited information about myself (e.g. name and age), using simple words and basic phrases.	I can convey personal information (e.g. about my family and hobbies), using basic phrases and formulaic expressions.	I can express simple opinions related to limited, familiar topics, using simple words and basic phrases in a restricted range of sentence structures, provided I can prepare my speech in advance.	I can express simple opinions about a limited range of familiar topics in a series of sentences, using simple words and basic phrases in a restricted range of sentence structures, provided I can prepare my speech in advance.	I can introduce myself including my hobbies and abilities, using a series of simple phrases and sentences.	I can make a short speech on topics directly related to my everyday life (e.g. myself, my school, my neighbor-hood) with the use of visual aids such as photos, pictures, and maps, using a series of simple words and phrases and sentences.
		I can give a simple explanation about an object while showing it to others using basic words, phrases and formulaic expressions, provided I can prepare my speech in advance.	I can convey simple information (e.g. times, dates, places), using basic phrases and formulaic expressions.	I can give simple descriptions e.g. of everyday objects, using simple words and basic phrases in a restricted range of sentence structures, provided I can prepare my speech in advance.	I can describe simple facts related to everyday life with a series of sentences, using simple words and basic phrases in a restricted range of sentence structures, provided I can prepare my speech in advance.	I can give a brief talk about familiar topics (e.g. my school and my neighbor-hood) supported by visual aids such as photos, pictures, and maps, using a series of simple phrases and sentences.	I can give an opinion, or explain a plan of action concisely giving some reasons, using a series of simple words and phrases and sentences.
W R I T I N G	Writing	I can write upper- and lower-case letters and words in block letters.	I can fill in forms with such items as name, address, and occupation.	I can write short texts about matters of personal relevance (e.g. likes and dislikes, family, and school life), using simple words and basic expressions.	I can write short texts about my experiences with the use of a dictionary.	I can write invitations, personal letters, memos, and messages, in simple English, provided they are about routine, personal matters.	I can write a simple description about events of my immediate environment, hobby, places, and work, provided they are in the field of my personal experience and of my immediate need.

160

B1.1	B1.2	B2.1	B2.2	C1	C2
I can talk in some detail about my experiences, hopes and dreams, expanding on what I say by joining together words, phrases and expressions I can readily use to make longer contributions.	I can give an outline or list the main points of a short story or a short newspaper article with some fluency, adding my own feelings and ideas.	I can give a prepared presentation with reasonable fluency, stating reasons for agreement or disagreement or alternative proposals, and can answer a series of questions.	I can give a fluent presentation, focusing on both the main points and related details. I can depart spontaneously from a prepared text and follow up interesting points raised by members of the audience, often showing remarkable fluency and ease of expression.	I can present clear, detailed descriptions of complex subjects integrating sub-themes, developing particular points and rounding off with an appropriate conclusion.	I can present a clear, smoothly flowing description or argument in a style appropriate to the context and with an effective logical structure which helps the recipient to notice and remember significant points.
I can talk about familiar topics and other topics of personal interest, without causing confusion to the listeners, provided I can prepare my ideas in advance and use brief notes to help me.	I can give a reasonably smooth presentation about social situations of personal interest, adding my own opinions, and I can take a series of follow up questions from the audience, responding in a way that they can understand.	I can develop an argument clearly in a debate by providing evidence, provided the topic is of personal interest.	I can clarify my viewpoints, and maintain conversation in debates on social issues and current affairs, integrating sub-themes or related cases.	I can express myself in clear, well-structured text, expressing points of view at some length.	I can write clear, smoothly flowing text in an appropriate style.
I can write a description of substantial length about events taking place in my immediate environment (e.g. school, workplace, local area), using familiar vocabulary and grammar.	I can report the outline or basic content of newspaper articles and movies, expressing my own opinions, using non-technical vocabulary and less complicated sentence structures.	I can write business documents (e.g. e-mail, fax, business letters), conveying degrees of emotion, in a style appropriate to the purpose, provided they are in my professional field.	I can write clear, detailed reports and articles which contain complicated contents, considering cause/effect and hypothetical situations, provided they are in my specialised field and of personal concern.	I can write about complex subjects in a letter, an essay or a report, underlining what I consider to be the salient issues. I can select style appropriate to the reader in mind.	I can write complex letters, reports or articles which present a case with an effective logical structure which helps the recipient to notice and remember significant points.

Exploring Language Frameworks

Skills		Pre-A1	A1.1	A1.2	A1.3	A2.1	A2.2
W R I T I N G	Writing	I can write down words provided they are pronounced letter by letter. I can copy what is written.	I can write short phrases and sentences giving basic information about myself (e.g. name, address, family) with the use of a dictionary.	I can write message cards (e.g. birthday cards) and short memos about events of personal relevance, using simple words and basic expressions.	I can write a series of sentences about my hobbies and likes and dislikes, using simple words and basic expressions.	I can write texts of some length (e.g. diary entries, explanations of photos and events) in simple English, using basic, concrete vocabulary and simple phrases and sentences, linking sentences with simple connectives like *and*, *but*, and *because*.	I can write my impressions and opinions briefly about what I have listened to and read (e.g. explanations about lifestyles and culture, stories), using basic everyday vocabulary and expressions.

B1.1	B1.2	B2.1	B2.2	C1	C2
I can write coherent instructions telling people how to do things, with vocabulary and grammar of immediate relevance.	I can write narratives (e.g. travel diaries, personal histories, personal anecdotes) in several paragraphs, following the order of events. I can write personal letters which report recent events in some detail.	I can write reasonably coherent essays and reports using a wide range of vocabulary and complex sentence structures, synthesising information and arguments from a number of sources, provided I know something about the topics.	I can write clear, coherent essays and reports with a wide repertoire of vocabulary and complex sentence structures, emphasizing important points, integrating sub-themes, and constructing a chain of argument, as long as I do not need to express subtle nuances of feelings and experience.		I can write summaries and reviews of professional or literary works.

9 The impact of the Common European Framework of Reference for languages on teaching and assessment at the language centres of the universities of Bonn and Göttingen

Ursula Hehl
Cologne University of Applied Sciences, Germany
Nicole Kruczek
University of Göttingen, Germany

Abstract

This paper presents an analysis of the impact of the Common European Framework of Reference for languages (CEFR) on university language teaching practice, based on a comparison of two German university language centres (Bonn and Göttingen), which focuses on the application of the framework in course organization, teaching and assessment.

As regards course organization, we shall briefly outline the general principles underlying the respective course programmes and curricula. Policies concerning placement and admittance to courses and the problems they pose, the question how much course time students should be granted to take learners from one level to the next, and aspects of learner autonomy are addressed in this section of the paper.

As far as teaching is concerned, our discussion revolves around teachers' knowledge about and implementation of the CEFR into their course practice, specifically as regards the action-oriented approach promoted by university language centres. We will argue that much remains to be done in terms of teacher training in order to ensure a more consistent application of the CEFR.

Our paper will further expound on how language centres refer to the CEFR in order to enhance the validity and reliability of their exams. In Göttingen, interactive and task-based formats are already used for testing purposes, while in Bonn a stronger integration of the action-oriented approach into assessment practices is still being worked on. The area of assessment reveals the most fundamental differences between the two language centres.

On the basis of this comparison and the conclusions we have drawn from it, we discuss constraints language institutions at universities are faced with and suggest ways of moving forward in order to render the CEFR more applicable to the specific purposes of university language centres.

Setting the scene

Since the joint declaration of the European Ministers of Education (Bologna Declaration of 19 June 1999) Germany's universities have committed themselves to restructuring their systems of academic tuition for both undergraduate and graduate students. In this process, new significance is being assigned to the acquisition of cross-disciplinary qualifications and the promotion of lifelong learning. Key competencies form the cornerstone of a goal-oriented curriculum and lay the foundation for sustainable success in a professional career, as the University of Göttingen proclaims on its website (http://www.uni-goettingen.de/en/192579.html). At the universities presented in our paper, every student enrolled in a Bachelor's or Master's degree programme must attend a certain number of courses as an integral and compulsory part of the professionalization syllabi, which is also the case with many doctoral degree programmes. Both universities therefore offer a broad range of key competency modules that enable students to individually shape their ability to perform in their chosen professions. Language competence provides a substratum for the development of such key competences, and language courses are often the most popular ones among students in the optional–compulsory range of modules. This attests to the enormous importance of the universities' language centres, which provide courses in a wide range of European and non-European languages. Self-directed language learning is an integral part of each course, as well as hybrid learning elements using a learning management system.

The University of Bonn Language Centre (SLZ) was founded in 1977 and has undergone a series of important developments since then. It is a subdivision of the department of Linguistics, Media Science and Musicology at the University of Bonn and to that extent is involved in research, primarily in the areas of language acquisition and teaching. Its main focus is the development and realization of language courses which are generally accepted as optional modules for Bachelor degree programmes at the university. At the time referred to in our analysis, regular course lessons were complemented by mandatory fortnightly meetings with a tutor, which were mainly intended to provide support in terms of self-directed learning. (N.B: Meanwhile, the tutorial system was abandoned. The information used in our paper dates from the summer semester 2011, when the system was still in use at the SLZ in Bonn.)

As a central institution, directly linked to the Vice-President for study and teaching, the purpose of the Centre for Languages and Transferable Skills (ZESS) is to provide all students of the university with a cross-disciplinary and academically relevant training in languages and key competencies such as linguistic and factual knowledge, methodological, personal and social competences.

For both centres, the publication the *Common European Framework of Reference for Languages: learning, teaching, assessment* (Council of Europe 2001) was a major source of inspiration when concepts had to be devised for the accreditation procedure of language modules. It was used to describe the courses in terms of objectives, the acquisition of key competencies and content.

In accordance with the Common European Framework of Reference (CEFR), the courses were given respective denominations to indicate the levels of language competence learners can achieve. Thus, General English courses ranged from CEFR Levels A2 to C1. At the ZESS, courses of English for Academic or Specific Purposes are offered from B1 to C1, teaching the pertinent subject-specific vocabulary, structures and text types. At the SLZ, courses of English for Academic or Specific Purposes are offered on so-called 'plus'-levels (B1+/B2+), which cover the upper ranges of the respective level and focus on transfer of the skills acquired in General English courses. This use of the term 'plus level' thus goes beyond North's definition of plus levels as 'characterized by a stronger performance in relation to the same features found at the criterion level, plus hints of features that became salient at the next level' (North 2007:657).

Students have to do a placement test before being assigned a place in one of the language modules. They are not allowed to register for courses other than those of the level indicated by their placement test result. Placement tests vary from language to language and are under constant revision.

Multilingualism and communication across the different languages taught are considered key features which ensure the high quality of language courses at both universities. Other aspects of quality control practised at the centres are in-house training for teaching staff, classroom observations and the establishment and constant adaptation of general guidelines. The language centres moreover participate in the UNIcert system. UNIcert is a language teaching and testing system for Higher Education. It certifies academic language competence in a non-standardized way and offers complementary university qualification (for further information see www.unicert-online. org).

Assessment is generally influenced by the learning situation and group dynamics, which in the cases presented here means that it is largely determined by the academic learning context and the aim to enable students to function as professionals internationally.

At the ZESS more refined assessment procedures have been established, which are characterized by university language testing conventions with a strong focus on task-based testing as defined by the GULT team (Chouissa, Dugovicova, Fischer and Virkkunen-Fullenwider 2011:15–24). These entail taking an integrative and holistic approach to the assessment of students' individual language competences. Exams consist of a series of micro-tasks which integrate as many skills and language aspects (grammar, vocabulary, style, register etc.) as possible. The basic structure of the exams is determined by a macro-context, a problem, project activity or at the very least related to a specific situation relevant to the students. On beginner levels, this basic idea is realized by integrating skills and embedding micro-tasks into an explicitly given situation. On advanced levels students are assessed both during the course on the basis of portfolios and at the end of semester by means of case studies, project work or global simulations.

Raising the issue

Course structures and curricula at university language centres refer more or less directly to the levels of competence set up in the CEFR, and, more specifically, learning objectives, key competencies to be acquired and course content are defined by the Common Reference Levels. Teachers are consequently expected to have some basic knowledge of the CEFR, its main ideas and the global scales. However, it appears that most practitioners seem to be using the CEFR intuitively in their everyday work. This raises the question of what this means in terms of the impact the framework has on language courses with respect to learning, teaching and assessment. A second important question in this respect is whether the CEFR is sufficiently known in countries of the EU and the rest of the world to use it for communication with external contacts.

In order to address these questions, we devized a questionnaire (see the Appendix) and conducted a survey on the use and impact of the CEFR in the two institutions. We distributed the questionnaire among teachers and coordinators, and, in the case of Bonn, the language course management. In Göttingen, the questionnaire was supplemented by personal interviews, as this seemed the more practical approach to collecting data there.

In designing the questionnaire, we wanted to focus on teachers' knowledge and implementation of the CEFR into their course practice and on further questions that arise in our own everyday practice: How reliable is a placement that does not take into account all the skills? How can we transfer the scales and competence levels in the CEFR to non-Indo-European languages?

How do we tackle the problem that learners have objectives which may contradict those formulated by us (e.g. getting credit points without having to put too much effort into the undertaking or pursuing the idea that progress has to be made by expanding one's knowledge of grammar)? How confident are teachers in applying the CEFR? In which ways can we develop a framework related to the CEFR to reflect the specific elements and requirements of language courses in an academic learning context?

We should add that the survey was not expected to yield statistically relevant data. Instead, we used it as a means of collecting comments and remarks from our colleagues which provide a more sustained picture of the present applications of the CEFR at language centres as well as some insight into its impact, its perceived and actual limitations and the potential and the demands for further development.

The CEFR in everyday practice

General remarks

As in all language centres known to us, the CEFR informs the definition of course levels, placement, the principles of teaching and learning, the choice of course materials and the final exams at both the ZESS and the SLZ, thus being instrumental in shaping the overall course programmes as well as individual course designs. It frames and permeates most activities in one way or another – sometimes directly, often in an indirect manner. The survey we conducted revealed that the members of the language course management, as well as the teachers working there on a freelance basis, recognize the enormous significance the CEFR has attained as the framework within which much of our work takes place. Tutors have been less unanimous in their acceptance of the CEFR, which may be due to the fact that they are neither teachers by training nor, more importantly, did they have much experience in teaching when they started working at the SLZ. They received a brief, general introduction to the CEFR when being initially trained for their job at the SLZ, while teachers and language course managers are expected to either possess detailed knowledge of the framework when they are accepted for a position at one of the centres or familiarize themselves with it on their own initiative. Still, they are supported in this by the quality management and frequently offered in-house training.

The level of significance coordinators at the ZESS ascribe to the CEFR seems to depend on their respective individual responsibilities; on the part of the questionnaire focusing on this issue, responses ranged from 3 to 6 (out of 6, where 6 is the highest level of significance). On average the coordinators feel that the CEFR is of considerable importance for their work. In both institutions, the CEFR is generally accepted as an instrument of communication between different languages, even as regards the non-European languages included in their range of courses. But its significance reaches far beyond this. It has shaped procedures and beliefs of how languages should be learned and taught. Even though this can safely be claimed for both language centres, there are differences in the individual interpretation of the global scales and the approach adopted from the CEFR. The interpretation varies between the institutions but also among the teachers practising and representing the institutions' interpretations. Teachers of different ages and from different cultural backgrounds may have been raised in quite diverse teaching traditions which can in turn account for noticeable divergences in their approaches to teaching. Another obvious reason for possible variations in the way the CEFR is applied is that freelance teachers often have little or no professional teacher training and have therefore not necessarily been introduced to the framework in a systematic way. This was corroborated by the results of our survey. However, it should be added that teachers at university language centres are generally required to have a university degree, preferably in a field related to language and teaching. In answer to our initial question how they were introduced to the CEFR, most of our colleagues explained that they had to familiarize themselves with the CEFR on their own through self study and practical experience. It is noteworthy that if they had discussed the CEFR during teacher training, it was mostly in courses of study for other languages than those they teach in the two institutions presented here. In this connection, it appears relevant that employers at language centres have only recently started asking for knowledge of the CEFR when hiring new teaching staff.

It should therefore come as no surprise that most of the persons asked describe their use of the framework as impressionistic rather than systematic, although a number of them claim that their way of using the CEFR is 'somewhere in between'. Some express the opinion that they feel they should strive for a more systematic application of the framework, but in terms of 'plus'-courses (language courses for special purposes) teachers maintain that it does not cover relevant areas satisfactorily yet, so that using it systematically for these courses would be artificial and potentially restrictive. This may be even more so as 'plus'-courses for the sciences (and to a lesser degree those focussing on academic communication) are now being re-designed as 'blended learning' courses at the SLZ in Bonn.

Course organization

In general, our survey revealed no significant differences in terms of background knowledge of and approach to the framework between teaching and course management staff. But the decisions made on the management level are of a more general nature and naturally have greater ramifications. They most directly concern matters of the general organization of courses, one of the areas where the CEFR has turned out to be of the utmost importance.

In Bonn, the CEFR provides a rationale for the centre's focus on communication, action orientation and learner autonomy. As postulated in the curriculum which is currently being developed for the SLZ, the centre aims to emphasize the aspect of what the CEFR calls 'savoir faire', i.e. 'the ability to carry out procedures' (Council of Europe 2001:11). To be more precise, there is a clear focus on teaching/learning to communicate in the foreign language and to acquire the skills required to become successful social agents at home and abroad in the different social contexts that are relevant to the individual and, more specifically, in the academic domain. For students, this will require a certain concentration on the mastery of academic and/or scientific discourses, complemented by the development of their intercultural competence. In order to achieve this, a second focus is placed on the aspect of 'learning to learn', on acquiring methods and strategies and reflecting on processes of learning in order to foster learner autonomy.

Learner autonomy is also an important theme in Göttingen. The language centre pays special attention to the teaching and testing of languages for specific and academic purposes and takes an interaction-focused, task-based approach to language testing. The ZESS understands its purpose to be the provision of excellent language training for academic purposes. In this context, language learning is believed to be an individual process based on using language in a given set of circumstances.

As regards the placement of participants, another important area of course organization, it is considered to be a great advantage of the framework that it helps to form learner groups that show a comparatively high degree of homogeneity, as it allows for a more effective categorization of students' levels of proficiency. However, as our survey revealed, it was generally felt that the placement of students in many cases is not as rigorous as would be requisite. At present, learners still show more or less pronounced differences in their mastery of the different skills. While in a general sense the receptive skills are usually well developed and often even go beyond the actual course level, productive skills need to be worked on to a varying degree – a phenomenon well known to language teachers. Coordinators and teachers believe that these sometimes very individual differences cannot sufficiently be taken into account by referring to the CEFR – and, perhaps even more importantly, are often not reflected in course materials such as textbooks. Thus, at the end of the course, it is not necessarily the case that the next level of proficiency has been reached, as assessment cannot entirely neglect the level of competence the group as a whole is able to demonstrate. In extreme cases, this may compromise both the validity and the reliability of assessment to a certain extent. Although the CEFR specifically mentions the possibility of individual profiles where skills development is uneven, teachers repeatedly refer to this problem and express their wish to have greater flexibility in addressing individual differences. The question remains how this can be achieved.

This problem is of course closely connected to the question of how much time learners need to reach the next level of language competence. It is answered in significantly different ways by the two language centres. In Bonn, a one-semester period (five class hours per week with a respective workload of 150 hours overall) is generally considered sufficient in order to move on from B1 to B1+ and so forth. Consequently, two semesters with a general language course in the first and a 'plus'-course in the second, are generally required to move on from one level to the next. In Göttingen at least two courses (for Indo-European languages) with an academic orientation are needed to obtain a level of language competence. These modules have a relatively fixed progression in terms of grammatical and linguistic competence along with topics and themes. For beginner modules in non-Indo-European languages which do not use Latin script, covering a level might require up to four courses (four class hours per week with a respective workload of 180 hours overall).

Even though the CEFR obviously cannot be adapted without alterations for non-Indo-European languages, teachers of these languages participating in the survey explained that they consider the framework very useful and would like to have more training in working with it. They stated that they had never needed knowledge of the CEFR before and have only started to familiarize themselves with it at the respective language centre. The CEFR has thus already proved to possess a certain potential as an instrument that can be used in establishing more coherent approaches to teaching languages not only of the Indo-European language families. However, in applying it to the tuition of non-Indo-European languages its level of abstraction has to be constantly monitored and, if necessary, adapted to the specific requirements of the language at stake.

Teaching

For teachers, the CEFR is most useful when making decisions on methodology and didactics; it specifically provides helpful guidance in applying communicative and/or action-oriented approaches.

In a language course, the specific circumstances that define the learning situation/context are shaped by both general and individual learning objectives. This is repeatedly mentioned by staff members as one of the areas where the framework is most helpful. Course content can be adapted to these objectives; the framework thus provides a useful guideline and basis for communication for all parties involved. Similarly, monitoring participants' progress is also mentioned as an aspect of both teaching and learning which by now heavily draws on the framework's Reference Level Descriptions and Can Do statements.

Staff members point out that in formulating learning objectives, these have to be adapted as far as possible to the individual needs of the group, rather than just follow descriptions taken from the framework. Internal differentiations are almost always necessary, particularly where a rather uneven profile of skills becomes apparent in individual learners. Viewed in this light, the CEFR level descriptions are in some cases taken to be too vague or general to fit course requirements. On the other hand, certain danger is seen that they might become too restrictive to take the reality of the course into account. A certain amount of insecurity in the application of the CEFR level descriptions needs to be considered here as well. Most teachers and tutors feel that they require further training in applying the CEFR in the various areas within which it has direct or indirect impact. And as only a handful of teachers use the documents related to the CEFR, such as the *Relating Language Examinations to the Common European Framework of Reference for Languages: Learning, Teaching, Assessment. A Manual* (Council of Europe 2009), workshops to familiarize staff members with those parts and related documents of the CEFR which may be relevant to their work could be one way to improve this situation.

In this respect it may be unfortunate that no clear picture emerges from our survey as regards the parts of the CEFR that are used most frequently. The Global Scale and the Descriptive Scheme are obvious sources of reference, as well as the Common Reference Levels and the Scales of Illustrative Descriptors. Additionally, teachers refer to the self-assessment grid, the material on activities and strategies (Council of Europe 2001: 43–100) and the Association of Language Testers in Europe (ALTE) Can Do statements (Council of Europe 2001:244–257). Coordinators also regularly consult the material on competences (Council of Europe 2001:101–130) and tasks (Council of Europe 2001:157–167) and are familiar with the *Manual* for relating language examinations to the CEFR. The *Manual for Language Test Development and Examining for use with the CEFR* (Council of Europe 2011) was not explicitly asked about because it was only published after the questionnaire's first version had been distributed.

In general it can be stated that the CEFR creates transparency of processes and procedures and provides orientation and support to management, teachers and learners. Course levels and individual levels of proficiency can be communicated and discussed more clearly and precisely than was the case before the CEFR was implemented.

Assessment

Operating under the general principle of action orientation, the ZESS practices a task-based approach which requires students to plan and structure their courses of action and keep focused on intended and possible outcomes. This is clearly reflected in assessment procedures. All in all, the CEFR is therefore just one point of reference as regards the design of final examinations. It clearly influences exam content, material for the reading and listening parts and the cognitive factors involved, which can be determined on the basis of level descriptors. The CEFR is considered to be helpful for evaluating and developing materials and for making decisions on a structural sequence of levels. Teachers at the ZESS tend to take the higher competence descriptions within a level as their point of orientation. The academic focus is given priority and shapes the way the level descriptors are interpreted.

At the SLZ the CEFR provides a useful basis for diagnostic tests as well as final course examinations, mostly in terms of helping teachers to find appropriate tasks for the respective levels and to formulate clear assessment criteria. Its focus on action orientation has been a major factor in motivating staff to strive to develop tasks that integrate different skills and language activities, reflecting a more authentic language use and foregrounding the productive aspects of language learning. However, the development of such language examinations is very time-consuming, so that the management is constantly confronted with one of their major constraints, arising from the fact that language centres typically work with freelance teachers for whom they are just one among a number of principals and whose time therefore can only be imposed upon to a rather limited extent.

The area of free text production, which is typically most difficult to assess, was mentioned as one where the framework was felt to be particularly useful. It obviously helps teachers/assessors feel more confident in determining what to expect of candidates on a given level. However, to what extent this can clearly refer to CEFR level descriptions is still an open question, as was pointed out above. Again, among other things, one possible solution to problems arising here may be to offer further training for teaching staff. This is all the more so since teachers in Bonn do not specifically refer to the CEFR's material on assessment (Council of Europe 2001:177–196) as being a valuable source of orientation. Since, interestingly, tutors in Bonn mention this chapter of the CEFR as being helpful, this once again may be a question of how experienced a person is in testing/assessing. On the other hand, teachers in Göttingen also use CEFR materials on assessment; in fact, these seem to be their main focus when reading the CEFR. A possible explanation for the response received from teachers in Bonn may be that at the time our survey was conducted, assessment there mainly consisted of designing the final exam, the range and format of which left colleagues comparatively little room for manoeuvre.

The guidelines provided to relate exams to the CEFR are frequently used and the framework seems to make exam writing easier. However, it is not always as easy and straightforward to ensure that a certain level of proficiency has been reached, as assessment more often than not is oriented towards what the group as a whole is able to do at a given point. Objectivity and fairness are in such cases positioned in an area of tension, the awareness of which, however, has been increased by using the CEFR. The specific circumstances of academic language learning and the needs of courses for special purposes thus require concessions in terms of adapting an abstract and generalized framework to the reality of the individual course. In Göttingen, exams are therefore structured in a way as to take the aims of the CEFR, UNIcert and the language itself into account; this leads to a certain profile of competence for each course. Tests accordingly consist of tasks covering the four skills (reading, listening, speaking and writing), each of which has to be at the specified level. So, generally speaking, at the ZESS the exams correspond clearly to a CEFR level. But in regard to topics and text characteristics the descriptors need to be adapted to an academic context in order to improve the exams' validity.

Thus, as far as general course organisation, teaching and assessment are concerned, the CEFR creates greater transparency of processes and procedures and provides orientation and support to management, teachers, examiners and learners. It is also an instrument that helps the teacher to adapt tuition and materials to the target group and facilitates monitoring their progress. Levels of courses and individual proficiency can be clearly communicated and discussed. Finally, it helps people in charge of language courses to communicate their decisions and assessments to students.

The comparison of the two language centres reveals many similarities in the use and the impact of the CEFR, but also some significant differences which, at least in part, can be attributed to the different stages the centres have arrived at in the process of implementing the UNIcert system. These are to be found for example in the degree of systematization as regards the application of the CEFR. Another area of pronounced differences is the aspect of self-directed learning and the ways in which it is promoted in the respective language centre. The action-oriented approach to teaching and learning is interpreted differently at the SLZ and the ZESS, where it has far greater significance and impact, and, consequently, assessment procedures also reveal important differences. At the ZESS, language learning and language testing are more closely interconnected; the measurement of language competence is embedded in authentic communicative situations based on the student's interests, if possible.

Problems and open questions

The description of the applications and the impact of the CEFR for everyday practice in the respective language centres has uncovered a number of problems and open questions, many of which have been and are still being discussed in other contexts as well. Most of them pose themselves for both centres described here – and quite likely a large number of similar institutions

– if to different degrees. For example, colleagues in Bonn mention the CEFR as an important instrument in helping learners to become more autonomous. However, it is not specified how this can be achieved or to what extent such an aim is pursued in the individual course. Of course, the self-assessment grid in the CEFR (Council of Europe 2001:26) directly comes to mind as a useful instrument for students wishing to evaluate their own linguistic competence. For that reason, it is used for language counselling in both centres.

In Bonn, the centre has largely given up working with the European Language Portfolio (ELP), because students on the whole showed little inclination to use it, so that at present the integration of e-learning units into the course work is the most important way of promoting learner autonomy. Here again, problems occur, as learners are often less than enthusiastic about engaging in this highly specialized way of language learning. It can be assumed that there are a number of reasons for this:

- e-learning units require students to spend additional time on language learning
- the aims and purposes of such units are not always transparent
- learners are unfamiliar with the Learning Management System (LMS)
- instructions for these units have not been formulated clearly and comprehensively
- e-learning units are not sufficiently 'communicative'.

Much remains to be done in order to train learners to become more autonomous. Students are often not willing to reflect on their practice, which, however, would be an important first step towards a greater degree of autonomy.

In this respect it also seems significant that the CEFR appears not to be known as widely as it needs to be in order to be useful beyond the area of actual language learning. Students are very often not really well informed about the framework and its applications, e.g. in autonomous learning. They seem to accept and even appreciate it as an institutional feature, but not as an instrument they can meaningfully apply to their own purposes. A problem closely connected to the question of students' acceptance of the CEFR is the fact that the adaptation of reference levels to textbooks and materials is still insufficient, among other things depending on whether the book is used at university or language schools. Teachers in both institutions feel that some tasks or even task formats are not suitable for students and that the academic orientation appears to be largely neglected. If this situation could be improved, students would quite likely find it easier and more meaningful to work with the framework, even for their very individual purposes.

A further impediment is created by the fact that potential employers often have never heard of the framework or the ELP, which largely reduces the range and importance of certification on the basis of the CEFR. It is generally felt that the framework is too little known in countries of the European Union and the rest of the world, which negatively affects communication with external contacts. Once this has changed, the impact of the CEFR, for example as a motivating factor for students, will be greatly enhanced.

Another problematic fact in the application of the framework is that teachers do not only see it as providing a guideline but a norm on which they have to develop their courses. Even if it was never meant to be normative, the CEFR strongly suggests itself as an instrument of standardization, which may be one of the greatest sources of problems in applying it to everyday course work. This is reflected in the common practice of using the CEFR as an argument for revizing language tests at university language centres. However, institutions and teachers do not always agree on what should be tested, and the CEFR's focus on language competence in use and the four skills is sometimes felt to neglect the importance of other competences teachers would like to see included in general language exams. Such 'shortcomings' are then quite often blamed on the CEFR – although in our view it remains open to discussion to what extent this problem is due to misinterpretations of the framework. However, it is certainly not free of inherent contradictions, such as the fact that on the one hand, as Green (2010) has claimed, teachers are encouraged to interpret the framework in quite individual and thus potentially divergent ways, which, on the other hand, interferes with one of the explicitly stated objectives of the CEFR, by restricting the 'comparability of outcomes from programmes purportedly situated at the same level' (2010:14).

In addition, there seems to be a widespread feeling among practitioners that the standard the CEFR provides is not reliable across languages, levels and institutions. As regards teachers' knowledge of the CEFR documentations, colleagues repeatedly claim that their significance is overstated and that they are too long and not always easy to understand. This impression decreases in proportion to the familiarization with the CEFR and its use in everyday practice.

Even though the CEFR had and still has great impact on the structure and operation of institutional procedures at the language centres presented here, there is thus still a long way to go before its full potential as an instrument of language learning, teaching and assessment has been realized.

Moving forward

By facilitating communication, enhancing transparency and thus enabling everybody involved in language learning, teaching and assessment to compare institutions and their course programmes, the CEFR has been most valuable in reducing the tension between the abilities learners are expected to demonstrate on account of institutional pressures and requirements and the abilities they need to acquire to become successful social agents in a globalized world where plurilingualism as a general ideal and language competence as a practical qualification are of ever increasing importance. This is reflected in the everyday practice at university language centres, even though much more can be done to exploit the enormous potential of the framework.

General curricula for all language courses should be designed which aim at a higher degree of integration of course programmes, classroom practice and assessment (Little 2011:382). The curriculum the ZESS has developed may be taken as a case in point, proving that this is a realistic demand to be made on university institutions of language learning in general, but specifically those who claim to use a particular framework of reference.

On a more general level, a series of Can Do statements need to be formulated to describe academic/scientific language competence on the different levels, likewise taking into account the specific vocabulary, functions, text types and forms, but also strategies and tasks to be performed by learners on a given level of competence. This, among other things, could be applied to improve placement in order to create groups that show a higher degree of homogeneity in the different skills or to use their heterogeneity in a more effective way. It would also facilitate the introduction of new language courses for university students. The problems that occurred in the attempt to establish an English C2 module at the SLZ were symptomatic of a deficit in terms of a sound reference level description for academic purposes. The teachers involved quickly found out that the students placed in this course showed a mastery of structures that left little to be taught here, but in respect to their active vocabulary participants revealed pronounced differences. This made it difficult to follow a common route, a problem which could be alleviated if the reference framework provided more input on an – academically defined – C2 level and its distinction from C1.

While most teachers in this study regard the CEFR as a useful instrument for language learners, not all agree. One problem seen in this respect is that it has been slow in gaining acceptance, in spite of its great potential. Another problem mentioned is that learners should concentrate on their individual progress rather than strive to achieve the objectives that are suggested by the framework. Methods of encouraging learners to monitor their own individual learning processes and reflect on their aims and the strategies they employ to achieve them still need to be refined. The 'autonomous learner' is very likely still more an ideal than a reality. But a greater involvement of students/ course participants in what happens in the classroom raises their awareness of their own responsibility for their individual learning processes.

It is now generally understood that perhaps the most important objective of any language learning and teaching activity is to enhance students' ability to communicate. The CEFR has proved to be helpful in putting an even clearer focus on this aim and taking it a step further through promoting the principle of action orientation, which, as North maintains, means that language is 'learnt for a social purpose' (North 2007:656). But in a university context, it is essential to adapt the action-oriented approach to the learners' specific requirements, taking into account the special discourse communities they have to move in. Discussion in this area is, however, rendered difficult by the fact that often no clear distinction is made between the communicative approach and the action-oriented approach, which in our opinion should not be taken to mean the same thing.

Although some teachers have applied interaction-focused and task-based methods and materials even before the CEFR made the action-oriented approach known and popular among a wider public, practitioners generally regard the framework as being successful in promoting action orientation in language learning and in having paved the way for implementing it as one of the guiding principles of the language courses offered. Teachers believe in it as a useful instrument for assessing and evaluating given materials and providing good indicators for developing their own interactive materials. In those courses which work with textbooks, the effect is of a more indirect nature. But even here teachers strive to use (additional) materials that render class work more interactive and action-oriented.

On the other hand, there remain a considerable number of users of the CEFR who feel compelled to single out grammar as a specific focus of their course work, which often does not leave them enough time for action-oriented activities. Both teachers with a more conservative approach and most students, who are trained to consider structures of the utmost importance and want to grasp them in theory before they apply them in practice, regard grammar as a central aspect of language learning that should be given far greater room than it is the case in modern language classrooms. The CEFR has not really been very successful in changing this attitude yet, the reason for this again being most likely that people know too little about it and thus of the value of the integrated approach to language learning/ teaching it promotes.

It has to be conceded that the quality of course books has improved with the implementation of the CEFR in terms of greater action orientation, even if, again, much remains to be done along these lines, for example by providing materials of greater authenticity, which could be an additional factor in enhancing learner motivation. The orientation towards skills and competences, however, is no longer an object of discussion among practitioners and many stakeholders. The emphasis on developing fluency in a foreign language is greatly appreciated by teachers. If course materials do not provide opportunities for action-oriented course work, they can be supplemented or modified accordingly. Experienced teachers seem to regard the CEFR as quite helpful here, but less experienced teachers and namely teaching assistants feel that it is difficult to find or develop appropriate materials. What is more, the topics suggested are considered to be somewhat old-fashioned and in need of adaptation. In university language courses, this can often be achieved quite easily in cooperation with the learners themselves, provided they are motivated to engage in such discussions. The development of specific e-learning materials for the different types of university language courses is another area that should be mentioned in this connection.

As some of the problems arizing in everyday practice at language centres quite clearly reveal, we need to aim at a more consistent interpretation of the Common Reference levels. In order to achieve this, teachers need to be guided and supported by familiarizing them systematically with the framework and the documents related to it. It might be considered helpful to use a teachers' portfolio for these purposes. Training seminars and workshops on the CEFR and its application in language teaching and testing appear to be of particular relevance when taking into consideration that at university language centres the teaching staff is usually also in charge of assessment, specifically in terms of designing final examinations for language courses. When it comes to certifying a certain level of language competence, many colleagues still feel that they need a clearer picture of what abilities candidates have to demonstrate so that a given level can be ascribed to them. Again, this decision is particularly difficult to make for 'plus'-courses. Another aspect of assessment that appears to need improvement is the fact that tests and examinations often quite typically consist of a mixture of what Lyle Bachman has called the 'ability' and the 'can do' approaches, which, as he maintains, should be clearly separated (Bachman 2011). But practitioners still seem to find this distinction difficult to make, which impairs the quality of their assessments. Increasing the assessment literacy of teachers should thus be a priority, given the great responsibility we have toward our course participants. For most Bachelor students, the final grade they achieve in their language courses is entered into their transcript of records and thus affects their overall result, so that this examination is of great importance to them. All parties involved, teachers/assessors, language course management and other stakeholders within and beyond the university, should keep in mind that university language courses which complement modular courses of studies lead to high-stakes examinations.

At this point it seems appropriate to address some of the major constraints university language centres operate under. A central problem consists in the question of staffing: how much input can you expect from freelance teachers in terms of time and effort in an increasingly difficult labour market? A further problem closely connected with this is the ever decreasing budget for language learning and key competencies available at universities. Even though stakeholders' expectations are continually raised, language teaching and learning does not appear to have the prestige and social status it would need to be sufficiently funded. Finally, bureaucratic constraints in terms of exam regulations should be mentioned, which still force us to use artificial modes of assessment that do not reflect the interactive, action-oriented approach to language teaching and learning we have already largely implemented in our everyday classroom practice. Even though we should doubtlessly strive for the 'politics of the possible, rather than the decontextualized affirmation of the ideal' (Byrnes 2007:642), we should also pursue the aim of making the ideal possible.

From a European perspective more cooperation between universities, university language centres and language teaching practitioners is needed to address the issues outlined above and, more specifically, to collaborate in order to further promote the CEFR as our common framework of reference. Comparing the two institutions' interpretation of the CEFR with those of others could reveal tensions and synergies and prevent the development of idiosyncratic uses which might be counter-productive as they would impede communication. But systems well founded on a meaningfully adapted framework of reference providing the basis for a continuous development could do much to enhance and promote such cooperation and remove internal and external constraints, thus working towards further reducing the tension between the abilities learners are expected to demonstrate and those they really need. Increased cooperation and constant dialogue among practitioners may also be the solution to the dilemma created by the fact that the CEFR aims at 'setting standards' while 'sustaining diversity', as stated in the ALTE motto, at not being an attempt at standardization in its own right, but enabling us to take a coherent approach to many, perhaps all languages, thus establishing comparability across languages and facilitating movement between cultures.

Note

The authors are grateful to the principals of the universities of Bonn and Göttingen for their support of the research discussed in this chapter.

References

Bachman, L (2011) *How do different language frameworks impact language assessment practice?,* keynote speech given at the ALTE 4th International Conference, Kraków, 2011.

Barth, T and Huschka, E (1998) Beschreibung der Leistungsstufen, in Eggensperger, K H and Fischer, J (Eds) *Handbuch UNICERT*, Bochum: AKS-Verlag, 81–91.

Byrnes, H (2007) Perspectives, *The Modern Language Journal* 91, 641–685.

Chouissa, C, Dugovicova, S, Fischer, J and Virkkunen-Fullenwider, A (2011) *Guidelines for task-based university language testing*, available online: gult. ecml.at

Council of Europe/Conseil de l'Europe (1998) *Modern Languages: Learning, Teaching, Assessment. A Common European Framework of Reference*, Strasbourg: Council of Europe.

Council of Europe/Conseil de l'Europe (2001) *Common European Framework of Reference for Languages: Learning, Teaching, Assessment*, Cambridge: Cambridge University Press.

Council of Europe/Conseil de l'Europe (2009) *Relating Language Examinations to the Common European Framework of Reference for Languages: Learning, Teaching, Assessment (CEFR). A Manual*, Strasbourg: Council of Europe.

Council of Europe (2011) *The Manual for Language Test Development and Examining for use with the CEFR*, available online: www.coe.int/t/dg4/linguistic/ManualtLangageTest-Alte2011_EN.pdf

Green, A (2010) Requirements for Reference Level Descriptions for English, *English Profile Journal* 1 (1), 1–19.

Language Policy Division, Council of Europe (2002) *Common European Framework of Reference for Languages: Learning, teaching, assessment. A Guide for Users*, available online: www.coe.int/T/DG4/Portfolio/documents/Guide-for-Users-April02.doc

Little, D (2011) The Common European Framework of Reference for languages: a research agenda, *Language Teaching* 44 (3), 381–393.

North, B (2007) The CEFR Illustrative Descriptor Scales, *The Modern Language Journal* 91, 656–659.

The European Ministers of Education (1999) *The Bologna Declaration of 19 June 1999*, available online: eu.daad.de/imperia/md/content/eu/bologna/bolognadeclaration.pdf

Appendix
Questionnaire

Questionnaire: Use and impact of the Common European Framework of Reference for Languages: Learning, Teaching, Assessment (CEFR)

1. What is your position?
- ❑ Member of the management
- ❑ Person responsible for language assessment, e.g. UNIcert
- ❑ Teacher
- ❑ Coordinator
- ❑ Tutor
- ❑ Other: Please specify _____

2. How familiar are you with the CEFR?
Choose a number from **6** (very familiar) to **1** (not familiar at all). ____

3. How have you been introduced to the CEFR?

Education/teacher training	
Workshop/seminar	
Self-study	
Other – please specify:	

Was knowledge of the CEFR mentioned as a requirement in your job interview?
❑ Yes   ❑ No

4. What significance does the CEFR have for your work?
Choose a number from **6** (great significance) to **1** (no significance). ____

5. In which areas of your work is the CEFR relevant?
Please explain what impact the CEFR has on these areas.

Area of work/Comments
course organization **(e.g. curricula, course programmes, communication, placement of course participants)**

communication with stakeholders
teaching (e.g. methodological/didactic considerations, setting learning objectives, monitoring progress)
choice and development of course materials
assessment (e.g. specification of content of examinations and assessment procedures, description of levels of proficiency in existing examinations, checking the validity)
other – please specify

6. **Which 'parts' of the CEFR do you mainly use?** Choose a number from **6** (very often) to **1** (not at all) to indicate how frequently you use the individual parts.

European Language Portfolio	
Complete text of the Framework document	
Global Scale	
Self Assessment Grid	
The Descriptive Scheme (Chapter 2)	
The Common Reference Levels (Chapter 3)	
Language activities and strategies (Chapter 4)	
Language competences (Chapter 5)	
The Scales of Illustrative Descriptors (Chapters 4 + 5)	
Language learning and teaching (Chapter 6)	

Tasks and their role in language teaching (Chapter 7)	
Linguistic diversification and the curriculum (Chapter 8)	
Assessment (Chapter 9)	
The DIALANG scales (Appendix C)	
The ALTE 'can do' statements (Appendix D)	
Manual for relating language examinations to the Common European Framework of Reference for Languages: Learning, Teaching, Assessment	

Do you use any of the CEFR-related documents?
❑ Yes   ❑ No

If yes, please specify: _____

7. **Would you describe your use of the framework as**
    ❑ **systematic?**
    ❑ **impressionistic?**

How, in your opinion, does this affect your work?

_____

_____

_____

_____

_____

8. **Has the level of your course book been adapted to the CEFR?**
    ❑ Yes   ❑ No

If yes, do you think that the level indicated is correct?
❑ Yes   ❑ No   ❑ Don't Know

If no, does this cause problems? Please specify.

_____

_____

_____

_____

_____

9. **What advantages and disadvantages do you perceive in working with the CEFR?**

Advantages	Disadvantages

10. **Are you familiar with other frameworks which could be alternatives to the CEFR?**
    ❑ Yes   ❑ No

    If yes: please specify. What possible advantages/disadvantages do these frameworks have in comparison with the CEFR?

    _____

    _____

    _____

11. **Do you think that the CEFR is a useful instrument for language learners?**
    ❑ Yes   ❑ No

    Please give reasons for your answer:

    _____

    _____

    _____

12. **One of the main objectives of the CEFR is to make the communicative approach to language teaching more action-oriented. In your opinion, how successful has it been in doing so?**

    _____

    _____

    _____

13. **Would you attend workshops and seminars on the use of the CEFR if offered by your institution?**
❑ Yes   ❑ No

If yes, what kind of further training should be offered?

_____

_____

_____

Thank you for your cooperation!

10 'Assessment recollected in tranquillity': the ECEP project and the key concepts of the CEFR

Enrica Piccardo
OISE University of Toronto, Canada

Abstract

A decade after the publication of the Common European Framework of Reference for languages (CEFR, Council of Europe 2001), practitioners' relationship with this fundamental tool is still rather ambivalent and certainly not homogeneous. Very often teachers feel hesitant, asking themselves if what they are doing is consistent with the CEFR guidelines. This scenario, with some minor variations, can be observed in several European countries. This contribution discusses some of the major concepts which constitute the new vision introduced by the CEFR, focusing on their impact on teaching practice. In particular, the data collected during the piloting phase of the project entitled *Encouraging the culture of evaluation among practitioners: The case of language teachers* (ECEP) is presented. These were quite homogeneous in various contexts despite differences in teaching/learning cultures. Finally, the article explains how the project builds on these results in order to produce a tool, *Pathways through assessing, learning and teaching in the CEFR* (Piccardo, Berchoud, Cignatta, Mentz and Pamula 2011), to support teacher educators in building a more complex vision of language teaching and learning.

Introduction

The choice of title which paraphrases William Wordsworth which paraphrases his ideal of 'emotion recollected in tranquillity' is not just a literary device. On the contrary, it is a way of trying and synthesizing several aspects relating to assessment which need particular attention and reflection.

Exactly 10 years after the publication of the CEFR (in its paper version), it is time to reflect on the vast and deep process of change that this document has started. A decade is a time span big enough to allow for reconsidering both the content and the structure of this document from a distance. It is also an opportune time for studying its impact so far and its potential for the future in the European context and beyond. This distance is necessary for getting clarity of vision, which is the basis for greater objectivity.

Other reasons justify the choice of title. Reflecting in tranquillity on assessment allows bringing out the numerous concepts implied in and related to this fundamental phase of the teaching/learning process. Assessment is a very complex endeavour, which involves different actors playing different roles, which requires different tools, each with a specific function and which implies choices at every stage (Bachman and Palmer 2010). No single solution – whether right or wrong – is provided to practitioners, but rather an intricate network where they are constantly at a crossroad and every choice they make has different consequences and implies different feedback.

Finally, the choice of this title aims at bringing the reader one step further. Practitioners see the big picture of assessment and perceive its underlying complexity and multitude of elements, in much the same way as the poet insists on the unity of the daffodils, on the fact that they formed altogether something like a living organism, even though he was aware of the fact that this unity was shaped by thousands of individual elements.

In keeping with what Lakoff and Johnson (1980) claim – that the laws of thought are metaphorical rather than logical – a 'literary' and metaphorical approach to assessment is in reality not odd or misplaced, but rather, it may help practitioners grasp the multidimensionality and complexity of this delicate aspect of their profession and mission.

The idea of building on different aspects to form an ensemble can in fact be better supported by a metaphorical vision than by a logical and strictly Cartesian one, where the focus would be on subdividing everything into discrete elements as much as possible in order to analyze them separately (Damasio 1994, 1999). The metaphorical approach would not deny any of the logical-rational implications of assessment; rather it would, in addition, allow some space for all the implications that somehow resist to complete rationalization, like, for instance, the issue of objectivity or balance between reliability and practicality.

The CEFR in reality: different scenarios

Before dealing with assessment specifically, we need to dedicate some space to the actual situation of the CEFR and to some scholarly discussions about its strengths and weaknesses, as well as to its impact in the contexts where it has been implemented.

Although extensive international studies on the impact of the CEFR on language teaching practices and language proficiency are still missing, an overview of different studies, articles and reports on the actual situation concerning the CEFR shows some common threads that appear to be very enlightening (Alderson 2002, Byrnes 2007, Coste 2007, Figueras 2007, Little, 2006, 2007, 2011, Morrow 2004, North 2007, Schärer 2007, Westhoff 2007). Similar concerns can be observed despite the difference of contexts and the variable impact of the CEFR, which depends on several factors relating both to institutional aspects and to the personality and professional vision of each individual practitioner.

We can definitely observe a consensus throughout on the fact that the CEFR has already played, and is still playing, a major role on the language learning and teaching landscape in Europe, and that even though a lot remains to be done, the impact is on the whole pretty encouraging. As Schärer (2007:11) observed:

> Evidence is emerging that the visions and concepts at the heart of the CEFR do have a predominately positive effect on learning and teaching, but also that a sustained effort over a long period of time will be needed to implement the visions and concepts into the daily school routine. Europe and the "state-of-the-art" in language education have changed profoundly since 1991 and 2001. Certainly not all credit can be attributed to the CoE [Council of Europe] and the CEFR. There is evidence, however, that their contributions have been considerable.

Nevertheless, some researchers underline how the CEFR 'is struggling to reach into classroom contexts' (Byrnes 2007:682) and even though 'it can proudly point to having been adopted at the highest policy levels of most of the Council's member states . . . its ability to change the frame of reference of teacher educators and their classroom practices at this point proves elusive' (ibid). Others (Coste 2007, Goullier 2007, Little 2006) point to the fact that the general knowledge of the CEFR is limited, thus resulting in a very partial implementation. Coste (2007, 2011) underlines how the CEFR has undergone a curious process he defines as 'reversed metonymy' (the whole – the CEFR – indicating a part, i.e. scales of descriptors of language proficiency, instead of the part indicating the whole as in a usual metonymy). Little stresses the fact that 'to date, its impact on language testing far outweighs its impact on curriculum design and pedagogy' (2007:648), thus pointing at a reduced implementation of the CEFR potential.

Moreover, several researchers (Alderson 2007, Hulstijn 2007, Little 2007) – sometimes coming from opposite perspectives – call for specific research that would integrate and refine the CEFR and introduce further developments. The increasing interest for – and use of – the CEFR beyond the European borders is also presently contributing to highlight strengths and weaknesses of the tool and to point at possible developments (Piccardo, Germain-Rutherford and Clément 2011). This quest for new reflection and research is the natural consequence of the process started by the CEFR, which implies innovation in language education and assessment at all levels, and is certainly welcome and timely. What should be stressed though is the need for the 'philosophy' of the CEFR to be understood by practitioners so that both dimensions of this tool, the testing and the pedagogic one – what Little (2007) calls respectively the vertical and the horizontal dimensions – are seen as more interdependent and mutually beneficial. As Byrnes explains:

> although both policy trajectories [top down from policy makers and bottom up from educators' level, editor's note] can realize noteworthy successes, their long-term ability to affect how countries enact multilingualism or plurilingualism and cultural identity in educational contexts now and into the future depends on a jointly constructed symbolic space whose creation, to the extent possible and as early as possible, involves all players (2007: 682).

This process is not seen as an easy one but ultimately as the most apt to realize the potential of the tool.

This very synthetic overview points to some of the concerns researchers expressed about the CEFR and its impact on the practice of language teaching and assessing in the different contexts. These concerns, together with shared observations deriving from the team members' professional experience in the field of teacher education, backed up the starting hypotheses of the four-year European project *Encouraging the Culture of Evaluation Among Practitioners: the case of language teachers (ECEP)* (http://ecep. ecml.at). They also helped us, the team members, decide if the material we intended to produce was potentially suitable to respond to some of the teachers' needs. All of us had been involved in teacher education for several years in four European countries (France, Italy, Poland and Germany) and had operated both within and outside our respective countries. What we had observed was very consistent beyond the differences of contexts and of teaching and assessing cultures: the CEFR remained only partially known and its different components were not seen as forming a synergy able to foster and scaffold an innovative vision of the teaching/learning process to be implemented into the class in an effective and relatively straightforward manner.

Our hypotheses

What has just been presented only reports the main trends of the situation we are faced with in the contexts where the CEFR has been officially introduced. It serves to somehow situate the investigation we had intended to conduct at the beginning of our project. Among those mentioned above, the studies published before 2008, the year in which the project began, also supported, among others, our hypotheses, which were essentially the following:

- Practitioners have often a very partial knowledge of the CEFR, which is limited to the grids, scales and tables, as these are the most accessible and intuitive parts of the document.
- There is a difficulty in integrating the CEFR into everyday practice. This could be due to its universal character together with the lack of targeted examples of how to bridge the gap between universality of theoretical assumptions and contextualized practice. Besides, we thought that the CEFR might be seen as an extra burden by practitioners.
- There is fundamentally a lack of targeted training with regard to the CEFR. For economic reasons mainly, training is usually limited to presentation of the document, often to multipliers, who in turn are called to present to other groups of teachers, the principles cascading from one level to the other and being homeopathically diluted.
- The fourth hypothesis is strictly linked to the previous one and completes it: not only is the economic reason detrimental to the quality of training but also, the lack of support and resources for training plays a major role.

These were the starting hypotheses and they were consistent with what can be seen as 'the general situation' concerning the CEFR. However, the aim of the ECEP project was to focus on assessment, mainly because one of the strengths of the CEFR is the idea of linking assessment to the entire teaching and learning process and to make practitioners aware of its complexity and of the need to make targeted choices at all steps (Tudor 2001). In our opinion, practitioners need a great deal of support in this delicate process, which appears to be crucial for introducing real innovation into language teaching and learning.

The largest part of our data therefore focused on assessment, as we wanted to study specifically the impact of the CEFR on the culture of evaluation in different contexts.

Data collection

Data was collected in four different countries (France, Italy, Germany and Poland) in the period between February and November 2008. The data collection was subdivided into two phases:

1. A piloting phase where a sample of teachers were asked to participate in a survey by completing a questionnaire followed by a 45-minute discussion on the answers and comments they had provided in the questionnaire. Participants' selection was done on the basis of the following criteria:

- type of school: junior secondary needed to be represented together with senior secondary
- profile of the school: a more innovative and a more traditional one

- experience in the profession: we deliberately chose some teachers who were not newly recruited and some others who were novice and were theoretically supposed to have undergone training for the CEFR or at least have been presented it

- gender of the practitioners: women being usually more numerous in the teaching profession, we tried to have more women than men (even though this was not possible in all contexts).

These samples were supposed to provide an initial, general, picture and to help us facilitate the focus groups.

2. A second phase where each member of the ECEP group conducted a series of focus groups specifically targeting the assessment dimension and the integration of the everyday practice of the CEFR.

Nearly 100 teachers in total participated in the research. A minimum of two focus groups was planned in each country (double in France as two members of the team were in that country and as the institutional representatives, principals and inspectors, were particularly interested in the study and encouraged participation) and this was not only honoured but also surpassed in most cases. Ten focus groups were conducted in Italy and France altogether with a fair number of participants each (six to 10 participants depending on the size of the school and the interest in the topic). Participation was a bit lower in the other two countries (Poland and Germany), either in terms of number of participants in each focus group or in terms of the difficulty in organizing focus groups in general, as often teachers seemed to perceive the exchange as an extra burden.

The questioning and discussion were guided by the five basic Wh-questions (who, what, when, where, how). To each of these guiding questions, the fundamental reflection on what impact the CEFR had had and how things had changed was systematically added.

Each focus group was recorded and transcribed. Recurrences and significant points in relation to the hypotheses were coded, sorted out, and later summarized. The summaries were used as a basis for devising the first draft of the 'guide' and a first sample of draft worksheets of the 'training kit'. These two components (guide and kit) would constitute the core of the future final publication of the ECEP project.

These drafts were submitted to a panel of 29 experts who each came from a different country of the Council of Europe, plus two project consultants. They all gathered in Graz in March 2009 to discuss the findings of the study. These experts also reported to the group about the impact of the CEFR in their contexts and on the issues and challenges practitioners were faced with. The input of the experts was highly important for finalizing the ECEP publication in terms of content as well as organization.

Impact of the CEFR on assessment

The results of the data allowed us to focus on the impact that the CEFR has had (and continues to have) on the assessment dimension of the teaching/learning process. In particular, in line with the title of the project (*Encouraging the Culture of Evaluation Among Professionals*), we wanted to investigate if the CEFR had modified the vision teachers had of the nature and role of assessment, if there was in this respect a 'before the CEFR' and an 'after the CEFR' and what exactly it consisted of. The most significant aspects that emerged from the data will be summarized hereafter.

The first big difference refers to the complexity of assessment in general and to the different components and implications of this phase of the teaching/learning process.

Teachers reported that they have become aware of the fact that assessing is a very complex process and that many aspects need to be taken into consideration; at the same time they said that they had realized how, before integrating the CEFR, the different components were hidden and how the whole process was somehow 'unconscious' to them.

The second form of awareness reported was the difference between assessing and grading. Teachers consistently stressed how intermingled these two processes had been beforehand. For some teachers, this distinction appeared to be very positive and relieving; for some others it was rather worrying and they felt pretty insecure about how to deal with it in practical terms.

Linked to this point was another important one. After the integration of the CEFR the possibility of giving specific grading to specific competences or to communicative activities related to task accomplishment instead of a global grade was seen by the vast majority of teachers as a very positive aspect.

Some of them pointed to the fact that a global scale was frustrating whereas specific, differentiated grades contributed to a sense of achievement. Only a minority of the teachers expressed a sense of insecurity, saying that differentiated grades would make the picture confusing and would not be really effective.

Another important aspect that had been greatly influenced by the introduction of the CEFR was the new vision of the oral component. Teachers recognized that the new stress on oral interaction as a communicative activity distinct from oral production was a real turning point in their practice and obliged them to reconsider not only the way they assessed communicative activities of production and interaction but also the methodology of teaching oral communication.

With respect to their relationship with institutional constraints and specifically the curriculum, teachers expressed a sense of freedom. The possibility of organizing contents and skills around tasks to be performed in a second language (L2) gave a sense of empowerment to a considerable number of practitioners who saw it as a way to set their creativity free and to plan and to really implement contextualized learning activities. On the other hand some other practitioners were puzzled by such a shift and felt not completely at ease, as they found it difficult to see how they would be able to follow the CEFR and the curriculum at the same time.

This diversified attitude of teachers, who were either excited or afraid, could also be observed in the two final important aspects on which the CEFR had had a great impact, i.e. the way errors should be considered and the responsibility of different stakeholders.

In spite of the different contexts and traditions where we collected our data, errors seemed to have a rather negative connotation everywhere. In some contexts more than in others certainly – for instance, in France errors seemed more stigmatized than in Italy – but on the whole, errors tended not to be seen in a constructive way (i.e. as part of the learning process). Teachers were unanimous in recognizing that the CEFR had fostered a change in this respect. Errors were seen as a sign of the ability – and willingness – to take risks. In this respect, a French teacher used a very interesting expression: 'erreur constructible', which stressed the new dynamic vision of the language learning process. The other aspect mentioned, the responsibility of the different stakeholders, was also generally recognized as an asset of the CEFR and a form of freedom for the teacher. By making the process more transparent and sharing the responsibility with the learners along a continuum which extends all the way to self-assessment, teachers felt themselves liberated from the weight of exclusive responsibility and therefore also from the fear of making mistakes.

Between new perspectives and doubts: the need for empowerment

The data presented above and the different reactions and reflections of practitioners provided a solid base for the project as it not only validated the hypotheses of the team members, but went well beyond that, by providing important insights into the paradigm shift that the CEFR was about to provoke in the assessment process and more generally in the language teaching process.

It is important to point out that during a later observation the results of the ECEP study were consistent with data provided by other studies. A Dutch study presented at the 4th ALTE conference (Krakow, 2011) by Moonen and de Graff (Utrecht University) and Corda (Leiden University), *Implementing the CEFR in Dutch secondary education: impact on FL teachers' educational and assessment practice* has particular relevance here. The reported increased awareness in different domains related to assessment, as well as the need for more targeted professional development, are only two examples of such consistency.

Using the same data presented above, I will try and summarize below the fundamental points that constitute the new perspectives and ideas the teachers whom we interviewed seemed to have gained from the CEFR and also to present the main challenges they were – and still are – faced with.

- *Assessment is complex and multidimensional.* There is not just one assessment but many assessments, i.e. different forms of assessment targeting many goals and justified by different reasons. Assessment involves many actors using different tools at different moments. It is a complex process with different implications.

- *Assessment can support and foster learning.* Assessment is no longer seen as the final moment of a process but rather as a fundamental pillar of the learning (and teaching) process able to play a steering role in the process itself.

- *Responsibility can be shared.* Teachers are no longer the only ones in charge of assessing, nor are they the only ones who bear the responsibility of the whole process. Learners share this responsibility to a greater or lesser extent. This involves an increase in transparency and awareness on both sides.

- *Making errors is a natural process.* In a dynamic perspective, the process of language learning becomes a trial-and-error one, where learners are encouraged to take risks and to reflect upon their own errors and mistakes. This awareness-raising journey is able to scaffold effective learning.

- *Profiles are dynamic.* In the process of learning languages nothing is static, learners construct their own profiles by increasing different competences in different languages and by acquiring targeted strategies.

- *Learning the language is not only about the language.* The action-oriented approach proposed by the CEFR stresses the need to learn languages to perform tasks that are more and more real-life tasks, where the language is a means rather than a goal in itself.

- *Freedom of adapting.* Practitioners are given great freedom of adapting, customizing and also creating according to their own needs, objectives and contexts. This freedom comes with a much higher level of awareness and responsibility for operating the most effective choices possible.

Nevertheless, teachers do not live in a utopian world but rather in a real one where constraints and obligations still play an important role. Therefore, they are still torn by several doubts and insecurities.

The first, and maybe major one, is the disconnect teachers feel between the institutional constraints and the freedom and flexibility advocated by the CEFR. One French teacher used the term 'schizophrénie' to better explain this feeling. They also feel a disconnect between the types of testing, i.e. the ideal ones and the required ones, which they exemplified with the need for testing oral activities, this being often in conflict with the institutional demand focusing on written tests. The second important problem teachers pointed out, was the time management issue. Teachers felt particularly worried by the time oral testing requires and also by the time they need to prepare targeted grids and to implement them adequately.

Finally, teachers expressed a certain need for training even though they were not specific. Moreover, they had a very unclear picture of what this training should look like, how it should be conducted, but also at a deeper level, what goals such training should pursue in the end.

On a more general level, beyond and above the specific domain of assessing, teachers testified that, overall, the CEFR has had great impact on teaching (and learning) practice at all levels, but also that this impact was not at all homogeneous from neither a quantitative nor a qualitative point of view. Practitioners seemed to perceive the great potential of this tool and, at a more or less conscious level, the force of innovation that is intrinsic to it. In general, they showed considerable interest in the CEFR but at the same time they acted very carefully when it was time to implement it. Some critical voices were also to be heard during the study. In particular, especially in more centralized contexts such as the French one, the CEFR was perceived as a new institutional constraint rather than an asset by some practitioners and in general this was the feeling that some of them expressed, especially when they felt they were 'left alone' with the CEFR. We noticed that some teachers, particularly the more experienced ones, feared the risk of the CEFR being just the last trend in language pedagogy, thus having to implement something that would be out of fashion pretty soon.

Finally, the complexity of the tool proved an obstacle everywhere, beyond the differences of context and of pedagogical tradition.

All that paved the way to our project, which was included in the four-year plan of the European Centre for Modern Languages called *Empowering language professionals*.

The ECEP project

The data presented above indicated that practitioners who have been in contact with the CEFR and have tried to implement it, have started a process: not only are they reflecting and asking themselves more and more questions but they have also started connecting different aspects of their reflection and trying (and sometimes struggling) to make sense of all these links and conceptual density and, above all, to really integrate it into their practice.

Bearing all this in mind, we set three main aims for the ECEP project:

1. Building self-confidence.
2. Developing a free and autonomous attitude.
3. Fostering professionalism.

Teachers' image and mission often suffer from social, technological and also political changes (Cachet 2009, Perrenoud 1996, 1999). This can be observed in many contexts, even if with slightly different connotations and characteristics. Education is not something neutral; on the contrary, it is often at the centre of political and ideological debates and practitioners may feel under pressure, as they need to adjust very quickly to deep and significant socio-political modifications such as the effect of new immigration policies or investment and budget changes. They may also feel anxiety with regard to their ability to effectively integrate new technological devices into their everyday practice. Faced with these expectations, practitioners may feel puzzled or overwhelmed. Building a sense of self-confidence appears therefore as the main and most urgent objective, if we share the idea that research in education needs to have an impact on practice.

A more self-confident practitioner is able to develop an autonomous attitude towards their own practice and also when it comes to dealing with external tools, institutional guidelines and constraints, suggested policies and innovations (Bandura 1995). In the case of the CEFR, for instance, an autonomous attitude would allow practitioners to avoid a 'for or against' position and to consider the proposed concepts – and contents – through the lens of their own context and vision of the teaching profession. Finally, professionalism is a fundamental aspect in the different domains but particularly in the teaching domain as quite a lot is expected from teachers, who are supposed to construct autonomously – and sometimes, unfortunately, without real support from their community – their own professional competences. The aim of the ECEP project was to help practitioners build their own professionalism, and therefore reinforce their status. In the case of the CEFR, which represents a major tool of innovation at an international level, such a process would in our opinion pass through four phases:

• awareness
• understanding
• appropriation
• implementation.

All four phases needed to be considered during the project, so that practitioners would feel supported in this delicate process, by the final product of the project itself.

The product resulting from the project would therefore be a practical and theoretical tool that aimed to facilitate observation of, and feedback on, practice. Its aim would be to provide training on the reflective approach, on the principles and backgrounds of the CEFR and the freedom it allows as well as on an integrated and contextualized approach to assessment.

The final product

The title chosen for the publication resulting from the ECEP project was *Pathways through assessing, learning and teaching in the CEFR* (Piccardo, Berchoud, Cignatta, Mentz and Pamula 2011). The choice of this title was justified by, and coherent with, the whole philosophy of the project, which, as previously mentioned, constantly stressed the need for practitioners to find their own way. The double publication consists of a guide and a kit and is integrated by more functional tools such as various indices, grids, schemes and examples of scenarios. Already, by observing the titles of the main chapters in the guide (*Reflexivity: an attitude leading to autonomy, Living (with) languages, Becoming more competent, Assessment*) it is evident that there is a tentative aim to focus on the main categories of the CEFR, which in turn represent a means for embedding the fundamental concepts addressed by this document. The guide proposes itself as a kind of Ariadne's thread to find a way through the labyrinth represented by the CEFR for some practitioners. In fact, as we all know, not only is there a lot behind a learner and teacher's performance, but, as the data revealed, there is also a lot beyond the present knowledge of the CEFR.

From the point of view of its function, the guide has a triple one, i.e. to be a mind map, a support for reflection and a resource to the training kit. The guide can be seen as a kind of mind map as it aims at helping readers grasp the links between the different concepts of the CEFR. It presents internal links as well as consistent links to the CEFR; every concept helps clarify, situate and contextualize the others. Finally, practical applications of the concepts presented and explained in the guide can be found in the kit where all worksheets include links to the guide itself and to the CEFR, so as to stress the circular approach adopted.

The guide is a support for reflection not only because of its link to the kit but also for the structure of the text itself. A reflective practitioner follows a non-linear approach: the CEFR is built in a non-linear way despite the graphical presentation, and so is the guide.

Concepts are explained, contextualized and linked to each other and this is organized in a recursive way, which helps readers explore things from different angles. Within *Pathways* several movements are made possible, both forwards and backwards (*CEFR–Guide–Kit–Own practice*). This helps to foster awareness as it supports the process of reconsidering both practice and theory at different moments and from different perspectives.

The guide constitutes a resource to the kit. By providing a first, easily accessible, explanation of the key concepts of the CEFR, the guide makes it easier to link theory to practice. It scaffolds reflective processes and fosters applied research and, in the long run, it provides practitioners with evidence of their ability (and of the feasibility) to implement the CEFR philosophy.

On the other side of the guide, and complementary to it, the kit provides a practical, customizable tool for grasping key concepts of the CEFR through clear understanding and reflection on these concepts and to practically consider their application, and applicability, to the different teaching and learning contexts and situations. It consists of over a hundred double worksheets (type A are more conceptual and type B are more practice oriented), in the same format in order to facilitate usage. They include links to the guide, the CEFR and other resources. Teacher educators, and through them teachers both in their pre-service and in-service teacher education, who are willing to share knowledge, reflection and know-how with colleagues, constitute the target group.

Scaffolding reflection and fostering professionalism: an example

As we could see from the analysis of the data, one of the main results of the implementation of the CEFR was a new awareness among practitioners of the complexity of the teaching/learning process. Even though they had not all the answers to their questions, they felt that they were dealing with something very rich in implications and consequences, which required a high degree of awareness to enable them to make targeted and effective choices.

The most emblematic for this new awareness is of course assessment as this is at the core of the CEFR, but potentially other key concepts can disclose a depth of implications for the practice of second language teaching. As a matter of fact this is precisely one of the aims of *Pathways* and of its implementation. Let us take assessment as the epitomizing key area for explaining the way *Pathways* was conceived and meant to help and scaffold reflection and awareness among practitioners.

Multidimensionality of assessment is an expression which may be appropriate to describe the way the CEFR considers – and deals with – this important aspect of the teaching/learning process. For the purpose of this paper I will briefly explain hereafter what this term exactly refers to. For a more detailed and complete explanation of this concept I refer the reader to Piccardo (in press 2012).

The three fundamental concepts of validity, reliability and feasibility constitute a sort of underlying foundation of every discourse in this area and they are necessarily evoked. But above these three fundamental categories, the CEFR emphasizes the two key questions it is concerned with:

'what is assessed?' and 'how is performance interpreted?' (Council of Europe 2001:178), thus providing a second layer, the possible uses of the CEFR, i.e. specifying the content of tests (what is assessed), formulating criteria capable of discriminating (how to interpret the performance) and consequently describing levels allowing comparison (how to compare). Both these layers – underlying principles and possible uses of the CEFR – encompass and go beyond the test itself and the performance during a test. In fact, chapter 4 of the CEFR (2001:43–100) focuses on descriptors of communicative activities, i.e. on what the learner can do at a precise moment, and descriptors of competences included in chapter 5 (2001:101–130) provide practitioners with a good basis for describing and categorizing what can be inferred through the performance, i.e. the competences, which the CEFR categorizes not only as linguistic competences but also as general competences. Moreover, the CEFR stresses a vertical dimension of language proficiency in general, and therefore also of assessment, by 'an ascending series of common reference levels for describing learner proficiency' (2001:16).

Finally, the use of strategies serves as a link to both the vertical and the horizontal dimension as learners use strategies to perform tasks and at the same time understand through their performance which strategies contribute most to the enhancement of their different competences and how they can progress more effectively in their language proficiency.

As the assessment process needs to be as accurate and as targeted as possible in order to be effective, several assessment tools and resources are necessary. Descriptors, grids, checklists, tables and scales all constitute possible ways of organizing data which are functional to the goal and target group of the assessment action. The format of presentation along with the type of tool chosen plays a big role not only because it increases effectiveness of assessment, but also because a targeted choice is necessary to answer the question 'how to present?', thus adding another layer to the process of assessing.

The CEFR does not only discuss principles, provide descriptors, care for both the horizontal and the vertical dimension of the learning process and present the different layers implied in the assessment, but it also multiplies the types of assessment by classifying them into 13 pairs, each pair being along a continuum. It is clear at this point that practitioners feel rather puzzled or overwhelmed by the wealth of perspectives and layers that the CEFR associates with assessment. The classification into 13 pairs may seem to add insult to injury, resulting in a feeling of discouragement and inadequacy, or in a tendency to refuse to question further and return to old habits.

The consideration of all these factors drove some of the choices made for *Pathways*. In the specific case of assessment, worksheets and passages of the guide were prepared for helping teachers differentiate between different types of grids, checklists and other assessment tools, between types of competences or of communicative activities, but above all to grasp the different layers and perspectives as well as the major implications of assessment. For this reason, the 13 assessment pairs were regrouped into four macro categories and practitioners were invited to compare pairs which dealt more with the distinction between, for example, competence and action or with the issue of objectivity, or with the question of timing and its influence on the assessment process.

At the same time, and in coherence with the fact that quite a lot of overlapping can be observed between these macro categories and also between the pairs and certain implications and layers I mentioned above, teachers are constantly invited to compare and contrast concepts but also to recognize overlapping and to see possible synergies.

Worksheets and guide chapters and paragraphs together with other parts of the publication should serve as signposts for helping teachers devise their own, targeted, path.

Recollection in tranquillity: towards a new vision

The introduction of the CEFR has already had a considerable impact on foreign/second language teaching all over the European continent and beyond. A process of transparency, coherence and quality assurance in language curricula and testing is being (or has already been) introduced. Nevertheless, the CEFR remains a rather obscure document *per se*, as the rich material it presents is not always easy to access without support and guidance. Practitioners are faced with many different tools and a wealth of concepts, which are not necessarily transparent or easy to access. The necessary mediation process between conceptual density and practical application is a very delicate one, which requires time, dedication and the availability of targeted tools. Supporting practitioners in their self-development process can do a lot.

The CEFR focuses on assessment as a driving force for introducing a paradigm shift into language pedagogy. In a similar way, reflection on assessment and its multidimensionality can start a process of change among practitioners if they have the possibility of grasping all the implications of their choices (Piccardo 2010a).

The CEFR is a complex document, which does not provide ready-made solutions but a wealth of options and resources and also some hints for possible usage. Such wealth runs the risks of remaining unexploited though, unless practitioners are encouraged to adopt a new perspective, a new complex vision of their profession.

According to complexity theory all elements are linked and interdependent. A change in one element of the system has consequences on all other elements. Starting to see the language teaching/learning process as a system allows practitioners to step away from a right or wrong perspective, from the quest of an impossible perfect solution. On the contrary, it allows them to enter into a new paradigm, where there are choices and a thorough reflection on the consequences of these choices. The process of reflection is potentially able to improve the whole system as it raises awareness among practitioners. Moreover, choices being necessarily context related, this awareness-building process is also able to focus on specific aspects related to each context.

The data collected for the ECEP project clearly showed that the CEFR is potentially able to set such a virtuous circle into motion provided that practitioners are supported in their journey towards accepting complexity, openness to risk-taking and a sense of freedom in approaching and implementing the CEFR in their practice. Practitioners need to work hard to construct their assessment building and they need help to see the single elements that form the big picture of assessment.

References

Alderson, J C (Ed.) (2002) *Common European Framework of Reference for Languages: Learning, Teaching, Assessment. Case studies*, Strasbourg: Council of Europe.

Alderson, J C (2007) The CEFR and the need for more research, *The Modern Language Journal* 91 (4), 659–63.

Bachman, L F, Palmer, A S (2010) *Language Testing in Practice*, Oxford: Oxford University Press.

Bandura A (1995) *Self-efficacy in Changing Societies*, New York: Cambridge University Press.

Byrnes, H (2007) Developing national language education policies: reflections on the CEFR, *The Modern Language Journal* 91 (4), 679–685.

Cachet, O (2009) Professionalisme des enseignants et complexité: vers une conception dynamique de l'agir, *Lidil* 39, 133–149.

Coste, D (2007) *Contextualising uses of the Common European Framework of reference for languages*, paper presented at the Council of Europe Policy Forum on use of the CEFR, Strasbourg 2007.

Coste, D (2011) Entretien avec Daniel Coste, Propos recueillis par Aline Germain-Rutherford et Enrica Piccardo, *Synergies Europe* 6, 15–19, available online: ressources-cla.univ-fcomte.fr/gerflint/Europe6/Europe6.html

Council of Europe (2001) *Common European Framework of Reference for Languages: Learning, teaching, Assessment*, Strasbourg: Council of Europe Publishing/Cambridge UK: Cambridge University Press.

Damasio A (1994) *Descartes' Error. Emotion, Reason and the Human Brain*, New York: Putnam.

Damasio A (1999) *The Feeling of What Happens, Body and Emotion in the Making of Consciousness*, New York: Harcourt Brace & Company.

Figueras, N (2007) The CEFR, a lever for the improvement of language professionals in Europe, *The Modern Language Journal* 91 (4), 673–675.

Goullier, F (2007) Impact of the Common European Framework of Reference for Languages and the Council of Europe's work on the new European educational area, in *The Common European Framework of Reference for Languages* (CEFR) *and the development of language policies:*

challenges and responsibilities, Strasbourg: Language Policy Division, 29–37.

Hulstijn, J H (2007) The shaky ground beneath the CEFR: quantitative and qualitative dimensions of language proficiency, *The Modern Language Journal* 91 (4), 663–667.

Lakoff, G and Johnson, M (1980) *Metaphors We Live By*, Chicago: University of Chicago Press.

Larsen-Freeman, D (2011) A complexity theory approach to second language development acquisition, in Atkinson, D (Ed.) *Alternative Approaches to Second Language Acquisition*, London and New York: Routledge, 48–72.

Larsen-Freeman, D and Cameron, L (2008) *Complex Systems and Applied Linguistics*, Oxford: Oxford University Press.

Le Moigne (1977) *La Théorie du système général: théorie de la modélisation*, Paris: Presses universitaires de France.

Little, D (2006) The Common European Framework of Reference for languages: Content, purpose, origin, reception and impact, *Language Teaching* 39, 167–190.

Little, D (2007) The Common European Framework of Reference for languages: perspectives on the Making of Supranational Language Education Policy, *The Modern Language Journal* 91 (4), 645–655.

Little, D (2011) The Common European Framework of Reference for languages: A research agenda, *Language Teaching* 44 (3), 381–393.

Machteld M, de Graaff, R and Corda, A (2011) *Implementing the CEFR in Dutch secondary education: impact on language teachers' educational and assessment practice*, paper presented at the ALTE 4th International Conference, Kraków, 2011.

Morin E (1990) *Introduction à la pensée complexe*, Paris: ESF.

Morrow, K (Ed.) (2004) *Insights from the Common European Framework*. Oxford: Oxford University Press.

North, B (2007) The CEFR: Development, theoretical and practical issues, *Babylonia* 1, 22–29.

North, B (2008) The Relevance of the CEFR to Teacher Training, *Babylonia* 2, 55–57.

Perrenoud, P (1996) Le métier d'enseignant entre prolétarisation et professionnalisation: deux modèles de changement, *Perspectives* XXVI (3), 543–562.

Perrenoud, P (1999) *Enseigner: agir dans l'urgence, decider dans l'incertitude. Savoirs et competences dans un metier complexe*, Paris: ESF Editeur.

Piccardo, E (2005) Complessità e insegnamento delle lingue straniere: ripensare un paradigma, *RILA*, 2–3, XXXVII, 75–92.

Piccardo, E (2007) Il ruolo della ricerca-azione nella didattica delle lingue-culture: verso una visione sistemica della classe, *RILA*, XXXIX, 3, 85–106.

Piccardo, E (2010a) From communicative to action-oriented: new perspectives for a new millennium, *CONTACT TESL Ontario* 36 (2), 20–35.

Piccardo, E (2010b) L'enseignant un stratège de la complexité: quelles perspectives pour la formation? in Baillat, G, Niclot, D and Ulma, D (Eds) *La formation des enseignants en Europe: approche comparative*, Bruxelles: de Boeck, 79–98.

Piccardo, E (2012 in press) Multidimensionality of assessment in the CEFR, *OLBI Working Papers* 4.

Piccardo E, Berchoud M, Cignatta T, Mentz O and Pamula M (2011) *Pathways*

Through Assessing, Learning and Teaching in the CEFR, Strasbourg: Council of Europe.

Piccardo E, Germain-Rutherford A and Clément R (Eds) (2011) Adopter ou adapter: le Cadre européen commun de reference est-il seulement européen? *Synergies Europe* 6.

Schärer, R (2007) The Common European Framework of Reference for Languages: multi-faceted and intriguing, *Babylonia* 1, 7–11.

Tudor, I (2001) *The Dynamics of the Language Classroom*, Cambridge: Cambridge University Press.

Westhoff, G (2007) Challenges and opportunities of the CEFR for reimagining foreign language pedagogy, *The Modern Language Journal*, 91 (4), 676–679.

11 Choosing certification exams: how frameworks may guide test users

Marylin Kies

Prolingua Language Centre, Luxembourg

Abstract

Proficiency frameworks such as the Common European Framework of Reference for languages (CEFR) (Council of Europe 2001) facilitate communication immensely, as they allow teachers, students, publishers, policy makers and examination boards to refer to common proficiency levels. The existence of these frameworks may, however, create the mistaken impression that measuring proficiency is straightforward. Institutional and professional test users in particular need to be aware that this is not the case, lest they assume that high-stakes certification exams pegged to a single proficiency level are necessarily equivalent. Given that aspiring students and employees choose the certification exams that are recognized by institutions and employers, these latter must set their policies wisely.

This study suggests how institutional and professional test users may use frameworks to autonomously decide which certification exams meet their requirements. Weir's (2005) socio-cognitive validity framework allows them to decide which exams are likely to provide trustworthy assessments, the Council of Europe's 2009 publication of their *Manual* relating language examinations to the CEFR allows them to judge the extent to which claims of linkage to the CEFR are substantiated, and the CEFR itself (Council of Europe 2001) or alternative proficiency frameworks allow them to decide which exams assess the skills they require and which level of certification they should require. Last but not least, proficiency frameworks such as the CEFR may also allow learners to evaluate their own level of proficiency and thus choose the level of certification that is most appropriate for them.

Introduction

The Council of Europe (CoE) has recognized that 'employers and admission authorities find themselves increasingly called upon to take decisions on the basis of qualifications, the status and value of which they have little or no reliable information on and are therefore unable to judge' (Council of Europe 2008:12). This is especially true of English for Speakers of Other Languages (ESOL) certification, which is most widely required and offered by the greatest number of professional certification boards. As Taylor (2004: 2) recognises:

> University admissions officers want to know how to deal with ...
> TOEFL, IELTS or CPE scores; employers need to know how to inter-
> pret different language qualifications previously achieved by potential
> employees; schools, teachers and students have to make choices about
> which test to take and they want to be clear about the relative merits of
> those on offer.

Test users are rarely knowledgeable of all the certificates on the market, and as the importance of foreign language ability grows on the job market, it is becoming imperative to understand exactly what each certificate means. Ideally, test users should be able to judge the suitability of certificates for their objectives, but few know even where to begin. Figueras and Melcion (2002) cringe at the prospect of admissions officers and personnel managers consulting pre-compiled lists of 'accepted' certificates, although this is already the case in certain contexts.

Who are the users of certification exams?

Although learners are the users of certification exams that first come to mind, learners are rarely in the position to choose the exam that they consider to be most appropriate. This choice is taken for them by those who require certification as proof of language proficiency, most typically academic or political institutions or prospective employers. Universities have long requested proof of language proficiency as a criterion for admitting foreign students, and this proof is increasingly taking the form of a certification exam. The same trend is appearing among employers, who have become reluctant to trust potential employees' self-evaluations or administer in-house language tests. Even political institutions have begun to require that aspiring residents or citizens present certification as proof of their language proficiency. For this reason this study will primarily address the needs of institutional and professional test users.

How do test users choose exams?

In spite of growing demand in Europe for 'coherence and transparency in language certification' (Figueras, North, Takala, Verhelst and Van Avermaet 2005:265) and the ever-greater role language certification plays as a qualification for job seekers (Figueras and Melcion 2002), test users rarely do serious comparison-shopping to choose one certificate over another. As already noted, learners are normally bound to follow the requirements set for them. However, even those setting the requirements – institutions and employers – frequently seek to avoid taking responsibility for this decision, likely because they consider themselves inadequately informed to do so. Institutions tend to choose exams on the basis of their reputation and notoriety. Academic institutions frequently choose exams recognized by the British Council, indicated by the Universities and Colleges Admissions Service (UCAS) as potentially satisfying the English languages requirements for study in the UK or those listed in the National Database of Accredited Qualifications compiled by Britain's Qualifications and Curriculum Authority (QCA). Finally, employers tend to copy the policies of their competitors or sector leaders under the assumption that they have made well-informed choices. In this state of affairs institutions and employers risk unjustly biasing against candidates and not recognizing which are the most qualified.

What do test users need to know about certification exams?

Personal experience working both in the university sector and in the provision of language training to professionals has allowed me to observe first-hand the types of questions that test users ask when choosing a certification exam. For example, learners usually wonder which level of certification they can hope to attain and need to know which exams will be recognized. This second point obviously depends on the policies set by institutions and employers, who in turn express doubts regarding the level of certification they should require, which exams assess the specific skills they require, which exams have been thoroughly linked to the CEFR and its proficiency levels, and finally, which exams are trustworthy in general.

Which frameworks can help them and how?

The Common European Framework of Reference for languages

The Common European Framework of Reference for languages (CEFR) presents 'a comprehensive, transparent and coherent frame of reference for language learning, teaching and assessment' (Council of Europe 2001:9) by defining six levels of language learner proficiency. 'To date, its impact on language testing far outweighs its impact on curriculum design and pedagogy' (Little 2007:648) and this impact on testing has generated considerable controversy. Undoubtedly, the intended assessment applications of the CEFR are ambitious:

1. specification of the content of tests and examinations: *what is assessed*
2. stating the criteria to determine the attainment of a learning objective: *how performance is interpreted*

3. describing the levels of proficiency in existing tests and examinations thus enabling comparisons to be made across different systems of qualifications: *how comparisons can be made*
(Council of Europe 2001: 178)

Experts however debate whether the CEFR is capable of achieving these applications. Its widespread success, empirical grounding, theoretical grounding and construct specifications have all been both praised and criticized. The popularity of the CEFR has produced mixed results. Fulcher (2004) attributes its rapid institutionalization to political applications and notes that the CEFR's noble aims of communication and mobility have instead produced minimum language requirements for immigrants, asylum seekers and aspiring citizens. He believes the CEFR has become such a powerful control instrument that it evades critical examination. Davidson and Fulcher (2007) worry that linkage to the CEFR is causing bureaucrats and educators to ignore local learners' needs and test impact.

North (2007) praises the empirical, European basis of the CEFR by recalling its origins in his Swiss research project (North 2000) in which teachers scaled descriptors calibrated on a common scale with known statistical properties. Statistical analysis demonstrated these descriptors to be not only valid, but also reliable upon replication and North and Schneider (1998) confirmed the unidimensionality of the scales from a psychometric perspective. North (2007) admits that some descriptors lack an empirical basis, but only those for C2, the phonological and orthographic control scales, and some subscales for sociolinguistic appropriacy.

Hulstijn (2007), however, rebuts that such empirical validity is irrelevant, as the CEFR must be underpinned by empirical evidence from L2 learners, not teachers. He laments the absence of empirical studies showing how learners progress through the levels and calls for an entirely new framework to replace the CEFR based on a theory of language development and supported by empirical learner data. Empirical weakness is also an issue for Fulcher (2004), who criticizes the CEFR's reference to the preceding CoE *Threshold, Waystage* and *Vantage* publications as they fail to indicate how well a learner must be able to execute performance at a given level. Thus, while the CEFR's empirical grounding is valid and reliable, its lack of reference to empirical learner data hinders its practical application in assessment.

The CEFR's theoretical grounding is often underestimated. North (2007) applauds its action-oriented approach and focus on content, experience and holistic activity over more traditional structure- and lexis-based models of language learning. The CEFR model innovatively categorizes language skills in terms of spoken and written reception (e.g., listening to a speech, silent reading), spoken and written production (e.g. oral and written presentations), spoken and written interaction (e.g. conversation, correspondence) as well as mediation (e.g. interpreting, translating) at higher levels. According to the *Manual*, this categorization developed from Brumfit's (1984) work 'encompasses educational and occupational activities more effectively' (Council of Europe 2009:28) than the preceding four-skills model.

Although second language acquisition (SLA) theory was not advanced enough to provide useful descriptions for the CEFR during development (North 2007), the CEFR is indirectly informed by Bachman's (1990) model of communicative language ability, as 'Strategies are . . . a kind of hinge between competences and the exigencies of the relevant task' (North 2007: 656). Moreover, Westhoff (2007:677) maintains that its underlying intuitive teacher judgements actually reflect recent SLA and cognitive psychology research. He cites theory by Myles, Hooper and Mitchell (1998), by Newell and Rosenbloom (1981) and experiments by Skehan (1998) showing that learners initially build lexical competence rather than rule knowledge to conserve space in working memory. He notes that the teachers involved in the scaling of the CEFR descriptors found this move toward rule knowledge to take place 'between levels B1.2 and B2.1'. Stoynoff (2009:2) even considers the CEFR to present its own SLA theory 'as a set of hierarchically arranged functions, situations, and the relative competence displayed . . . across a range of ability levels'.

In contrast, Fulcher (2004) cites North to emphasize that the CEFR is practically atheoretical, as 'what is being scaled is not . . . learner proficiency, but the teacher/raters' perception of that proficiency' (North 2000:573). Alderson (2007) similarly considers the absence of a theory of comprehension to be one of the framework's greatest weaknesses, as receptive abilities cannot be diagnosed in terms of the CEFR without a means for identifying their underlying mental operations. Moreover, according to Weir (2005: 209), the CEFR:

> . . . is premised on an incomplete and unevenly applied range of contextual variables; little account is taken of the nature of cognitive processing at different levels of ability; and performance of the 'Can-dos' is rarely criterion-related to actual quality of performance.

Not all see lack of reference to SLA theory as a weakness, however, and even Fulcher recognizes the opportunity this offers. Davidson and Fulcher (2007) consider the CEFR to exemplify 'effect-driven' rather than the 'model-driven' test development which has dominated applied linguistics. Moreover, although many believe direct grounding in SLA theory would strengthen the CEFR, this remains unlikely until SLA theory is unified and consolidated.

In contrast with Fulcher (2004), Weir (2005) values the CEFR's grounding in the *Threshold, Waystage* and *Vantage* publications for the detailed specifications they provide. He nonetheless finds the CEFR's lack of comprehensive specifications to hinder the development of tests at different levels and the establishment of equivalence among exams at the same level or among different forms of the same exam (see also Bachman 1990, Bachman and Palmer 1996, Davidson and Lynch 2002).

Efforts to link assessments to the CEFR have already borne this out. For example, Hawkey and Barker (2004) found the CEFR's functional competence descriptors inadequate to develop a common writing scale and used corpus analysis to distinguish candidates at different levels. Similarly, during work on the DIALANG framework, Alderson (2007) found the descriptors to lack sufficient detail for test development. During the same project, Huhta, Luoma, Oscarson, Sajavaara, Takala and Teasedale (2002) used the *Waystage, Threshold* and *Vantage* publications to overcome the CEFR's abstraction.

Not only content specifications have been found inadequate. Davidson and Fulcher (2007) cite Pawlikowska-Smith (2000) to lament a lack of reference to setting, audience, topic, task length, time constraints and purpose of communication. They also report a lack of reference to the quality of test task performance, inconsistency in references to situations, a lack of distinction among levels and finally among roles (e.g., requesting and providing services are equated in spite of the latter's greater difficulty). This myriad of inadequacies indicates a clear agenda for improvement.

In spite of all these perceived weaknesses, the *Common European Framework of Reference for Languages: learning, teaching, assessment* (Council of Europe 2001) remains a framework of great importance to test users. Indeed, the Table 2 it presents on pp. 26–27 serves as the self-assessment tool in the CoE's European Language Portfolio, of which 102 models have been accredited. Just as this table allows learners to evaluate their own proficiency levels, it can consequently also allow them to decide which level of certification is most suitable for them. Similarly, test users such as institutions and employers setting the level of certification to require as a minimum acceptable level of proficiency will find the CEFR equally useful but need to base such high-stakes decisions on a greater range of descriptors. Moreover, as employers and institutional staff often lack a sufficient understanding of linguistics to be able to adequately describe the type of language skills they require, the consultation of a number of proficiency scales specifically addressing practical, academic and professional skills as well as the CEFR's categorization of linguistic abilities in terms of spoken and written production, spoken and written interaction and reading and listening comprehension may be of help in identifying these needs and consequently allowing institutions and employers to decide which certification exams assess them adequately.

However, as Taylor (2004:5) has recognized, on its own the CEFR does not offer sufficient insight into differences among exams situated at the same level. She believes such distinctions require 'a multifaceted framework which asks (and answers) a range of questions about each test's characteristics' (Taylor 2004:5).

The Council of Europe's Manual

Fortunately, the CoE's *Relating language examinations to the Common European Framework of Reference for Languages: Learning, teaching, assessment (CEFR) A Manual* (Council of Europe 2009) can also assist test users in choosing the most appropriate certification exams for their needs. Although originally written to 'help the providers of examinations . . . situate their examination(s) in relation to the CEFR' (2009:1), a basic understanding of the five-step process it recommends for making claims of linkage to the CEFR can allow test users to evaluate the worth of such claims by an exam board.

A pilot version of the *Manual* appeared following the publication of the CEFR as part of a series of publications to assist test providers in validating the linkage of their language exams to a given CEFR level. The definitive version was published in 2009. The *Manual*'s authoring group (Council of Europe 2007) expresses its aim as helping exam providers develop, apply and clearly report procedures to situate their work in relation to the CEFR. Curiously however, the aims stated in the *Manual* (2009) are dominated by *non*-aims:

- *not* [to] provide a general guide how to construct good language tests or examinations
- *not* [to] prescribe any single approach to constructing language tests
- *not* [to] require the test(s) to be specifically designed to assess proficiency in relation to the CEFR
- *not* [to] provide a label, statement of validity or accreditation that any examination is linked to the CEFR. Any such claims and statements are the responsibility of the institution making them.

(Council of Europe 2009:1–2; emphasis added)

Indeed, this sort of guidance without prescription is a hallmark of the CoE's language policy, as expressed in the introduction to the CEFR (Council of Europe 2001:xi):

> We have NOT set out to tell practitioners what to do or how to do it . . .
> It is not the function of the CEF[R] to lay down the objectives that users should pursue or the methods they should employ [emphasis in original].

As the *Manual* directives are non-prescriptive, exam profiles and *focuses* at a given CEFR level may vary qualitatively (Council of Europe 2009) to suit local contexts and pedagogic traditions. The *Manual* (2009) warns that CEFR-linked exams may also vary quantitatively, as the proficiency range for each CEFR level is actually quite wide. The *Manual*'s disclaimers seem to even counter its aims when asserting: 'Neither is it the intention of this Manual to tell language professionals what their standards should be, *or how they should prove linkage to them*' (2009:4, emphasis added). According to Figueras et al, an exam may at most be technically linked to a CEFR level by stating for example, that 'a score of 45 on the test is the minimum score for which a qualification at B1 is awarded' (2005:269). The *Manual* authors (2009) admit the need to further address the validation of cut-off scores and provide calibrated performance samples and test items for all widely studied European languages.

The *Manual* (2009) outlines the process for relating a test to the CEFR through standard setting, which involves setting a cut score. This procedure has both influenced and been influenced by various efforts to link tests to the CEFR (Huhta et al 2002, Kaftandjieva and Takala 2002, North 2002, Papageorgiou 2007). Figueras et al (2005: 272) recognize that applying 'the same label for two qualitatively different things must mean that they are interchangeable in some respect' and worry that the unidimensionality of the CEFR scales implies that all tests can be ranked on a single continuum. This suggests that in spite of the *Manual*'s caveats, tests at the same CEFR level should be practically interchangeable, although unfortunately 'the existence of [the] manual and associated support materials cannot possibly ensure that all tests claiming to be, say, B1 really are B1 . . .' (Little 2007: 649).

The *Manual*'s (Council of Europe 2009) linking process comprises five steps: familiarization, specification, standardization training/benchmarking, standard setting and validation. Familiarization involves training to ensure that those involved with the exam clearly understand the levels and illustrative descriptors. Participants rank the descriptors through various activities to identify characteristics of and distinctions between the levels. Specification involves auditing in depth the exam's coverage in terms of CEFR Chapters 4 and 5 and forms are completed to describe the characteristics of each test component. This process may reveal inadequate coherence with the CEFR categories or between outdated test specifications and recently administered tests (Council of Europe 2009). In standardization training and benchmarking, participants observe samples of performance benchmarked to the CEFR (such as those provided by the CoE) to refine their assessment of local performance. Local samples are then benchmarked and these samples are used for training and future assessment practice. Finally, validation requires ongoing quality monitoring to judge whether the standard setting procedure is trustworthy. In contrast with Weir's (2005) socio-cognitive framework, the *Manual* (2009) focuses on the validity of how the exam has been related to the CEFR.

North (2006) has noted that these procedures reflect the process of design, implementation and evaluation characteristic of any quality management system. *Manual* users are invited to decide which of the techniques suggested are most suitable for their context. It should, however, be noted that the five-step process the *Manual* outlines is presented as a one-off procedure to be conducted in order to establish CEFR linkage. However, the criteria examined are more indicative of solid CEFR linkage if they address the ongoing activities of exam boards, and therefore it is suggested that test users apply them as such when evaluating certification exams.

Weir's socio-cognitive validation framework

Finally, Weir's *Language testing and validation: An evidence-based approach* (2005) is made use of in this study as a means for allowing test users to question the overall validity of any certification exam by distinguishing and recognizing its different aspects.

Weir articulates overall test validity into context validity, theory-based validity (referred to as cognitive validity in subsequent publications), scoring validity, criterion-related validity, consequential validity and consideration of test taker characteristics. Weir's definition of validity is grounded in Bachman's concept of intended interpretation and use as:

> ... the extent to which a test can be shown to produce data, i.e. test scores, which are an accurate representation of a candidate's level of language knowledge or skills. In this revision, validity resides in the scores on a particular administration of a test rather than in the test *per se* (2005:12).

Thus validity depends not only on how test performance is linked to intended interpretation and use, but also on how the scores produced reflect this link. Weir argues that tests should always arise from explicit specifications reflecting the context within which the tasks are performed as well as the linguistic and cognitive abilities required. He cautions that none of the six aspects of validity may be considered superior to another. Insufficiency of any aspect will cast doubt on the soundness of overall test score interpretation, which Weir refers to simply as validity.

Weir's (2005) framework does not use the term 'reliability' as Weir considers distinguishing reliability from validity to be unhelpful, given that the former actually provides validity evidence. He therefore uses the term 'scoring validity' to emphasize this important but single aspect in building a global validity argument. Similarly, Stoynoff (2009) has observed that reliability and validity are increasingly superimposed, with reliability coefficients increasingly cited to support test developers' claims of construct and content validity.

As mentioned above, Weir (2005) adopts a 'collection of evidence' approach to support test score interpretation and use. Similar approaches were previously adopted by Kane (1992, 2002) and Mislevy, Steinberg and Almond (2002). The different forms of evidence represent complementary, not alternative means for building an evidential basis for test interpretation through triangulation. The six criteria in Weir's (2005) socio-cognitive framework will now be briefly outlined.

Context validity requires creating test conditions that assess realistic language use. While tasks may not be fully authentic, they should reflect the target situations as closely as possible. Moreover, an adequate sample of ability is required to allow for accurate assessment. Weir (2005) expresses concern regarding topic choice and suggests that topics must be familiar, inoffensive and suited to the students' age and ability level. Clarity is essential to tasks, rubrics and assessment criteria, and test administration must be standardized down to the smallest detail.

Weir's introduction of theory-based (subsequently cognitive) validity emphasizes that while 'the actual cognitive operations involved in accessing executive resources are not susceptible to direct investigation, theory-based validity nonetheless remains a primary concern' (2005:87). Chapelle, Enright, and Jamieson (2008) recall the 1990s conviction that language proficiency theory should form the basis for score interpretation for large-scale tests with high-stakes outcomes (Messick 1994). This conviction emerged from repeated efforts to model second-language (L2) acquisition. As early as the 1980s, Canale and Swain's (1980) work had advanced a conceptualization of the L2 construct which was elaborated and extended by Bachman (1990), Bachman and Palmer (1996) and Chapelle, Grabe and Berns (1997), Kramsch (1993). However, as Chapelle, Enright et al note:

> ... articulating an appropriate theory of language proficiency is [still] a divisive issue in language assessment: agreement does not exist on a single best way to define language proficiency to serve as a defensible basis for score interpretation (2008:1–2).

High-stakes certification exams should, however, make at least some reference to the body of SLA theory that has developed. In his socio-cognitive validation framework, Weir (2005) refers primarily to Bachman's (1990) communicative language ability model to assess theory-based validity, and he lists distinct considerations to be applied to reading, writing, listening and speaking assessment on the basis of the cognitive processes they engage.

As regards scoring validity, Weir (2005) addresses the need for grading to respect explicit benchmark criteria, the importance of consistency in deciding whether the set criterion has been met and the minimum criteria required of a passing candidate. Productive tasks raise issues such as the use of band scales, holistic scoring, real-time assessment, compensation strategies, multiple marking and marker standardization.

Weir (2005) defines criterion-related validity as a proven relationship between test scores and an external criterion measuring the same ability or a close relationship between test scores from different test versions administered to the same candidates on different occasions. He attributes the lack of published criterion-related studies partly to the difficulty involved in demonstrating the scoring validity of alternate test forms.

Consequential validity represents one of the newer elements in validation schemes. Here it encompasses three areas: differential validity addressing whether construct under-representation or construct-irrelevant components differentially affect test takers (American Educational Research Association, American Psychological Association, National Council on Measurement in Education 1999); washback addressing impact on teaching, learning and use; the test's overall effects on society.

Finally, in discussing consideration of test taker characteristics, Weir (2005) observes that stress should be minimized to optimize performance although exam boards generally consider some emotional response to be inevitable and indicative of real-life conditions. Special needs candidates must also be accommodated, although such accommodations are felt to jeopardize generalization to performance in the real world.

Although non-specialist test users may not be familiar with these concepts or the related terminology, a selection of the most pertinent criteria therein may be made comprehensible to them. Offering test users this elementary understanding of test validity allows them to examine certification exams more critically in terms of various validity criteria. What's more, by analysing the aspects of validity considered they are put in a position to measure the extent of what they typically refer to as the exam's trustworthiness.

How can the frameworks be made accessible?

The reason why test users avoid taking their own decisions regarding certification exams is that they lack the expertise necessary to analyze exam characteristics. It would therefore not seem possible for test users to make use of the frameworks listed above, given that all of them were conceived for language professionals. Not only are the frameworks not readily available to non-specialists, they are also very lengthy and most importantly, they make use of concepts and terminology which are beyond the grasp of most test users. It is however true that not all of the content in these frameworks is necessary for the purposes of test users, only select general concepts. Furthermore, in most cases these concepts may be expressed in simpler terms without making use of the jargon that is employed by language testing specialists. It is however true that by selecting and simplifying the content of the frameworks, much of the spirit of the original documents is lost, and such unforeseen use may not meet the approval of their authors. This is undoubtedly the greatest *caveat* underlying these proposed guidelines for test users.

Applying the frameworks in practice

Using the CEFR

As seen above, the CEFR addresses a number of questions posed by test users. Most obviously, the CEFR's Table 2 is the foundation of the CoE's European Language Portfolio and for years has allowed learners to evaluate their current level of language proficiency. However, the descriptors within this self-assessment tool can equally assist learners in autonomously choosing the appropriate level of certification to aim for (see Council of Europe (2001:26–27) or a reproduction of Table 2 as a response to the question posed by learners: 'Which level of certification is right for me?' visible at: http://dl.dropbox.com/u/38997837/Frameworks%20for%20test%20users.doc).

Similarly, institutions and employers must decide which level of certification to require of aspiring candidates, a decision of utmost impact which sometimes appears to be taken too lightly. Alderson (2007:662) has indeed expressed concern that minimum proficiency requirements may not always be set appropriately, as:

> There are claims that school leavers must achieve B1, that university degrees in languages must be at level C2, and that migrants wishing to become citizens of a given country must attain level A2 or B1/2 without any thought being given to whether these levels might be achievable or justified.

Such decisions call for a more in-depth understanding of the CEFR levels than any single scale can provide and should involve careful consideration of at least a 'big ten' of overall proficiency scales: the scales for overall spoken interaction, overall spoken production, overall written production, overall written interaction, overall listening comprehension, overall reading comprehension, general linguistic range, grammatical accuracy, sociolinguistic appropriateness and spoken fluency.

Ideally, additional CEFR scales addressing the specific skills required should also be consulted. For example, the practical skills involved in residency or citizenship applications are reflected in the scales for understanding conversation between native speakers, reading instructions, transactions to obtain goods and services as well as understanding a native speaker interlocutor. The academic skills required of university or technical school applicants are addressed in the scales for creative writing, reports and essays, processing text and note taking. Finally, the professional skills required of potential employees are captured in the scales for correspondence, public announcements, formal discussion and meetings, sustained monologue (putting a case) and listening to announcements and instructions. Although the 'big ten' scales and those addressing practical, academic and professional skills are scattered throughout the text of the CEFR (Council of Europe 2001), they have been brought together in this study to allow institutions and employers to decide: 'Which level of certification should we require?' and are visible at the link above.

Last but not least, the CEFR can assist institutions and employers in deciding which certification exams test the skills they require for their context. Achieving this requires an analysis of certification exams on the basis of past test papers, exam board publications and any available independent research. The acquisition of these materials constitutes an analysis in itself, as the more these are found to be available, the more likely it is that the claims made by the examination board will be defensible. Unfortunately, institutional and professional test users may lack the ability to clearly conceptualize the skills they require in terms of linguistic proficiency, and the CEFR can assist them by offering its model of proficiency in terms of the six categories of spoken and written production, spoken and written interaction and reading and listening comprehension and by describing practical, academic and professional skills in terms of the specific scales mentioned in the previous paragraph and reproduced with their descriptors in the link. Once the users have conceptualized their proficiency requirements using one of these approaches, they can then examine the test tasks and quantify the tasks found to evaluate each proficiency category or specific skill of interest.

Using the *Manual*

According to the CoE, the *Manual* was created to help exam providers align their exams to the CEFR (Council of Europe 2009), given that ever more frequently 'reference may be made to the CEFR . . . merely for the purpose of recognition on "the educational market" without real application of its basic values and concepts' (Council of Europe 2008:9). According to Bonnet (2007), the claims by exam boards that their examinations demonstrate linguistic competence at a given CEFR level cannot always be trusted, and indeed Taylor and Jones (2006:2) warn that 'simply to assert that a test is aligned with a particular CEFR level does not necessarily make it so'.

The problem is that when setting their recognition policies, institutions and employers tend to presume equivalence among certificates at the same CEFR level, while they should instead be asking themselves 'How can I be sure that your B1 . . . is my B1?' (Alderson in Figueras et al 2005:271). Fortunately, by analysing past test papers, exam board publications and any available independent research for a given exam in light of the concepts presented in the *Manual*, test users may evaluate the value of that exam's linkage claims. For the purposes of institutions and employers, the *Manual*'s most pertinent concepts may be summarized into seven questions that may be posed of any certification exam. If an analysis of past test papers, exam board publications and independent research allows a test user to answer 'yes' to a question, this offers substantiation of that exam's linkage to the CEFR. The extent of linkage may thus be measured in terms of how many of the following questions can produce a 'yes' answer for a given certification exam:

1. Is there evidence that the item writers, examiners and raters possess in-depth knowledge of the CEFR?
2. Are the exam's development and assessment procedures and the rationale for results reporting clearly documented?
3. Does the certification exam assess all six CEFR categories (spoken interaction, written interaction, spoken production, written production, reading comprehension, listening comprehension)?
4. Do examiners of speaking and writing receive training in benchmarking (accurate distinction of levels) and standardization (agreed, reliable judgements)?
5. Is the standard-setting procedure (to determine who passes and fails) described and justified?
6. Are the test items piloted and pretested to calculate their difficulty?
7. Have results from the exam been compared to an external analysis or alternative test?

Using Weir's *Language Testing and Validation*

Beyond specific concerns regarding linkage to the CEFR, the staff of institutions and employers setting certification recognition policies often express a more general interest in the extent of an exam's overall trustworthiness. This rather vague term used by non-specialists may be interpreted as a reference to the complex concept of text validity, which Weir (2005) unpacks into the more specific aspects of context validity, scoring validity, theory-based validity, criterion-related validity, consequential validity and the extent to which the exam takes test taker characteristics into consideration. Although Weir's framework is intended for language professionals, the most relevant concepts therein for institutions and employers may again be simplified and expressed in the form of questions (a form often also used in Weir 2005) to pose of a certification exam through an analysis of past test papers, exam board publications and any available independent research. Once again, every time a test user is able to answer 'yes' to a question for a certification exam, this offers substantiation of that exam's claim of validity. The extent of the exam's validity may thus be measured in terms of how many of the following questions (condensed from Weir, 2005 and approved by the author, A/N) can produce a 'yes' answer:

Context validity:

1. Do the tasks simulate relevant, real-life use of the target language?
2. Does the certification exam avoid biasing against students who may be unfamiliar with the response format(s)?

3. Are the marking criteria clear to both the markers and the candidates?
4. Are the timings and the topics addressed appropriate?
5. Is the administration of the exam standardized?

Scoring validity:

1. Is examiner subjectivity reduced to a minimum?
2. Are the abilities rewarded those the exam purports to measure?
3. Is marking demonstrably consistent across markers and across exam sessions?
4. Is the pass/fail cut-off set with reference to a clear criterion?
5. Is passing determined by meeting a criterion rather than by attaining a mark within a given range (e.g., the top 33%)?

Theory-based validity:

1. Reading – Does the exam test both careful reading and scanning for information?
2. Writing – Is assessment based on multiple realistic writing tasks of various types?
3. Listening – Is listening assessed independent of other abilities using multiple discrete items?
4. Speaking – Does the exam test speaking in realistic situations and focus assessment on overall proficiency, not simply grammar?

Criterion-related validity:

1. Have the exam scores been related to an external criterion?
2. Has the reliability of the exam across sessions been demonstrated?
3. Has the test been linked to an external benchmark?

Consequential validity:

1. Is the exam free of bias toward candidates due to their gender, cultural background, native language or cognitive style?
2. Are the exam's effects on teaching, learning and the academic environment likely to be positive?
3. Is the exam likely to have a positive effect on society?

Consideration of test taker characteristics:

1. Does the exam accommodate candidates with special needs?
2. Does the exam put candidates at ease?
3. Is it possible for exam candidates to familiarize themselves with the exam?

It should be noted that comprehensive illustrations of how Weir's (2005) framework may be applied are available in a series of four volumes: *Examining Writing* (Shaw and Weir 2007); *Examining Reading* (Khalifa and Weir 2009); *Examining Speaking* (Taylor (Eds) 2011); *Examining Listening* (Geranpayeh and Taylor (Eds) forthcoming 2013).

Conclusions

The time has come to recognize that no amount of research and development by testing specialists can guarantee the appropriate use of certification exams. This depends on the decisions taken by test users, and their needs must consequently be taken into consideration. Rather than simply assuming that test users are incapable of evaluating the merits of exams and choosing accordingly, an effort must be made to allow non-specialists to acquire an elementary understanding of the characteristics of interest to them.

However, it goes without saying that reducing and simplifying the content of frameworks for the purposes of test users presents considerable risks as well as advantages. On the negative side, a significant amount of information and detail is obviously lost, and the simplification of the concepts may lead to misinterpretation of the frameworks' original intent. On the positive side however, in this way the content of the frameworks may be made accessible to non-specialists who play an important role in setting minimum language proficiency and certification exam recognition policies. Test users who are empowered by this understanding are also put in the position to autonomously choose the exams that are best suited to their specific context and needs, rather than relying on blanket recommendations which may be unduly influenced by market forces.

References

Alderson, J C (2007) The CEFR and the need for more research, *Modern Language Journal* 91, 659–663.

American Educational Research Association, American Psychological Association, National Council on Measurement in Education (1999) *Standards for Educational and Psychological Testing*, Washington DC: Author.

Bachman, L F (1990) *Fundamental Considerations in Language Learning*, Oxford: Oxford University Press.

Bachman, L F and Palmer, A (1996) *Language Testing in Practice*, Oxford: Oxford University Press.

Bonnet, G (2007) The CEFR and education policies in Europe, *Modern Language Journal* 91, 669–75.

Brumfit, C J (1984) *Communicative Methodology in Language Teaching*, Cambridge: Cambridge University Press.

Canale, M and Swain, M (1980), Theoretical bases of communicative approaches to second language teaching and testing, *Applied Linguistics* 1, 1–47.

Chapelle, C A, Grabe, W and Berns, M (1997) Communicative language proficiency: Definitions and implications for TOEFL 2000, *TOEFL Monograph* 10, 1–25.

Chapelle, C A, Enright, M K and Jamieson, J M (Eds) (2008) *Building a Validity Argument for the Test of English as a Foreign Language (TOEFL)*, New York: Routledge.

Council of Europe (2001) *Common European Framework of Reference for Languages: Learning, Teaching, Assessment*, Cambridge: Cambridge University Press.

Council of Europe (2007) *Introduction and feedback from the pilot phase*, presentation at the policy forum The CEFR and the development of language policies: challenges and responsibilities, Strasbourg, 6 February 2007.

Council of Europe, Language Policy Division (2008) *Recommendation of the Committee of Ministers to member states on the use of the Council of Europe's Common European Framework of Reference for Languages (CEFR) and the promotion of multilingualism*: available online: www.coe.int/t/dg4/linguistic/

Council of Europe (2009) *Relating Language Examinations to the Common European Framework of Reference for Languages: Learning, Teaching, Assessment (CEFR) A Manual*, Strasbourg: Language Policy Division.

Davidson, F and Fulcher, G (2007) The Common European Framework of Reference (CEFR) and the design of language tests: A matter of effect, *Language Teaching* 40, 231–241.

Davidson, F and Lynch, B K (2002) *Testcraft: a teacher's guide to writing and using language test specifications*, New Haven, CT: Yale University Press.

Figueras, N and Melcion, J (2002) The Common European Framework in Catalonia, in Alderson, J C (Ed.) *Common European Framework of Reference for Languages: Learning, Teaching, Assessment. Case Studies*, Strasbourg: Language Policy Division, 13–23.

Figueras, N, North, B, Takala, S, Verhelst, N and Van Avermaet, P (2005) Relating examinations to the Common European Framework: a Manual in *Language Testing* 22 (3), 261–279.

Fulcher, G (2004) Deluded by artifices? The Common European Framework and harmonisation, *Language Assessment Quarterly* 1 (4), 253–266.

Geranpayeh, A and Taylor, L (Eds) (forthcoming 2013) *Examining Listening: Research and Practice in Examining Second Language* Listening, Studies in Language Testing volume 35, Cambridge: UCLES/Cambridge University Press.

Hawkey, R and Barker, F (2004) Developing a common scale for the assessment of writing, *Assessing Writing* 9, 122–59.

Huhta, A, Luoma, S, Oscarson, M, Sajavaara, K, Takala, S and Teasedale, A (2002) A diagnostic language assessment system for adult learners, in Alderson, J C (Ed.) *Common European Framework of Reference for Languages: Learning, Teaching, Assessment. Case Studies*, Strasbourg: Council of Europe, 130–146.

Hulstijn, J H (2007) The shaky ground beneath the CEFR: Quantitative and qualitative dimensions of language proficiency, *The Modern Language Journal* 91, 663–667.

Kaftandjieva, F and Takala, S (2002) Council of Europe Scales of Language Proficiency, in Alderson, J C (Ed.) *Common European Framework of Reference for Languages: Learning, Teaching, Assessment. Case Studies*, Strasbourg: Language Policy Division, 106–129.

Kane, M (1992) An argument-based approach to validity, *Psychological Bulletin* 112, 527–535.

Kane, M (2002) Validating high-stakes testing programs, *Educational Measurement: Issues and Practice* 21 (2), 31–41.

Khalifa, H and Weir, C (2009) *Examining Reading: Research and Practice in Assessing Second Language Reading*, Studies in Language Testing volume 29, Cambridge & New York: UCLES/Cambridge University Press.

Kramsch, C (1993) *Context and Culture in Language Testing*, Oxford: Oxford University Press.

Little, D (2007) The Common European Framework of Reference for languages: Perspectives on the making of supranational language education policy, *The Modern Language Journal* 91, 645–655.

Messick, S (1994) The interplay of evidence and consequences in the validation of performance assessments, *Educational Researcher* 23 (2), 13–23.

Mislevy, R J, Steinberg, L S and Almond, R G (2002) Design and analysis in task-based language assessment, *Language Testing* 19, 477–496.

Myles, F, Hooper, J and Mitchell, R (1998) Rote or rule? Exploring the role of formulaic language in classroom foreign language learning, *Language Learning* 48, 323–362.

Newell, A and Rosenbloom, P S (1981) Mechanisms of skill acquisition and the law of practice, in Anderson, J R (Ed.) *Cognitive Skills and Their Acquisition*, Hillsdale, NJ: Erlbaum, 1–55.

North, B (2000) *The Development of a Common Framework Scale of Language Proficiency*, New York: Peter Lang.

North, B (2002) A CEF-Based Self-assessment Tool for University Entrance, in Alderson, J C (Ed.) *Common European Framework of Reference for Languages: Learning, Teaching, Assessment. Case Studies*, Strasbourg: Language Policy Division, 146–166.

North, B (2006) *The Common European Framework of Reference: development, theoretical and practical issues*, paper presented at the symposium A New Direction in Foreign Language Education: The Potential of the Common European Framework of Reference for Languages, University of Foreign Studies, Osaka, Japan, March 2006.

North, B (2007) The CEFR illustrative descriptor scales, *The Modern Language Journal* 91, 656–9.

North, B and Schneider, G (1998) Scaling descriptors for language proficiency scales, *Language Testing* 15 (2), 217–262.

Papageorgiou, S (2007) *Relating the Trinity College London GESE and ISE examinations to the Common European Framework of Reference: Final project report, February 2007*, London: Trinity College London.

Pawlikowska-Smith, G (2000) *The Canadian Language Benchmarks 2000: English as a Second Language – for Adults*, Ottawa, ON: Centre for Canadian Language Benchmarks.

Shaw, S D and Weir, C (2007) *Assessing Writing: Research and Practice in Assessing Second Language Writing,* Studies in Language Testing volume 26, Cambridge: UCLES/Cambridge University Press.

Skehan, P (1998) *A Cognitive Approach to Learning Language*, Oxford: Oxford University Press.

Stoynoff, S (2009) Recent developments in language assessment and the case of four large-scale tests of ESOL ability, *Language Teaching* 42 (1), 1–40.

Taylor, L (2004) Issues of test comparability, *Research Notes* 15, 2–5.

Taylor, L (Ed.) (2011) *Examining Speaking: Research and Practice in Assessing Second Language Speaking,* Studies in Language Testing volume 30, Cambridge: UCLES/Cambridge University Press.

Taylor, L and Jones, N (2006) Cambridge ESOL exams and the Common European Framework of Reference (CEFR), *Research Notes* 24, 1–4.

Weir, C J (2005) *Language Testing and Validation: An Evidence-based Approach,* Hampshire: Palgrave Macmillan.

Westhoff, G (2007) Challenges and opportunities of the CEFR for reimagining foreign language policy, *The Modern Language Journal* 91, 676–9.

Section Three
Frameworks and practical issues

12 Towards a new phonological control grid

David Horner
École Nationale de la Statistique et de
l'Administration Économique, Paris, France
Consultant to University of Cambridge ESOL
Examinations, United Kingdom

Abstract

While the Common European Framework of Reference for languages (CEFR) (Council of Europe 2001) devotes considerable time and effort to describing oral productive competence, it is surprising that of the 32 different grids proposed to assess it, only one covers pronunciation. Moreover, the grid raises important issues relating to: intelligibility and its lack of dependence on accent; the impact of 'effort', irritation, and the hearer's listening skills; and whether we know enough about how phonological features are acquired, or which are most salient for hearers to establish truly relevant pronunciation descriptors at the different CEFR levels. The CEFR phonological control grid is critically reviewed in this paper with reference to the available research literature on pronunciation and terms commonly used in phonological descriptors. Another grid is proposed as a first step towards a more significant revision, in particular the removal of all reference to accent and 'effort'. Intelligibility is maintained on condition that oral examiners receive considerable training with a variety of accents.

Introduction

This article addresses an important area of language assessment which this author believes to be inadequately dealt with by the Common European Framework of Reference for languages (CEFR) (Council of Europe 2001), namely pronunciation. While the CEFR devotes considerable time and effort to describing the various elements which together make up oral productive competence (especially in chapter 4 (Council of Europe 2001:43–100)), of the 32 different grids of descriptors proposed for the assessment of oral productive competence, only one covers pronunciation. Given the importance of a sufficiently intelligible pronunciation in the negotiation of successful communicative outcomes, this is, to say the least, surprising, although, in the wider context of language teaching, perhaps not. As Derwing and Munro (2005:380) put it: '. . . much less research has been carried out on L2 pronunciation than on other skills such as grammar and vocabulary, and instructional materials and practices are still heavily influenced by commonsense intuitive notions.'

Table 1 The CEFR phonological control grid

PHONOLOGICAL CONTROL	
C2	As C1.
C1	Can vary intonation and place sentence stress correctly in order to express finer shades of meaning.
B2	Has acquired a clear, natural, pronunciation and intonation.
B1	Pronunciation is clearly intelligible even if a foreign accent is sometimes evident and occasional mispronunciations occur.
A2	Pronunciation is generally clear enough to be understood despite a noticeable foreign accent, but conversational partners will need to ask for repetition from time to time.
A1	Pronunciation of a very limited repertoire of learnt words and phrases can be understood with some effort by native speakers used to dealing with speakers of his/her language group.

Source: Council of Europe (2001:117)

This grid raises a number of issues relating to, in particular: the presence or absence of accent (does it disappear after B1?); the nature of intelligibility and its relationship to accent, comprehensibility and the listener's familiarity with accents; 'effort' (also called 'strain' in the CEFR) and whether it can be adequately defined or quantified; the fact that the majority of situations where English is now spoken in the world concern at least one non-native speaker (NNS) (Graddol 2006) and to what extent we should take this into account, for example via the Lingua Franca core (Jenkins 2000); and whether we know enough about how phonological features are acquired to be able to establish pronunciation descriptors for the different CEFR levels, or whether we need to rely on phonological components which have demonstrably an effect on intelligibility.

In what follows, I shall examine the CEFR phonological control grid, looking in the first section at the common, yet to my mind still nebulous concept of intelligibility and the associated area of accent; in the next section at the enticingly attractive concept of 'effort' (or 'strain') and the overlapping idea of 'irritation' (related to the notions of error gravity or error tolerance); before going on to discuss what is known about pronunciation hierarchies; and then considering whether the CEFR phonological control grid satisfies its own criteria for good descriptors. The following section is a summary of the findings outlined in the earlier sections; and the final section is the conclusion, in which an alternative grid is proposed.

Accent and intelligibility

The CEFR grid (given in Table 1) suggests that accent disappears beyond B1. Yet, as Trask (1996:4) puts it, 'every speaker of a language necessarily speaks it with some accent or other'. Indeed, there is a fruitful and growing body of research to explain why learners retain their accents. Accent is influenced not only by biological limitations on sound production, but also by sociolinguistic realities: speakers speak the way they do because of the social or regional groups they belong to or desire to belong to. Accent is an essential marker of social belonging. Indeed, even in NS situations, there is considerable evidence that accent is perhaps the last vestige of permissible discrimination (see Milroy and Milroy 1985, Wolfram and Schilling-Estes 1998). Mugglestone (1995) has shown how Received Pronunciation became both a mark of socioeconomic power and status and a gate-keeping tool to exclude non-RP speakers; and Lippi-Green (1997) has similarly shown how accent is used in American English to discriminate against speakers of non-prestige varieties.

The pull of identity is also strong for NNSs of a language. Jenkins (2000) illustrates the importance of identity through the tendency toward accent convergence, even when it means speaking English with more deviant pronunciation, when she describes how NNS pairs of the same first language (L1) pronounce English with a greater number of deviations than do pairs of speakers from different L1s. Similarly, Gatbonton, Trofimovich and Magid (2005) have shown how ethnic group affiliation is a critical factor in pronunciation accuracy, where social pressure from home communities or other students who speak their L1 may lead learners to avoid being seen as disloyal to their primary ethnic group by adopting non-standard pronunciation.

Under the circumstances, including the notion of accent may well be misplaced: accent is something we have and we hold on to, something we change and manipulate according to our circumstances. But it is not something that we can willingly cast aside once we reach B1. Research suggests indeed that accent will remain in all but exceptional cases: while some adult learners may occasionally achieve native-like speech patterns, this would appear to be restricted to a very small number of highly motivated individuals (Moyer 2004) and to those with special aptitude (Ioup, Boustagi, El Tigi and Moselle 1994). Studies of ultimate attainment in general suggest that achieving NS-like pronunciation after early childhood is exceedingly rare (Flege, Munro and Mackay 1995, Scovel 2000). In fact, there is no reason to believe that this goal is achievable, at least in classroom settings.

More central to the issue is to what extent accent interferes with intelligibility. The degree of intelligibility of a learner's speech seems to have become the yardstick by which to measure it. However, what exactly do we mean by intelligible speech? The concept seems to have begun with Abercrombie, who defined it as 'a pronunciation which can be understood with little or no conscious effort on the part of the listener' (1956:93). Although this has the merit of emphasising the role of the hearer in the notion of intelligibility (a point we shall underline again and again), as we shall see in the next section, it still leaves us with the problem of defining effort in any meaningful way.

The key issue, surely, is to what extent a speaker's intelligibility impacts negatively on the passage of his or her message: to what extent is it a barrier to communication? But even this leaves us with the issue of determining whether the barrier comes from the spoken production of the speaker or the listening skill of the hearer, or both.

In both cases, of course, the issue of accent will be crucial. As we have already emphasised, losing one's accent – even a regional accent – is an exceptional event, but the situation becomes more complicated when the accents in question are non-native. Native speakers (NS) can generally adapt readily to other accents when they have a lifetime's experience of dealing with such situations. The intuitive assumption that NS varieties of English are *not* mutually intelligible has some support from research which shows that understanding in NS communication is often more complex than one would expect (see Cutler, Dahan and van Donselaar 1997).

In other words, it is significantly easier to understand an accent you are used to than one that you are not used to. It is important therefore to determine whether and to what extent tolerance to foreign accent is greater among NNS, and whether poor pronunciation still represents a barrier to understanding. Under the circumstances, however intuitively attractive it might be, using accent as a measure of intelligibility in descriptors, and, above all, relating this to terms like 'effort' and 'strain', makes little sense unless the examiners are extensively exposed to varieties of accents: intelligibility, as we shall see, is as much a question of the hearer's ability to listen as it is of the speaker's ability to pronounce.

As already mentioned, however, English is not spoken only by and between native English speakers. Graddol (2006) estimates that the balance is about ¾ NNS-NNS and ¼ NNS-NS for English. Its role as an international *lingua franca* means it is frequently used in presentations by NNS and in conversations between NS and NNS, and wholly between NNS. The requirement for intelligibility, and of the adherence to a common and shared standard becomes thus more problematic (always assuming one can agree on what such a common standard should be; Deterding (2005), for example, argues that emphasising prestige models is counterproductive since it does not help learners to understand the speech (NS or NNS) they are likely to encounter). However, it should not be forgotten that speakers who engage often in such exchanges will also gather considerable exposure to different varieties of English, and we have already mentioned the essential role exposure plays in intelligibility.

And this is the crux of the matter when it comes to intelligibility: NNS of

English are no different from NS in this respect and usually good at decipher-ing the English they are used to hearing, and much less so when faced with 'non-standard' varieties (e.g. when they move from recorded course book dialogues to listening to real native speakers). This may be one reason why learners in countries where films and TV programmes are not dubbed are so often thought to be significantly better at English than learners in countries where this is not the case. Yet little work has been done with NNS listen-ers (but see Jenkins 2002). Preliminary studies indicate, however, that NNSs often find a fellow L1 speaker easier to understand than someone from a dif-ferent L1 background (Major, Fitzmaurice, Bunta and Balasubramanian 2002, Smith and Bisazza 1982). And, unsurprisingly, there is some evidence to suggest that listeners can benefit from training to improve their skills at listening to accented speech (Derwing, Rossiter and Munro 2002).

In short, the intelligibility issue is not just one of pronunciation: it is also one of listening comprehension and familiarity with accents. Field (2005: 401), in a typically interesting article, defines intelligibility much more pre-cisely but also narrowly to include only the production side of the interaction, restricting it:

> to features of the speech signal . . . it refers to the extent to which the
> acoustic-phonetic content of the message is recognizable by a listener.
> On this analysis, intelligibility forms part of a wider construct of com-
> prehensibility. The distinction helps to position the present study within
> an area of specifically phonological enquiry. It also serves to separate
> perceptual evidence at phoneme, word, and tone-group levels from
> higher level evidence such as world knowledge, which originates outside
> the signal.

However useful this may be in terms of a research paradigm identifying those features of production that need to be investigated, it fails to deal with our current preoccupation, which is how to assess intelligibility when listener bias (due to such factors as previous experience of the accent) is present.

Trudgill (2005), for instance, has argued that NNS' comprehension of NS English is dependent on their ability to pronounce its phoneme distinctions. Similarly, Levis (2005), following Kachru (1986) and Bamgbose (1998), has devised grids of possible NS-NNS interaction patterns in which he introduces the complicating concept of 'nativized varieties' of English (i.e. NNS varie-ties spoken in second language settings, as, for instance, in India). He then classifies 'accepted' varieties of English like prestige varieties of American or British English as inner-circle varieties, while the 'nativized' varieties are classed as outer-circle. This leads him to conclude that:

> In U.S. university settings, for example, graduate teaching assistants
> from outer-circle countries such as India are routinely tested for spoken

> English proficiency, even when their English proficiency is otherwise indistinguishable from inner-circle graduate students. It seems evident that such testing is conducted because outer-circle speakers have unfamiliar accents, not a lower proficiency in English' (Levis 2005:374).

However, if intelligibility is about being understandable, as Levis (2005) remarks, it is also necessary to recognise that communication can be successful even when foreign accents are quite strong, and that there is no clear correlation between accent and intelligibility (Derwing and Munro 2005, Munro and Derwing 1995, 1999). These researchers identify three aspects of foreign-accented speech: (a) the extent to which the speaker's intended utterance is actually understood by a listener (intelligibility), (b) the listener's perception of the degree of difficulty encountered when trying to understand an utterance (comprehensibility, which we identify below as 'effort' or 'strain'), and (c) how much an L2 accent differs from the variety of English the listener is familiar with (accentedness). Derwing and Munro claim (2005:386) that 'one of the most robust findings in studies examining the relationships among these dimensions is that they are partially independent. Although listeners who find specific L2 utterances to be both unintelligible and incomprehensible always perceive such samples as heavily accented, the reverse is not necessarily true.' It is not unusual, in other words, to assign good comprehensibility ratings to speech samples that are also rated as heavily accented. In addition, studies requiring listeners to transcribe learners' speech indicate that some heavily accented speech samples are completely intelligible, while others are not (Derwing and Munro 1997, Munro and Derwing 1995). This can in part, but not entirely, be ascribed to the absence or presence of context.

Scheuer (2005:116) draws the same conclusion that 'foreign accent and unintelligibility are not synonymous'. Similarly, Johansson (1978:6, author's italics) points out that 'speech can be severely distorted and yet be intelligible . . . [t]o be communicatively effective, the message must get across swiftly and unambiguously and *without undue demands upon the receiver*'. This, however, brings us to the nebulous notion of 'effort' on the part of the listener (see the next section).

Jenkins (2000) proposes that many NNS lack the language proficiency to handle speech other than through bottom-up processing, whereas NS are essentially top-down processors. Although this is probably an oversimplification, it does suggest that NNS will be more reliant on segmental rather than suprasegmental features; i.e. the very aspects of pronunciation which a strong accent typically distorts.

Yet, as Levis (2005) remarks, despite a paucity of research evidence for the belief that suprasegmentals rather than segmentals are important in promoting intelligibility, over the past 25 years this is where the emphasis has been in teaching. Yet the importance of suprasegmentals for communication in English as an international language (EIL) is uncertain (Jenkins 2000, Levis 1999); nor is it certain that all suprasegmentals are equally learnable. Pennington and Ellis (2000), for example, found that although some elements of intonation, such as nuclear stress, appear to be learnable, other elements, such as pitch movement and the intonation of sentence tags, are not. As Field (2005:401–402) sums it up, the problem is that 'it is by no means easy to determine which features of pronunciation should be prioritised on the grounds that they enhance a learner's intelligibility'.

Counter-intuitively, perhaps, there is evidence that NNS judges and instructors evaluate foreign learners' errors considerably more severely than do NS and non-instructors. For instance, Koster and Koet (1993:69) compared the different ways in which Dutch non-native teachers of English and English native speakers evaluated Dutch-accented English, and found that the former were stricter than the latter. A similar severity in NNS teachers of English composition was also attested in Hughes and Lascaratou (1982) and Sheorey (1986). Likewise, Galloway (1980) and Schairer (1992) found that NS who did not teach Spanish were more lenient judges of English-accented Spanish than those who did. Fayer and Krasinski (1987:321) also found that Spanish-speaking judges of Puerto Rican-accented English were stricter than native speakers of English, and suggested that 'nonnatives, no matter what their proficiency level, are embarrassed by their compatriots' struggles in the nonnative language'.

Unfortunately, the evidence suggesting that NNS are harsher judges, although strong, is not conclusive, other studies suggesting that there is no real difference. Munro, Derwing and Morton (2006), for example, in a study where listeners from native Cantonese, Japanese, Mandarin, and English backgrounds evaluated the same set of 48 foreign-accented English utterances from native speakers of Cantonese, Japanese, Polish, and Spanish, found that the different listener groups showed moderate to high correlations on intelligibility scores and comprehensibility and accentedness ratings: the groups tended to agree on which of the speakers were the easiest and most difficult to understand, and the listeners did not consistently find speech produced in their own accent more intelligible.

Intelligibility, then, is a much less robust indicator than we would like it to be: however much we may feel intuitively that it should be an essential aspect in assessing a learner's pronunciation, it has to be admitted that we do not all have equal tolerance to foreign accents. Both as individuals and as members of social or cultural groups, we tend to be less tolerant of certain errors that may be perceived as much less serious by other individuals and social groups (teachers are notoriously intolerant of 'minor' grammatical errors, for example). The even hazier concept of 'irritation' rears its head here (see next section), but there would appear to be no obvious way to account for it.

This does not, of course, necessarily mean that intelligibility should not appear as a criterion in assessing pronunciation. But it does underline the necessity of training oral examiners to become accustomed to other accents and to overcome their personal, social, cultural and professional prejudices. (See Taylor and Galaczi (2011:209–214) for a review of the effects of rater training.)

In conclusion, accent, if it impacts negatively on intelligibility – i.e., if it is a barrier to comprehension – needs to be taken into account in any assessment of speaking proficiency. However, because intelligibility is as much a case of the listener's familiarity with other varieties of English (whether NS or NNS), examiners need to be trained to develop this familiarity. Moreover, given the global context within which English functions, we cannot ignore the experience or the reactions of NNS to non-'standard' (NS as well as NNS) English. Surprisingly, given the research findings, this last factor should induce us to be more rather than less demanding in our expectations of learner proficiency in the speaking skill.

The question that remains, however, is whether there exists a means of gauging the degree of (un)intelligibility. Dating back to the first discussions of intelligibility, yet appearing only at A1 in the CEFR phonological grid, one way that has been mentioned is the degree of effort required of the hearer (sometimes termed 'strain' on the hearer), and the related idea of the amount of 'irritation' felt by the hearer; an idea emerging from research into hearer reactions to NNS speech. It is to a discussion of the relevance and practicality of these that we shall now turn.

Effort and irritation

As already mentioned, the issue of 'effort' is related to Abercrombie's definition of 'intelligible' as 'a pronunciation which can be understood with little or no conscious effort on the part of the listener' (1956:93). However, like intelligibility, one person's perception of 'effort' (sometimes called 'strain on the listener') is not the same as another's. Our reaction to the effort required to understand someone is related to our experience of hearing speakers of other languages speak ours, to the situation in which the conversation is taking place, and to our inherent patience. Research into how foreign, intelligible or irritating an accent is has shown that this depends, at least to some extent, on the raters' own linguistic background. Calloway (1980), Flege (1984) and Thompson (1991), for instance, have shown that linguistically experienced listeners are more reliable than inexperienced judges in estimating L2 learners' speech intelligibility, irritation and/or accentedness.

Moreover, we need to make an effort to understand someone for several interrelated reasons (their poor control of grammar, limited lexis, tiredness, etc.) which inevitably interact with both a strong accent and the discourse context; but can we distinguish between each of these to decide which one is forcing us to make an effort? Unsurprisingly, therefore, Gass and Varonis (1984:81) found that a native speaker's familiarity with 'the topic of discourse', with 'nonnative speech in general', with 'a particular nonnative accent' and with 'a particular nonnative speaker' all facilitate 'the native speaker's comprehension of nonnative speech'. This implies that communicative efficiency is reduced if familiarity with any of these four elements is absent. This effect is likely to be particularly strong if some of these features are combined. Similarly, the fluency and other non-phonological elements have also been shown to influence perceptions of accent (Anderson-Hseih and Koehler 1988, Garcia Lecumberri and Gallardo del Puerto 2003, Munro and Derwing 1995).

I suspect that the issue of 'effort' is closely related to that of 'irritation'. There would appear to be no generally accepted and applicable technical definition of the term, but it would seem to have emerged from a body of research in the 1980s related to error gravity and error tolerance (see Eisenstein (1983) and Ludwig (1982) for reviews and Rifkin and Roberts (1995) for a critical assessment). The early research in this area explicitly claimed that there was a link between intelligibility and 'irritation' (Johansson 1978, Magnan 1983, Piazza 1980); whereas other researchers considered irritation to be at least partially socially determined (Vann, Meyer and Lorenz 1984), thus allowing for the possibility that NS production could be both intelligible and irritating. Yet, the notion of irritation itself remained undefined. Santos (1988), however, suggests that it is linked to notions of acceptability: i.e. the degree to which errors violate target norms, whether implicit or explicit. Horner (1987), for example, found that French native speakers judged harshly the absence of subjunctive forms in obligatory occurrences or the overuse of 'ça', while Santos (1998) found NS English teachers were most irritated by double negatives. This research also agrees with those of van den Doel's (2006) findings that stigmatised phonetic forms (e.g. substituting of / ð/ and /θ/ by /t/ or /d/) were judged very negatively. The error gravity research was able to show, therefore, that certain errors were perceived as serious by NS or NNS or both, for reasons more closely related to social acceptability than linguistic correctness or intelligibility.

Indeed, several studies found that irritation – or intolerance to error – was a more important factor in creating negative reactions in hearers than other, more 'traditional' aspects of language competence. A study by Piazza (1980: 424–426), for example, into the reactions of French secondary school pupils to grammatical mistakes made by American learners of French found that '[i]rritation was judged more severely than lack of comprehensibility', especially in spoken language. This is supported by findings from van den Doel's mammoth 2006 study of NS reactions to Dutch pronunciation. He found that:

> intelligibility is not the sole criterion used by native speakers in decid-
> ing whether a particular pronunciation error is acceptable. *Respondents'*
> *emotive reactions to certain stigmatised realisations indicate that factors*
> *such as irritation or amusement also play a part in prioritising certain*
> *errors over others.* Moreover Respondents' comments indicate that,
> across different groups of native speakers, some errors are clearly
> and consistently more irritating than others (van den Doel 2006: 287,
> author's italics).

Significantly, this finding could be taken to indicate that foreign accents
are not only judged on the basis of intelligibility, but also by L1 standards
for acceptability, at least where NSs are involved. It also gives us the beginnings of a definition of irritation: unacceptable or stigmatised phonological
realisations. However, without research into what is considered inappropriate (by whom? in what circumstances?) or whether realisations which are
stigmatised by NS because socially or regionally connotated are equally not
tolerated by NNS. To my knowledge, there is no research to support this in
one way or the other.

In short, irritation would appear to be a significant factor in the perception by NS of both socially or regionally stigmatised varieties of NS English
and of NNS varieties. The research, however, does not allow us to identify
which elements are actually not tolerated.

In conclusion, it is possible, if not probable, that irritation plays a role
in our perceptions of both the language proficiency and the personality of
a learner. In the current state of affairs, however, we are not in a position
to identify or quantify which elements of pronunciation lead to intolerance on the part of the hearer. It cannot therefore be used to assess speaking
proficiency.

Equally, because it involves an interaction with a variety of other factors
– both linguistic and non-linguistic – the notion of 'effort', although super-
ficially attractive, is not easily restricted to dealing solely with accent. And
once again, we are brought back to the fact that the degree of 'effort' required
of a hearer depends not only on the speaker's control of phonological features, but also crucially on the hearer's familiarity with the speaker's variety
of English and the topic of the conversation. If it is to be included in an assessment grid for pronunciation, therefore, it needs to be accompanied by training for examiners which will familiarise them with this accent in particular
and foreign accents in general.

It is interesting that the CEFR grid only includes 'effort' at A1, whereas
accent and intelligibility persist up to B1. Yet what makes an accent? What
makes a learner more or less intelligible? In short, what is pronunciation and
at what stages of proficiency (from A1 to C2) would one expect learners to
master these different elements? This brings us to the idea of pronunciation
hierarchies; i.e. which aspects of pronunciation: are deemed to be more or

less important; or more or less irritating; have been shown to be more or less difficult to acquire; or acquired in one order rather than another; and/or have been shown to have an impact on intelligibility?

It is to a discussion of this concept that we shall turn in the next section.

Pronunciation hierarchies

There is a great deal of agreement on what constitutes the construct underlying the assessment of phonological control. According to the CEFR (Council of Europe 2001:116), for instance, it includes 'skill in the perception and production of': the phonemes and allophones of the language; its distinctive features; syllable structure, consonant clusters, etc.; word stress; prosody; sentence stress and rhythm; intonation; and features of linking (strong and weak forms, assimilation, elision, etc.).

In terms of a pronunciation hierarchy, however, if we accept the construct outlined above, then we also need to decide whether – and to what extent – each feature is relevant at each level. The CEFR agrees (Council of Europe 2001:116), but only states that:

> users of the Framework may wish to consider and where appropriate state:
> * what new phonological skills are required of the learner;
> * what is the relative importance of sounds and prosody;
> * whether phonetic accuracy and fluency are an early learning objective or developed as a longer term objective.

Van den Doel's (2006) study is of great interest here as he found that errors involving word stress were considered to be among the most important, whereas much less significance was accorded to the avoidance of weak and contracted forms, and intonation errors were rated among the least important (surprising given that previous research had found that prosody tended to be perceived more negatively by NSs). There was a general tendency for phonemic errors to be ranked more highly than sub-phonemic. (Nevertheless, there were counter-examples where respondents' comments indicated that these errors were either stereotyped foreign pronunciations (such as the use of uvular-r) or realisations associated with stigmatised L1 varieties of English (such as schwa insertion in film, or substitutions of /ð/ and /θ/ by /t/ or /d/).

The centrality of word stress is supported by Field's (2005) study of NS and NNS groups of listeners who transcribed recorded material in which the variables of lexical stress and vowel quality were manipulated. He found that NS and NNS responded in very similar ways: for both groups, the loss of intelligibility depended to a large extent on the direction in which stress was shifted and whether changes in vowel quality were involved. When stress was shifted leftward, the impact was considerably less than when it was shifted to the right. (Interestingly, for Spanish speakers, the word stress shift and accompanying change in vowel quality actually enhanced intelligibility, presumably because this brought the stress patterns closer to their interlanguage variety.)

Equally, Bond and Small (1983, cited in Field (2005)) found that when NS were asked to repeat back speech containing pronunciation errors, they were three times more likely to detect and reproduce an example of misplaced word stress than one of a mispronounced phoneme.

Jenkins (2000, 2002) in her work on English as a lingua franca, derived from her analyses of NNS conversations, has also made recommendations based on the idea we emphasised earlier that a large proportion of the interactions in English take place between NNS. She proposes a lingua franca core of phonological features which are essential to maintain intelligibility among both NNS and NS. Interestingly, she argues that consonant sounds (except for /ð/ and /θ/ and dark 'l') are more important than vowels/diphthongs (except for vowel length contrasts); and she emphasises the importance of nuclear (tonic) stress (see also below, Hahn 2004). Most other areas of pronunciation are then designated non-core, and these include, in particular, weak forms and contractions.

Van den Doel's (2006) research is additionally interesting in that it also suggests that factors other than strictly phonological features need to be taken into account when attempting to establish pronunciation hierarchies. In addition, I would suggest, establishing a hierarchy of phonological elements for each proficiency level ought to be a reflection of research into areas like: which aspects of pronunciation are deemed to be more or less important (by whom? To a large extent this was answered above by van den Doel and Jenkins.); which aspects of pronunciation are deemed to be more or less irritating (by whom? We have seen that a considerable amount of work still needs to be done here.); which aspects of pronunciation have been shown to have an impact on intelligibility? (Again, we have shown that this is a more complex issue than is generally recognised); which aspects of pronunciation have been shown to be more or less difficult to acquire (and to what extent are these affected by the learner's L1?); which aspects of pronunciation have been shown to be acquired in one order rather than another (and to what extent are these affected by the learner's L1?). These last two points are crucial in deciding whether and to what extent we can make assessment grids generalisable across all or a broad range of languages.

Yet to my knowledge, there is no authoritative acquisition order for elements of pronunciation, although there has been work for individual languages reflecting learners' difficulties with pronouncing English (Swan and

Smith 2001). Hopefully, the work currently being undertaken under the English Profile Programme will be revealing in this respect.

What little we know, therefore, would appear to suggest that phonetic realisations and word stress should be among the first to be taught and mastered, whereas prosody, features of linking, rhythm and intonation are less important and can be mastered later. Indeed, the paucity of research related to pronunciation, and indeed the lack of fundamental principles relating to phonological phenomena makes me doubt the presence of intonation, in particular, at any but the very highest levels. Levis (2002), for example, found NS could distinguish meanings in only three of five intonation contours. Before learners are taught the patterns of English speech, researchers and teachers must ensure that the information they provide is accurate. This point also takes us back to the choice of variety of English: different varieties use different patterns for the same thing, and English is changing (see the widespread use among younger Britons of rising intonation in statements). If such is the case, how do we assess learners' proficiency?

On the other hand, Hahn (2004), in a study in which Korean accented mini-lectures (each identical except for the use of nuclear stress – tonic or sentence stress) were played to three groups of undergraduate college students found that the group who heard the lecture with the appropriate use of nuclear stress understood significantly more of the lecture and rated the speaker more favorably than the other groups.

An interesting ancillary question is to wonder whether there is a hierarchy reflected in the CEFR phonological control grid. A brief look at it clearly shows an overt hierarchy of phonological components which learners are expected to master as they progress in proficiency, and which we can summarise as follows in Table 2:

Table 2 The pronunciation hierarchy reflected in the CEFR phonological control grid

CEFR level	Descriptors
C2	The ability to use intonation and prominence correctly and to express fine nuances of meaning.
C1	The ability to use intonation and prominence correctly and to express fine nuances of meaning.
B2	Clear and natural use of intonation, stress, and sounds.
B1	Intelligible, although a foreign accent is sometimes detectable. Pronunciation errors may occasionally occur.
A2	Pronunciation is sufficiently intelligible, despite a strong accent. The speaker may sometimes have to repeat what they said.
A1	Intelligible with effort.

The grid seems to have got the place of intonation right, leaving it till the upper ranges. However, as shown by van den Doel (2006), the feature identified by native speakers as most important was word stress. Yet this only appears – perhaps, since the term can just as easily cover prominence – under 'stress' at B2. There is no other mention, unless it is also subsumed under 'pronunciation errors', in which case the term is far too vague. As was suggested in the previous section, the importance of word stress in terms of both 'irritation' and intelligibility would argue for it appearing explicitly and early.

The research indicates that intonation is less relevant to NNS and that even NS find other aspects of pronunciation to be more important. It is therefore right to find it in the upper levels. That this is the case is borne out by research indicating that NSs and NNSs do not grade NNS pronunciation according to the same criteria: the former tend to react to suprasegmentals, whereas the latter are more sensitive to segmental features (Anderson-Hseih and Koehler 1992, Johansson 1978:9–15, 123, van den Doel 2006). This finding may go some way to explaining the fact that Dutch high school students' judgements of the overall proficiency of Dutch speakers of English were found to depend more closely on how good their accents were thought to be (Meijer 2010).

In short, the following elements have been identified as key to intelligibility in NNS speech, be it with NS or other NNS: word stress and phonemes, with consonants being more important than vowels/diphthongs, and nuclear stress. One would therefore expect that they be taught earlier and more thoroughly than other components. Non-core elements include: weak forms, contractions, rhythm, prosody and, to a lesser extent, intonation.

Once it has been established which components of phonology should be included in a phonological control grid, however, they need to be realised as descriptors. It is to this that we turn in the next and final sections.

Does the grid satisfy the criteria for good descriptors?

The CEFR (Council of Europe 2001:205–207) requires five qualities from language proficiency descriptors. It argues that they need to be: (1) *positive*, to serve as learning objectives and not just means of assessment; (2) *definite*, i.e. avoid vagueness; (3) *clear*, i.e. that the meaning be transparent and the descriptor written in simple syntax; (4) *brief*, in our terms, when we would expect assessment to take place in real time; this is essentially because 'a descriptor which is longer than a two-clause sentence cannot realistically be referred to during the assessment process. Teachers consistently seem to prefer short descriptors' (2001: 207); and (5) *independent*, i.e., essentially, that each sub-criterion should have independent integrity; in other words that it 'could serve as an objective rather than having meaning only relative to the formulation of other descriptors on the scale' (2001:207).

There is little doubt that the grid meets its own objectives of being positive, definite, brief, and clear, at least in so far as it uses simple syntax. It is less obvious, however, that it be transparent and independent.

As we showed earlier, the literature on intelligibility offers no wholly robust definition other than that the learner's speech be understandable. Under the circumstances, it is hard to see what might distinguish between 'clear' and 'intelligible'. (Both are defined in the *Concise Oxford Dictionary* (Oxford University Press 1995) as being 'easy to understand' and each is given as a synonym of the other in *Roget's Thesaurus* (Collins Reference 1998)). To be intelligible, surely you need to be clear, and if you are clear, then surely you are intelligible. Nor does the research support the contention that accent be linked to intelligibility, or that it might be expected to disappear beyond B1; on the contrary.

Moreover, as we have seen, the evidence is strong that perceptions of clarity are linked to the listener's experience of dealing with NNS speech. Proposing that these terms can distinguish between levels is therefore unconvincing. For the same reasons, using 'effort' as a criterion of differentiation between levels – and more particularly that 'effort' should only be palpable at A1– seems to be fraught with difficulties.

There is also the issue of 'natural': can one seriously propose that a learner can progress beyond a pronunciation that is 'clear and natural'? How can you be better than 'natural'? Surely 'natural' implies a capacity to perform at the same level as that which is 'natural' in that language; i.e. at that of a NS. To suggest, therefore, that a learner has attained such a level at B2, seems, at best, unrealistic.

And finally, to what extent does the CEFR grid reflect the independence (if any) of the various phonological elements it itself uses to define phonological competence, i.e. phonemes and allophones; distinctive features; syllable structure, consonant clusters, etc.; word stress; prosody; sentence stress and rhythm; intonation; and features of linking? The grid would seem to group elements together. Until B1, no distinction is made: pronunciation is seen as a monolith, or as something whose elements cannot be distinguished until a certain level of proficiency is achieved. B2 introduces a threefold split between sounds, stress and intonation, but without splitting any of these elements into their constituent parts. C1 and C2 highlight the use of prominence and intonation, but again without identifying which elements are being emphasised, other than to 'express fine nuances of meaning'. This hardly allows us to assess the independence of the phonological elements. This lack of independent integrity among the sub-components in the CEFR grid for phonological control is clearly linked to the issue of pronunciation hierarchies discussed in the previous section.

In conclusion, although the grid meets some of its own criteria for good descriptors, problems remain with the restricted range of accent and 'effort', the use of the terms 'clear and natural' at B2, and the lack of clear differentiation between the various components of phonology as defined by the CEFR itself and leading to a lack of internal independent integrity of the items. Accent, as we have seen, cannot be restricted to the lower levels: the norm is that an easily identifiable accent will persist into C2. 'Effort', as we saw in section 2, is not a readily quantifiable measure and is as much dependent on listener as on speaker characteristics. And, it will be necessary to make better use of what we know about pronunciation hierarchies to establish, at worst, learning objectives at the different CEFR levels that we can then translate into descriptors for assessment.

In the next section we shall summarise our findings from the four sections of the article before going on to concrete proposals in the final section.

Summary

Accent is something which very few adults succeed in losing. Beyond any biological barriers that might exist to acquiring a native-like control of the phonological features of a foreign language, accent is too essential a marker of personal, social, ethnic or regional identity to be easily abandoned. Reference to accent in phonological control grids is therefore misplaced.

Although there is considerable intuitive agreement that accent impacts on intelligibility and that intelligibility is a key factor in assessing a speaker's ability to successfully communicate, there are considerable technical difficulties in defining it or in converting the intuitions into usable descriptors. This stems from two factors highlighted by the research: on the one hand, the fact that, counter-intuitively, neither accent nor intelligibility would appear to be necessarily linked to comprehensibility; and on the other, the degree of intelligibility is as much a question of the listener's familiarity with the speaker's oral production as with the speaker's actual speech.

This has two quite separate repercussions: (i) the need to train oral examiners to become familiar with unfamiliar accents; and (ii) the desperate need for further research into what renders speech more or less intelligible.

'Effort', 'strain', 'irritation', and, more positively, 'tolerance' have all been suggested as means of measuring intelligibility indirectly: the more unintelligible the speech, the greater effort the listener needs to make. Again, anyone who has worked extensively with Oral Examiners will know that such labels appeal intuitively because they reflect perceived realities. Unfortunately, defining or quantifying these terms is notoriously difficult. As we have already mentioned, listeners' perception of intelligibility or 'effort' are as much a function of their own experience with NNS and unfamiliar accents as they are of the speaker's actual phonological control. In both cases, moreover, it has been shown that perceived effort often results from the interaction with factors other than those which are purely phonological, including grammatical and lexical control, fluency, familiarity with the topic of discourse, context, cotext, situation of utterance and tiredness. Moreover, listeners can be irritated by productions which may or may not be deviant, but which violate socially accepted norms. That the degree of irritation can lead to more negative assessments of the speaker's performance than other aspects of their speech is significant when it comes to assessment. However, research in this area is mostly dated and deals rarely with speech. Further research would certainly help our understanding of the phenomenon.

Any mention of intelligibility or effort, therefore, needs to be accompanied by the extensive training of Oral Examiners to familiarise them with different varieties of NNS speech.

We also looked at pronunciation hierarchies; i.e. what do we know about either the order of acquisition of phonological features, or their importance in spoken production? Unfortunately, the answer to the first question is 'very little', and research here will not (yet) help us construct a phonological control grid. On the other hand, we do know more about the relative importance of different phonological features in terms of intelligibility. Before trying to use them in an assessment grid, however, we need to decide what target proficiency we are aiming at: NS-like or best NNS. The available evidence on the perseverance of accented production, together with the fact that some 75% of the English spoken takes place entirely in exchanges between NNS argues strongly for the latter. The question is open, however, as to what a definition of best NNS actually is.

The research on which phonological features are most – and least – useful for NNS to master is sometimes contradictory (especially on the relative importance of the suprasegmentals), but this is most often due to the failure to distinguish between the different constituents. What we do know emphasises the primary importance of word stress and phonemics, and the relative lack of importance attached to weak forms, contractions and suprasegmentals. On the other hand, it has been shown that nuclear sentence stress (prominence) is both important in comprehension of messages and teachable, both of which would argue for this also being included in a grid. Intonation, however, has been shown to be a highly complex phenomenon and one would expect it to appear late.

What is especially interesting in many of these findings is that there is little difference in judgements between NS and NNS listeners. Highlighting these findings in a phonological grid should therefore cover the other 25% of NS–NNS interactions. It is to the construction of such a grid that we turn in the final section.

Conclusion: towards a new phonological control grid

The discussion so far leads us to a conclusion which emphasises two essential axes in the development of any functional (and functioning) phonological control grid: on the one hand, and while awaiting more, much-needed research on the subject, a grid that reflects what is known about pronunciation, and on the other, the importance of the training and regular retraining of examiners so that they have sufficient experience of dealing with NNS accents to overcome the listener's bias against intelligibility brought about by unfamiliarity.

From the summary, it can be seen that certain elements need to be removed from the grid and others highlighted. Among the former are references to accent and 'effort'. There is also a strong case for removing intelligibility, but, given its predominance in the pedagogical literature, this may be premature. Among the latter are word stress, phonemic control and prominence; intonation also, perhaps, but only at the highest levels. There are good theoretical arguments for including such features as prosody and rhythm, but the available research does not yet allow us to identify where.

Thus, a preliminary grid can be outlined as follows, simplifying the technical terms for a non-technical audience of Oral Examiners. Hence, phonemics becomes 'sounds' and prominence 'sentence stress'. I have also preferred 'understood' to intelligible at lower levels.

This, in turn, needs to be checked against the CEFR global proficiency scale (see Table 3) to ensure that it would enable the learner to achieve these levels of communicative spoken competence (Council of Europe 2001:24).

The C2 requirements would appear to be more demanding than those proposed here. However, providing an equivalent phonological descriptor would align the phonological grid against the NS benchmark which we earlier eschewed. It may be for this reason that the original CEFR grid makes C1 the ceiling level. The C1 requirements are met by the proposed grid, as are those of B2. The B1 demands of the proposed grid are probably slightly higher than those required on the global scale. The possibility that the listener may need to ask for clarification is absent from the global scale at A2. We can either remove it from the proposed scale, or maintain it for potential situations which go beyond the direct exchange of information. The A1 scales agree.

On the whole, therefore, it seems sensible to leave the proposed descriptors as they are. However, they do need to be converted into a more user-friendly form. For ease of use, therefore, it could be bullet-pointed as in Table 4. Note that at B2 and above, four elements of assessment are suggested, whereas at B1 and below there are only three. It is this mix that should help an examiner convert a level into a grade. However, one essential question remains:

Table 3 Summary of the CEFR global proficiency scale: speaking only

CEFR level	Descriptors
C2	Can express him/herself spontaneously, very fluently and precisely, differentiating finer shades of meaning even in more complex situations.
C1	Can use language flexibly and effectively for social, academic and professional purposes. [. . .] Can express him/herself fluently and spontaneously.
B2	Can interact with a degree of fluency and spontaneity that makes regular interaction with native speakers quite possible without strain for either party.
B1	Can deal with most situations likely to arise whilst travelling in an area where the language is spoken.
A2	Can communicate in simple and routine tasks requiring a simple and direct exchange of information.
A1	Can interact in a simple way provided the other person talks slowly and clearly and is prepared to help.

Table 4 Proposed new phonological control grid descriptors: bullet-pointed for ease of use

CEFR level	Descriptors
C2	• Pronunciation is easily intelligible. • Mispronunciations are rare. • Sentence stress is used successfully most of the time. • Intonation is used successfully most of the time.
C1	• Pronunciation is easily intelligible. • Mispronunciations are rare. • Sentence stress is used successfully most of the time. • Intonation patterns are used but not always effectively.
B2	• Pronunciation is intelligible. • Mispronunciations occur but do not interfere with understanding. • Sentence stress is used but not always successfully. • Basic intonation patterns are common but not used successfully all the time.
B1	• Sufficient control of sounds to be intelligible. • Sufficient control of word stress to be intelligible. • Mispronunciations occur, but only occasionally interfere with understanding.
A2	• Sufficient command of sounds to be understood, but with some difficulty. • Sufficient command of word stress to be understood, but with some difficulty. • The interlocutor may need to ask for repetition or clarification.
A1	• Sufficient command of sounds to be understood, but not all of the time and with some difficulty. • Sufficient command of word stress to be understood, but not all of the time and with some difficulty. • The interlocutor will need to ask for repetition or clarification.

Table 5 Proposed new phonological control grid operational form to allow grading

Phonological control	A2		B1		B2
	1	2	3	4	5
Sounds	1. Not always understood.		1. Intelligible. 2. Mispronunciations occur which interfere with understanding.		1. Intelligible but mispronunciations do not interfere with understanding.
Word stress	1. Not always understood.		1. Intelligible. 2. Mispronunciations occur which interfere with understanding.		1. Intelligible but mispronunciations do not interfere with understanding.
Need for clarification	1. Yes. 2. No.				
Sentence stress and intonation					1. Sentence stress used not always successfully. 2. Intonation used not always successfully.

do these descriptors refer to outcomes; i.e. do they describe the end range of the level? If this is the case, identifying the descriptor as the end value of the range complicates grading, since, in educational settings, you cannot normally give a binary grade: has acquired/has not acquired. In situations where an actual grade is required, therefore, a grid like the following is suggested (seen in Table 5), which reflects a widespread educational reality where the theoretical class level is, for instance, B1, but where the actual range of levels is much wider. The grid could enable a teacher to give a mark out of 20 for pronunciation by multiplying the two horizontal criteria by the number of marks given vertically (from 1 for a pupil at the bottom of the A2 range to 5 for pupils achieving B2).

Thus, to obtain a grade of 20, a good pupil would get a mark out of 5 at a Level B2 for each of the four vertical components. He or she would get 17, say, if they mixed elements of B1 and B2.

In this article I have used the available research literature on pronunciation and terms commonly used in phonological descriptors to critically review the CEFR phonological control grid. In particular this has meant the removal of all reference to accent – accent is assumed to be present throughout the CEFR range – and 'effort'. Despite considerable misgivings, intelligibility has been maintained, but with the proviso that Oral Examiners need considerable exposure to, and marker training with, a variety of accents, with specific focus on developing the ability to understand unfamiliar accents and to be able to abstract away from factors which cause 'irritation'. The causes and real impact of this element, however, require further research.

It goes without saying that this is only a first step. A great deal of research still needs to be done on defining intelligibility, and on identifying at what stages in the learning process the different components of phonological competence can be actually acquired. It is to be hoped that the English Profile Programme will supply at least the beginnings of a response to this question.

References

Abercrombie, D (1956) Teaching pronunciation, in Abercrombie, D, *Problems and Principles: Studies in the Teaching of English as a Second Language*, London: Longman, 28–40.

Anderson-Hseih, J and Koehler, K (1988) The effect of foreign accent and speaking rate on native speaker comprehension, *Language Learning* 38 (4), 561–613.

Anderson-Hseih, J and Koehler, K (1992) The relationship between native speaker judgements of nonnative pronunciation and deviance in segmentals, prosody and syllable structure, *Language Learning* 38 (4), 561–613.

Bamgbose, A (1998) Torn between the norms: innovations in world Englishes, *World Englishes* 17, 1–14.

Bond, Z and Small, L H (1983) Voicing, vowel and stress mispronunciations in continuous speech, *Perception and Psychophysics* 34, 470–474.

Bresnahan, M J, Ohashi, R, Nebashi, R, Liu, W Y and Shearman, S M (2002) Attitudinal and affective response toward accented English, *Language and Communication* 22, 171–185.

Calloway, D R (1980) Accent and the evaluation of ESL oral proficiency, in Oller Jr., J W and Perkins, K (Eds) *Research in Language Testing*, Rowley, Massachusetts: Newbury House, 102–115.

Council of Europe (2001) *Common European Framework of Reference for Languages: Learning, Teaching, Assessment*, Cambridge: Cambridge University Press.

Cutler, A, Dahan, D and van Donselaar, W (1997) Prosody in the comprehension of spoken language: a review, *Language and Speech* 40, 141–201.

Cutler, A, Weber, A, Smits, R and Cooper, N (2004) Patterns of English phoneme confusions by native and non-native listeners, *Journal of the Acoustical Society of America* 116, 3,668–3,678.

Delamare, T (1996) The importance of interlanguage errors with respect to stereotyping by native speakers in their judgements of second language learners' performance, *System* 24, 279–297.

Derwing, T M and Munro, M J (1997) Accent, intelligibility, and comprehensibility: evidence from four Lls, *Studies in Second Language Acquisition* 19, 1–16.

Derwing, T M and Munro, M J (2005) Second language accent and pronunciation teaching: a research-based approach *TESOL Quarterly* 39 (3), 379–397.

Derwing, T M, Rossiter, M and Munro, M J (2002) Teaching native speakers to listen to foreign accented speech, *Journal of Multilingual and Multicultural Development* 23, 245–259.

Deterding, D (2005) Listening to Estuary English in Singapore, *TESOL Quarterly* 39 (3), 425–440.

Eisenstein, M (1983) Native reactions to non-native speech: a review of empirical research, *Studies in Second Language Acquisition* 5, 160–176.

Fayer, J M and Krasinski, E (1987) Native and nonnative judgements of intelligibility and irritation, *Language Learning* 37, 313–325.

Field, J (2005) Intelligibility and the listener: the role of lexical stress, *TESOL Quarterly* 39 (3), 399–423.

Flege, J E (1984) Factors affecting degree of perceived foreign accent in English sentences, *Journal of the Acoustical Society of America* 84, 70–79.

Flege, J E, Munro, M J and Mackay, I R A (1995) Factors affecting strength of perceived foreign accent in a second language, *Journal of the Acoustical Society of America* 97, 3,125–3,134.

Galloway, V B (1980) Perceptions of the communicative effects of errors in Spanish, *Modern Language Journal* 64, 428–453.

Garcia Lecumberri, M L and Gallardo del Puerto, F (2003) English FL sounds in school learners of different ages, in García Mayo, M P and García Lecumberri, M L (Eds) *Age and the Acquisition of English as a Foreign Language*, Clevedon: Multilingual Matters, 115–135.

Gass, S and Varonis, E M (1984) The effect of familiarity on the comprehensibility of nonnative speech, *Language Learning* 34, 65–89.

Gatbonton, E, Trofimovich, P and Magid, M (2005) Learners' ethnic group affiliation and L2 pronunciation accuracy: a Sociolinguistic Investigation, *TESOL Quarterly* 39 (3), 489–511.

Graddol, D (2006) *English Next*, London: the British Council.

Hahn, L D (2004) Primary stress and intelligibility: research to motivate the teaching of suprasegmentals, *TESOL Quarterly* 38, 201–223.

Horner, D (1987) The perception of error gravity by French native speakers, *Franco-British Studies* 3, 73–86.

Hughes, A and Lascaratou, C (1982) Competing criteria for error gravity, *ELT Journal* 36, 175–182.

Ioup, G, Boustagi, E, El Tigi, M and Moselle, M (1994) Re-examining the critical period hypothesis: a case study of successful adult SLA in a naturalistic environment, *Studies in Second Language Acquisition* 16, 73–98.

Jenkins, J (2000) *The Phonology of English as an International Language*, Oxford: Oxford University Press.

Jenkins, J (2002) A sociolinguistically-based, empirically-researched pronunciation syllabus for English as an international language, *Applied Linguistics* 23, 83–103.

Johansson, S (1978) *Studies in Error Gravity: Native Reactions to Errors Produced by Swedish Learners of English*, Gothenburg: Acta Universitatis Gothoburgensis.

Kachru, B (1986) *The Alchemy of English: The Spread, Functions, and Models of Non-native Englishes*, New York: Pergamon.

Koster, C J and Koet, T (1993) The evaluation of accent in the English of Dutchmen, *Language Learning* 43, 69–92.

Levis, J M (1999) The intonation and meaning of normal yes-no questions, *World Englishes* 18 (3), 373–380.

Levis, J M (2002) Reconsidering low-rising intonation in American English, *Applied Linguistics* 23, 56–82.

Levis, J M (2005) Changing Contexts and Shifting Paradigms in Pronunciation *TESOL Quarterly* 39 (3), 369–377.

Lippi-Green, R (1997) *English With an Accent: Language, Ideology and Discrimination in the United States*, New York: Routledge.

Ludwig, J (1982) Native speaker judgments of second-language learners' efforts at communication: a review, *Modern Language Journal* 66, 274–283.

Major, R C, Fitzmaurice, S F, Bunta, F and Balasubramanian, C (2002) The effects of nonnative accents on listening comprehension: implications for ESL assessment, *TESOL Quarterly* 36, 173–190.

Magnan, S S (1983) Age and sensitivity to gender in French, *Studies in Second Language Acquisition* 5, 194–212.

Meijer, A (2010) *If you're so smart, why do you sound so Dutch? Experiences of university lecturers teaching in English*, paper presented at the Amsterdam Conference on Pronuniciation, 2010.

Mey, J (1998) *Concise Encyclopedia of Pragmatics*, Oxford: Elsevier Science.

Milroy J and Milroy L (1985) *Authority in language: Investigating language prescription and standardization*, London: Routledge and Kegan Paul.

Moyer, A (2004) *Age, Accent and Experience in Second Language Acquisition*, Clevedon: Multilingual Matters.

Mugglestone, L (1995) *'Talking proper': The Rise of Accent as Social Symbol*, Oxford: Clarendon.

Munro, M J and Derwing, T M (1995) Foreign accent, comprehensibility, and intelligibility in the speech of second language learners, *Language Learning* 45, 73–97.

Munro, M J and Derwing, T M (1999) Foreign accent, comprehensibility and intelligibility in the speech of second language learners, *Language Learning* 49, 285–310.

Munro, M J, Derwing, T M and Morton, S L (2006) The mutual intelligibility of L2 speech, *Studies in Second Language Acquisition* 28, 111–131.

Pennington, M and Ellis, N (2000) Cantonese speakers' memory for English sentences with prosodic cues, *The Modern Language Journal* 84 (3), 372–389.

Piazza, L G (1980) French tolerance for grammatical errors made by Americans, *Modern Language Journal* 64, 422–427.

Rifkin, B and Roberts, F D (1995) Error gravity: a critical review of research design, *Language Learning* 45 (3), 511–537.

Ryan, E B (1983) Social psychological mechanisms underlying native speaker evaluations of non-native speech, *Studies in Second Language Acquisition* 5, 148–159.

Ryan, E B and Sebastian, R J (1980) The effects of speech style and social class background on social judgements of speakers, *British Journal of Social and Clinical Psychology* 19, 229–233.

Ryan, E B, Carranza, M A and Moffie, R W (1975) Mexican American reactions to accented English, in Berry, J W and Loaner, W J (Eds) *Applied cross-cultural psychology*, Amsterdam: Swets & Zeitlinger, 174–178.

Santos, T (1988) Professors' reactions to the academic writing of non-native speaking students, *TESOL Quarterly* 22, 69–90.

Schairer, K E (1992) Native speaker reaction to non-native speech, *Modern Language Journal* 76, 309–319.

Scheuer, S (2005) Why native speakers are (still) relevant, in Dziubalska-Kołaczyk, K and Przedlacka, J (Eds) (2005) *English Pronunciation Models*, Oxford: Peter Lang, 213–228.

Scovel, T (2000) A critical review of the critical period research, *Annual Review of Applied Linguistics* 20, 213–223.

Sheorey, R (1986) Error perceptions of native-speaking and non-native speaking teachers of ESL, *ELT Journal* 40, 306–312.

Smith, L E, and Bisazza, J A (1982) The comprehensibility of three varieties of English for college students in seven countries, *Language Learning* 32, 259–269.

Swan, M and Smith, B (2001) *Learner English*, Cambridge: Cambridge University Press.

Taylor, L and Galaczi, E (2011) Scoring validity, in Taylor L (Ed.) *Examining Speaking: Research and Practice in Assessing Second Language Speaking*, Studies in Language Testing volume 30, Cambridge: UCLES/Cambridge University Press, 171–233.

Thompson, Y (1991) Foreign accents revisited: The English pronunciation of Russian Immigrants, *Language Learning* 41 (2), 177–204.

Trask, R (1996) *A Dictionary of Phonetics and Phonology*, London: Routledge.

Trudgill, P (2005) Finding the speaker-listener equilibrium: segmental phonological models in EFL, in Dziubalska-Kołaczyk, K and Przedlacka, J (Eds) (2005) *English Pronunciation Models*, Oxford: Peter Lang, 213–228.

van den Doel, R (2006) *How Friendly are the Natives? An Evaluation of Native-speaker Judgements of Foreign-accented British and American English*, Utrecht: LOT.

Vann, R J, Meyer, D E and Lorenz, F O (1984) Error gravity: a study of faculty opinion of ESL errors, *TESOL Quarterly* 18, 427–440.

Wolfram, W and Schilling-Estes, N (1998) *American English: Dialects and Variation*, Language in Society 24, Oxford, Blackwell.

13 The empirical validity of the CEFR Fluency Scale: the A2 level description

Katrin Wisniewski

Technical University Dresden, Institute for Romance Studies, Germany

Abstract

Even if the Common European Framework of Reference for languages (CEFR) (Council of Europe 2001a) is in widespread use, there remains much work to do concerning the empirical validation of its scale system. It is unclear if it actually reflects the reality of learner language, and it is not empirically shown that the scales – being neither derived from a model of communicative language ability nor based on the analyses of empirical test language – describe language well enough to justify their use in language testing.

In this paper, the CEFR A2 level description for fluency is analysed with the aim to find evidence for its adequacy and usefulness for the description of empirical learner language (Italian and German, N=19). In a process of operationalization, 'scale variables' are derived from the descriptors which are used for various quantitative analyses.

Evidence is gathered from multiple validity-related perspectives: the A2 level descriptors must be relevant in that they mirror what speakers actually do. Furthermore, learner productions should be meaningfully captured with the descriptors. Another aspect regards the relationship of the scale to objective fluency measures. To guarantee practicality, then, raters should be able to implement the descriptors unambiguously.

Results show that the appearance of some aspects of the CEFR A2 fluency level description seems dependent on the task type and the target language. Convergence between the scale variables is rather weak and inconsistent, which makes it hard to plausibly describe learner productions with the scale variables. Further difficulties relate to construct validity as there are concepts in the scale which probably do not relate to fluency, but other aspects of second language (L2) competence. The ratings in this sample are shown to be related to, but not fully explained by the A2 fluency level description, thus leaving space for speculations about other motivations for the rating decisions.

Introduction

The Common European Framework of Reference for languages (CEFR) (Council of Europe 2001a) has become the most important reference document in all matters of language teaching, learning and assessment throughout Europe. The CEFR *scale system* has to be considered one of the very few methodologically sophisticated reference tools of its kind. Despite its enormous success and its overwhelming distribution, the CEFR has received much critical attention. Some have criticized the lack of theoretical coherence, others emphasized problems regarding empirical validity (Bausch 2003, Fulcher 2004, Hulstijn 2007, Hulstijn, Alderson and Schoonen 2010, Weir 2005). This contribution takes up the criticisms regarding the still missing evidence for the adequacy and the appropriateness of the CEFR scales for the description of empirical learner language. To date, it has not been demonstrated that the scales can capture authentic learner behaviour in a consistent and meaningful way.

In this exploratory case study, which is based on the analysis of empirical learner language, a cross-linguistic (Italian and German) multi-method design is adopted with the aim to analyse the relationship between the A2 fluency level description and the language learners produced in an oral examination (N=19). Fluency was chosen as it is one of the most common rating criteria in oral language tests, and it is believed to be something human raters agree upon relatively easily (Koponen and Riggenbach 2000, North 2000).

This study looks at learner language through the eyes of the (operationalized) CEFR Fluency Scale descriptors in order to find out how useful the scale is for describing language produced in an authentic testing situation. This approach does not aim at detecting 'criterial features' of pre-defined CEFR levels (Hawkins and Buttery 2010). On the contrary, in quite a critical perspective, the existence of the CEFR levels is not taken for granted here, but considered something empirical evidence has to be collected for. Thus, the test taker's production is attributed a central role.

It is believed that to be the basis for the development of fair and valid measurement instruments, the CEFR scale contents must 'match' learner productions in that they describe relevant linguistic features (Alderson 1991). Furthermore, level descriptions must not contain elements that hide theoretically or empirically contradictory assumptions about the construct. It should be possible to differentiate between speakers who fit a level description and others who don't sufficiently well. Furthermore, the descriptors have to prove their relevance for the construct of fluency. It is necessary for the CEFR scales which are often used as a rating tool to be understandable and useful for human raters. In addition, the more or less explicit claim of the CEFR scales to work comparably (if not equally) across (European) languages and tasks is to be an object of the analyses.

The problem of CEFR scale validity

There are a number of difficulties users encounter when they work with the CEFR scales. For example, they are fragmentary, mentioning single concepts on single scale levels only. Many descriptors are very vague, while others are subjective (e.g. Fluency Scale: C2, 'ease of expression'; B1+, 'relative ease') or self-referential (Fluency Scale: B2, 'Can interact with a degree of fluency . . .') (Council of Europe 2001a:129).

Many of these problems are connected with the methodology that was chosen for scale calibration in the so-called 'Swiss Project' (North 2000, Schneider and North 2000). In the sophisticated procedure, a considerable number of scales then used in very different assessment contexts and for differing purposes were the basis for the choice of the most useful descriptors for practitioners to come to reliable decisions. To put it in very simple terms, these scales were analysed, descriptors were improved, and the best ones were calibrated with the help of a multi-faceted Rasch model. The Fluency Scale, for example, is derived from 23 original scales (Schneider and North 2000), only one of which was developed in a data-driven way (Fulcher 1996).

The two main problems with this procedure are first, the CEFR scales are not derived from (or automatically compatible with) a model of foreign language ability, for which they have been described as being 'essentially theory free' (Brindley 1998:188, Fulcher 2003:112). Second, the scales are based exclusively on practitioners' (i.e. teachers') impressions. This is acknowledged by the CEFR authors themselves: 'If the framework of reference is objectively scaled with a measurement model, then that is an objective scaling of a subjective consensus . . . The most that can be said is that it maps that proficiency with objective scale values in terms of categories, perceptions and conventions which are shared by the group of raters concerned' (North 2000:71).

It certainly is reasonable to include expert knowledge. In the case of the CEFR scales, though, this happened not only at the expense of theoretical coherence, but it led to the exclusion of the learner's perspective as well. In the process of scaling the CEFR descriptors, no empirical language was analysed to check the validity of the CEFR scales with regard to learner varieties. As Alderson puts it, 'if descriptors are to be meaningful characterizations of ability, then they should be able to be related to actual performance' (1991:74). Even if the CEFR scales are not assessor-oriented (Alderson 1991), they tend to be used in a great variety of testing and teaching contexts without being changed much, as is shown by the rating grid used in the 'Swiss Project', for example, which can be found in the CEFR as 'Table 3' (Council of Europe 2001a:28–29).

While there is much criticism, there do not seem to be studies that look at the validity of the CEFR scales from an empirical perspective. The newer reference level description projects initiated by the Council of Europe (CoE) (e.g., English Profile Programme; *Profilo della lingua italiana*) are based on impressive amounts of empirical data. These projects, though, do not aim at scale validation, but at an *illustration* of the CEFR reference levels by finding 'criterial features' (asking how could we better characterize learner language if we took CEFR level validity for granted?). In this study, on the contrary, it is considered crucial to first find empirical evidence for the possibility of describing learner language in a meaningful way with the CEFR Fluency Scale (asking does the CEFR A2 level description for fluency describe what learners really do in terms of fluency?).

What is fluency?

Fluency is one of the most readily used rating criteria in language tests, and it is a feature of particular relevance in lay perceptions of someone's second language (L2) competence. Despite (or maybe because of) this, there is a noticeable heterogeneity in the conceptions of fluency (Koponen and Riggenbach 2000).

First of all, the importance attributed to the phenomenon is dependent on language *theory*. In theoretical accounts that sustain the separation between performance and competence (e.g. in generativist approaches), fluency tends to be completely ignored as a mere performance phenomenon (e.g. Chomsky 1995). In usage-based approaches, on the contrary, fluency receives considerably more attention (e.g. Tomasello 2000). As far as *models* are concerned, many researchers make use of Levelt's model of spoken language production (1989, 1999) or its adaptation to the bilingual speaker by De Bot (1992). Recently, Segalowitz (2010) has developed a very comprehensive multi-factorial model of fluency as an open dynamic complex system. On a more *operational* level, there is a broad variety of features that are considered crucial for determining fluency; while some researchers define it in a very broad way, nearly equating it with L2 competence itself (Fillmore 1979), others focus on temporal aspects of spoken language, describing fluency as 'smoothness of speech' or 'low order fluency' (Lennon 2000; see Koponen and Riggenbach 2000 for an overview). Still others emphasize the influence of lexical knowledge on fluency (Hilton 2008).

There are doubtlessly some aspects to be considered no matter which approach towards fluency is being adopted. First of all, it is of major importance to keep the *perspectivity of the phenomenon* in mind: the smoothness of cognitive processes (cognitive fluency) is something different from observable fluency characteristics of produced speech (utterance fluency) which again might differ considerably from what a hearer actually notices as (dis-)fluent speech (perceived fluency; Lennon 1990, Segalowitz 2010). Secondly, L2 fluency is strictly dependent on first language (L1) fluency; it has been shown that there are only a very small number of measures that can capture specific characteristics of the former (De Jong, Schoonen and Hulstijn 2009, Derwing, Munro, Thomson and Rossiter 2009, Segalowitz 2010). Furthermore, a speaker's use of communication strategies plays an important role (Dörnyei and Kormos 1998, Kormos 2006). As early as 1983, Pawley and Syder have emphasized the meaning of formulaic sequences (see also Wray 2002) for the smooth production of speech: if a speaker can make use of pre-fabricated chunks he has memorized as a whole (automatized/ proceduralized), there is no need to process language in a 'rule-based' way, as Skehan called it (1996). Using chunks thus means (not only) saving time for a (not only) L2 speaker. Further issues that might affect someone's fluency are task characteristics, e.g. their difficulty, the planning time available, and the familiarity with the task (Foster and Skehan 1996, Mehnert 1998, Ortega 1999, Skehan 2001, 2004, Tavakoli and Skehan 2005).

The study

Aims: aspects of scale validity

This study aims at finding evidence for the adequacy and usefulness of the CEFR Fluency Scale (2001a:129) for the description of empirical learner language produced in a language test with the target languages Italian and German.

The study consists of two conceptually different analytic blocks. The first one forms the heart of the study, directly addressing the relationship of learner language with the CEFR scale without involving human ratings. This approach was adopted in order to avoid argumentative circularity as it is not possible to validate aspects of a CEFR scale if one makes use of ratings that come in between the scale and the learner productions and are themselves based on the CEFR. It is certainly interesting and important, but it cannot be considered sufficient to report rating reliability when one aims at validating a rating scale (Connor-Linton 1995, Lumley 2005, Weigle 1994). In this first and central unit of analysis, aspects of *utterance fluency* will be confronted with operationalized descriptors of the A2 fluency level description.

It is believed that the CEFR scale descriptors ought to mirror what learners really do in order to justify the often high-stake decisions that are taken on this basis: if the CEFR descriptors are not relevant in this sense, they cannot be useful for assessment purposes, and fairness and validity will be compromised (*criterion of relevance*).

Then, it will be important to find out if there really are learners whose L2 productions could be described in a reasonable way by the operationalized CEFR descriptors (see the Method section). In this approach, scale content is taken very seriously: learner language is analysed strictly through the eyes of the CEFR level description (*criterion of convergence*).

If there really are learners whose productions 'match' the A2 fluency descriptors, these ought to be clearly distinguishable from other test candidates' productions. The scale level description is only useful if it helps to differentiate the targeted speakers from others. This does not necessarily imply a relationship to second language acquisition progression, of course, which the CEFR avoids claiming (Council of Europe 2001a, North 2000, Schneider and North 2000). But if there are speakers one could describe as being typical A2 performers (criterion of convergence), they should be different from other speakers in terms of the CEFR scale descriptors (*criterion of distance*).

The Fluency Scale (2001a:129) is very fragmentary and is not derived from a model-based (or even theory-based) construct, as mentioned above. That is why a possible relationship of the scale variables (see the Method section) to more objective (or at least more common) fluency measures is still to be searched for (*construct criterion*).

While it is crucial to directly relate performances to the CEFR scale, a rating scale does not come without someone who uses it. For the CEFR Fluency Scale to be useful, it should also be possible for human raters to implement the descriptors (and nothing else) in an unambiguous way when assessing performances (*criterion of practicality*). This cannot be taken for granted as research has shown that there is great variability in how human raters judge performances even if they are trained and use analytic scales (see Eckes 2008, Lumley 2005, Wisniewski 2010). In the second analytic block, therefore, the focus is on *perceived fluency*.

Data

In this study 19 language tests for Italian (N=10) and German (N=9) as L2 carried out in the KOLIPSI project were analysed. In KOLIPSI (initiated by the European Academy of Bolzano (EURAC)) roughly 1,500 pupils were tested for their writing skills, and a smaller sample (N=100) of pupils took part in an oral examination as well. In addition, questionnaires for pupils, teachers, and parents were administered in order to find out possible non-linguistic factors of influence on the pupils' L2 competences in multi-lingual South Tyrol (Abel, Vettori and Wisniewski forthcoming). Candidates for the present study were chosen carefully; they form a very homogeneous group of 17–18-year-old pupils with a number of variables controlled (e.g. L2 experience, languages of schooling, amount of L2 contact, school marks). Their productions were rated in a double-blind procedure with very high inter-rater agreement (see the Method section).

The oral examination consisted of a short warm-up conversation with the interviewer followed by a monologue production task in which test takers were asked to describe one out of four pictures. In the second (dialogic) exercise the candidates discussed one of two topics ('horoscopes' or 'reality TV shows').

Throughout test construction, administration and evaluation, intensive quality management was carried through and international quality guidelines and codes of practice were adhered to (Abel et al forthcoming, Association of Language Testers in Europe 1994, Bachman and Palmer 1996, Council of Europe 2009, Fulcher 2003).

Method

The test productions chosen for this study were transcribed following CHAT transcription conventions in the editor ELAN developed by the Max Planck Institute in Nijmegen.

To analyse aspects of scale validity, the descriptors had to be operationalized, i.e. they needed to be brought into a measurable form. This was a rather complex and somewhat speculative procedure, because the fragmentary character of the CEFR scales means that single characteristics might be found only on single CEFR levels. Therefore, it is not possible to formulate hypotheses about the value of specific features throughout the scale (e.g. moving up from A1 to C2), but each single level is supposed to have its own characteristics. Furthermore, there are some subjective and very vague expressions in the descriptors which can hardly be translated into something objectively measurable.

This can be illustrated by a closer look at the process of operationalization of the A2 level description for fluency which says: 'Can construct phrases on familiar topics with sufficient ease to handle short exchanges despite very noticeable hesitation and false starts' (Council of Europe 2001a:129). First of all, there are some problems regarding translation: 'phrases' is translated with 'espressioni' in Italian (Council of Europe 2002), but in German with 'Redewendungen' (Council of Europe 2001b) which is something different from a simple phrase in that it suggests a higher level of idiomaticity. Another translation difficulty resides in the choice of the German 'häufig' (meaning 'frequent') for the originally English term 'noticeable'; referring to pause phenomena, noticeable pausing does not only imply the number, but also the length of pauses. Thus, translations lead to somewhat different possible interpretations of the scale descriptors. For the analyses in this study, therefore, the English original was referred to in the case of doubt. Some formulations had to be excluded for their subjectivity (e.g. 'sufficient ease').

The remaining operationalizable aspects of the A2 level descriptions which could be termed 'scale variables' regard the extent of pausing, the complexity of the utterances ('phrases') and the number of false starts. The scale variables are:

- mean length of pauses (in seconds)
- number of pauses per minute speaking time
- number of clauses per AS-unit (Foster, Tonkyn and Wigglesworth 2000)
- number of false starts per minute speaking time.

Transcripts were coded in the multi-layer standoff annotation format provided by ELAN. Transcriptions were not only coded according to CEFR scale features, but also with regard to a considerable number of research-based measures for the analysis of construct validity. The coding was partially done double-blind to check inter-coder reliability. The inter-coder reliability for hesitation phenomena (C=.917 and κ = .697) and strategies (C=.899 and κ =.773) was satisfactory.

For the analyses, several statistical procedures were applied (e.g., cluster analysis, discriminant analysis) which will be described in the Results section.

Results

Relevance of the A2 fluency level description

For the scale variables to be of *relevance*, a necessary condition is that they be observable in empirical learner language. This refers mainly to the presence of pauses and false starts for the A2 fluency level. Simple descriptive statistics show that there is no lack of pauses, however, but it is hard to observe false starts, especially in the monologue task: 12 out of 19 learners do not produce any false start in this exercise (dialogue task: 6), while none utters more than two (dialogue task: maximum 5). This probably has to do with the fact that without the threat of being interrupted by the interviewer and with a convenient amount of planning time allowed, candidates plan their utterances more thoroughly. Therefore, it cannot be assumed that reference to the number of false starts can help assess someone's fluency across types of tasks.

Convergence and distance: Is there something like 'A2 fluency'?

In order to discover if the scale variables convey a coherent picture of fluency on the A2 level, correlations among them were calculated. The analysis showed that correlations are generally weak. Only two were significant (p<.05), i.e. the correlation between false starts and the mean length of pauses for German (only task 2, Pearson's R =−.796) and the correlation between the utterance complexity and the number of pauses for German (only task 1, Pearson's R=−.772). As was to be expected, correlations were always positive between the number and the length of pauses, but on the other hand there were inverse correlations between tasks (i.e. positive for one, negative for the other task) and also between languages.

We would expect CEFR scale variables of one level description to be related to each other, and that should be the case independently of the target language or the task type. As the sample size in this study is very small generalizsations are difficult to make, but the findings here seem to indicate rather weak and inconsistent relationships between the scale variables.

To find out if there really is something like an 'A2 fluency' (*criterion of convergence*), i.e. if someone's production could be described reasonably with scale variables only, in a second step, cluster analyses were carried out. The aim of these cluster analyses was to group together candidates who behaved in a similar way with regard to the scale variables, maximizing their distance to others. Candidates who would best fit the A2 fluency description are searched for. Hierarchical cluster analyses (Ward method) were followed by non-hierarchical procedures (k-means). The analyses were carried out separately for the target languages.

The clustering is much easier in the first task than in the second. Not only are the clusters completely homogeneous from a statistical viewpoint ($F<1$, variance inside the clusters is constantly lower than the variance between the clusters) but also for both Italian and German, it is possible to find speakers who actually produce utterances that are not very complex while they make frequent long pauses (false starts were excluded because they were too low in number, see above). The clustering seems also plausible from a scale content-based view.

The same is not true in the second exercise: even if statistical homogeneity is complete ($F<1$), the results are not very plausible with regard to the scale content. For both languages, false starts do not occur in the way predicted by the scale; the candidates who make many and also long pauses have a lower number of false starts. In Italian, the ones who pause often also have more complex utterances, which again does not correspond to the A2 level description.

The cluster analyses helped to detect structure in the data. In order to check the statistical plausibility of these cluster solutions, in a second step discriminant analyses were carried through. With the help of these, it is possible to analyse how much variance is unaccounted for if scale variables are used to distinguish between the cluster solutions. The discriminant analyses can help to understand, in other words, how important scale variables (as compared to other, unknown factors of influence) are for the discrimination between speakers clustered as 'A2' and other speakers.

Results show that the variance can be significantly reduced ($p<.05$) for both languages and both tasks if analysed separately (see Table 1; in task 1, 'false starts' were excluded). It is important to keep in mind that the discriminant analyses can only show the strength of the cluster solutions in terms of their statistical quality, whereas in respect of contents, the incoherence commented upon is not resolved with this procedure.

Table 1 Results of discriminant analyses of cluster solutions

	Task 1 (monologue)	Task 2 (dialogue)
ITA	$\Lambda = .204$, p=.016	$\Lambda = .199$, p = .004
GER	$\Lambda = .093$, p=.005	$\Lambda = .267$, p = .003

The results of these analyses which regard the *convergence and distance criteria* of scale validity show that the A2 level description actually does describe something real, although there are some serious problems. Above all, they confirm the above-mentioned suspicion about including false starts in the level description. Not only are false starts a rather rare phenomenon – less fluent speakers (i.e. speakers who could otherwise easily be identified as 'A2' in terms of fluency) obviously cannot be said to produce more false starts. It might well be partly a matter of personal conversational preference: the ones who pause often without producing false starts might be oriented towards accuracy rather than towards a well-flowing conversation (Robinson 2001, Skehan 2001).

The fact that it is not possible to meaningfully conduct these analyses across languages and tasks points at the difficulty of generalizing the scale level description. The Fluency Scale is found in chapter 5 of the CEFR (Council of Europe 2001a:129) (see also North 2000, Schneider and North 2000), so it is meant to be useful for the description of aspects of learners' L2 communicative competence independently of the task type. Furthermore, the CEFR claims to be useful for all (European) languages. Findings indicate, though, that the scale contents might be of different importance in different languages.

Does the A2 level description really measure fluency?

In this part of the study, further evidence for convergent validity was searched for. While the results of the previous section focus on the scale variables themselves, here the aim was to examine the relationship of the scale with objective fluency measures. Before presenting the results of these analyses conducted in order to examine the explanatory power of the A2 level description as an indicator of fluency (and nothing else), some preliminary remarks are necessary.

First of all, with regard to the scale variable 'number of pauses per minute speaking time' it is important to keep in mind that there is no linear relationship between the number of pauses a speaker makes and fluency, as many studies have shown (e.g. Towell, Hawkins and Bazergui 1996). Pausing is a multi-causal phenomenon, and a very complex one (see for example Fulcher 1996). Furthermore, none of the scale variables are L2 specific (Derwing et al 2009); this is to say that they presumably cannot distinguish between a speaker's fluency in her native language and the same phenomenon in an L2. Thirdly, complexity and fluency should possibly be considered as two separate constructs, as suggested by studies about the relationship between complexity, accuracy, and fluency (Ellis and Barkhuizen 2005, Robinson 2001, Skehan 2001). This would mean that while the 'false starts' variable leads to an empirical coherence problem, the complexity aspect might *a priori* not belong to the fluency construct.

For the analysis of the relationship of the A2 Fluency Scale variables with fluency as a (heterogeneous) construct, first of all correlations between the former and a considerable number of fluency measures were calculated (Ejzenberg 2000, Iwashita, McNamara and Elder 2001, Kormos and Dénes 2004, Lennon 1990, Rohde 1985, Segalowitz 2010, Towell et al 1996). Among these there were general time-related measures like the mean length of runs (number of syllables per second in stretches of speech between pauses >.250ms), the speech rate (syllables/minute, pauses included) and the articulation rate (syllables per minute, pauses excluded), some measures regarding the amount of speaking in time like the phonation–time ratio (speaking time divided by task duration [minus interviewer's speaking time] in per cent), measures that capture the position of pauses (at clause boundaries or inside phrases), measures that regard breakdown fluency (abandoning a message or giving up after searching for an expression), measures regarding the frequency of long pauses (>2 seconds) and some statistics about hesitation phenomena like filled pauses, self-repair, phonetic lengthenings of word endings, repetitions, reformulations and others. The last group of measures regarded strategies like switching into the L1, circumlocutions, foreignizing, or asking for help (Dörnyei and Scott 1997).

Results show a clear difference between scale variables: the number and the mean length of pauses not surprisingly correlate significantly (p<.05) with many time-related measures of fluency. The most consistent correlations (significant for each of the two languages and also across languages) regard the phonation–time ratio, the mean length of runs and the number of pauses longer than 2 seconds (per syllable) a speaker makes (see Table 2). None of the scale variables seems to be connected with the speed of speech, as there are no correlations whatsoever for articulation rate (number of syllables/time spent speaking in seconds).

Table 2 Correlations of scale variables with time-related measures of fluency

		phonation–time ratio	speech rate	mean length of runs	long pauses/ syllable
T1	pauses/minute	−0.795		−0.906	.766
	mean length of pauses	−0.631	−0.680		.905
	complexity				
	false starts				
T2	pauses/minute	−0.741		−0.928	
	mean length of pauses	−0.614			.833
	complexity				
	false starts				

The results also show that the time-related scale variables (number of pauses/minute and mean length of pauses) correlate only with a very small number of measures that do not target temporal aspects of fluency. Most of these correlations hold only for either Italian or German (exceptions: mean length of pauses and message abandonment in task 2, R=.467; mean length of pauses and the strategy of switching into the L2 in task 1, R=.525), while none are consistent across tasks.

Table 2 also shows that the other two scale variables, the complexity and the number of false starts, do not correlate with any of the temporal fluency measures. This result alone would not automatically render these variables problematic, as of course there are many aspects playing a role in fluency. Yet if the other aspects of fluency are taken into account, there are still no consistent correlations, none valid across tasks, and there is not even one that holds across both languages.

Summing up the outcomes of the correlation analyses, it turned out that only two of the four scale variables consistently measured aspects of fluency (number and mean length of pauses); with very few exceptions, these correlations were very high only for temporal aspects of fluency. The complexity of utterances and the number of false starts do not correlate with any fluency measures regarding strategies, hesitation phenomena, breakdown phenomena or temporal aspects across languages or tasks, though there are single correlations to be found. So far, these results indicate that the A2 level description, when operationalized as was done here, might measure something that has been termed 'low order fluency' which can be exhaustively described with time-related measures (Kormos and Dénes 2004, Lennon 2000).

To further explore the relationship between the A2 level description and a possible construct of fluency, T-tests were carried through. The aim was to check the plausibility of the cluster solutions. The same variables as for the correlation analyses were used to find out if there were significant differences between the 'A2 clusters' and the other clusters in terms of fluency measures.

Findings show that the amount of time spent speaking as expressed by the phonation–time ratio, the mean length of runs and the number of long pauses are the most powerful measures (p<.05, see Table 3).

Table 3 t-tests; p<.05 for measures of fluency and A2 scale variables

	Task 1 (monologue)	Task 2 (dialogue)
ITA	phonation–time ratio (p=.04) filled pauses (p=.048)	phonation–time ratio (p=.011) mean length of runs (p=.002) long pauses (p=.047) speech rate (p=.002) boundary pauses (p=.017)
GER	phonation–time ratio (p=.042) mean length of runs (p=.029) long pauses (p=.045) speech rate (p=.001)	phonation–time ratio (p=.001) mean length of runs (p=.003) long pauses (p=.003)

This reinforces the results of the correlational study: the strongest link between the operationalized A2 description and the objective measures applied pertains to temporal aspects of fluency.

Practicality: How do raters implement the A2 level description?

The following analyses address the practicality criterion of the A2 level description validity. To be a useful basis for assessing learners' fluency, the scale must not only fit real learner productions and be in line with a coherent fluency construct. It is also very important that practitioners/raters be able to 'translate' scale content into their decisions. Let us suppose that the 'A2 clusters' – as objectively and directly derived from the CEFR scale as possible – really correspond well to the A2 level description. How do ratings relate to these clusters?

The tests used for this study were rated by at least two raters. Each rater assessed each test twice with the help of a rating grid very similar to Table 3 of the CEFR (Council of Europe 2001a:28–29); the Fluency Scale content was not changed, but re-structured in a more assessor-oriented way (Alderson 1991). For this sample the productions with the highest agreement between ratings were used (Italian: task 1 Cronbach's α =.933, task 2: α =.954, N = 10. German: task 1 α =.964, task 2: α = 923, N = 9). In addition, a questionnaire was developed in order to find out decision-leading features of the productions and characteristics of the scale(s) that seemed most important to the raters (Wisniewski 2010). Raters were trained in a one-day workshop, regular follow-up meetings were held, and all recommendations of the publication *Relating Language Examinations to the Common European Framework of Reference for Languages: Learning, Teaching, Assessment Manual Preliminary Pilot Version* (Council of Europe 2009) were followed. Table 4 shows that many productions that were objectively clustered as 'A2' were also rated as such.

For Italian, task 1 ratings are not very much in line with the 'A2 cluster' – the only candidate rated A2 is not to be found in the cluster, although there is another speaker rated B2 that could be described well with A2 scale characteristics.

Why is the candidate who was rated A2 not in the target cluster? Possibly, the raters relied on additional information for their decision. A closer look at this speaker shows that she has an extremely high percentage of phrase-internal pauses (40%) which tend to be considered as disfluent – this might have influenced the raters' decisions to consider this speaker only an A2 even if she did not make many pauses and speaks in a rather complex way. In the same setting, i.e. first task Italian, there is one speaker who was rated B2 while at the same time he would have to be considered much more dis-fluent

Table 4 Ratings and candidates clustered as 'A2'

	Clustered candidates	Rating	Mean of ratings
ITA, T1	1	B1	2.5
	2	B1	2.67
	3	B1	3
	4	B2	3.75
ITA, T2	1	A2	2
	2	A2	2
	3	B1	2.75
	4	B1	3
GER, T1	1	A2	2
	2	A2	2
	3	A2	2.25
	4	B1	3
GER, T2	1	A2	2
	2	A2	2.25
	3	A2	2.25
	4	B1	3

in terms of the A2 scale variables. This candidate has a very low 'breakdown fluency' as compared to the other speakers, and he manages to keep going rather smoothly (high mean length of runs); these factors might constitute an explanation for the strongly differing rating.

In the other 'settings', the ratings and the cluster solutions fit quite well together, with a general tendency of the clusters being somewhat too 'wide': they do include all speakers rated A2, but regularly also learners who were thought to be a little better than that (B1). This is probably caused by the statistical procedures applied.

Though this looks encouraging, literature on variability of rating behaviour tells us that very often raters construct idiosyncratic models of L2 competence, basing their decisions on subjective theories especially when problems with the measurement instrument occur (Arras 2009, 2010, Eckes 2008, Milanovic, Saville and Shuhong 1996, Wisniewski 2010). In other words, it is very possible that the ratings are in accordance with the objective clusters while at the same time based on aspects of L2 fluency that are not in the scale.

To find out how much variance between the candidates rated A2 and the other speakers the scale variables alone can account for, a stepwise discriminant analysis was carried through (see Table 5). The procedure shows that the scale variables can reduce the variance in a significant way, but there remains a considerable amount of roughly 40% of unexplained variance. Scale variables are not very helpful to explain the difference between the speakers that were rated A2 and the others for the first task and the Italian language. The most important variable for the raters was the number of pauses per minute (all settings).

Table 5 Wilks' Lambda for scale variables

	Task 1 (monologue)	Task 2 (dialogue)
ITA	$\Lambda = .880, p = .841$	$\Lambda = .394, p = .008$
GER	$\Lambda = .413, p = .016*$	$\Lambda = .400, p = .017$

Obviously, there were factors of influence on the raters' decisions that are not defined by the A2 level. To discover these, a second stepwise discriminant analysis was conducted (see Table 6). All uncorrelated variables used for the construct-related part were integrated.

Table 6 Wilks' Lambda for objective fluency measures

	Task 1 (monologue)	Task 2 (dialogue)
ITA	pauses in phrases [$\Lambda = .484, p = .019$]	pauses at boundaries [$\Lambda = .293, p = .002$]
GER	long pauses [$\Lambda = .410, p = .016$] deadends [$\Lambda = .165, p = .004$] repetitions [$\Lambda = .061, p = .004$] pauses in phrases [$\Lambda = .016, p = .001$]	long pauses [$\Lambda = .285, p = .004$]

Even after the discriminant analysis a rather high amount of variance for the monologue task in Italian remains unexplained, while the concept of the pause position helps to reduce this to roughly 48%. The concept of the position of pauses seems to have played a role for the ratings as well as the number of long pauses (only in German).

Factors influencing rating decisions vary between tasks and languages. Though not in the centre of the analyses, a tentative solution to aspects raters might have had on their minds when assessing the performances can be offered. Only a different research design would allow the further exploration of the raters' behaviour, but this is not part of the research question addressed in this contribution. Subjective theories might have had an impact on the ratings as well as something that is neither to be found in the A2 level description nor captured by the fluency measures used in the analyses and that might or might not be related to fluency.

Conclusion

The CEFR scales are made for practitioners, and it would have been completely unrealistic to wait for the dissolving of all theoretical disputes before the implementation of the scales (Jones and Saville 2009). On the other hand, in the last years we could observe a willingness to accept a certain reification of the CEFR scale system – the validity of which has not yet been shown in a sufficient way – despite the CEFR authors' definition of the *Framework* as an open document that is to be considered a work in progress (Council of Europe 2001a:8).

Even if some aspects of the A2 level description in this study turned out to be rather problematic, a constructive approach is being adopted, and concrete if cautious suggestions about possible solutions will be offered. Before doing that, it is necessary to emphasize that generalizations from a sample as small as the one used here are very problematic. Results should therefore be interpreted with caution.

First of all, in various steps of the analysis, the 'false starts' have turned out to be a problematic scale description feature in the sample. Not only is their appearance task-dependent, but the inclusion of this phenomenon as indicative of a relatively low level of fluency might be misleading even from a construct perspective. The 'false starts' variable is also the main factor to inhibit a plausible and coherent clustering of candidates in terms of the scale variables (even if the complexity variable also causes trouble here).

Furthermore, the evidence for *convergence* among the four scale variables is very weak, as suggested by low and partly even contradictory correlations. Thirdly, a detailed analysis of the relationship between what is in the A2 level description and common objective measures of fluency revealed that two of the scale variables probably do not have very much to do with fluency (complexity and false starts), as there are only sporadic correlations to be found, none of which is valid for each language separately *and* across them. Given that research suggests complexity to be something different from fluency, it might be necessary to rethink the descriptor formulation ('phrases'). Another reason to do that is the poor translation which here can lead to considerable misunderstandings of the scale.

What remains in the A2 level description if 'false starts' and 'complexity' are left out is a pure temporal characterization of fluency. In principle there is no problem about that, of course, but it might be beneficial to reconsider the construct of fluency that one intends to integrate in the CEFR or to at least define it in the text of the document, as there is no information on the meaning and characteristics of fluency to be found there.

Another constant difficulty regards the poor generalizability across different tasks and languages. In contrast to the scales to be found in chapter 4 of the CEFR (Council of Europe 2001a:43–100) which relate to concrete 'communicate activities', the chapter 5 (Council of Europe 2001a:101–130) scales (where fluency is found) rather implicitly claim to work not only across languages, but also across different tasks.

The results regarding scale *practicality* suggest that while ratings (perceived fluency) do have to do a lot with the 'objective' clustering, the raters' decisions do not seem to be based exclusively on the CEFR scales, leaving very much space for speculation about the possible decisive factors for the ratings. This is probably not exclusively due to the wording of the scale, as rating variability even among trained raters is a well-known phenomenon.

Something worth reconsideration concerns the gap between the information in the CEFR text and the contents of the CEFR Fluency Scale. All the users only learn that fluency is a 'generic qualitative factor which determines the functional success' (Council of Europe 2001a:128). There is no information about any of the characteristics of fluency. This is probably due to the fact that while in the CEFR text or 'descriptive scheme' a competence model is suggested, the same is not true for the scale descriptors. As North (2000) notes, 'relating proficiency categories that are meaningful for teachers and assessors to a competence model has been, to say the least, difficult' (2000:53). Thus, much room is left for contradictions between the scale(s) and the CEFR text which compromizes the coherence of the CEFR (fluency) approach as a whole.

Further studies with larger samples and for more target languages are needed to confirm these conclusions. Another constraint of this study resides in the fact that nothing is known about the candidates' L1 fluency. Anyhow, this corresponds to realistic assessment situations where very often we do not know the candidate's fluency in the L1. In a larger research project, more levels (B1 and B2) and constructs (vocabulary range and accuracy) are being analysed for the same sample and with the same procedure. Again, it would be preferable to cover the whole CEFR scale and the whole range of competence features in order to find out more about the empirical validity of the CEFR scale system.

References

Abel, A, Vettori, C and Wisniewski, K (forthcoming) *Die Südtiroler SchülerInnen und die Zweitsprache: eine linguistische und sozialpsychologische Untersuchung*, Bolzano: Eurac.

Alderson, C J (1991) Bands and scores, in Alderson, C J and North, B (Eds) *Language Testing in the 1990s*, London: British Council/Macmillan, 71–86.

Arras, U (2009) What's on a rater's mind? Die Erforschung von Beurteilungsstrategien und ihre Bewusstmachung durch Schulungsmaß nahmen als Voraussetzungen für die Testvalidität, *Zeitschrift für Angewandte Linguistik* 50, 33–45.

Arras, U (2010) Subjektive Theorien als Faktor bei der Beurteilung fremdsprachlicher Kompetenzen, in Berndt, A and Kleppin, K (Eds), *Sprachlehrforschung: Theorie und Empirie – Festschrift für Rüdiger Grotjahn*, Frankfurt: Lang, 169–179.

Association of Language Testers in Europe (1994) *The ALTE Code of Practice*, available online: wwwalteorg/cop/indexphp

Bachman, L F and Palmer, A (1996) *Language Testing in Practice*, New York: Oxford University Press.

Bausch, K R (Ed.) (2003) *Der Gemeinsame Europäische Referenzrahmen für*

Sprachen in der Diskussion Arbeitspapiere der 22 Frühjahrskonferenz zur Erforschung des Fremdsprachenunterrichts, Tübingen: Narr.

Brindley, G (1998) Describing language development? Rating Scales and SLA, in Bachman, L F and Cohen, A (Eds) *Interfaces Between Second Language Acquisition and Language Testing Research*, Cambridge: Cambridge University Press, 112–140.

Chomsky, N (1995) *The Minimalist Program*, Cambridge: MIT Press.

Connor-Linton, J (1995) Looking behind the curtain: what do L2 composition ratings really mean? *TESOL Quarterly* 29 (4), 762–765.

Council of Europe (2001a) *Common European Framework of Reference for Languages: learning, teaching, assessment*, Cambridge: Cambridge University Press.

Council of Europe (2001b) *Gemeinsamer europäischer Referenzrahmen für Sprachen: lernen, lehren, beurteilen*, Berlin ua: Langenscheidt.

Council of Europe (2002) *Quadro comune europeo di riferimento per le lingue: apprendimento, insegnamento, valutazione*, La Nuova Italia: Oxford.

Council of Europe (2009) *Relating Language Examinations to the Common European Framework of Reference for Languages: Learning, Teaching, Assessment Manual Preliminary Pilot Version*, retrieved 10 August 2011 from www.coe.int/lang

De Bot, K (1992) A bilingual production model: Levelt's 'speaking' model, *Applied Linguistics* 13, 1–24.

De Jong, N H, Schoonen, R and Hulstijn, J (2009) *Fluency in L2 is related to fluency in L1*, paper presented at the Seventh International Symposium on Bilingualism (ISB7), Utrecht, The Netherlands.

Derwing, T M, Munro, M J, Thomson, RI and Rossiter, M J (2009) The relationship between L1 fluency and L2 fluency development, *Studies in Second Language Acquisition* 31, 533–557.

Dörnyei, Z and Kormos, J (1998) Problem-solving mechanisms in L2 communication: a psycholinguistic perspective, *Studies in Second Language Acquisition* 20, 349–385.

Dörnyei, Z and Scott M L (1997) Communication Strategies in a Second Language: Definitions and Taxonomies, *Language Learning* 47 (1) 173–210.

Eckes, T (2008) Rater types in writing performance assessments: a classification approach to rater variability, *Language Testing* 25 (2), 155–185.

Ejzenberg, R (2000) The juggling act of oral fluency: a psycho-sociolinguistic metaphor, in Riggenbach H (Ed.) *Perspectives on Fluency*, Ann Arbor: University of Michigan Press, 287–314.

Ellis, R and Barkhuizen, G (2005) *Analysing Learner Language*, Oxford: Oxford University Press.

English Profile Programme, available online: http://www.englishprofile.org/

Fillmore, C (1979) On fluency, in Fillmore, C, Kempler, D and Wang, W (Eds) *Individual Differences in Language Ability and Language Behaviour*, New York: Academic Press, 85–101.

Foster, P and Skehan, P (1996) The influence of planning and task type on second language performance, *Studies in Second Language Acquisition* 18 (3), 299–323.

Foster, P, Tonkyn, A and Wigglesworth, G (2000) Measuring spoken language: a unit for all reasons, *Applied Linguistics* 21 (3), 354–375.

Fulcher, G (1996) Does thick description lead to smart tests? A data-based approach to rating scale construction, *Language Testing* 13 (2) 208–238.

Fulcher, G (2003) *Testing Second Language Speaking*, London: Longman/ Pearson Education.

Fulcher, G (2004) Deluded by artifices? The Common European Framework and harmonization, *Language Assessment Quarterly* 1 (4), 253–266.

Hawkins, J A and Buttery, P (2010) Criterial features in learner corpora: theory and illustrations, *English Profile Journal* 1 (1), 1–23.

Hilton, H (2008) The link between vocabulary knowledge and L2 fluency, *Language Learning Journal* 36 (2), 153–166.

Hulstijn, J H (2007) The shaky ground beneath the CEFR: Quantitative and qualitative dimensions of language proficiency, *The Modern Language Journal* 91, 663–667.

Hulstijn, J, Alderson, J C and Schoonen, R (2010) Developmental stages in second-language acquisition and levels of second-language proficiency: are there links between them?, in Bartning, I, Martin, M and Vedder, I (Eds) *Communicative Proficiency and Linguistic development: Intersections Between SLA and Language Testing Research*, available online: eurosla.org/monographs/EM01/EM01home.html

Iwashita, N, McNamara, T and Elder, C (2001) Can we predict task difficulty in an oral proficiency test? Exploring the potential of an information-processing approach to task design, *Language Learning* 51, 401–436.

Jones, N and Saville, N (2009) Scales and frameworks, in Spolsky, B and Hult, F M (Eds) *The Handbook of Educational Linguistics*, Oxford: Oxford University Press, 495–509.

Koponen, M and Riggenbach, H (2000) Overview: varying perspectives on fluency, in Riggenbach H (Ed.) *Perspectives on Fluency*, Ann Arbor: University of Michigan Press, 5–24.

Kormos, J (2006) *Speech Production and Second Language Acquisition*, Mahwah: Erlbaum.

Kormos, J and Dénes, M (2004) Exploring measures and perceptions of fluency in the speech of second language learners, *System* 32, 146–164.

Lennon, P (1990) Investigating fluency in EFL: a quantitative approach, *Language Learning* 40, 387–417.

Lennon, P (2000) The lexical element in spoken second language fluency, in Riggenbach H (Ed.) *Perspectives on Fluency*, Ann Arbor: University of Michigan Press, 25–42.

Levelt, W (1989) *Speaking. From Intention to Articulation*, Cambridge: MIT.

Levelt, W (1999) Producing spoken language: a blueprint of the speaker, in Brown, C and Hagoort, P (Eds) *The neurocognition of language*, Oxford: Oxford University Press, 83–122.

Lumley, T (2005) *Assessing Second Language Writing: The Rater's Perspective*, Frankfurt: Lang.

Mehnert, U (1998) The effects of different lengths of time for planning on second language performance, *Studies in Second Language Acquisition* 20 (1), 83–106.

Milanovic, M, Saville, N and Shuhong, S (1996) A study of the decision-making behavior of composition markers, in Milanovic, M and Saville, N (Eds) *Performance Testing, Cognition and Assessment*, Cambridge: Cambridge University Press, 92–114.

North, B (2000) *The Development of a Common Framework Scale of Language Proficiency*, Oxford: Peter Lang.

Ortega, L (1999) Planning and focus on form in L2 oral performance, *Studies in Second Language Acquisition* 21 (1), 109–148.

Pawley, A and Syder, F H (1983) Two puzzles for linguistic theory: nativelike selection and nativelike fluency, in Richards, J C and Schmidt, R W (Eds) *Language and Communication*, London: Longman, 191–226.

Profilo della lingua italiana, available online: www.lanuovaitalia.it/profilo_ lingua_italiana/origini.html

Robinson, P (2001) Task complexity, task difficulty, and task production: exploring interactions in a componential framework, *Applied Linguistics* 22 (1), 27–57.

Rohde, L (1985) Compensatory fluency: a study of spoken English produced by four Danish learners, in Glahn, E and Holmen, A (Eds) *Learner Discourse*, Copenhagen: University of Copenhagen, 43–69.

Schneider, G and North, B (2000) *Fremdsprachen können – was heißt das? Skalen zur Beschreibung, Beurteilung und Selbsteinschätzung der fremdsprachlichen Kommunikationsfähigkeit*, Chur, Zürich: Rüegger.

Segalowitz, N (2010) *Cognitive Bases of Second Language Fluency*, London: Routledge.

Skehan, P (1996) A framework for the implementation of task-based instruction, *Applied Linguistics* 17, 38–62.

Skehan, P (2001) Tasks and language performance assessment, in Bygate, M, Skehan, P and Swain, M (Eds) *Researching Pedagogic Tasks, Second Language Learning, Teaching and Testing*, Harlow: Longman, 167–185.

Skehan, P (2004) *A Cognitive Approach to Second Language Learning*, Oxford: Oxford University Press.

Tavakoli, P and Skehan, P (2005) Strategic planning, task structure, and performance testing, in Ellis, R (Ed.) *Planning and Task Performance in a Second Language*, Amsterdam: John Benjamins, 239–273.

Tomasello, M (2000) First steps towards a usage-based theory of language acquisition, *Cognitive Linguistics* 11 (1/2), 61–82.

Towell, R, Hawkins, R and Bazergui, N (1996) The development of fluency in advanced learners of French, *Applied Linguistics* 17 (1), 84–119.

Weigle, S C (1994) Effects of training on raters of ESL compositions, *Language Testing* 11 (2), 85–106.

Weir, C (2005) Limitations of the Common European Framework for developing comparable examinations and tests, *Language Testing* 22 (3), 281–300.

Wisniewski, K (2010) Bewertervariabilität im Umgang mit GeRS-Skalen. Ein- und Aussichten aus einem Sprachtestprojekt, *Deutsch als Fremdsprache* 3, 143–150.

Wray, A (2002) *Formulaic Language and the Lexicon*, Cambridge: Cambridge University Press.

14 Rating scale design: a comparative study of two analytic rating scales in a task-based test

Bart Deygers, Koen Van Gorp, Lucia Luyten and Sien Joos

Katholieke Universiteit Leuven, Belgium

Abstract

The Certificaat Nederlands als Vreemde Taal (CNaVT) or 'Certificate of Dutch as a Foreign Language', develops a suite of five domain-related task-based language tests, one of which is the test of Dutch for Academic Purposes. To ensure the representativeness of the task and the rating scale, the CNaVT is in the process of reshaping its rating scales.

The aim of this study was to develop and validate a new polytomous rating scale which incorporates both the Common European Framework of Reference for languages (CEFR) (Council of Europe 2001) and the opinions of subject specialists. In the research design both the existing dichotomous and the newly developed polytomous scales were used by four novice raters who each rated 125 written and spoken performances on the test of Dutch for Academic Purposes. The data emerging from the rating process was analyzed both qualitatively (semi-structured focus groups were conducted with the raters after the rating process) and quantitatively. Whereas the quantitative analysis indicates that the dichotomous scale is more reliable, the qualitative data offers a slightly different perspective, favouring the polytomous scale.

Rating scale development: general issues

The reliability and validity of different rating scale types have been the focus of linguistic research since the 1980s (see Barkaoui 2010 for an overview). In a more recent study Lumley (2002:268) stresses the 'somewhat limited validity' of rating scales because of their 'inability to describe texts adequately'. The idea that any formalized description of language will be unable to fully grasp all the subtleties of a real-life performance is also shared by Fulcher, Davidson and Kemp (2010), who subdivide the authors' rating scales according to their construction process. The authors distinguish between measurement-driven rating scales and performance-driven scales. Measurement-driven scales are descriptions of linguistic performance that have been composed by language experts. Typically, measurement-driven rating scales are not based on real-life performances and since their abstract level descriptors may be distant from actual performance, these rating scales may lose any direct relationship with real performance. According to Fulcher et al (2010:7):

> This [measurement-driven] approach to scale design is primarily iden-
> tified with the creation of the Common European Framework of
> Reference [. . .]. Although the scale is empirically derived, it is not based
> on performance data, as there is no reference to the performance of
> learners or test takers on specific tasks, or even perceptions of the value
> of performances.

Performance-driven rating scales, on the other hand, are constructed by closely analyzing and describing real-life performances, but may suffer from descriptional complexity (Fulcher et al 2010).

Rating scales can be subdivided according to the construction process, but categorisation can also be led by the way a scale yields a score, which can be holistic or analytic. In the former approach, raters judge a performance as a whole, whereas the latter compels raters to take into account separate features of language, such as grammar, vocabulary and structure (Alderson, Clapham and Wall 1995). In previous studies analytic scales have often proven to be more reliable than holistic ones (Barkaoui and Knouzi 2011, Knoch 2009, Weigle 2002) and to offer richer diagnostic information for second language (L2) learners. Holistic scales, on the other hand have shown to be more authentic and quicker to use than their analytic counterparts (Knoch 2009, Weigle 2002).

To date, the effects of employing a holistic or an analytic rating scale have been researched with mixed results (Barkaoui 2010), but ultimately, it is not the rating scale but the user of the scale, the rater, who has the final say (Lumley 2002). Naturally, the descriptors' complexity and their level of abstraction will influence the quality of the judgments (Alderson et al 1995, Fulcher et al 2010), but it is the rater who interprets the wording in the scale and who must maintain consistency of interpretation throughout the rating process. In order to enhance the reliability of the judgement, rater training is an effective tool (Lumley 2002, Shohamy, Gordon and Kraemer 1992, Weigle 1994) as it can influence future raters' behaviour and their interpretation of the criteria.

Combining a concern for rating scale type and rater expertise, Barkaoui (2010) studied the effect of using one type of scale together with both novice and experienced raters. Because of the way they are organized and subdivided, analytic scales were found to result in less conflicting decisions than holistic scales. Especially when performances are judged by novice raters, analytic scales are more reliable than holistic ones, since they increase self-consistency and focus the attention on the criteria at hand. Barkaoui notes that the type of rating scale steers the rater's judgement, implying that the type of scale directly influences the validity and reliability of the test.

In the study at hand both rating scales force the rater to make a number of smaller judgements based on a series of criteria and both rating scales are analytic rather than holistic. In the dichotomous scale, which is currently used by the Certificaat Nederlands als Vreemde Taal (CNaVT) or 'Certificate of Dutch as a Foreign Language', the rater is asked to judge a performance according to a series of criteria that are scored in a binary way. Polytomous scales, on the other hand, are not binary and share their architecture with band descriptors, similar to those found in the Common European Framework of Reference for languages (CEFR) (Council of Europe 2001) scales. As such, dichotomous rating scales force the rater to make a series of pass/fail decisions, whereas polytomous scales allow for more scoring options.

Context and general aims of the study

Since language testing is a practice that makes claims about real-life language ability based on performances which have often been gathered in artificial settings, the CNaVT has purposefully moved away from indirect testing towards a direct, task-based approach (Ellis 2003, Gysen and Van Avermaet 2005). In order to minimize the gap between test performance and real-life ability, the CNaVT assesses whether a candidate can perform a real-life task representing an external criterion. As such, it has adopted the Task-Based Language Assessment paradigm (Van Gorp and Deygers in press) and it links in with Bachman's Can Do typology of language tests (Bachman 2011).

The CNaVT offers a suite of five profile-based tests which fit three domains: societal, professional and educational. The distinction between a profile-based test and a domain-based test is the scope and specificity of its context. Within one domain (i.e. the academic domain), the CNaVT distinguishes two profiles (i.e. Dutch for Academic Purposes – Students and Dutch for Academic Purposes – Teachers). The domains and profiles of the CNaVT were established in 2000 after an extensive needs analysis (Van Avermaet and Gysen 2006), based on the principles of Long (2005). This needs analysis determined to what end and in which contexts the CNaVT target audience uses Dutch. The profiles that emerged from the needs analysis encompassed a number of task types that could be considered representative within a specific domain.

One of the tests in the CNaVT suite, the test of Dutch for Academic Purposes (Students), determines a candidate's ability to use and adapt language according to situational requirements (Davies 2001:143) within an academic context. A college student, for example, should be able to send formal and informal emails, participate meaningfully in class, be a skilled writer and so on. Similar to the other profiles, the test of Dutch for Academic Purposes has been constructed with target language use, not language level as first priority. The test was therefore not specifically constructed for a given language level. Rather, it addresses tasks that are considered representative for the target language use. After test construction, an expert panel linked the test of Dutch for Academic Purposes (Students) to the B2 level of the CEFR. Since the 2008 CEFR alignment, the academic profile has been routinely checked and kept up to date, both in terms of content and in terms of cut-off score, which is monitored by means of a Rasch analysis after each test administration.

The pool of raters employed by the CNaVT may change from one test administration to the next, so novice raters are a common occurrence. Since novice raters appear to judge more reliably when using analytic scales and since analytic scales offer richer feedback data for L2 learners, the CNaVT to date uses a dichotomous analytic rating scale. This scale gives the rater a series of criteria to score either 1 or 0. The pass/fail logic shows that the rating scale was not designed to identify various language levels within one test but to make the distinction between test takers that are able to function in the target setting and those that are not.

When administering authentic task-based language tests, subject specialists may assist in determining task types and refining tasks that have been developed (Douglas 2000, 2001). In 2009, the subject specialists of the test of Dutch for Academic Purposes addressed an issue concerning the validity of the profile's dichotomous rating scale. According to them, the rating scales occasionally caused performances to be judged differently in the test than they would in real life. More concretely, the subject specialists assumed the scales might induce rater leniency when judging formal aspects of language. This concern, raised by the subject specialists, instigated a redevelopment of the existing dichotomous rating scale as well as the development of a new polytomous scale. This new scale was to address the subject specialists' concerns, but also those of the end users, who wished for the rating scale to be linked to the CEFR more transparently. Following the redevelopment, a study was conducted to compare the reliability and the validity of the polytomous and dichotomous scales employed.

Research questions

The primary reason for conducting the study was to scrutinize the dichotomous rating scale of the test of Dutch for Academic Purposes (Students) and compare it to an alternative – polytomous – scale that addressed the needs and concerns raised by the CNaVT's subject specialists. These specialists had stressed the need for a rating scale that took into account their 'tacitly known criteria' (Jacoby and McNamara 1999:224) and operationalized formal aspects of academic language. Additionally, the end users of the test of Dutch for Academic purposes had requested a clearer link between the rating scales and the CEFR.

Before the rating scales could be compared, a new rating scale had to be composed. This new rating scale was to meet the needs of the subject specialists and was to consider the relevant CEFR descriptors as reference points. Depending on the task, different CEFR scales were taken into account. Most widely used were the scales for productive activities and strategies (Council of Europe 2001:57–65), receptive activities and strategies (Council of Europe 2001:65–72), interactive activities and strategies (Council of Europe 2001:73–84) and linguistic competences (Council of Europe 2001:108–118). The challenge here was to create valid and reliable rating scales that did not suffer from the 'descriptional inadequacy' sometimes associated with measurement-driven scales (Fulcher et al 2010).

The second goal of the study was research-based and included two research questions, which were investigated both qualitatively and quantitatively:

1. Is the new polytomous rating scale as reliable as the existing dichotomous scale?
2. Is the new polytomous rating scale as valid as the existing dichotomous scale?

Development of the CNaVT scale

Subject specialist involvement

In the present study the subject specialists' involvement in the rating scale development process consisted of two phases. In the first phase, subject specialists participated in an online questionnaire and in focus groups so as to generate rating criteria. In a second phase, the subject specialists offered feedback on the draft of the rating scale.

In order to determine the criteria to be used in a rating scale for a test of Dutch for Academic Purposes, two focus groups of domain experts were held, and an online questionnaire was administered to domain experts. The first focus group consisted of seven respondents, the second of six. Each focus group was attended by professionals employed within the academic target domain. All of them were regularly involved with student instruction and assessment of performances. Table 1 shows the professional background of the participants.

Table 1 Participants' professional background

Position	N
Language tutor in preparatory classes of Dutch for Academic Purposes	4
Academic staff (languages)	2
Academic staff (other subjects than languages)	3
Researcher	4

First, the focus group participants were asked to scrutinize the tasks of the test of Dutch for Academic purposes. By doing so, they got a thorough grasp of the task content, which allowed them to make more meaningful comments concerning the tasks' rating scales. After this, the respondents were asked to voice the criteria they would employ when judging a performance on a note-taking task (audio input), a summarizing task (written input) and an argumentative speaking task (visual schematized input). The purpose of this was to tap into the subject specialists' real-life indigenous criteria (Jacoby and McNamara 1999). These are criteria that are often intuitively but not always consciously known by a group of people functioning within a specific field. A group of doctors, for example, might agree that a certain academic presentation is insufficient, although they may not immediately know why this is the case.

Having identified their criteria based on the task only, the subject specialists then received student performances on the same tasks. The subject specialists were invited to refine or adjust their criteria. The criteria, which had been heavily content-focused after the first 'blind' run, now became more focused on form.

Since each focus group served as a check of the other, the results from both focus groups were compared. Both focus groups showed an identical trend towards focus on form. A third source of information concerning intuitive rating criteria by academic staff was an online questionnaire comprising 178 subject specialists (see Table 2 for distribution according to profession).

Offering similar questions as the ones asked in the focus groups, the purpose of the questionnaire was to check the generalisability of the conclusions drawn from the focus group. The data of the questionnaire largely replicates the criteria that had been identified in the focus group. The tendency to focus as heavily on form as on content was sustained. Table 3 lists the criteria that had been identified by the respondents for the three task types.

After a first draft rating scale had been composed based on the criteria that had been identified by the focus group members and by the respondents of the questionnaire, the focus groups were invited again to offer feedback on the redesigned rating scale. Because subject specialists were consulted on

Table 2 Distribution of questionnaire respondents according to profession

Position	N
Language tutor in preparatory classes of Dutch for Academic Purposes	34
Academic teaching position (languages)	41
Academic teaching position (other subjects than languages)	50
Researcher	57
Other	6

Table 3 Respondents' criteria for three task types

Note-taking task	Summarising task	Argumentative task
Skill: Integrated writing	Skill: Integrated writing	Skill: Integrated speaking
Expected performance: notes	Expected performance: written summary	Expected performance: argumentative speaking
Audio input	Written input	Schematised input

Criteria	%	Criteria	%	Criteria	%
Content (accuracy)	27.8	Structure	16.9	Structure	18.5
Grammar	11.3	Content (accuracy)	15	Content (accuracy)	16.1
Structure	10.7	Summarizing skills	13.4	Grammar	10.6
Spelling	4.8	Grammar	13.1	Argumentation	9.6
Vocabulary	4.4	Style	6.7	Pronunciation and fluency	7.5

several occasions throughout its composition, the polytomous scale went through an iterative and dialogic development process.

The subject specialist input led to a number of important changes in the rating scale design, the most important one being the increase of the relative importance of formal aspects of language. The polytomous scale takes into account similar formal criteria as the dichotomous scale but their relative weight in comparison with content is greater than in the dichotomous scale. As such, the polytomous scale focuses on getting the message across appropriately in an academic context.

The CEFR and the development of the polytomous scale

Whereas the original dichotomous rating scale presents two options for each criterion, the polytomous scale offers four, ranging from unsatisfactory to excellent. The B2-target level occupies the third level in the scale (Table 4).

The criteria for each task were based on the parameters that were identified by the subject specialists who attended the focus groups and those who filled out the online questionnaire. For the argumentative speaking task, the following criteria were operationalized: register (a criterion that was stressed by

Table 4 Polytomous rating scale layout

Target level +1	C1
Target level	B2
Target level −1	B1
Target level −2	A2

the focus group members, but not by the respondents of the questionnaire), content, argumentation, structure and cohesion, vocabulary, grammar and pronunciation and fluency. The wording for each level was adapted from the CEFR according to the requirements of the task. Even though the CEFR 'was not designed specifically for test specifications and language testing contexts' (North 2004 in Papageorgiou 2010:273), it remained a crucial point of reference during the rating scale composition process.

After the scale had been composed and approved by the subject specialists, it was trialled in two pilot studies (see below). First, four raters used the scales to rate a total of 250 performances. After this, they were invited to offer feedback on the usability and interpretability of the scale. The raters reported vagueness of the level descriptors as the main problem when using the polytomous scale. Based on the feedback, the scales were reformulated and the scales were piloted again with a second team of novice raters. During rater training, the raters were given the chance to think about alternative wording to make the scales more easily interpretable.

The rewritings focused on simplifying the sometimes overly abstract CEFR-based descriptors and on marking the borders between levels more clearly. Vagueness was avoided as much as possible by replacing such terms as 'adequate' and 'nearly perfect' with more readily interpretable alternatives that can be grouped into four categories: concrete insertions, subjective insertions, discriminating insertions and exemplary additions.

Concrete insertions are additions to the CEFR descriptors that serve to give the rater a better foothold. One such insertion in the criterion argumentation is 'the argumentation is unconvincing and cannot be maintained without the interlocutor's help' (target level -2). A subjective insertion takes on the perspective of the novice rater when listening to concrete performances: 'the structure is consistent and perfectly aligned with the content. 'The audience has no problem following the presentation' (Target level) / 'Every now and then, the audience may lose track of the presentation' (Target level -1). Discriminating additions serve to make the borders between two performance levels more clear. In one instance, the wording changed from 'The performance is largely understandable' to 'The performance is only partly understandable' (Target level -1). Exemplary additions are concrete grammatical markers of ability. They are syntactic structures that should be mastered at a given level and increase rater confidence because they are

Table 5 Dichotomous scale for 'Structure and Cohesion'

	1	0
The text is well structured. It has a clear organization and uses cohesive devices		

Table 6 Polytomous scale for 'Structure and Cohesion'

Structure and cohesion	
The presentation's structure is consistent and perfectly aligned with the content. The audience has no problem following the presentation. *The presentation shows a varied and correct use of cohesive devices and structuring strategies. The presentation's structure supports its content.*	A
The presentation is coherent and for the most part logically structured. Every now and then, the audience may lose track of the presentation. *Cohesive devices are mostly used correctly. Largely coherent even though some parts of the communication are not always effective.*	B
The presentation shows 'jumpiness' and/or is occasionally lacking in cohesion. *Cohesive devices are limited to common linear linking words. Due to lack or misuse of cohesive devices, the internal cohesion may be insufficient.*	C
The presentation hardly shows structure or cohesion. *Fragmentary or inadequately structured to such an extent that the intended message is difficult to understand.*	D

concretely observable: 'in complex structures grammatical flaws may occur even though common grammatical structures (e.g. conjugation, inversion, and subclause) are mostly correct.' / 'The performance shows mastery of basic grammatical patterns (simple clauses, main word order).'

By the time of its completion, the polytomous rating scale had received input from the CEFR, from subject specialists, from raters and from test developers. This resulted in a four-point scale which focuses on getting the message across adequately in an academic context. Tables 5 and 6 show the descriptors for rating 'Structure and Cohesion' in a presentation task in the dichotomous scale (Table 5) and the polytomous scale (Table 6).

Piloting of the polytomous CNaVT scale

Research design

As discussed above, the rating scale research served to gather information on the usability of the scales. Additionally, the research compared the dichotomous scale to the polytomous scale in terms of reliability and validity.

The quantitative data-collecting process involved four novice raters who were paired. For both rating scales, the raters received a two-day training session, which has been shown to positively influence rater reliability (Knoch 2009). After the training, the raters received a *decision booklet*, which enlisted a number of rating pitfalls and showed how to go about them as a rater (Knoch 2009).

Each pair of raters rated the same task performances (N = 250). The first pair of raters rated 125 task performances (75 integrated writing tasks and 50 integrated speaking tasks, clustered in 25 tests) first with the polytomous scale and subsequently with the dichotomous one. In order to monitor the influence of one rating scale on the next, the second dyad took the reverse order and started out by rating their 125 performances with the dichotomous scale first and the polytomous one next. All performances used in this research had been preselected so as to guarantee varying levels of linguistic ability, geographical dispersion and a wide array of first languages (L1s).

Since the raters ware paired throughout the rating process and each pair judged the same 125 performances twice, the main variable was the rating scale used. Each scale was used to rate a total of 250 task performances and was used by two pairs of raters in two different sequences. The data gathered is the result of four different setups: rater A/B polytomous, rater A/B dichotomous, rater C/D dichotomous and rater C/D polytomous (Table 7).

Table 7 Quantitative research design

Raters A/B Performance 1–125	Raters C/D Performance 126–250
Polytomous	Dichotomous
↓	↓
Dichotomous	Polytomous

For each different setup, the same data analysis occurred, i.e. a Pearson correlation to determine the strength of the connection between the ratings of each rater dyad. Secondly, Cohen's Kappa was calculated, so as to illustrate the measure of agreement between the raters (Council of Europe 2009).

After the rating procedure was concluded, the qualitative data was gathered. The first four raters were invited to a semi-structured focus group to discuss the usability and interpretability of the rating scales and the level descriptors. Based on their comments the rating scales were adjusted and a second group of five raters was called upon. During their training, this second group of raters helped to adjust level descriptors that were considered multi-interpretable. After this, they rated additional performances (N = 76) and took part in a new semi-structured focus group which served to determine whether the changes to the level descriptors had increased the rating scale's usability.

Findings

Quantitative findings

Raters A and B rated their 125 tasks with the polytomous scale first, yielding a medium positive relationship ($r = .47$, $p < .01$), a fair inter-rater agreement ($K = .30$) and an α of .76. When considering the data closely, little correspondence between the judgements can be found around the cut-off score. Rater A agrees with 40 of the 65 performances that rater B considers adequate. Of the 25 remaining performances, rater A considers 10 to be insufficient and 15 to be excellent. There is no real consistency to be found in the cases of non-agreement. The unsatisfactory correlation and the low measure of rater agreement may indicate that the polytomous scale allows for multi-interpretability.

Next, raters A and B rerated the 125 tasks using the dichotomous model. Here, the correlation shows a strong positive relationship ($r = .82$, $p < .001$), the rater agreement is moderate ($K = .59$) and the reliability has increased slightly ($\alpha = .77$). Around the cut-off, there is more agreement between the raters than there was when using the polytomous scale. When closely examining the 90 performances that rater A considers sufficient, there are 25 performances considered less than adequate by rater B. Rater B's severity is consistent however, so the pattern around the cut-off score is less random than it was when using the polytomous scale.

So as to get a grip on the effect of the order in which the scales were used, raters C and D took the reverse order from raters A and B and began rating their performances with the dichotomous scale first and the polytomous one next. The ratings of raters C and D, rating different performances than raters A and B, also showed a strong positive relationship when using the dichotomous scale ($r = .94$, $p < .001$) as well as an increased reliability ($\alpha = .86$). The inter-rater agreement was moderate ($K = .54$), but after removing 13 items out of 56 items with a negative Item-Total Correlation (no negative ITCs were observed for raters A and B when using the polytomous scale), the inter-rater agreement was perfect ($K = 1$).

The data emerging from the polytomous rating process of raters C and D shows a lower correlation than was the case when using the dichotomous scale ($r = .79$, $p < .001$). The measure of rater agreement is fair ($K = .35$) and the reliability remained unchanged ($\alpha = .86$). When examining the items clustered around the cut off score however, little to no agreement is to be found.

Qualitative findings

Contrary to what Knoch (2008) found in her study, the raters who took part in this study showed no tendency to neglect the outer bands of the polytomous scale. During the focus group after the rating process, they did report other effects from using a polytomous scale. One such effect was the subjective judgement of time spent rating exams. The four novice raters involved in the focus group reported having spent at least 50% more time when using the polytomous scale. In reality, using polytomous scales to rate performances indeed took longer, but the difference was roughly 20%. All respondents claimed that the polytomous scale required them to consider the performance and the descriptors more thoroughly, required them to reflect more. The continual conscious reflection could be what caused the respondents to believe the polytomous scale to be disproportionately time-consuming. If anything, this implies that the respondents did not discard the outer bands of the scale but rather took them into account for every performance.

When asked about their preferred scale in general and for their preferred scale to assess written performances, all raters opted for the dichotomous one, stating that it appeared to be faster than the polytomous one. Additionally, they appreciated the sense of certainty the dichotomous options induced, as opposed to the confusion sometimes induced by a polytomous scale. The limited number of available options in the dichotomous rating scale makes this type of scale easier to memorize than its multi-faceted counterpart, but according to the respondents it is also what makes it too crude an instrument. Three out of four novice raters taking part in the current study considered the polytomous scale ideal for assessing speaking tasks. According to the raters, the polytomous scale's advantages are also its downsides: because it is in line with one's intuitive judgement, it may lead to subjective rating. The raters feared that their experience with rating was too limited to allow for intuition to influence their judgement. For that reason, they preferred more guidance. Also, since the polytomous scale allows for more detailed judgement, the raters reported, it may cause doubt. In short, the novice raters involved in this pilot found the polytomous rating scale too vague.

Since the raters reported the occasional vagueness of the level descriptors in the polytomous scale as the cause of the doubt when rating, the descriptors for oral production were rewritten (noted in the Research design section). These rewritten descriptors were piloted in a small-scale trial which served to check whether it would be possible to improve the strong aspects of the polytomous scale while diminishing its negative effects. The trial involved five novice raters who rated a total of 76 oral performances using rewritten level descriptors.

After rating 76 oral production tasks, four out of five raters partaking in the semi-structured focus group reported preferring the polytomous scale for oral production to the dichotomous one. The raters who preferred the polytomous model did so because they no longer believed the rating scale to be too vague or too abstract. Additionally, they reported it to allow for fine-grained distinctions between language levels.

Discussion

The extent of the difference in terms of reliability (α) and rater agreement (K) between both scales can be clearly observed in Table 8, which shows that the rater agreement is consistently lower when using the polytomous scale. Raters A and B, who started off with the polytomous scale show less agreement on the polytomous scale than raters C and D, who may have benefited from the sequence effect. Still, irrespective of the order in which the performances were rated, the dichotomous scale emerges as the most reliable option. This implies that even if the sequence of rating would have had an impact on the reliability of the rating, it would not necessarily have benefited the dichotomous scale. Indeed, the reliability indexes of raters C and D are highest for the dichotomous scale, which was used first. So, even if the order in which the scales were used would have had an effect, the dichotomous scale consistently outperforms the polytomous one in terms of rater correspondence and inter-rater agreement.

Table 8 Reliability indexes of polytomous and dichotomous scales

Raters A/B Performance 1–125		Raters C/D Performance 126–250	
Polytomous		Dichotomous	
	r = .47		r = .94
	K = .30		K = .54
	α = .76		α = .86
↓		↓	
Dichotomous		Polytomous	
	r = .82		r = .79
	K = .59		K = .35
	α = .77		α = .86

The quantitative differences between both scales are to some extent mathematically explainable. Indeed, it is normal for correlations to be more robust as the number of options decreases. Likewise, it is a known fact that 'unweighted kappa coefficients decrease with the number of categories' (Brenner and Kliebst 1996:199) and that impressionistic descriptors provide 'a wider window for rater interpretation of the meaning of the descriptors, but [. . .] inevitably results in lower inter-rater reliability' (Knoch 2008: 61). Therefore, even though the differences in reliability indices for both rating scales should not be ignored, the quantitative data should be supplemented with qualitative input, which offers information on the validity and interpretability of the scales.

In the focus groups conducted with the first team of novice raters, they reported a sense of certainty caused by dichotomous options and the confusion the CEFR-based polytomous descriptors sometimes caused. This may help to explain the quantitative differences between both scales. Additionally, the qualitative follow-up study shows that the process of actively exploring and refining the rating scale together with prospective raters affects rating behaviour. The rewritings focused on simplifying CEFR-based descriptors and on marking the borders between levels more clearly. Vagueness was avoided as much as possible by using the concrete insertions, subjective insertions, discriminating insertions and exemplary additions discussed above.

Conclusion

This study compared a polytomous to a dichotomous analytic rating scale in terms of reliability and validity. The polytomous rating scale was developed in close conjunction with subject specialists and consists of CEFR-like level descriptors, whereas the dichotomous (also the scale which is currently in use) is made up of a series of binary options. Even though the dichotomous scale includes descriptors concerning the formal aspects of language, the focus is on the content, on getting the message across. The polytomous scale focuses on getting the message across appropriately, thereby giving a larger proportional weight to formal aspects of language, such as structure, register and grammatical accuracy.

Both rating scales were piloted with two pairs of novice raters. Each pair rated 125 performances, the first pair starting off with the polytomous scale and switching to the dichotomous one, the other pair using the reverse order. The results from the quantitative data show the dichotomous scale to be consistently more reliable, irrespective of the order in which the raters used the scales.

Overall, the raters preferred the dichotomous scale to the polytomous one, because having two instead of four categories made them feel more certain about their decision-making process, but also because it was less intuitive and less vague. The vagueness of the polytomous descriptors most likely stemmed from the fact that they had been composed together with subject specialists as well as testing specialists and that they had been based on CEFR descriptors, which may appear too vague for novice raters, even after rater training. The fact that the polytomous scales were considered to leave too much room for interpretation and that these scales proved to be less reliable than their dichotomous counterparts, links in with Bachman's observation that 'vagueness in task specification inevitably leads to vagueness in measurement' (Bachman 2002:458).

The raters' preference for the dichotomous scale did contain one important exception, since they preferred the polytomous scale for assessing speaking. In a follow-up study, five new novice raters were called upon to assess speaking tasks by means of the polytomous scale, which had been adjusted in line with the results from the first pilot. During the rater training for the second pilot, the raters were invited to comment on the scale descriptors in order to help reformulate them by using words they could grasp more easily. The wording of the new scales consequently moved away from the CEFR terminology and became more tangible for novice raters. The process of thinking about the rating scale and making it 'more detailed, empirically-developed' did result 'in subsequent changed rating behaviour' (Knoch 2008: 62). The raters involved in this second pilot (containing only oral production tasks) largely preferred the polytomous scale – which they had helped rewrite – to the dichotomous one. Future quantitative analyses will be necessary to investigate whether this effect has also improved the reliability of the rating scale.

Even though this study has reaffirmed the statistic robustness of the dichotomous scale, the subject specialists and the raters involved in both pilot studies indicated its limitations regarding authenticity and validity. After revising the polytomous scale together with the end users, its interpretability had improved.

Further quantitative research will be needed to determine the reliability of the rewritten polytomous rating scales. If the reliability indexes in a new large-scale pilot are satisfactory, the scales for written production will be rewritten parallel to those for speaking.

References

Alderson, C J, Clapham, C and Wall, D (1995) *Language Test Construction and Evaluation*, Cambridge: Cambridge University Press.

Bachman, L F (2002) Some reflections on task-based language performance assessment, *Language Testing* 19, 454–476.

Bachman, L F (2011) *How do different language frameworks impact language assessment practice?* plenary talk at ALTE 4th International Conference, Kraków, Poland, July 2011.

Bachman, L and Palmer, A (2010) *Language Assessment in Practice*, Oxford: Oxford University Press.

Barkaoui, K (2010) Explaining ESL essay holistic scores: a multilevel modeling approach, *Language Testing* 27, 515–535.

Barkaoui, K and Knouzi, I (2011) *Rating scales as frameworks for assessing L2 writing: examining their impact on rater performance*, paper presented at ALTE 4th International Conference, Kraków, Poland, July 2011.

Brenner, H and Kliebst (1996) Dependence of weighted kappa coefficients on the number of categories, *Epidemiology* 7, 199–202.

Cohen, J (1960) A coefficient for agreement for nominal scales, *Education and Psychological Measurement* 20, 37–46.

Colpin, M and Gysen, S (2006) Developing and introducing task-based language tests, in Van den Branden, K (Ed.), *Task-based Language Education: From Theory to Practice*, Cambridge: Cambridge University Press, 151–174.

Council of Europe (2001) *Common European Framework of Reference for Languages: Learning, teaching, assessment*, Cambridge: Cambridge University Press.

Council of Europe (2009) *Relating Language Examinations to the Common European Framework of Reference for Languages: Learning, Teaching, Assessment (CEFR) A Manual*, Strasbourg: Language Policy Division.

Davies, A (2001) The logic of testing languages for specific purposes, *Language Testing* 18, 133–147.

Douglas, D (2000) *Assessing Languages for Specific Purposes*, Cambridge: Cambridge University Press.

Douglas, D (2001) Language for specific purposes assessment criteria: where do they come from? *Language Testing* 18, 171–185.

Ellis, R (2003) *Task-Based Language Learning and Teaching*, Oxford: Oxford University Press.

Fulcher, G, Davidson, F and Kemp, J (2010) Effective rating scale development for speaking tests: Performance decision trees, *Language Testing* 28, 5–29.

Gysen, S and Van Avermaet, P (2005) Issues in functional language performance assessment: The case of the certificate Dutch as a foreign language, *Language Assessment Quarterly* 2, 51–68.

Jacoby, S and McNamara, T (1999) Locating competence, *English for Specific Purposes* 18, 213–241.

Knoch, U (2008) The assessment of academic style in EAP writing: The case of the rating scale, *Melbourne Papers in Language Testing* 13, 34–67.

Knoch, U (2009) Diagnostic assessment of writing: A comparison of two rating scales, *Language Testing* 26, 275–304.

Long, M (2005) *Second Language Needs Analysis*, Cambridge: Cambridge University Press.

Lumley, T (2002) Assessment criteria in a large-scale writing test: What do they really mean to the raters? *Language Testing* 19, 246–276.

McNamara, T (2006) Validity in language testing: the challenge of Sam Messick's legacy, *Language Assessment Quarterly* 3, 31–51.

McNamara, T and Roever, C (2006) *Language Testing: The Social Dimension*, Malden, MA: Blackwell Publishing.

Norris, J M (2009) Task-based teaching and testing, in Long, M H and Doughty C J (Eds) *The Handbook of Language Teaching*, Malden, MA: Wiley-Blackwell, 578–594.

Norris, J M, Brown, J D, Hudson, T D and Bonk, W (2002) Examinee abilities and task difficulty in task-based second language performance assessment, *Language Testing* 19, 395–418.

Papageorgiou, S (2010) Investigating the decision-making process of standard setting participants, *Language Testing* 27, 261–282.

Sawaki, Y (2007) Construct validation of analytic rating scales in a speaking assessment: Reporting a score profile and a composite, *Language Testing* 24, 355–390.

Shohamy, E (1996) Language testing: matching assessment procedures with language knowledge, in Birenbaum, M and Dochy, F (Eds), *Alternatives in Assessment of Achievements, Learning Processes and Prior Knowledge*, Boston, MA: Kluwer Academic Publishers, 143–159.

Shohamy, E, Gordon, C and Kraemer, R (1992) The effect of raters' background and training on the reliability of direct writing tests, *Modern Language Journal* 76, 27–33.

Skehan, P (1996) A framework for the implementation of task based instruction, *Applied Linguistics* 17, 38–62.

Skehan, P (1998) *A Cognitive Approach to Language Learning*, Oxford: Oxford University Press.

Spence-Brown, R (2001) The eye of the beholder: authenticity in an embedded assessment task, *Language Testing* 18, 463–81.

Van Avermaet, P and Gysen, S (2006) From needs to tasks: Language learning needs in a task-based approach, in Van den Branden, K (Ed.) *Task-Based Language Education: From Theory to Practice*, Cambridge: Cambridge University Press, 17–46.

Van den Branden, K (Ed.) (2006) *Task-Based Language Education*, Cambridge: Cambridge University Press.

Van Gorp, K and Deygers, B (in press) Task-based language assessment, in Kunnan, A (Ed.) *The Companion to Language Assessment*, New Jersey: Wiley-Blackwell.

Weigle, S C (1994) Effects of training on raters of ESL compositions, *Language Testing* 11, 197–223.

Weigle, S C (2002) *Assessing Writing*, Cambridge: Cambridge University Press.

Wigglesworth, G (2008) Task and performance based assessment, in Shohamy, E and Hornberger, N H (Eds), *Encyclopedia of Language and Education*, New York: Springer, 111–122.

Wu, W M and Stansfield, C W (2001) Towards authenticity of task in test development, *Language Testing* 18, 187–206.

15 Who, what, where, WENS: the native speaker in the Interagency Language Roundtable Scale

Rachel L Brooks
Federal Bureau of Investigation

Beth Mackey
Department of Defense

Abstract

The reference to the Well Educated Native Speaker (WENS) in the United States' Interagency Language Roundtable Skill Level Descriptions has been called into question by second language acquisition practitioners inside and outside the government, as evidenced by the interest in this topic within the Interagency Language Roundtable (ILR) community in the USA. Following a discussion of the definition of a native speaker, the paper contextualizes the issues surrounding the role and characteristics of the well-educated native speaker within the Skill Level Descriptions. The authors explain how the ILR scale, which is functional in nature, is used by the United States Government to test native and non-native speakers of a language. Using authentic test samples, the paper illustrates the different profiles of native and non-native speakers at the ILR Level 2+ and Level 3 border. Drawing upon their extensive experience in testing speaking, reading and listening, the authors demonstrate how the ILR Skill Level Descriptions can successfully be applied to rate all speakers of a language.

Introduction

The Interagency Language Roundtable (ILR) Skill Level Descriptions were developed in the 1950s because the US State Department needed to evaluate and document the language proficiency of its Foreign Service Officers. The proficiency framework describes a progression of functional linguistic ability, from day-to-day survival needs to a description of language use characterized by sophisticated and complex manners. At the top of the scale (ILR

Level 5) is the ideal speaker, described as 'functionally equivalent to that of a highly articulate, well educated native speaker' (ILR 1985).

The 'native speaker' is not only used as the reference point for the top of the scale; it is also referred to within the skill level descriptions as an interlocutor and a reference point. For example, from the Speaking definitions at Level 1 (ILR 1985): 'A "native speaker" must often use slowed speech, repetition, paraphrase, or a combination of these to be understood by this individual. Similarly, the native speaker must strain and employ real-world knowledge to understand even simple statements/questions from this individual.' This 'native speaker' is meant to be a person who has natively acquired the language, a first language speaker living in a country where the language was spoken. The Skill Level Descriptions further define 'native speaker' as follows:

> Unless otherwise specified, the term 'native speaker' refers to native speakers of a standard dialect. 'Well-educated,' in the context of these proficiency descriptions, does not necessarily imply formal higher education; however, in cultures where formal higher education is common, the language-use abilities of persons who have had such education is considered the standard. That is, such a person meets contemporary expectations for the formal, careful style of the language, as well as a range of less formal varieties of the language (ILR 1985).

As the United States Government (USG) uses the term 'native speaker' in different settings, it is no wonder that there is significant confusion over the use of the concept in a rating scale. However, ambiguity over what is meant by the term in the government context does not mean that the term is used inappropriately. Some of the USG's operational needs demand a higher level of proficiency than most educational or professional contexts. High-level language users have to be able to tailor language, persuade and advise in diplomatic or politically sensitive contexts. They have to be able to blend into other cultures seamlessly and without detection. Language at this level is simply not described in other frameworks or standards.

The ILR community has recently reaffirmed its commitment to retaining the 'native speaker' model in their definitions. Simply eliminating the 'native speaker' concept without some other way to reference the model for functional language ability leaves the ILR Skill Level Descriptions without a manner to describe language ability at Level 5. Disambiguating the USG's usage of 'native speaker' will instead help to inform the stakeholders of what it means and does not mean, clarifying misunderstandings surrounding the term. Thus, people who are native speakers by acquisition who do not reach the highest ILR levels can understand what the rating implies and does not imply.

The native speaker in literature

In second language acquisition literature, the concept of the 'native speaker' has been nebulous and elusive (Davies 2003, Maher 2001). Nevertheless, many teachers and researchers refer to the concept of the native speaker, assuming a common understanding of its definition (Maher 2001). In fact, almost every area of linguistics employs the native speaker concept in some form. Sociolinguists are interested in native speaker/native speaker interactions (Fasold 1984). Theoretical linguists use native speakers as the arbiters of phrase acceptability (Chomsky 1957). Computational linguists try to build computer models that identify and parse language chunks as a native speaker would (McEnery and Wilson 2001). Applied linguists investigate what contributes to or prevents native speaker-level language attainment (Firth and Wagner 1997).

If such varied research utilizes the construct of native speaker, then one would expect that its definition and parameters would be well established. However, there does not seem to be a universally accepted way to describe a native speaker. Davies (2003) explores many of the term's uses. Is it a speaker of a language spoken in the land of his or her birth? Is it a person who speaks the language of his or her mother during formative years? Does one have to complete school in the language to be classified as a native speaker? Is it the language a person speaks best? Is it a speaker who is perceived as native by other native speakers? Are there certain linguistic features that must be attained to a certain level of consistent accuracy?

Whereas references in the 19th and early 20th century took for granted that native speakers had but one understood meaning, Paikeday (1985) proposed dual definitions for the native speaker, with one referring to how the language was acquired and the other referring to competent, proficient, or ideal speakers of the language. The definition of native speaker in the popular sense refers to the language acquisition method, 'a person who has a specified language as the mother tongue or first learned language' (1985: 9–10). This first definition implies continuity of language use and learning since birth or at least within the critical period or the onset of puberty (operational definitions of what this means being still debated). Woolf (1973) specified further demographic requirements for the native (English) speaker as 'a native speaker of English and hav[ing] at least a bachelor's degree from a reputable college or university' (1973:10, quoted in Paikeday 1985). Paikeday also recognized the second, idealistic sense of the native speaker as 'one who is a competent speaker of a specified language and who uses it idiomatically' (1985:10), or in the usual way, including structure, syntax and grammar. The authors acknowledge that neither definition of native speaker presumes the other.

In an effort to further clarify what each of these definitions means, Paikeday encounters numerous theoretical issues that prevent clear conclusions. As to the latter definition, native speakers are better described as more proficient than competent speakers; however, what level of proficiency is needed for native status is not established. Native speakers who are proficient users of the language can 'make immediate and intuitive judgments of a linguistic (and related cultural) kind' (Paikeday 1985:74) as they are deemed the arbiters of grammatical acceptability. Native speakers by acquisition may be capable of making judgments of some simple grammatical structures, but are not capable *de facto* of making evaluations of advanced matters; therefore, they must be highly educated (the extent to which is undefined). Moreover, errors committed by native speakers are often not judged as serious as those same mistakes made by non-natives. The ambiguity and social baggage attached to the term native speaker leads Paikeday to conclude that it is of no relevant use to linguists, rather proficiency should be the focus. Since proficiency is variable, 'the proficiency of any speaker of a language at any given point in time could be tested objectively on the basis of criteria we could lay down for achieving the purpose for which the proficiency is required' (Paikeday 1985:87–88).

Davies' (2003) discussions on the nature, usefulness, and existence of the native speaker have formed the foundation for the understanding and use of the concept in applied linguistics. Davies investigated psycholinguistic, linguistic, and sociolinguistic aspects of the concept of a native speaker, as well as applied aspects of language such as native speaker specific knowledge, communicative competence, and intelligibility. Davies' goal was to determine whether being a native speaker was solely a self-ascribed term for identity, or rather an objective, definable reality.

Davies describes the linguistic competence of a native speaker in terms of three distinct grammars: the idiolectal grammar (an individual's personal set of grammatical rules), the shared grammar between a group of native speakers (the standard grammar of a language), and the grammar of a human's capacity (Chomsky's Universal Grammar (Chomsky 1965)). Emphasis is placed on the need for exploration of the shared, standard grammar for defining the native speaker. Davies described four knowledge types related to language ability: metalinguistic, discriminating, communicational (relating to competence), and skills (relating to performance). In a different view, metalinguistic knowledge is viewable as pure, while the latter three knowledge types refer to control or proficiency, with skill being the true representation of language proficiency in a productive language skill such as speaking. Communicative competence distinguishes levels of native speakers, as experiences with language and culture are generalized into an ability to articulate linguistic ability within a range of situations, paying careful attention to notions of appropriateness beyond personal experience.

Where language proficiency testing is concerned, Davies (2003) examines the utility of the native speaker as a measurement yardstick. A performance equivalent to general native speakers (a developmental measure) demonstrates a certain level of mastery; however, it lacks discrimination between average speakers and exceptional speakers, who are capable of superior levels of language skill (an attainment measure). Still, Davies states that it is needed as a model and a goal, although the average or typical native speaker is not useful as a measure.

Ultimately, Davies describes the native speaker as a person who (a) acquires the language as a child, (b) has intuitions of productiveness and acceptability of the grammar of his or her own idiolect, (c) has intuitions of the standard language grammar as distinct from idiolect grammar, and (d) produces fluent, unrehearsed discourse employing a massive array of vocabulary with an extensive ability to display communicative competence, encompassing both demographic and ideal notions of the native.

When posed with the question as to whether or not a learner can be a native speaker, Davies states that it is possible to meet all of the above criteria except for (a), childhood acquisition, because it is contrary to the definition of a second language learner. Davies therefore acknowledges that theoretically there is a distinction between the demographic and ideal concepts in the native speaker, but does not consider the two to be mutually exclusive. He suggests that with enough practice and contact, most of the criteria can be met, though it is difficult and rare. The criteria themselves mostly describe the differences typically encountered between natives and non-natives, but do not explain why a non-native would be prohibited from native-speaker status.

Davies (2004) finds that differences between native speakers and high-achieving non-natives are typically psycholinguistic rather than socio-linguistic. Accent aside, non-natives have less speed and confidence in grammaticality judgements.

Davies asserts that there is no test to distinguish native from non-native psychological differences at this time, leaving the distinction to autobiography only. According to this idea, a policy that excludes non-natives based wholly on the assumption that a non-native could not reach the native speaker ideal may be unjustified based on research to date, though he concedes that even high-level learners are very unlikely to achieve the native speaker ideal. In conclusion, becoming a native speaker is in many ways a social issue, one of confidence and identity (Davies 2003).

The continuing usage of the native speaker has been challenged not only by Paikeday (1985), who declared the native speaker dead, and Davies (2003) who considered whether or not the native speaker was a myth or reality, but also by other applied linguists. Rampton (1990) suggested that the varying meanings of native speaker and mother tongue be replaced by other terms, such as language expertise, language inheritance, and language affiliation. Butcher (2005) gives a history of the term's origins and uses, noting that many meanings for 'native' are negative, stemming from colonialism. Moreover, 'speaker' is a unilateral term, which places no emphasis on communication. Butcher recommends that 'native speaker' be used only to refer to how a language was acquired. Ortega (2010) proposed that native speakers as an acquisition goal be replaced by 'the bilingual speaker'. Lantolf and Frawley (1985) agreed that the native speaker only exists as an abstract type. Many of the critics of how the term 'native speaker' is used in speaking proficiency assessment (e.g. Jenkins 2006) are outside of the field of language testing, and criticize that the term native speaker appears in testing criteria or constructs without a closer examination of what it means (or does not mean) to the examination authorities, and what its role is to the construct of the test (Taylor 2006).

Much of the doubt that arises from using the native speaker concept in language testing is that it assumes that the native speaker's attributes and performance is definable as measurable criteria: a yardstick. In reality, native speakers cannot be considered as homogenous, even though there is often an assumption that they are (Bachman 1990). Even considering the different types of native speakers, both the native acquirers and the ideal speakers, there is variation. In Hamilton, Lopes, McNamara and Sheridan (1993), the homogeneity of native speakers is explored by reviewing three studies examining native speaker performance on the *International English Language Testing System (IELTS)* exam. In Hamilton (1991), no significant difference was found between native speaker students from three different concentrations within a vocational school, but the range of native speaker results on the *IELTS* Reading sub-test varied between 10 and 27, with a maximum score being 37. Sheridan (1991) conducted a similar study with a writing test that showed comparable results. Lopes (1992) replicated Hamilton's study, but with three more highly educated groups of native speakers (junior barristers, post-graduate students, and academic staff). In this instance there was a significant difference between the groups of native speakers, though no group had perfect scores. Brooks and Brau (2007) examined native speaker performances on Arabic, Mandarin and Spanish speaking assessments, and found wide variation between the performances, ranging from ILR 2+ to ILR 5.

The native speaker in the Interagency Language Roundtable

Not only does the ambiguity in how the term native speaker is used result in confusion, but confusion also arises from the 'shorthand' used when USG personnel refer to the ILR scale. The fact is, native speakers vary in their language proficiency. The use of the term native speaker has proved to be both useful and problematic for Federal Government Testing. Inside the Federal Government, the native speaker serves as a practical model against which language proficiency is measured, allowing raters to make judgements as to what is correct and appropriate in language use. In addition, Federal Government agencies, such as the Federal Bureau of Investigation (FBI), require speaking test raters to be native speakers of the test language and to score an ILR Level 5 on a Speaking Proficiency Test. The use of the term native speaker in a general, academic sense is confused with what a native speaker means in the Federal Government context, and often leads to criticism of the Federal Government's reliance on the native speaker concept. Further explication of the Federal Government's native speaker is needed to avoid such confusion.

When the 'native speaker' is mentioned in reference to the ILR Skill Level Descriptions, it typically refers to the 'native speaker' that appears at the top of the ILR scale in ILR Level 5. As mentioned previously, the use of 'native speaker' in this context is really a shortened version of the full reference in the ILR (1985): 'speaking proficiency [which] is functionally equivalent to a highly-articulate "native speaker" (ILR 1985). This 'native speaker' is not an average person who has learned the language in a native context, but is an ideal user of the language. ILR's Level 5 'native speaker' is often referred to in Federal Government materials as the well-educated 'native speaker' (WENS). The concept of the ILR Level 5 WENS is also referred to by the condensed level title 'Functionally Native Proficiency'. The title implies that the speaker only needs to function like a 'native' to receive this score, even though most natives do not function at this level. Out of the approximately 3,000 speakers the FBI tests every year, there are only a handful of people who receive ILR Level 5.

In the ILR Level 5 description, the phrase 'functionally equivalent' is interpreted to mean that a person does not need to have acquired the language as a first language (L1) to receive a score of ILR Level 5; one does not need to be a native speaker, one only needs to function in a manner equivalent to a WENS. Although it is extremely rare, there are cases where a non-native speaker has received an ILR 5. 'Functionally equivalent' also refers to the functional nature of the ILR scale. It does not mean that the examinee only needs to be able to complete the functions that a WENS can complete to receive an ILR Level 5, but that the examinee must complete them in a manner equivalent to the WENS, including all aspects of WENS speech.

The Level 5 'native speaker' also needs to be 'highly articulate'. By 'highly articulate', the ILR means a speaker who not only does not make any errors or mistakes, but also consistently and appropriately employs the language to its fullest capacity. Speaking in an ILR Level 5 manner involves conveying complex ideas in a clear and precise manner and using sophisticated strategies to tailor the message to a wide variety of audiences, doing so in an effortless and natural manner. The ILR Level 5's vocabulary is nuanced and precise, employing terms that fit the meaning exactly. The structures employed are complex when appropriate, and do not include errors often made by native speakers. The fluency has no noticeable hesitations or restarts, and the pronunciation is standard for the language. The message that the speaker conveys, including the direct and meta-messages, suits the situation perfectly and is highly effective for achieving the speaker's purpose. This type of language is one that few normal native speakers ever attain, and one that is not typically attained though routine life interactions. The development of 'highly articulate' speech must be extensively practised and cultivated. The profile of the person that most likely would attain an ILR Level 5 is a 'highly articulate well-educated native speaker', but this does not mean that all well-educated native speakers are highly articulate. Raters recognize that ILR Level 5 is a range. There are a variety of ways that 'highly articulate' speech may manifest itself, all of which are correct.

Much of the misperception about the WENS comes from the phrase 'well-educated'. Often, 'well-educated' is taken to mean someone who has completed higher education, perhaps a Bachelor's or Master's degree. However, most university graduates typically score between ILR Levels 2+ and 4. Moreover, ILR speaking tests do not consider a person's background when assigning a rating. The ILR Skill Level Descriptions, in fact, note that:

> 'Well-educated,' in the context of these proficiency descriptions, does not necessarily imply formal higher education; however, in cultures where formal higher education is common, the language-use abilities of persons who have had such education is considered the standard. That is, such a person meets contemporary expectations for the formal, careful style of the language, as well as a range of less formal varieties of the language (ILR 1985).

A speaker with no formal education whatsoever can receive ILR Level 5; a speaker with a PhD will not necessarily receive ILR Level 5. (For a related discussion of the native speaker concept in the Common European Framework of Reference for languages, see Jones, this volume.)

Testing in the United States Government

The ILR Skill Level Descriptions provide a scale that is functional in nature. The primary purpose of the ILR Skill Level Descriptions is to describe how language professionals use their language proficiency, ranging from Level 0, No Proficiency, through Level 5, Functionally Native Proficiency. Because it is accepted that not all native speakers are homogenous, a 'native speaker' level in and of itself is not sufficient. There must be a way to distinguish between higher levels of language proficiency. The USG employs professionals with highly developed language proficiencies in order to fulfil specialized mission demands. These personnel require proficiency levels beyond what would be expected by the average speaker of the language. For example, diplomats working for the Department of State need to be able to negotiate policy effectively using the appropriate cultural and sociolinguistic strategies to convey their message. Covert operatives need to be linguistically imperceptible when working undercover. Effectively tailoring to a range of audiences, maintaining the appropriate tone during a debate, and presenting an unconventional, complex idea in a manner where nuance or meaning could adversely affect its acceptance are all tasks that are carried out by Government positions. As a consequence, the ILR scale needs to make distinctions between proficiencies of high-level speakers. For most language learning and professional purposes, reaching ILR Level 3 (General Professional Proficiency) is more than sufficient. There are positions, however, that require greater depth and breadth, and the ILR scale therefore distinguishes between this basic, professional level that begins at Level 3 up through the advanced professional Level 4, through to Level 5, where we expect the range of language associated with the 'highly articulate, well educated native speaker'.

The original purpose of the ILR scale was to test second language adult learners represented initially by the Foreign Service community and extended to 'the feds' in general, local government entities, and anyone who wished to build a test based on the scale. In today's USG, the ILR scale is used to assess all types of language speakers – no matter where their language was acquired. Agencies across the USG use the ILR Skill Level Descriptions to describe the language proficiency of native speakers and language learners. Because of the functional nature of the ILR scale, this has worked well for the government. The ILR scale permits the distinctions between higher levels of speaking proficiency. While individuals who hold a doctorate in nuclear physics or marine biology would be considered 'well educated', they may or may not meet the other requirements of the ILR language proficiency scale, such as the 'use (of) functional rhetorical speech' (Level 4) or they may not display 'a breadth of vocabulary and idiom, colloquialisms and pertinent cultural references', expected at Level 5.

These distinctions inevitably result in conflict for those who self identify as 'native speakers' and they feel that any score below a Level 5 is a slight to their identity as a language speaker. These distinctions also concern second language learners, who believe that the 'functionally equivalent to a highly-articulate native speaker' (FE HA WENS) standard is unattainable. The challenge for the USG is to educate the language community and ensure that the needs for language skills are accurately linked to the ILR scale, and that testing accurately measures language proficiency on that scale. Whether examinees are second language learners, heritage or native speakers has no bearing on their score. Their ability to use the language is assessed independent of the acquisition process.

The theoretical native speaker in practical language testing

Not all native speakers are exemplary speakers of the language, and in fact, the distribution of outcomes by examinee type helps to exemplify the variety of outcomes that may result from language testing. It is true that some speakers can and do exceed well beyond their expected range. However, examinees still consider themselves members of these groups by their demographic characteristics.

The typical high school learner in the United States receives two or three years of classroom study, and reaches a proficiency level of 0+ to 1+ (Rifkin 2003). Language majors, particularly those who have included immersion experiences as a part of their studies, often reach anywhere between the 1+ and 2+ levels, sometimes attaining Level 3. Heritage speakers have a wide range of outcomes as well, depending on how much the language was used at home, travel experiences, and formal education in the language in addition to home use. Heritage speaker outcomes typically range between the 2 and 3 levels. Even native speakers who are born, raised, and educated through all of their developmental years in a native-speaking environment typically reach ILR Levels 2+ to 3+. In order to receive a score beyond this level, even the native speaker must become a learner of his or her own native language, developing a sophisticated and precise lexicon, cultivating skill in employing pragmatic and sociolinguistic strategies that are culturally appropriate and highly effective, and practising this skill in order to improve the fluidity of speech across a broad range of contexts. Opportunities to develop linguistic skills to this level are rare, and are not emphasized in even higher-level education. This is partially why so few ever attain the FE HA WENS level.

The ILR community defines proficiency as the functional ability to accomplish communication tasks through unrehearsed language. Therefore, ratings are determined by evaluating whether or not examinees have met all of the requirements in the description, without regard to how the language was acquired. The ILR scale is non-compensatory in nature. The traditional formats for assessing speaking proficiency in this manner are the Oral Proficiency Interview (OPI) and the Speaking Proficiency Test (SPT). Explorations of two sample performances from official USG OPIs illustrate the irrelevance of language acquisition method: native speaker performance that fails to reach the Level 3 standard is contrasted with a non-native speaker who demonstrates successful performance in a supported opinion task. Level 3 samples were selected due to the importance of this level to the USG, and similar distinctions can be found in OPIs at other levels.

ILR Level 2 and 3 are the most critical levels in the Federal Government context. An examination of the OPI performances of two individuals, one native speaker and one non-native speaker, is provided to illustrate the functional nature of the scale. The full ILR Skill Level Description for Speaking is included in Appendix A. Transcripts of the interview samples can be found in Appendix B. A word of caution, however, must be provided: we run the risk of oversimplification by providing only one sample performance from one Level 3 task from a longer interview. It is important to keep in mind that overall scores are always given by comparing the *full* language sample to the *full* ILR Descriptions only.

Level 2, Limited Working Proficiency, is characterized by the ability to satisfy routine social demands and limited work requirements. Level 2 speakers can execute a range of functions such as conduct routine work-related interactions and they are able to participate in personal interactions with facility. Level 3 speakers, on the other hand, show greater depth and breadth of ability. They are able to speak the language with sufficient structural accuracy and vocabulary to participate effectively in most formal and informal conversations in practical, social and professional topics. Level 2 and Level 3 speakers differ in their control of organization, with Level 2 speakers using minimal coherence. Level 3 speakers, who are able to clarify, support opinions, justify decisions and deliver extended monologues, use cohesive discourse. Level 2 speakers control basic structures and often show weakness, whereas Level 3 speakers effectively use language structures to convey meaning accurately. There are also notable differences in vocabulary between Levels 2 and 3. Level 2 speakers use vocabulary that is appropriate in high-frequency settings, while Level 3 speakers use the language clearly and relatively naturally to elaborate concepts freely and make ideas easily understandable. Level 2 speakers speak with confidence but not facility; a speaker at Level 3 speaks readily and fills in pauses suitably. Differences are also apparent between these levels in terms of pronunciation: Level 2 speakers often miscommunicate due to pronunciation, but Level 3 speakers' errors virtually never interfere with understanding. Differences in levels of socio-cultural awareness can also be noted, with Level 2 speakers comfortable in social situations, and Level 3 speakers are able to be effective across social, practical and professional topics.

Sample performances are provided (Appendix B) to illustrate language performances on a typical Level 3 task to support an opinion. The samples are excerpted from authentic OPIs given by one government agency. The first sample is from an interview with a non-native speaker of English who successfully demonstrates Level 3 proficiency on this task. The second sample is from an interview with a native speaker of English. He is also given a supported opinion prompt, yet his performance on this task fails to meet the Level 3 standard. We hope that by providing a native performance at Level 2+ and a non-native performance at Level 3, we can exemplify the functional nature of the ILR scale and the irrelevance of the source of a speaker's language proficiency.

John (name changed), the non-native speaker, is asked to comment on global warming (see Appendix B for an excerpt from this OPI). He provides a clear argument, with an opening idea, supporting details and restatement of his main idea. He effectively uses cohesive elements (*if we maintain that course of action, eventually . . .*) to organize his discourse. He shows command of language structures, but does make some minor errors (*there are change in how we do*) but these do not impede understanding. His use of vocabulary is adequate for general professional use, although it lacks precision (*. . . that Al Gore came with his presentation . . .*). John uses fillers, hesitations, and restarts, but these do not impede the flow of the conversation. His pronunciation is clear and understandable. John's tone is appropriate to the task. He demonstrates command of a more formal tone and he is also able to employ some colloquial expressions (for example, *in a nutshell*). On this task, and on other Level 3 tasks during the OPI, John successfully meets the Level 3 standard for speaking proficiency.

Mark (name changed), a native speaker of English, is also asked to support an opinion on the topic of the environment (see Appendix B for an excerpt from this OPI). His performance shows inconsistent performance at Level 3 on this task. Because he was also unable to show consistent and sustained performance across all the Level 3 tasks in the OPI, but he did demonstrate performance that substantially exceeds Level 2, he was awarded an overall score of Level 2+. Mark's response to the interviewer lacked overall organization of his argument. While ideas were linked, the logic was weak. He did show solid command of structures (subordinate clauses used with effect) but did have some awkwardness. Mark's vocabulary was not consistently clear nor elaborate. He employs semantically vacuous words (*delegate those kinda things* and *those kind of environmental things*), or everyday, nonprofessional terms (*I think it's good to have . . .* and *use it all up*). His fluency, however, was good and his pronunciation clear and understandable. In terms of his social/cultural appropriateness, however, he hedges the argument and does not present a professional tone (*Kinda, I guess*).

Conclusion

The goal of this paper was to further the discussion regarding the functional nature of the ILR scale, and the role of the FE HA WENS within that system. The USG's OPIs are designed to assess how well speakers perform across a variety of functions and topics. The samples we provided illustrated the functional nature of the scale as well as the relationship between the scale and the native speaker concept. The samples also serve to illustrate the fact that the ILR scale serves as a standard to rate native and non-native language proficiency.

The ILR's WENS is a reality, and a necessary construct as an ideal for measuring proficiency. Since the USG's focus on proficiency measurement is the examinee's functional ability, the native speaker concept is mostly irrelevant, except that the WENS is how we refer to the ideal speaker. Perhaps, in hindsight, a less ambiguous term than native speaker would have helped to avoid such confusion. Though most people who acquired the language as native speakers are not ILR FE HA WENSs, their proficiency scores are not a reflection on their identity as a native speaker or their educational levels. Their scores are a measure of their language proficiency according to the functional descriptions that comprise the ILR scale.

Acknowledgements

The authors would like to acknowledge the contributions of Mika Hoffman, Defense Language Institute, Christina Hoffman, Foreign Service Institute, Pardee Lowe Jr, Department of Defense, Victoria Nier and Maria Brau, Federal Bureau of Investigation.

References

Bachman, L F (1990) *Fundamental Considerations in Language Testing*, Oxford: Oxford University Press.

Brooks, R L and Brau, M M (2007) *Adult native and heritage speakers: How different are they?*, paper presented at the American Association of Applied Linguistics, Costa Mesa, California, 2007.

Butcher, C A (2005) The case against the 'native speaker', *English Today* 21 (2), 13–24.

Chomsky, N (1957) *Syntactic Structures*, New York: Walter de Gruyter.

Chomsky, N (1965) *Aspects of the Theory of Syntax*, Cambridge, MA: MIT Press.

Davies, A (2003) *The Native Speaker: Myth and Reality*, Bilingual Education and Bilingualism, Clevedon: Multilingual Matters, 2nd edn.

Davies, A (2004) The native speaker in applied linguistics, in Davies, A and Elder, C (Eds), *The Handbook of Applied Linguistics*, Malden, MA: Blackwell Publishing, 431–450.

Fasold, R W (1984) *Introduction to Sociolinguistics: the Sociolinguistics of Society Volume 2*, Cambridge, MA: Wiley-Blackwell.

Firth, A and Wagner, J (1997) On discourse, communication, and (some) fundamental concepts in SLA research, *The Modern Language Journal* 81 (3), 285–300.

Hamilton, J (1991) *Native and non-native speaker performance on the IELTS Reading test*, unpublished MA thesis, University of Melbourne.

Hamilton, J, Lopes, M, McNamara, T and Sheridan, E (1993) Rating scales and native speaker performance on a communicatively oriented EAP test, *Language Testing* 10 (3), 337–353.

Interagency Language Roundtable (1985) Interagency Language Roundtable Skill Level Descriptions for Speaking, available online: govtilr.org/Skills/ILRscale2.htm

Jenkins, J (2006) The times they are (very slowly) a-changin', *ELT Journal* 60 (1), 61–62.

Lantolf, J P and Frawley, W (1985) Oral-proficiency testing: a critical analysis, *The Modern Language Journal* 69 (4), 337–345.

Lopes, M (1992) *Native speaker performance on the IELTS reading test*, unpublished MA thesis, University of Melbourne.

Maher, J C (2001) The unbearable lightness of being a native speaker, in Elder, C E, Brown, A, Grove, E, Hill, K, Iwashita, N, Lumley, T, McNamara, T and O'Loughlin, K (Eds), *Experimenting with Uncertainty: Studies in Honour of Alan Davies*, Studies in Language Testing volume 11, Cambridge: UCLES/ Cambridge University Press, 292–303.

McEnery, T and Wilson, A (2001) *Corpus Linguistics: An Introduction*, Edinburgh: Edinburgh University Press.

Ortega, L (2010) *The bilingual turn in SLA*, plenary presented at the American Association of Applied Linguistics, Atlanta, Georgia, 6 March 2010.

Paikeday, T M (1985) *The Native Speaker Is Dead!: An Informal Discussion of a Linguistic Myth with Noam Chomsky and Other Linguists, Philosophers, Psychologists, and Lexicographers*, Toronto: Paikeday Pub.

Rampton, M H (1990) Displacing the 'native speaker': expertise, affiliation, and inheritance, *ELT Journal* 44 (2), 97–101.

Rifkin, B (2003) Oral proficiency learning outcomes and curricular design, *Foreign Language Annals* 36, 582–588.

Sheridan, E (1991) *A comparison of native/non-native speaker performance on a communicative test of writing ability (IELTS)*, unpublished MA thesis, University of Melbourne.

Taylor, L (2006) The changing landscape of English: implications for language assessment, *ELT Journal* 60 (1), 51–60.

Woolf, H B (1973) Definition: practice and illustration, *Annals of the New York Academy of Sciences* 211 (1), 253–258.

Appendix A

ILR Skill Level Descriptions: Speaking Proficiency (ILR 1985)

Speaking 2+ (Limited Working Proficiency, Plus): Able to satisfy most work requirements with language usage that is often, but not always, acceptable and effective. The individual shows considerable ability to communicate effectively on topics relating to particular interests and special fields of competence. Often shows a high degree of fluency and ease of speech, yet when under tension or pressure, the ability to use the language effectively may deteriorate. Comprehension of normal native speech is typically nearly complete. The individual may miss cultural and local references and may require a native speaker to adjust to his/her limitations in some ways. Native speakers often perceive the individual's speech to contain awkward or inaccurate phrasing of ideas, mistaken time, space and person references, or to be in some way inappropriate, if not strictly incorrect.

Examples: Typically the individual can participate in most social, formal, and informal interactions, but limitations either in range of contexts, types of tasks or level of accuracy hinder effectiveness. The individual may be ill at ease with the use of the language either in social interaction or in speaking at length in professional contexts. He/she is generally strong in either structural precision or vocabulary, but not in both. Weakness or unevenness in one of the foregoing, or in pronunciation, occasionally results in miscommunication. Normally controls, but cannot always easily produce general vocabulary. Discourse is often incohesive.

Speaking 3 (General Professional Proficiency): Able to speak the language with sufficient structural accuracy and vocabulary to participate effectively in most formal and informal conversations in practical, social and professional topics. Nevertheless, the individual's limitations generally restrict the professional contexts of language use to matters of shared knowledge and/or international convention. Discourse is cohesive. The individual uses the language acceptably, but with some noticeable imperfections; yet, errors virtually never interfere with understanding and rarely disturb the native speaker. The individual can effectively combine structure and vocabulary to convey his/her meaning accurately. The individual speaks readily and fills pauses suitably. In face-to-face conversation with natives speaking the standard dialect at a normal rate of speech, comprehension is quite complete. Although cultural references, proverbs and the implications of nuances and idiom may not be fully understood, the individual can easily repair the conversation. Pronunciation may be obviously foreign. Individual sounds are accurate: but stress, intonation and pitch control may be faulty.

Examples: Can typically discuss particular interests and special fields of competence with reasonable ease. Can use the language as part of normal professional duties such as answering objections, clarifying points, justifying decisions, understanding the essence of challenges, stating and defending policy, conducting meetings, delivering briefings, or other extended and elaborate informative monologues. Can reliably elicit information and informed opinion from native speakers. Structural inaccuracy is rarely the major cause of misunderstanding. Use of structural devices is flexible and elaborate. Without searching for words or phrases, the individual uses the language clearly and relatively naturally to elaborate concepts freely and make ideas easily understandable to native speakers. Errors occur in low-frequency and highly complex structures.

Appendix B

Excerpts from two Oral Proficiency Interviews

Sample Performance by 'John'

John provides a response to the following prompt: 'John, an increasing number of scientists and environmental specialists warn that our planet is in grave danger of global warming, that will radically alter life on earth. Many large corporations in the U.S. are opposing stricter environmental laws to protect their profits while environmentalists feel that tighter regulations are needed. What is your opinion on this topic?'

Mark provides a response to the following prompt: 'I'd like to get your opinion on the topic of the environment, more specifically, what you think about government intervention to encourage or penalise businesses for their pollution emissions? What is your opinion on this topic?'

Table 1 Transcription key

Symbol	Explanation
( )	Transcriber didn't hear these sounds or syllables pronounced but they may have been there
(/)	Transcriber heard the first option but the speaker may have pronounced the second option
[ ]	Non-speech notations

Table 2 Non-native speaker (John)

Tester	John
	I'm a little bit familiar with it, when I went to graduate school at Denver University,
Mm hm	
	I took one or two courses in the uh, global economy slash global war(n/m)ing issues dealing with the economy and growth in advance(d) countries as well as less develop(ed) countries,
Mm hm	
	And the professor who's teaching that he's relatively well known Barry Hughes
Mm hm	
	He wrote a book. And we debated and we studied. So naturally I may have my own opinion formed, based on what I research(ed) and read in that classroom and outside. I really think global war(n/m)ing and (e)specially now th- that Al Gore came with his presentation,
Mm hm	
	And acknowledging that hey folks we have serious problems, the answer is yes, we do have problems, but I'm also, very much, encouraged by the fact that science and technology has always played a key role in um, environmental issues
Mm hm	
	As well as other areas but now that the topic is focused on, *[inhales]* eh, global uh environmental issues and uh harms or warnings, there are specific science and technology, there are machineries, there are change of how we do, agricultural activities,
Mm hm	
	Uh, industrial activities, that have enabled us to really make a impact,
Mm hm	
	Even though, some argue well it's a small impact, but I still believe that the impact if we maintain that course of action, eventually, we'll be successful at it
Okay well *[inhales]*	
	Corp-corporations by the way, fight it because sure it's gonna cost them millions and billions of dollars to
Mm hm	
	Retool (d/th)eir style, their machinery, and whatever output they put into the uh environment, but I think they're also becoming much more responsible than they have been in the past, so, that's in a nutshell my perspective and opinion
Laughs okay	
	On the subject. {SAMPLE ENDS}

Table 3 Native speaker (Mark)

Tester	Mark
	[inhales] Yeah um, I think it's it's really important that the the government does delegate those kinda things because, *[inhales]* I know especially in the the mindset of, trying to make money as quickly as possible in any way, possible, *[laughs]* um, it's really easy to overlook those kind of, environmental things especially when it doesn't, affect the, the present, or even the immediate future um, so I think it's good to have those people that are in in positions to look long term, and recognise the dangers and threats of, of certain, behavior, and then, um yeah try and delegate what what should be done, *[inhales]* um I think it's I mean it's important obviously for, for us as we grow older as well as for (our) future gener- generations to be able to, *[inhales]* enjoy, uh I guess this planet, *[laughs]*,
Mm hm	
	As much as possible before, um, we use it all up um, so yeah I think it's really important that the government does do that,
Mm hm	
	And *[trails off]*
[soft] Okay	{SAMPLE ENDS}

16 Foreign language mediation tasks in a criterion-referenced proficiency examination

Ágnes Dévény
Budapest Business School, Hungary

Abstract

Is foreign language mediation an independent language skill and part of our conception of language proficiency? There have been heated debates in professional circles on the role and function of mediation and whether it can be considered a legitimate language examination subtest. In Hungary language examinations often include a mediation task, which gains justification from tradition and from some recent needs analyses results. However, there has not been any scientific research verifying that mediation is an independent language skill, and part of the candidate's language competence. The Common European Framework of Reference for languages (CEFR) (Council of Europe 2001) describes mediation as one of the language activities but does not define it as an independent language skill. The aim of the present research project is to investigate whether foreign language mediation is an independent language skill that can be measured by specific criteria, and which behaves fundamentally in the same way in the test battery as other subtests, and as part of a foreign language examination it contributes to a more complex assessment of the test takers' language proficiency. The research methods included:

- descriptive and statistical analyses of more than 27,000 test results (intersubtest, subtest-final test score correlations, reliability analyses, factor analyses, multiple regression analyses, cluster analyses)
- interviews with experts on the difficulties of measurement and the methodological problems they face in preparing learners for doing written mediation examination tasks
- longitudinal surveys following the students' preparatory work for the task.

The paper presents how the results of the research verified the hypotheses investigated and discusses several important pedagogical implications deriving from the study.

Introduction

Is foreign language mediation an independent language skill? Is it part of our conception of language proficiency and a segment of the language learners'/ users' language competence? Can it be measured just like other language skills? There have been heated debates in professional circles on the role and function of mediation and the debates have not abated yet (Bárdos 1997, 2005, Heltai 2001, Szabari 2001).

The notion of foreign language mediation

Experts interpret and explain the concept of mediation in many different ways and their opinions vary, reflecting the different views of specialists in the field of bilingualism/multilingualism (Alderson 2001, Bárdos 2005, Einhorn 1998, Fekete, Major and Nikolov 1999).

As language proficiency models do not interpret the notion of mediation unambiguously, it is important for the purposes of this study to define mediation, its relation to translation theories and translation science, and to describe how it differs from other definitions of translation. In the current article, foreign language mediation is defined as follows: mediation is a skill which facilitates mediation activity in the course of which the information in source language (SL) text is successfully processed while using appropriate mediation strategies such as summarising, paraphrasing and rewording, in a manner in which the essential information content of the SL text is successfully switched into the target language (TL). Transfer is successful if it is accomplished with appropriate linguistic, lexical and stylistic tools without causing essential distortion to information content. The aim of foreign language mediation is not the translation of the SL text word for word, but to reflect the intention and the message of the original text. Therefore, a successful mediation strives to ensure that the message remains clear in the target text.

Very few experts in applied linguistics consider any type of mediation (mostly translation) as part of language competence/proficiency. Palmer (1917) used translation in language teaching, emphasising the importance of exercises that teach the ability to think in the target language and their aim involved mediating TL culture as well. Lado (1961:26) wrote that 'a fifth skill is the ability to translate, which should be tested as an end itself and not as a way to test mastery of the language'. Harris (1969) opposed translation, arguing that it hindered foreign language acquisition because of first language to second language (L1–L2) interference. Oller (1979) accepted translation as part of pragmatic testing techniques if it reflected real-life situations. Cummins (2005) opposed monolingual language teaching programmes. In his view there was no scientific evidence that translation hindered effective foreign language acquisition; on the contrary, empirical evidence (e.g. Orellana, Reynolds, Dorner and Meza 2003) has confirmed the pedagogical usefulness of translation. Rivers and Temperley (1978:325) claim that 'translation is both a skill and an art, of considerable practical and aesthetic value in the modern world' and either type (L1–L2, L2–L1) of translation 'may be an advanced activity to test the ability to transfer meaning comprehensively and elegantly from one language code to the other' (1978:326). They do not agree with the concept that translation as a teaching device hinders 'the development of the ability to think directly in the new language' (1978:326). Stern (1992:76) introduced a major distinction between two broad types of communication skills: intralingual and crosslingual (mediating) skills, so in his model mediation appears as part of second language proficiency on Level 2 (skills).

Mediation in the Common European Framework of Reference for languages (CEFR) appears among *Language activities* (Council of Europe 2001:14). It is important to note that although mediation is not considered in the CEFR as an independent language skill (it does not appear in an explicit way as an element of communicative language competence or language proficiency), it is treated on a par with reception, production and interaction. The CEFR (2001:14) even emphasises that:

> in both the receptive and productive modes, the written and/or oral activities of *mediation* make communication possible between persons who are unable, for whatever reason, to communicate with each other directly. Translation or interpretation, a paraphrase, summary or record, provides for a third party a (re)formulation of a source text to which this third party does not have direct access. Mediating language activities – (re)processing an existing text – occupy an important place in the normal linguistic functioning of our societies.

The last idea is extremely important, as former models of language competence have acknowledged the social and cultural embeddedness of language activities, but very few of them position such activities in multilingual circumstances.

Mediation as an examination task

Debates in professional circles can become even more heated when experts have to decide whether a mediation task (e.g. in a written mediation test) can be considered a legitimate language examination task (Fekete 2001, 2002, Klaudy 1984, 1986a, 1986b, 1990). The scientific investigation of bilingualism/multilingualism in education and testing, as well as the interpretation of the notion of foreign language mediation, are especially delicate topics as they conceal the diversity and distinctness of opinions and theories of language skills and abilities. Opponents of bilingual examinations do not regard any type of mediation as an independent language skill and an element of language knowledge, and do not accept the concept that by testing and measuring this skill we can get a more complex idea of the candidate's foreign language proficiency. On the contrary, many of them fear the negative washback effect of the mother tongue on foreign language acquisition (Nikolov, Fekete and Major 1999). Contradictory views are reflected in the fact that whereas a mediation task was completely left out from school-leaving (maturity) examination tasks in Hungary, several bilingual and monolingual examination systems have been accredited in that country since the beginning of the accreditation procedures in 1999 (Alderson 2001, Einhorn 1998, Nikolov et al 1999). The acceptance of bilingual examination systems was only justified by some needs analyses and Hungarian language examination traditions, but there was not any empirical research verifying that foreign language mediation is an independent language skill, which is part of the candidate's language competence.

The principal argument of the opponents of the mediation task is its negative washback on teaching practice, and the difficulties of its evaluation arising from the complex nature of the skill. The negative impact cannot be considered as a generally acceptable counter-argument in all cases. According to Bachman and Palmer (2000:102–104) a language test can be useful and reasonable if it corresponds in demonstrable ways to language use in a specific target language use domain and is based on certain procedures of needs analysis.

A Hungarian national survey (Teemant, Varga and Heltai 1993) and some surveys with smaller scope (Dévény and Szőke 2007, Major 2000, Silye 2004) were conducted mainly in the field of professional language usage during the last decade. The results of these surveys show that mediation is verified as a real-life domain of language usage, so it is justifiable as a test task, but they do not produce any evidence of acknowledging it as an independent language skill.

Posing the problem

The aim of the current research is to present an empirically supported argument that foreign language mediation is an independent language skill that can be measured by specific criteria, and that as part of a foreign language examination it contributes to a more complex assessment of the test takers' language knowledge.

In accordance with the theme of this paper, three main fields of the academic literature were surveyed. A brief study of related disciplines revealed various interpretations of language use and proficiency in evolutional psychology, cognitive psychology, psycholinguistics, sociolinguistics and pedagogy. Evolutional psychology studies the location of language skills and abilities in the human brain. According to Szathmáry's (2001, 2002) Language AmoeBa (LAB) hypothesis, 'language amoeba is the neural activity pattern that essentially contributes to processing of linguistic information, especially syntax. It is a sort of dynamic manifestation of Chomsky's language organ. It finds its "habitat" in the developing human brain' (2002:42). While linguistic approaches focus on the formal structures of languages and language use (Chomsky 1965), cognitive psychology, as a subdiscipline of psychology, investigates human cognition, focusing on language acquisition, language comprehension and language production (Kintsch 1974, Levelt 1989, Pinker 1994). Based on Broadbent's (1958) cognitive approach, the dominant paradigm in the area is the information processing model of cognition, which envisions mental processes as software running on a computer that is the human brain. Language, along with thinking, intelligence, creativity and problem solving, is a primary mental knowledge representation system (Csapó 1992), and language proficiency is also part of cognition. Psycholinguistics, combining the disciplines of psychology and linguistics, studies the relationship between the human mind and language. It examines the processes that occur in the brain while producing and perceiving both written and spoken discourse, the ways of storing lexical items and syntactic rules in the mind, as well as the processes of memory involved in the perception and interpretation of texts. The processes of speaking and listening, language acquisition and language disorders are also analysed by psycholinguistics (Gósy 1999). Sociolinguistics is the study of interrelationships between language and society. In Gumperz's view (1971:223), it is an attempt to find correlations between social structure and linguistic structure, while also observing any changes that occur. The appearance of the notion of communicative competence in some studies of sociolinguists can be considered an important step towards defining the elements of language proficiency, but attempts to specify the exact meaning of communicative competence have not been very successful, probably because of its complex and all-encompassing nature (Wardhaugh 1986, 2006). Wardhaugh (2006:384) writes that:

> if an important part of the linguistic competence of language users is their ability to handle variation and the various uses of language in society, then the competence that needs to be explained is one that encompasses a much wider range of abilities: it is *communicative competence*, of which linguistic competence is but a part. (authors italics)

In the second phase of the literature review the most important models of language proficiency in language pedagogy were surveyed with special attention to the models which include any type or form of foreign language mediation (e.g., Bárdos 2000, 2005, 2006, Stern 1983, 1992). As in this research project foreign language mediation skill was studied through linguistic outputs generated in testing or examination situations, the third field surveyed was the notion of foreign language measurement, evaluation and testing, to show their place in language pedagogy.

From the perspective of language assessment, the following research questions guided the study:

- What is the construct validity of the written mediation task in the language examination under investigation?
- Is mediation a reliable examination task in the language examination under investigation?
- Are there any subskills in written mediation tasks that appear in other subtests as well?
- What does the inter-subtest correlation of the written mediation task show compared with other examination tasks?
- What are the special criteria in the assessment of the written mediation task?

From the perspective of teaching, the guiding research questions were:

- What is the role of mediation in language usage and language instruction?
- What are the distinguishing features in teaching foreign language mediation and are these features reflected in the evaluation criteria of the mediation task?
- How are students/candidates prepared for the mediation examination task?
- What are the special difficulties that instructors and students have to face?

Based on the research questions the following hypotheses were formed:

- the special language skills that appear and can be measured in written mediation tasks are not present in other subtests, therefore bilingual language examinations can measure skills that are not measurable by monolingual examination systems
- written mediation tasks have special measurement criteria on the basis of which they can be evaluated.

In order to answer the research questions and to support the hypotheses four different research studies were conducted: (1) statistical analyses of the examination results; (2) interviews with language teachers; (3) a longitudinal survey of students' opinions; (4) analysis of documents showing the changes in the description and evaluation criteria.

The scope of this paper does not allow a discussion of all questions posed above. Instead, the focus will be on the assessment-related research questions.

The background of the research

For the present research project the examination system of the Budapest Business School (BBS) was chosen, a bilingual, criterion-referenced, Language for Specific Purposes (LSP) examination system, where along with the traditional language skills (speaking, writing, reading comprehension, listening comprehension), mediation skills are also measured at different levels of the examination. The examination tasks of the complex intermediate (B2) exam at the time of the research were the following:

1. Written examination:
   * grammar test
   * reading comprehension test
   * writing test (generally a business letter)
   * written mediation test from Hungarian to the target language.
2. Listening comprehension test.
3. Oral examination:
   * introductory conversation
   * oral mediation task (mediation of a newspaper article into Hungarian)
   * speaking test (conversation on vocational topics)
   * situation.

The written mediation test focused on in the present study, as an intermediate examination task, involved the following: the examinee had to mediate a written text in Hungarian of approximately 150 words, with an output of approximately 100 words in the target language. The requirement was not a word-for-word translation of the text but it involved a summarising element. Candidates were not allowed to use a dictionary.

At this point it is important to emphasise that the present research project was *not* part of the research and development activity of the language examination centre. Since the time of the research the test battery of the B2 examination has been changed and the written mediation task has been omitted from the examination system of the BBS.

Methods of the research

The characteristics of the sample

Research study one: Examination results

For the statistical analysis of the examination results the examination scores of those candidates were chosen who took the intermediate LSP exam in the BBS examination centre from 2000 to 2007. The population comprised

17–35-year-old males and females, typically college and university students (97–98%). The remaining 2–3% were employees from different areas of the economy. The size of the sample was slightly different in each examination period, but it ranged typically from 1,000 to 2,000, totalling to 27,832 candidates in 18 examination periods.

Research study two: Teacher interviews

Eight teachers from the Foreign Language Institute of the BBS were interviewed; they were accredited examiners of the language examination centre of the BBS as well. The teachers were considered suitably qualified; as a group they had 15–33 years of experience in teaching in higher education and 10–22 years of experience in teaching LSP. All of them took part in developing the BBS language examination system and had extensive test-writing experience.

Research study three: Student survey

The longitudinal survey consisted of three questionnaires. One hundred and sixty-six students from 13 groups, all of them second-year students, who were preparing for the language examination, took part in the first phase of the research conducted at the beginning of November 2005. In the second phase, at the beginning of March 2006, 137 students took part in the survey from the same groups. The third phase of the research was in May 2006, immediately after the students had taken the written examination. Eighty-eight students from the above-mentioned groups completed the questionnaire this time. Additionally, 69 students from other different groups who formerly did not take part in the longitudinal survey were asked to participate. Any differences between the answers from the groups from the longitudinal research and the answers originating from the control group were focused on here. This also helped to address the question whether the longitudinal survey had any influence on the preparatory work of the groups.

Research study four: Document analysis

Official and non-official documents were collected from the period 2000–07 showing the changes in the description and evaluation criteria of the intermediate written mediation task. The documents show the different versions proposed by the experts, and those that were translated into practice.

Research instruments and methods of data analysis

Qualitative instruments for oral interviews, questionnaires and document analysis were used; the analysis of test batteries was quantitative. The methods of data analysis involved:

- descriptive and inferential statistics generated with the statistical software SPSS (analysis of validity and reliability aspects of the tests, inter-subtest correlations, subtest-final score correlations, reliability index of the subtests, factor analysis, multiple regression analysis, cluster analysis)
- analysing interviews with qualitative methods and with qualitative data analysis management and model-building software (ATLAS.ti)
- some questions from the questionnaires were analysed statistically (SPSS) and open-ended questions were analysed with ATLAS.ti software.

Results

Results of the statistical analyses

As noted earlier, statistical analyses of the examination scores were carried out in order to investigate the relationship between the results of the sub-tests. Although different types of statistical analyses, e.g. confirmatory factor analysis (CFA) have been used in psychology and other social sciences to support measuring abilities, personality traits etc., the concept of using statistical analyses to support the existence of an independent foreign language skill is not considered a usual approach in language pedagogy. In classical and modern test theories statistical analyses were used largely for solving different testing and test construction problems.

The statistical analyses were used to confirm the hypothesis that the written mediation examination task can measure a skill or a complexity of subskills that cannot be measured with other examination tasks, thus demonstrating that besides the traditional language skills an *independent foreign language mediation skill* exists. Statistical analyses in this paper will be illustrated with the results of *one examination period* (January 2005) and the results of all 18 exam periods will be summarised separately. Table 1 shows the main characteristics of the chosen examination period.

As Table 1 indicates, the means of the scores of the oral examination tasks are higher than the means of the written examination tasks. The examinees achieved the lowest scores on the listening comprehension test (x=9.52; 48% of the possible maximum score of 20). The mean of the scores of the written mediation task is the second lowest (x=5.81; 58% of the possible maximum score of 10). The standard deviation (SD) in the case of the written mediation task is the lowest (1.994), ranging from the minimum (0) to the maximum (10) score for the task. The distribution of scores of nearly all examination tests (except for the listening comprehension) is negatively skewed as would be expected in the case of criterion-referenced tests.

Table 1 Descriptive statistics of the examination test scores (Sample period: January 2005) (n = 1,669)

	Grammar test	Reading comp.	Writing test	Written mediation	Listening comp.	Introductory conv.	Speaking	Situation	Oral mediation
Total score on task	20	20	20	10	20	20	20	20	10
Mean	10.78	12.12	12.31	5.81	9.52	15.53	13.21	14.72	7.26
SE of Mean	.088	.090	.093	.049	.096	.076	.101	.100	.050
Median	11	12	12	6	9	16	14	15	8
Mode	10	13	12	6	9	18	14	20	8
SD	3.610	3.680	3.814	1.994	3.917	3.093	4.116	4.073	2.038
Variance	13.030	13.544	14.549	3.975	15.341	9.564	16.943	16.588	4.153
Skewness	-.170	-.148	-.103	-.207	.385	-.643	-.455	-.757	-.585
SE of Skewness	.060	.060	.060	.060	.060	.060	.060	.060	.060
Kurtosis	-.561	-.415	-.414	-.280	-.412	.085	-.284	.268	-.110
SE of Kurtosis	.120	.120	.120	.120	.120	.120	.120	.120	.120
Range	19	19	20	10	19	16	20	20	10
Minimum	1	1	0	0	1	4	0	0	0
Maximum	20	20	20	10	20	20	20	20	10

Internal correlations as a way of assessing the construct validity of tests

Construct validity is a form of test validation which essentially involves assessing to what extent the test is successfully based upon its underlying theory (Alderson, Clapham and Wall 1995:183). In order to investigate the construct validity of the mediation task – the inter-subtest and the subtest – final test scores correlation coefficients of the examination tasks were calculated.

Inter-subtest correlations

The idea behind inter-subtest correlation of test components is that if two test components correlate very highly with each other, we might assume that the two test components are *not* testing different traits or skills. It means that one of them might be superfluous.

At first the Pearson correlation coefficient was calculated to see the overlap between the subtests. The optimal value in the case of inter-subtest correlation is between .3–.5, which means a 9–25% overlap of variance between two subtests (Alderson et al 1995:184). The results (Table 2) show that except for the Grammar test, all other subtests' inter-subtest indices are in the ideal range. But even in the case of the Grammar test the overlap is only about 30% of variance of the two subtests.

The problematic point of the measurement is that test results do not always show a normal distribution, as examinees who sit for a criterion-referenced proficiency exam are supposed to be well prepared, so the distribution curve can be negatively skewed (see Table 1). That is why the non-parametric correlation was considered as well. The correlation matrix showed nearly the same results as the parametric analysis.

The means of the inter-subtest correlations of the 18 examination periods show a desirable overlap between the different subtests – an approximately 18–25% overlap of variance (Table 3). The only exception is the Grammar test which shows an average of 36% overlap of variance. The Grammar test, as it does not measure an independent language skill, behaves in the same way for all examination periods.

Subtest–total test scores correlation

According to classical test theory of language testing, the correlations between each subtest and the whole test might be expected to be higher – possibly around +.7 or more – since the overall score is taken to be a more general measure of language ability than each individual component score (Alderson et al 1995:184). The subtest–total test scores correlation (Table 4) is calculated because it shows the impact of the subtest on the total (overall) test scores of the examination.

Table 2 Inter-subtest correlation matrix of written mediation (L1 → L2) task. Comparison of the results of the parametric and non-parametric analysis (January 2005) (n=1,669)

Subtests	M	SD	Parametric analysis				Non-parametric analysis			
			r Pearson Corr.	p	R^2	Overlap of variance %	r Spearman's rho	p	R^2	Overlap of variance %
Grammar test	10.78	3.610	.561**	.000	.315	31	.550**	.000	.302	30
Reading Comp.	12.12	3.680	.424**	.000	.179	18	.416**	.000	.173	17
Writing test	12.31	3.814	.459**	.000	.210	21	.445**	.000	.198	20
Listening Comp.	9.52	3.917	.461**	.000	.212	21	.450**	.000	.202	20
Introductory Conv.	15.53	3.093	.367**	.000	.134	13	.361**	.000	.130	13
Speaking test	13.21	4.116	.341**	.000	.116	12	.345**	.000	.119	12
Situation	14.72	4.073	.386**	.000	.148	15	.394**	.000	.155	16
Oral mediation	7.26	2.038	.338**	.000	.114	11	.340**	.000	.116	12

** Correlation is significant at the 0.01 level (2-tailed).

Table 3 Overlapping of skills measured by written mediation (L1 → L2) task with skills measured by other subtests
[Mean of inter-subtest correlations of 18 examination periods (%)]

Subtests	r	p	R^2	Overlap of variance (%)
Grammar test	.598	.000	.357	36
Reading Comp.	.493	.000	.243	24
Writing test	.507	.000	.257	26
Listening Comp.	.461	.000	.212	21
Introductory Conv.	.417	.000	.173	17
Speaking test	.426	.000	.181	18
Situation	.437	.000	.190	19
Oral mediation (L2-L1)	.420	.000	.176	18

As Table 4 shows, the correlation coefficients in the case of the Grammar test (r=.671), Reading comprehension test (r=.691), Writing test (r=.616) and Listening comprehension test (r=.637) are on the low side. In the case of all other tests, including the Written mediation test (r=.726), they are above the optimal .7 value. These results show a rather strong correlation between the subtests and the total scores and show how important these subtests are in the test battery. Non-parametric analysis in each case shows a lower correlation coefficient of the written mediation test but it is near to the desired value.

Table 5 shows the subtest–total score (minus self) correlation of the Written mediation task (L1 → L2) in the 18 examination periods. The correlation coefficients are generally between .6 and .7, a bit lower than the optimal, but convincingly higher than the inter-subtest correlation coefficients.

The correlation analyses indicate that the written mediation test does not behave in a different way when compared with the other examination tasks, and does not show such a high common proportion of variance with them that would indicate that the mediation task measures the same skills as the other examination tasks (subtests). This indicates that neither the written mediation task nor the other examination tasks can be omitted from the test battery.

Reliability analysis of the subtests

Test reliability refers to the extent to which test scores are consistent. According to classical item analysis in test construction it is useful to calculate the reliability index (coefficient Alpha) of test items in order to know which test item increases or decreases the reliability of the whole test. Those items that decrease the reliability of the test should be omitted.

In this case each subtest was considered as an item of the whole test (examination) battery and the reliability indices of subtests (Table 6) were calculated.

Table 4 Subtest–total test scores (minus itself) correlation matrix (January 2005) (n=1,669)

	Max. test score	r Total test score minus itself	p	M of subtests	SD of subtests	M Total test score minus itself	SD Total test score minus itself
Grammar test	20	.671**	.000	11.81	3.427	88.75	22.276
Reading Comp.	20	.691**	.000	12.34	4.150	88.21	21.654
Writing test	20	.619**	.000	12.33	3.469	88.23	22.406
Written mediation (L1-L2)	10	.726**	.000	5.55	1.996	95.00	23.218
Listening Comp.	20	.637**	.000	10.24	3.656	90.31	22.214
Introductory Conv.	20	.778**	.000	14.90	3.617	85.66	21.788
Speaking test	20	.780**	.000	12.38	4.484	88.17	21.047
Situation	20	.773**	.000	14.24	4.364	86.31	21.177
Oral mediation (L2-L1)	10	.763**	.000	6.76	2.349	93.80	22.866

** Correlation is significant at the 0.01 level (2-tailed).

Table 5 Subtest–total score (minus self) correlation of written mediation tasks (L1 → L2) in 18 examination periods

		r	p	M	SD	M Total test score minus Mediation score	SD Total test score minus Mediation score	N
1	Sep 2000	.676	.000	4.88	2.237	89.95	26.069	229
2	Jan 2001	.668	.000	5.88	2.241	91.92	27.253	360
3	May 2001	.642	.000	6.27	2.134	98.46	21.735	2,072
4	May 2002	.646	.000	5.75	2.140	97.63	21.599	2,754
5	Jan 2003	.605	.000	5.86	2.182	96.21	20.480	1,630
6	May 2003	.595	.000	5.70	2.034	97.86	20.306	2,577
7	Sep 2003	.608	.000	5.56	2,065	94.02	19.519	1,180
8	Jan 2004	.601	.000	5.20	2.156	96.91	20.378	1,532
9	May 2004	.584	.000	5.39	1.928	94.90	20.367	2,540
10	Sep 2004	.606	.000	6.07	1.927	93.23	19.681	1,280
11	Jan 2005	.726	.000	5.55	1.996	95.00	23.218	1,669
12	Mar 2005	.581	.000	5.81	1.994	95.45	20.551	319
13	May 2005	.596	.000	5.75	2.047	97.95	21.670	2,286
14	Sep 2005	.656	.000	5.91	1.950	89.99	19.449	1,399
15	Jan 2006	.632	.000	5.92	2.193	97.81	22.802	1,596
16	May 2006	.706	.000	6.16	2.124	98.41	22.931	1,922
17	Sep 2006	.608	.000	5.24	2.191	90.28	24.404	1,103
18	Jan 2007	.672	.000	5.74	2.226	98.62	23.655	1,384

Table 6 Reliability analysis of subtests (January 2005) (n=1,669)

	Item-total statistics			
	Scale mean if item deleted	Scale variance if item deleted	Corrected item-total correlation	Cronbach's Alpha if item deleted
Grammar test	90.47	369.586	.656	.850
Reading Comp.	89.13	377.324	.579	.858
Writing test	88.94	381.048	.524	.864
Written mediation (L1-L2)	95.44	422.064	.581	.862
Listening Comp.	91.73	376.122	.541	.862
Introductory Conv.	85.72	382.069	.678	.849
Speaking test	88.04	351.327	.683	.848
Situation	86.53	350.619	.698	.846
Oral mediation (L2-L1)	93.99	413.115	.681	.856

Full test reliability statistics

	Cronbach's Alpha	N of cases	N of items
	.869	1669	9

Figure 1 Omitting written mediation (L1 → L2) tasks from the test battery, Cronbach's Alpha coefficient (18 examination periods)

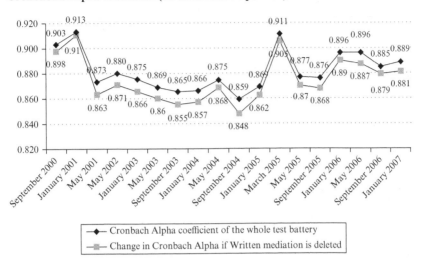

The results in Figure 1 show that if the Written mediation test were deleted from the test battery the reliability index (Cronbach Alpha) of the test batteries would decrease in all examination periods. It means that the total scores of the whole examination and thus the examination itself would be less reliable.

Factor analysis

The procedure of factor analysis is used to reduce the number of variables accounting for test performance by identifying the common underlying factor (or factors) shared by a series of tests in the test battery.

The results of the Kaiser-Meyer-Olkin (KMO) (≥0.8) and Bartlett's Test showed that the data was suitable for factor analysis. The principal component analysis (PCA) method was used in this research project as it 'gives us a way of discovering factors that underlie language performance and ways of testing the relationship among them' (Hatch and Lazaraton 1991:489). PCA initially attempts to fit as much of the data from the correlation matrix of all variables entered, into a single principal component; in other words, it attempts to explain through the first factor as much of the variability in the data as possible. Once this has been done it trawls through the data again, looking for the second component which will explain as much of the remaining variance as possible (Green and Weir 2001:113).

In the case of the presented examination period all subtests loaded

Table 7 Factor analysis (January 2005) (n=1,669)

	Component matrix (a)				
	Component				
	1	2	3	4	5
Grammar test	**.763**	.274	−.152	−.359	−.040
Reading Comp.	**.687**	.267	.441	−.379	.198
Writing test	**.642**	.326	−.523	.166	.398
Written mediation (L1-L2)	**.690**	.371	−.151	.067	−.563
Listening Comp.	**.656**	.319	.422	.488	.076
Introductory Conv.	**.751**	−.453	−.012	.158	−.009
Speaking test	**.759**	−.481	−.049	−.088	.030
Situation	**.776**	−.466	.028	.012	−.050
% of variance	51.435	14.320	8.683	7.187	6.564

**% Total variance explained by 5 factors
88.188**

Extraction method: Principal Component Analysis.　　　　　　　　KMO = .863

a. 5 components extracted.

positively on the first factor with .642 or above (Table 7), which can be considered as an indication of a substantial link between them. They all load on the same factor as the first factor represents *general linguistic ability* (Green and Weir 2001:115).

More complex procedures can be followed, such as rotation of the factors to see if any clearer solutions present themselves in order to reveal the underlying factors or components. In analysing test results Varimax rotation is the most commonly used procedure (Green and Weir 2001:117). The result of the Varimax rotation of test scores (Table 8) showed that the different subtests representing different language skills fell on different factors with rather high factor loadings, except for the Grammar test which does not represent a separate language skill.

Written mediation appears in the third factor in the observed examination period (January 2005) and accounts for 15% of variance of the test battery.

In the 18 examination periods foreign language mediation tests appear in the second to fifth factors. It mostly falls on the second and third factors. Factor loadings are between .730 and .911. On average, in all 18 examination periods, foreign language mediation tests account for 17% of variance. In all cases the factors correlate well with total test scores.

To summarise, the results of the factor analysis show that foreign language mediation skill represented by written mediation tasks is one of the components of general language ability. It can be clearly separated from other language skills with its high loading of variance and on average it explains 17%

Table 8 Factor analysis – Varimax rotation (January 2005) (n=1,669)

	Rotated component matrix (a)				
	Component				
	1	2	3	4	5
Grammar test	.287	**.586**	**.485**	**.388**	−.019
Reading Comp.	.218	**.875**	.116	.084	.294
Writing test	.191	.140	.187	**.925**	.169
Written mediation (L1-L2)	.199	.159	**.900**	.175	.230
Listening Comp.	.200	.239	.206	.167	**.887**
Introductory Conv.	**.842**	.064	.131	.144	.208
Speaking test	**.858**	.223	.106	.147	.013
Situation	**.862**	.179	.161	.078	.127
% of variance	30.423	16.206	14.875	14.012	12.673

**% Total variance explained by 5 factors
88.188**

Extraction method: Principal Component Analysis.   KMO = .863
Rotation method: Varimax with Kaiser Normalization.

a. Rotation converged in 6 iterations.

of the variance of the language skills in the test battery, so it represents an important part of language knowledge.

Multiple linear regression analysis (Method FORWARD)

Multiple regression analysis reveals the common subskills between media-tion tests and other subtests. The problematic point was to keep reliability of variables in the test battery on nearly the same level. (The test battery con-tains subtests that are subjectively scored, so it was important to elaborate and use a system of evaluation criteria that increases the objectivity of evalu-ation of these tests. Surveying the elaboration of this system is beyond the scope of this paper.)

The whole process and all the steps of multiple linear regression analysis of the test scores of the examination period under research cannot be presented here, so only the model summary (Table 9) representing the most important result of the analysis will be shown in this paper.

In this case (January 2005), Introductory conversation and the Speaking task on a vocational topic were dropped from the model. The model summary reveals that approximately 41% of the variance of the written mediation test can be explained by the help of other variables. It indicates the presence of common subskills. The remaining 59% indicates the existence of subskills that are only present in mediation skill.

Multiple regression analyses revealed the common subskills (the

Table 9 Model summary of regression analysis (January 2005) (n=1,669)

		Model summary		
Model	R	R Square	Adjusted R Square	Std. Error of the estimate
1	.561(a)	.315	.315	1.650
2	.613(b)	.376	.375	1.576
3	.630(c)	.397	.396	1.549
4	.637(d)	.405	.404	1.539
5	.638(e)	.407	**.405**	1.537

a Predictors: (Constant), Grammar test
b Predictors: (Constant), Grammar test, Listening Comp.
c Predictors: (Constant), Grammar test, Listening Comp., Writing test
d Predictors: (Constant), Grammar test, Listening Comp., Writing test, Situation
e Predictors: (Constant), Grammar test, Listening Comp., Writing test, Situation, Reading Comp.
f **Dependent Variable: Written mediation (L1-L2)**

proportion of variation in the dependent variable explained by the regression model) between mediation tasks and other tasks. On average 54% of the variance of the mediation task is not explained by other examination tasks so it represents subskills that can only be attributed to foreign language mediation skills.

Cluster analysis

Clustering is the assignment of a set of observations into subsets (called *clusters*) so that observations in the same cluster are similar in some sense. Cluster analysis sorts through the raw data and groups it into clusters. A cluster is a group of relatively homogeneous cases or observations. Objects in a cluster are similar to each other. They are also dissimilar to objects outside the cluster, particularly objects in other clusters. Thus this method seemed to be suitable to see how the different subtests relate to each other (Figure 2).

When observing the 18 examination periods in each case the Written mediation test formed an independent cluster.

Summarising the results of the cluster analyses, they also confirmed that foreign language mediation is an independent language skill as mediation tasks are distinctly separate from other examination tasks forming an independent cluster.

Summary of statistical analyses and results

Table 10 presents a summary of the results of the various statistical analyses of examination scores.

Figure 2 Cluster analysis – Dendrograms using Average and Single Linkage (January 2005) (n=1,662)

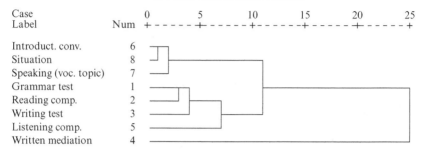

Hierarchical cluster analysis

Dendrogram using Average Linkage (between groups)

Rescaled distance cluster combine

Case Label	Num	0	5	10	15	20	25

Introduct. conv.	6
Situation	8
Speaking (voc. topic)	7
Grammar test	1
Reading comp.	2
Writing test	3
Listening comp.	5
Written mediation	4

Hierarchical cluster analysis

Dendrogram using Single Linkage

Rescaled distance cluster combine

Case Label	Num	0	5	10	15	20	25

Introduct. conv.	6
Situation	8
Speaking (voc. topic)	7
Grammar test	1
Reading comp.	2
Writing test	3
Listening comp.	5
Written mediation	4

Results of the interviews with teachers/examiners

This part of the research project dealt with the progress of the preparatory work for the written mediation task. The teachers (accredited examiners) expressed their opinions in structured interviews focusing on the following questions:

- What are the skills or subskills that are measured by the mediation task?
- Is mediation a valid and reliable examination task?
- Would they change anything in the task or its measurement criteria?

Their answers on the process of the preparatory work can be compared with the students' opinions on the same topic.

Table 10 Statistical analyses indicate the presence of an independent mediation skill

Analyses	Results
1. Inter-subtest correlation 2. Subtest–total score correlation	The *written mediation task* **does not behave in a different way** when compared with the other examination tasks, and **does not show such a high common proportion of** variance with them that would indicate that the mediation task measures the same skills as the other examination tasks (subtests). It was obvious that neither the *written mediation task* nor the other examination tasks can be omitted from the test battery.
3. Reliability coefficients of subtests	The **omission** of the *written mediation task* **would reduce the reliability of the whole test battery**.
4. Factor analysis	Foreign language mediation skill represented by written mediation tasks **is one of the components of general language ability**. It can be clearly separated from other language skills with its high loading of variance and **on average it explains 17% of the variance in the test battery** so it represents an important part of language knowledge.
5. Multiple linear regression analysis	It **revealed the common subskills** (the proportion of variation in the dependent variable explained by the regression model) **between *mediation tasks* and other tasks**. On average **54% of the variance of the mediation task is not explained by other examination tasks** so it represents subskills that can be attributed only to foreign language mediation skill.
6. Cluster analysis	It confirmed that *foreign language mediation* is an independent language skill as mediation tasks are distinctly separate from other examination tasks forming **an independent cluster**.

The interviews indicated that experts consider written mediation an authentic and productive examination task which, due to its complexity, requires multifold activities from the examinees. They think it is a good measuring instrument of language knowledge, and would like to give it a greater emphasis in the test battery. They find the task especially important as it mobilises nearly all language competences. When executing the task a specific, new quality is born from the complex operation of bilingualism and the traditional language skills which is a characteristic feature only of foreign language mediation. The preparatory work on the part of the teachers can be considered very purposeful, relying on the individual and collective work of the students. Their approach is practical and purpose-oriented, their role is positive and supporting during the whole process but they hardly deal with affective factors such as the students' anxiety or distress in relation to this examination task.

The results of the longitudinal survey

The longitudinal survey followed the process of the preparatory work for the written mediation task from the viewpoint of students. Not only can the process of the instruction and skill development be traced from the answers to the questionnaires, but also how the results of this work serve the final goal, the successful examination. During this process students have to confront a number of problems and difficulties. The picture of the preparatory work drafted by the teachers in the interviews and by the students in the longitudinal survey can be compared to each other.

Both teachers' and students' opinions naturally show a different level of consciousness. Uncovering the anxiety, fears and difficulties that can be attached to the examination task created an important part of the research. Students' answers reflect convincingly the purposeful pedagogical work that results in increasing independence, consciousness and satisfaction for the students. It is surprising, however, that despite of the painstaking preparatory work the fears and anxiety from the examination task only decreases slightly.

Results of the document analysis

It was clear from the analysis of official and non-official documents that as new standpoints based on experience emerged, the examination team endeavoured to clarify and define the best possible description, measurement criteria and descriptors for the mediation task (Table 11).

Table 11 Changes and main problem points in the measurement criteria of the intermediate mediation task (2000–07)

	Criterion 1	Criterion 2
Official version/1	mediation of content	sociocultural competence
Suggested version/1	mediation of information content	language strategies serving mediating information content, [global (text-level) information transfer]
Suggested version/2	mediation of the message of the text (without damaging the transfer of information)	applying language strategies (serving the mediation of the content – vocabulary, language/grammar structures, etc.)
Official versions/2 & 3 (change in descriptors)	mediation of content	applying language strategies (serving the mediation of the content – vocabulary, style, language structures, etc.)

Main problem points:
1. Length, authenticity, genre, style, LSP content, function of SL text.
2. Need for real communicative situation – knowing the aim, role, function, genre, audience, etc. of TL text.

The most striking changes appeared in the length of the mediation task as the input text was shortened from the original 1,000 to 150 words. This did not correspond with the opinion of some experts who suggested increasing the length and the role of the task in the test battery. Evaluation of the mediation skill needs a set of special criteria. The validity, reliability and objectivity of the task can be increased by a more elaborate and precise system of measurement criteria.

Based on the idea of the extended SL text, a new system of evaluation criteria was elaborated consisting of three criteria instead of two in which – along with Criterion 1 and Criterion 2 (see Table 11) – the criterion of sociocultural competence was reintroduced based on the idea that the communicative function of mediation is very important, and this criterion was missing from the evaluation criteria of the mediation task at the time of the research mainly because the text was too short for evaluating its sociocultural competence.

Conclusions and recommendations

The aim of this research project was to investigate by empirical methods whether foreign language mediation is an independent language skill that can be measured by specific criteria, whether it is as legitimate as traditional basic language skills and whether its usage as an examination task contributes to a more complex notion of the test takers' language knowledge. The research findings supported the hypotheses:

- The written mediation examination task measures a segment of language knowledge independently; skills appearing in it are not present in other examination tasks. Foreign language mediation is an independent language skill; therefore bilingual language examinations can measure skills that are not measurable by monolingual examination systems.
- Skills appearing in the written mediation task have special measurement criteria on the basis of which this task can be evaluated. The objectivity, validity and reliability of the evaluation of the task can be increased by a more precise definition of measurement criteria.

Pedagogical implications

As foreign language proficiency and the ability of communication between cultures and languages have become an important economic and strategic factor, assuring equal opportunities to Hungarian students in the international labour market is a basic task of tertiary education language curricula. Institutions in tertiary education should adjust to the needs of the labour market. Therefore an overall, large-scale needs analysis is indispensable to gauge the language skills necessary for employees in different professions and positions.

It is important to renew professional debates on the construct of language proficiency and examine whether the strict rejection of mediation as an examination task is well founded.

It may be reasonable to re-examine the theoretical background of the accreditation of language examination systems carefully because if we acknowledge foreign language mediation as an independent skill, it is questionable whether monolingual and bilingual examinations correspond to each other in value.

In accordance with the results it would be worthwhile rethinking the theoretical background and practice of the school-leaving examination (maturity exam) if we want to get an overall picture of candidate's language proficiency. Because of the especially complex nature of the mediation skill it would only be advisable to reintroduce the measurement of mediation skill at the higher level of proficiency.

Developing foreign language mediation skills is not equal to the training of professional translators and interpreters. It is a different area, so it would be advisable to include the methods of mediation-skill-development in teacher training courses. Suitable materials for instruction and practice files should be developed to assist the teacher trainers' and language teachers' work. It would be advisable to alleviate teachers' and examiners' fear of tests involving subjective evaluation by developing their knowledge of the theory of testing.

Topics for further research

This research project cannot be concluded at this point as several questions have emerged during the investigations that are worthy of future study. The following topics can be suggested for further research:

- exploring skills/subskills in mediation e.g. by using think-aloud protocol
- the influence of L1 reading deficiencies on foreign language mediation skill
- comparing oral and written mediation tasks, exploring common subskills and differences
- the washback effect of the different examination tasks on the language curricula
- how (code-)switching between languages, especially switching to the mother tongue influences examinees' foreign language performance during the examination
- exploration of bridging strategies and problems arising from their

application in the process of teaching and learning foreign language mediation

* contrasting teachers' consciousness with their students' routine in the process of preparation for an examination task or skill development.

References

Alderson, J C (2001) *The lift is being fixed. You will be unbearable today*, script of Plenary Session, 10th Hungarian Macmillan Conference, Budapest, 2001.

Alderson, J C, Clapham, C and Wall, D (1995) *Language Test Construction and Evaluation*, Cambridge: Cambridge University Press.

Bachman, L F and Palmer, A S (2000) *Language Testing in Practice*, Oxford: Oxford University Press.

Bárdos, J (1997) *A nyelvtanítás története és a módszerfogalom tartalma*, Veszprém: Veszprémi Egyetemi Kiadó.

Bárdos, J (2000) *Az idegen nyelvek tanításának elméleti alapjai és gyakorlata*, Budapest: Nemzeti Tankönyvkiadó.

Bárdos, J (2005) *Élő nyelvtanítás-történet*, Budapest: Nemzeti Tankönyvkiadó.

Bárdos, J (2006) A nyelvtudás-fogalom metamorfózisai: kritikai elemzés. In: *Porta Ligua-2006. Utak és perspektívák a hazai szaknyelvoktatás és – kutatásban*, Debrecen. Debreceni Egyetem ATC.

Broadbent, D E (1958) *Perception and Communication*, London: Pergamon Press.

Chomsky, N (1965) *Aspects of the Theory of Syntax*, Cambridge, MA: MIT Press.

Council of Europe (2001) *Common European Framework of Reference for Languages: Learning, Teaching, Assessment*, Cambridge: Cambridge University Press.

Csapó, B (1992) *Kognitív pedagógia*, Budapest: Akadémiai Kiadó.

Cummins, J (2005) *Teaching for Cross-Language Transfer in Dual Language Education: Possibilities and Pitfalls*, paper presented at TESOL Symposium on Dual Language Education: Teaching and Learning Two Languages in the EFL Setting, Turkey, 2005.

Dévény, Á and Szőke, A (2007) Milyen nyelvtudást vár el a munkaadó a munkavállalótól, in *Stratégiák 2007 és 2013 között. Tudományos Évkönyv 2006*, Budapest: BGF, 319–330.

Einhorn, Á (Ed.) (1998) *Vizsgatárgyak, vizsgamodellek I*, Budapest: Országos Közoktatási Intézet.

Fekete, H (2001) Az írásbeli nyelvvizsga a számok tükrében. Az ITK ORIGÓ angol középfok, *Nyelvi Mérce* 1 (2) 54–58.

Fekete, H (2002) Az írásbeli nyelvvizsga a számok tükrében. Az ITK ORIGÓ német középfok, *Nyelvi Mérce* 1 (2) , 45–56.

Fekete, H, Major, É and Nikolov, M (Eds) (1999) *English Language Education in Hungary*, Budapest: The British Council Hungary.

Green, R and Weir, C (2001) *Using Statistics for the Analysis of Test and Evaluation Data*, manuscript used on ISLC course at University of Reading.

Gósy, M (1999) *Pszicholingvisztik*, Budapest: Corvina Kiadó.

Gumperz, J J (1971) *Language in Social Groups*, Stanford, CA: Stanford University Press.

Harris, D P (1969) *Testing English as a Second Language*, New York: McGraw-Hill Book Company.

Hatch, E M and Lazaraton, A (1991) *The Research Manual: Design and Statistics for Applied Linguistics*, New York: Newbury House.

Heltai, P (2001) Iskolai tantárgy-e az idegen nyelv?, *Nyelvi Mérce* 1, 1–2.

Kintsch, W (1974) *The representation of meaning in memory*, Hillsdale, NJ: Lawrence Erlbaum Associates.

Klaudy, K (1984) Hogyan alkalmazható az aktuális tagolás elmélete a fordítás oktatásában?, *Magyar Nyelvőr*, 1,083.

Klaudy, K (1986a) A fordítás helye és szerepe a nyelvoktatásban: a „valódi" fordítás a középiskolai nyelvoktatásban, in Lengyel, Zs. (Ed.), in *Az idegen nyelvi nevelés-oktatás néhány iránya és lehetősége*, Budapest: Oktatáskutató Intézet.

Klaudy, K (1986b) A fordítás oktatásának elméleti alapjai. *Felsőoktatási Szemle* XXXV, 5.

Klaudy, K (1990) Átváltási műveletek a fordításban, *Idegen Nyelvek tanítása* 2.

Lado, R (1961) *Language Testing*, London: Longmans, Green and Co. Ltd.

Levelt, W J M (1989) *Speaking: From Intention to Articulation*, Cambridge, MA: The MIT Press.

Major, É (2000) Milyenfajta angol nyelvtudásra van szükség a nyelvigényes munkakörökben? Vizsgálat a munkaadók elvárásainak felmérésére, in *Modern Nyelvoktatás*, 2000, április, VI/1, 33–49.

Nikolov, M, Fekete, H and Major, É (Eds) (1999) *English language Education in Hungary. A Baseline Study,* Budapest: The British Council Hungary.

Oller Jr, J W (1979) *Language Tests at School: a Pragmatic Approach*, London: Longman.

Orellana, M F, Reynolds, J, Dorner, L and Meza, M (2003) In other words: Translating or "para-phrasing" as a family literacy practice in immigrant households, *Reading Research Quarterly* 38 (1), 12–34.

Palmer, H E (1917) *The Scientific Study and Teaching of Languages*, Oxford: Oxford University Press, 2nd edn.

Pinker, S (1994) *The Language Instinct*, New York: W Morrow and Co.

Rivers, W M and Temperley, M S (1978) *A Practical Guide to the Teaching of English as a Second or Foreign Language*, New York: Oxford University Press.

Silye, M F (2004) *A szaknyelvoktatás és a szaknyelvi tudást felhasználók igényeinek elemzése és megjelenítése egy angol szaknyelvoktatási program-modellben*, unpublished PhD thesis, Budapest: ELTE, PPK.

Stern, H H (1983) *Fundamental Concepts of Language Teaching*, Oxford: Oxford University Press.

Stern, H H (1992) *Issues and Options in Language Teaching*, Oxford: Oxford University Press.

Szabari, K (2001) Anyanyelvtudás, idegennyelvtudás, nyelvi közvetítés. *Nyelvi Mérce*. Nyelvvizsgáztatók és Nyelvtanárok Lapja 1 (1–2), Budapest: ITK.

Szathmáry, E (2001) Origin of the human language faculty: the language amoeba hypothesis, in Trabant, J and Ward, S: *New Essays on the Origin of Language.* Berlin: Mouton de Gruyter, 41–51.

Szathmáry, E (2002) Az emberi nyelvkészség eredete és a „nyelvi amőba", *Magyar Tudomány,* 2002/1:42.

Teemant, A, Varga, Z and Heltai, P (1993) *Hungary's Nationwide Needs Analysis of Vocationally-Oriented Foreign Language Learning: Student, Teacher, and Business Community Perspectives,* Budapest: Művelődésügyi és Közoktatási Minisztérium, a Munkaügyi Minisztérium, az Egyesült Államok Tájékoztatási Hivatala és az Európa Tanács Modern Nyelvek Szekciója.

Wardhaugh, R (1986) *An Introduction to Sociolinguistics,* New York: Blackwell

Wardhaugh, R (2006) *An Introduction to Sociolinguistics,* Cambridge: Blackwell, 5th edn.

17 ILR-based verbatim translation exams

Maria M Brau
Federal Bureau of Investigation, United States

Abstract

The Interagency Language Roundtable (ILR) Language Skill Level Descriptions (SLDs) define the tasks and functions required for each skill level on an ordinal scale of 0 to 5. ILR-based tests assign scores by reference to the descriptions. The ILR Translation Performance SLDs define the required tasks by characterizing the source texts that an individual must deal with successfully at a given level. Based on these characterizations, the Federal Bureau of Investigation has developed testing instruments to assess translation performance. This paper discusses how the tests were developed and reviews the ensuing test validation study.

Background: the ILR

The Interagency Language Roundtable (ILR) is a loose association of United States Government agencies that hire personnel with multiple language skills. It dates from the mid-1950s, when the State Department's Foreign Service Institute (FSI) began sponsoring informal meetings with represent-atives from other agencies to discuss issues related to language acquisition and language testing. In 1972, the General Accounting Office recommended a more formal organization as a means to encourage further coordination among the participating agencies.

The ILR obliged by setting up various committees and a regular meeting schedule: once a month, from September to June. There has been little change since then. Attendance by government representatives is still voluntary, and members of professional associations, academics, and private individuals are also welcome. It remains unfunded and without by-laws. One reason for its continued existence is that most agencies find it useful to have a forum where language issues are examined, research findings shared, and common problems addressed (Frith 1975, Herzog 2003, ILR 1985).

The organization is best known for developing a criterion-referenced system to measure functional language proficiency based on a 0 to 5 ordinal scale. The first set of ILR Skill Level Descriptions (SLDs) characterize proficiency levels in four language skills (speaking, listening, reading, and writing). In 1985, they were approved by the Office of Personnel Management (OPM) as the official standard for government-wide use.

This original set of SLDs has been extremely influential in the government language community, where the ILR ordinal scale is widely understood and referenced. Because the descriptions were designed for assessment purposes, government agencies have developed various testing instruments that assign language proficiency levels along the ILR scale, notably the Oral Proficiency Interview (OPI). The interview technique, originally developed by the Foreign Service Institute (FSI) to assess speaking proficiency, was refined and aligned to the ILR descriptions to serve as the model for the OPI (Lowe Jr 1978). The OPI Manual has undergone several revisions, and has been adapted for use at other agencies. This test has become so entrenched that an ILR speaking score is usually enough to provide a telegraphic evaluation of an individual's overall language proficiency. Outside government, the speaking descriptions developed by the American Council on the Teaching Foreign Languages (ACTFL) represent an adaptation of the OPI and the ILR scale for use in academic contexts (Lowe Jr 2011).

At the Department of Defense (DoD), the ILR SLDs for listening and reading have been used by the Defense Language Institute Foreign Language Center to produce successive versions of the Defense Language Proficiency Test (DLPT), administered across the government to assess listening and reading skills. Similar instruments have been developed by other agencies.

All of these ILR-based tests rely on a series of prompts intended to obtain responses that provide evidence of consistent performance at a given level. For the production skills (speaking and writing), questions that link functions and tasks to level requirements are the means used to elicit responses. For the receptive skills (listening and reading), passages are selected that conform to the text types prescribed in the SLDs as appropriate for each level and questions are then framed to elicit a response. To facilitate passage selection, a text typology developed by DoD is often used (Child 1987a). In all cases, responses are holistically rated by comparison to the corresponding SLDs and a score representing the level is assigned. ILR scores are then used by government managers to match an individual's language skills to work requirements. Hiring, promotions, duty assignments, and awards depend on ILR scores in language-related positions.

Development of the ILR SLDs for Translation and Interpretation

With language acquisition as its focus, the ILR initially showed little interest in specifically addressing assessment of translation and interpretation.

The ILR minutes from the mid 1970s to the early 1980s, for instance, do not record any discussion of translation or interpretation. At best, reading and speaking tests were used to identify qualified candidates from a population whose native language was usually English. For translation (defined as conveying the meaning of written materials in one language to written materials in another language), a reading comprehension test in the foreign language was considered sufficient. For interpretation (defined as conveying speech in one language to speech in another language), a speaking test in the foreign language served the purpose. The inadequacy of these instruments for assessing translation skills was admittedly obvious, and by the late 1980s, some agency representatives were arguing that the 'combined skills' merited separate consideration (Lowe Jr 1987).

At the Federal Bureau of Investigation (FBI), where there was less interest in language acquisition (unlike other agencies, the FBI does not run a language school), the need for a translation test construct became urgent as the demand for translators increased and applicants whose native language was not English became more numerous. Thus, by the early 1990s, the FBI developed guidelines called the *Provisional Interagency Language Roundtable Skill Level Descriptions for Translation*, but did not officially present them to the ILR for approval. Concomitantly, DoD personnel developed another set of descriptions for 'translation proficiency' that were published as ILR SLDs for 'Translation (Congruity Judgment)', although they had not received ILR approval. This latter set applied the typology that had been developed by DoD for the selection of reading test passages to the selection of passages for translation tests. Most importantly, it introduced the term 'congruity judgment' to describe 'the skill unique to translation' (Cascallar, Cascallar, Lowe and Child 1996, Stansfield, Scott and Kenyon 1992).

To allow for further discussion of these issues, ILR members interested in translation and interpretation were organized as a Special Interest Group (SIG), but no further progress was made towards preparation of Translation SLDs until government requirements for translation and interpretation services grew exponentially in the wake of the 11 September 2001 attacks. Government managers who had to hire qualified personnel for translation and interpretation tasks found that they could no longer rely on reading and speaking tests, self-assessments on the part of applicants, or submission of sometimes unverifiable credentials as selection tools.

In response to the surge, the SIG was constituted as the ILR Committee for Translation and Interpretation (the T&I Committee), on par with the two original ILR Committees (Training and Testing). Pardee Lowe (DoD) and Maria Brau (FBI) were appointed co-chairs of the new T&I Committee. The new group was given the task of developing guidelines for assessment of translation and interpretation skills.

In 2002, the T&I Committee presented to the full body the 'Translation

(Congruity Judgment)' SLDs previously developed by DoD personnel, on the grounds that these represented a useful assessment tool. However, the document was not approved by the full body. The T&I Committee was instructed to draft a new document, appointing a Sub-Committee to accomplish the task. In 2005, the current set of ILR SLDs for Translation Performance was approved by the full body of the ILR (ILR 2005). Almost immediately, the T&I Committee appointed another Sub-Committee to begin work on a set of ILR SLDs for Interpretation Performance SLDs, which were approved by the full body in 2007 (ILR 2007).

The ILR SLDs for Translation Performance

As stated in the Preface (ILR 2005), the ILR Translation Performance SLDs are specifically intended for use in government settings, where on-the-job ability to complete translation tasks successfully is subject to evaluation before and after hiring, and where there is the risk that wrong or imprecise information conveyed to decision-makers may have unfortunate, perhaps disastrous, consequences. Accordingly, the document is written in clear, nontechnical language, and the Preface addresses various issues concerning the translation process with which managers may not be thoroughly familiar, particularly if they are not language practitioners.

The Preface stresses that testing prerequisite language proficiency skills (reading the source language and writing the target language) may be used for screening purposes, but that translation skills *must be tested separately*. This view is supported by a study conducted by the FBI that correlated reading and translation scores in Arabic for a population of 1,400 examinees. It found that reading comprehension in the source language was not a reliable predictor of translation performance (Lunde and Brau 2005). Translation skills are defined in the Preface as the ability to 'choose the equivalent expression in the target language that both fully conveys and best matches the meaning intended in the source language' (ILR 2005). Borrowing from the earlier DoD document, this ability is referred to as 'congruity judgment', normally dependent on successful application of a translation methodology and, as stated in the preface, it follows that a translation test must measure 'the individual's ability to exercise congruity judgment' (ILR 2005).

The descriptions that follow the Preface conform to the familiar 0 to 5 ILR scale, where levels are characterized in terms of performance and level 3 is always designated as the Professional Level. According to the SLDs, it is at this level that the necessary skills align to enable production of a reasonably accurate and reliable translation. Because performance below level 3 does not require much use of congruity judgment, the descriptions posit that 'translation is not possible' at levels 0+ to 1+, and that at levels 2 and 2+ products 'should not be considered professional translations' (ibid). Therefore, terms other than 'translation' had to be used in the descriptions for the lower levels. After much discussion, 'render' was chosen for levels 2+ and 2, and 'transfer' for levels 1+ and below. Though 'render' and 'transfer' are often used as synonyms for 'translation', this distinction in terminology avoids reference to 'translation' for the lower levels and is intended to separate professional from non-professional performance.

At each level, the texts appropriate for that level are characterized, and examples of document types that can serve as likely sources for the texts at level are also provided. With maximum performance ratings tied to the prescribed text complexity for a given level, assessment depends on more than error deductions. Tests used by the American Translators Association exemplify this approach (Angelelli 2009). Regardless of how accurate or well written the product, the individual cannot receive a rating higher than the level assigned to the source text. Based on these guidelines, testing instruments that assess translation performance may be and were developed.

FBI ILR-based translation tests

The Verbatim Translation Exams (VTEs) developed by the FBI follow the by-now accepted procedures prescribed for ILR-based tests: prompts designed to elicit performance that will be rated according to skill level descriptions. The prompts consist of passages that are selected to meet the translation text specifications assigned to a level.

Before development started, FBI personnel had to decide levels to be tested, test duration, number of passages, passage length, and rating procedures. Since the FBI's requirements call for individuals performing at translation skill levels 2+ and above, the decision was made to include items at levels 2, 2+, 3, and 4, with level 2 serving as a filtering device. Testing level 5 was not considered feasible, as the ILR Descriptions define level 5 in terms that are difficult to measure by means of a single translation test.

Time constraints placed on test administration determined test duration: in the FBI applicant test battery, the maximum time allotted for translation testing is 90 minutes. Within those time limits, the decision was to select four passages, short enough for all four to fit single-spaced in one page. Each passage would be a prompt for only one level, thereby ensuring that text characteristics for that level be densely packed within the passage. A single, longer text was discarded as an option because text characteristics are likely to vary over the length of the passage. For similar reasons, topics had to vary. Furthermore, the subject matter of the passage (whether political, financial, legal, etc.) or text type (letter, report, editorial, etc.) would not determine the level. Rather, the only determinant would be the level characteristics exemplified by a text. (Examples are provided below, under Guidelines for selection of passages.)

Assuming the selected passages represented the prescribed characteristics for texts at a given level, it was hypothesized that the examinee's performance would deteriorate as the complexity of passage prompts increased. Rating would thus follow the familiar level check/probe process, with the final score corresponding to the highest level attained.

Guidelines for selection of passages

The VTEs currently exist in 24 languages: Albanian, Arabic, Bosnian, Bulgarian, Chinese, Croatian, Farsi, French, German, Hebrew, Hindi, Italian, Japanese, Korean, Pashto, Polish, Portuguese, Russian, Serbian, Spanish, Turkish, Ukrainian, Urdu, and Vietnamese. (Eastern and Western Armenian, Dari, Romanian, and Somali are in preparation.) All of the tests have at least two parallel forms, each consisting of four passages that must be: (a) authentic; (b) valid; (c) on a variety of topics; and (d) of increasing complexity. The FBI approaches test validation projects by providing evidence that supports their use in government operations. In this context, valid means that the passage represents material which FBI employees have translated in the course of their work. Letters, manuals, police reports, court papers, legislation, policy statements or financial documents usually contain suitable samples. Secret or confidential information is edited out before use, as well as names and dates.

Guidelines for selection of VTE passages were derived from the ILR Descriptions. As noted, the ILR characterizes texts appropriate for each level. The level 2 description reads:

> **Able to render into the target language some straightforward, factual texts in the standard variety of the source language.** Can typically render accurately uncomplicated prose (such as that used in short identification documents, simple letters, instructions, and some narrative reports) that does not contain figurative language, complex sentence structures, embedding, or instances of syntactic or semantic skewing ... To the extent that faulty expression may obscure or distort meaning, accuracy will suffer.

Accordingly, the following guidelines were prepared for use in selecting passages at level 2:

- CONTENT: straightforward narration, description, directions, instructions, simple explanation
- PURPOSE: to convey factual information
- LEXICON: everyday usage; a minimum of words with multiple meanings; technical terms, if any, do not demand special knowledge or expertise
- STRUCTURES: basic, high-frequency complex, with few modifiers
- STYLE: expository, without unusual stylistic devices

- CONGRUITY JUDGMENT: minimally required
- TOPIC: any subject matter is appropriate which is encountered on a regular basis by FBI translators in the course of their work.

Several sample passages in English, the common language of those submitting selections, were also provided for each level. Among those illustrating level 2:

(1) At approximately 12:18 PM, an explosion occurred under the World Trade Center in New York City. The explosion killed six people and injured more than one thousand. Twenty-five of the one thousand were injured as a direct result of the explosion. The remainder of the injuries happened in the aftermath of the explosion and consisted of smoke inhalation and cuts or bruises due to falls.

(2) Evidence containing blood should be completely dried before it is packaged and shipped to the laboratory for analysis. To avoid direct contact and exposure to these materials in the courtroom, evidence should be placed in a sealed, transparent package and labeled appropriately.

(3) Duration of the agreement. The initial duration of this agreement is for two (2) years and is renewable on an annual basis, until one of the parties terminates it according to the conditions provided below.

At level 2+, performance is limited to 'straightforward texts dealing with everyday matters that include statements of fact as well as some judgments, opinion, or other elements which entail more than direct exposition, but do not contain figurative language, complex sentence structures, or instances of syntactic or semantic skewing'. For level 3, the source texts contain 'not only facts but also abstract language, . . . implications, many nuances . . . usually . . . situations and events which are subject to value judgments of a personal or institutional kind'. Texts that include figurative language, complex sentence structures, or instances of syntactic or semantic skewing are no longer barred at level 3.

The guidelines for level 3 passage selection are as follows:

- CONTENT: varied, some socio-cultural references
- PURPOSE: varied
- LEXICON: professional terminology
- STRUCTURES: complex
- STYLE: complex syntax, stylistic devices, formulaic expressions
- CONGRUITY JUDGMENT: required
- TOPIC: same as for level 2.

Below are two of several samples illustrating level 3:

(1)   It is the policy of the Department of Justice that all acquisitions which allow unescorted contractor access to Government facilities or sensitive information contain, as appropriate, requirements for appropriate personnel security screening by the contractor. To the maximum extent practicable, contractors shall be made responsible for security screening, except that personnel may vary from one acquisition to another, depending on the type, context, duration and location of the work to be performed.

(2)   It is misleading to suggest that affirmative action as practiced in the American university admissions process is a subtle thumb on the scale to help those whose circumstances have given them few advantages. In fact, the preferences typically accorded to affirmative education beneficiaries in university admissions at elite schools are hardly a subtle thumb. A heavy hand would be a more accurate description.

No set of detailed guidelines are provided for level 4. However, it is made clear that texts at this level demand detailed decoding and rearrangement prior to translating. The following exemplifies a level 4 passage:

INCONTESTABILITY: This policy shall be incontestable, except for non-payment of premiums, after two years from its date of issue. No statements made by any person insured under this policy relating to his insurability shall be used in contesting the validity of the insurance with respect to which such statement was made after such insurance has been in force prior to the contest for a period of two years during such person's lifetime nor unless it is contained in a written instrument signed by him.

Contributors are warned against submitting texts for level 4 that may appear 'difficult' to translate because they contain highly specialized material (usually technical or scientific) that demands subject matter expertise or research on the part of the non-expert. Typically, these texts do not require the use of congruity judgment: field-specific vocabulary is precise by definition, syntax generally simple, and the intended meaning purposefully made clear. An example illustrating this type of unacceptable passage is provided in the guidelines:

The MTMM correlations were analyzed using exploratory factor analysis. Principle axes were extracted, with squared multiple correlations on the diagonal, without iteration. On the basis of a screen test, three factors were identified. These factors were then rotated obliquely, using the direct oblimin rotation and least squares hyperplane fitting.

Verbatim Translation Exams validation study

Since the VTEs were designed to have high construct and face validity, the passages used came directly from authentic FBI translation assignments. To support the claims for construct validity, a group of FBI linguists was asked to choose and submit passages from work they had completed. For face validity, the linguists were also asked to verify that the assignments were representative of their typical tasks. To address content validity, the passages were chosen not only to reflect a range of ILR translation skill levels, but also a representative range of topics.

By the time tests in 15 languages had been completed, funding was granted for an analytical validation study. Several approaches to test validity were then considered to ensure that test results accurately represented translation ability. Before beginning to collect research data, an extensive review of existing translation tests was conducted to explore the possibility of a concurrent validation approach (FBI 2006). The survey of the validation status of existing translation exams included assessments from the National Accreditation Authority for Translators and Interpreters (Australia), the Faculty of Modern and Medieval Languages, University of Cambridge (United Kingdom), the Monterey Institute of International Studies (United States), the American Translators Association (United States), the Association of Translators and Interpreters Ontario (Canada), United Nations Educational, Scientific and Cultural Organization (International), the European Union (Europe), Lingua Learn (United Kingdom), Clemson University (United States), and the Institute of Translation and Interpreting (United Kingdom). Since none of the translation tests in use had undergone a statistical validation process, the decision was to validate the methodology to be used for the VTEs, i.e. that test passages represented the prescribed levels and, concomitantly, that performance would likely deteriorate as complexity increased.

The ensuing VTE validation study reflected how the tests were used in government contexts. On the basis of a background questionnaire, 80 participants representing the typical demographics of government translators were recruited for each language. They were administered a translation self-assessment, an English Writing Test, and both forms of the VTE. The tests were independently double-rated by experienced FBI raters.

Initially, the tests were evaluated for bias against groups of examinees. Examinee attributes considered in the analysis included citizenship, language acquisition environment, education, professional language experience, gender, age, and primary and secondary languages. Age, gender, and primary language, of particular interest to the FBI since they are considered discriminatory for hiring purposes, showed no significant effect ($p < .05$) on test outcome. Those attributes that impacted the test outcome were typically factors that would impact language proficiency. None of these were unexpected. For example, if the examinees had parents who spoke the language at home, or if they had learned it as children with education provided in the target language, then they encountered more success on the translation exam.

Second, a Generalizability (G) study analyzed sources of variance in ratings due to different factors or facets of the tests. In particular, the interaction between rater, form, and passage was analyzed. No significant differences were found between performances on the two forms in relation to the contribution from test taker variability. For each of the 15 languages, the set of two parallel forms was examined for mean differences in scores across forms and passages, aggregating across raters. Overall, no significant differences were found between performances on the two forms. Specifically, mean overall scores were virtually identical between the two forms. ILR plus levels were converted to integers, with the plus representing 0.6. For example, the mean overall score for French Form A was 1.999 and Form B was 1.990. Mean scores generally increase across passages, supporting the intended feature of test construction that the passages should increase in difficulty and have higher possible ratings as the test progresses (e.g. passage 3 can be scored only up to level 3, whereas passage 1 can only be scored up to level 2).

A passage-by-passage analysis investigated whether or not passages functioned at the intended level, i.e., whether the passages demonstrated increased levels of translation complexity. To determine this, researchers calculated the percentage of examinees that successfully translated the passage at the level, with the expectation that a) as passages became more difficult, a smaller percentage of examinees would be able to accurately translate the passage and b) that examinees would be able to translate less complex passages successfully but not progressively more complex passages. Passages selected for levels 2 and 4 generally behaved at level, i.e. showed a progression from less to more difficult, but passages at levels 2+ and 3 did not always do so. Figure 1 illustrates the percentage of participants for the three languages that were able to translate successfully the four test passages, i.e., the passage passing rates.

Following the G-study, a Decision (D) study explored the generalizability coefficients found for the interaction of passage, form, and rater, with attention paid to the rater reliability coefficients. The generalizability coefficients were expressed in the form of phi-coefficients, as reliability indicators for each of the potential rater and passage combinations. Generally, the D-study revealed that the combination of two raters and four passages resulted in a phi-coefficient of 0.7 or higher, which is generally acceptable for tests of this type.

The study confirmed the effectiveness of the methodology used, but yielded recommendations that more passages at each level be added. Because of the testing time limits mentioned above, longer tests are not feasible, and four passages continue to be used. However, errant passages (i.e., those that

Figure 1 Passage passing rates

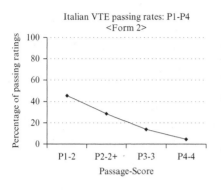

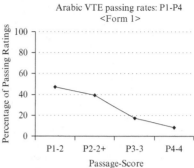

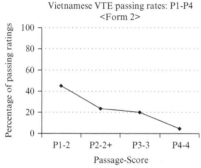

did not follow the pattern of progressive difficulty to translate accurately), have been replaced, and new forms prepared for three languages. Following the same methodology, additional VTEs were prepared in nine additional languages, and six more are in development. Because of the difficulties posed in making precise borderline distinctions between levels 2+ and 3, eliminating the level 2+ passage and replacing it with a second level 2 passage is being considered.

At present, a project to automate rating is in progress. Further research on passage behaviour is planned, using applicant examinee production.

Note

The author would like to state that this article is not an official Federal Bureau of Investigation document.

References

Angelelli, C V (2009) Using a rubric to assess translation ability, in Angelelli, C V and Jacobson, H E (Eds) *Testing and Assessment in Translation and*

Interpreting Studies, American Translators Association Scholarly Monograph Series XIV, Philadelphia: John Benjamins Publishing Company.

Cascallar, E C, Cascallar, M I, Lowe, P and Child, J R (1996) Development of new proficiency based skill level descriptions for translation: theory and practice, in Milanovic, M and Saville, N (Eds) *Performance Testing, Cognition and Assessment: Selected Papers from the 15th Language Testing Colloquium*, Studies in Language Testing volume 3, Cambridge: UCLES Cambridge University Press, 292–313.

Child, J R (1987a) Language proficiency and the typology of texts, in Byrnes, H and Canale M (Eds) *Defining and Developing Proficiency: Guidelines, Implementation and Concepts*, Lincolnwood, IL: National Textbook Co.

Child, J R (1987b) Language Proficiency and Translation, in Gaddis Rose, M (Ed.) *Translation Excellence: Assessment, Achievement, Maintenance. American Translators Association Scholarly Monograph Series*, Binghamton: University Center at Binghamton (SUNY).

Federal Bureau of Investigation (2006) *Verbatim Translation Exam (VTE) Validation Project Methodology*, Washington, DC: Author.

Frith, J R (May 1975) Cooperation among governmental agencies in the language field, *ADFL Bulletin* 6 (4),15–17.

Herzog, M (2003) An overview of the history of the ILR Language proficiency skill level descriptions and scale, *Interagency Language Roundtable*, available online: govtilr.org/Skills/IRL%20Scale%20History.htm

Interagency Language Roundtable (ILR) (1985) *Interagency Language Roundtable Skill Level Descriptions*, available online; govtilr.org

Interagency Language Roundtable (ILR) (2005) *Interagency Language Roundtable Skill Level Descriptions for Translation Performance*, available online: govtilr.org/Skills/AdoptedILRTranslationGuidelines.htm

Interagency Language Roundtable (ILR) (2007) *Interagency Language Roundtable Skill Level Descriptions for Interpretation Performance*, available online: govtilr.org/Skills/interpretationSLDsapproved.htm

Lowe, Jr, P (1978) *Manual for LS Oral Interview Workshops*, Washington, DC: Government Language School.

Lowe, Jr, P (1987) Revising the ACTFL/ETS Scales for a new purpose: rating skill in translating, in Rose, M G (Ed.) *Translation Excellence: Assessment, Achievement, Maintenance. American Translators Association Scholarly Monograph Series*, Binghamton: University Center at Binghamton (SUNY), 53–61.

Lowe, Jr, P (2011) Is it possible to align CEFR and the ACTFL/ILR for Speaking Assessment? Tops, Bottoms, and Middles, in Tschirner, E (Ed.) *The ACTFL Proficiency Guidelines and the Common European Framework of Reference*, Tuebingen: Stauffenburg.

Lunde, R M and Brau, M M (2005) *Correlation between reading and translation ability*, paper presented at the World Congress of Applied Linguistics, Madison, Wisconsin, 2005.

Stansfield, C W, Scott, M L and Kenyon, D M (1992) The measurement of translation ability, *Modern Language Journal* 74, 455–467.

18 Developing diagnostic tests for young learners of EFL in grades 1 to 6

Marianne Nikolov and Gábor Szabó
University of Pécs, Hungary

Abstract

Recently, the number of children learning English as a foreign language (EFL) has increased exponentially around the world. However, outcomes and classroom practices often fail to reflect how children learn languages (Nikolov 2009a, 2009b, Nikolov and Mihaljević Djigunović 2006, 2011). Thus, it is necessary to shift from *testing of learning* to *testing for learning* (e.g., Black and William 1998, McKay 2006, Nikolov and Szabó 2011, Teasdale and Leung 2000), a key issue in the young learner classroom, to help teachers scaffold their pupils' development. The paper presents the first results of a large-scale study involving over 2,000 pupils (ages 6 to 13) learning English in 154 groups in 26 public schools in Hungary. The study aimed to develop, pilot, and validate new diagnostic tests for young learners in the four basic skills and to place the tests on a scale of difficulty corresponding to the A1 and A2 levels of the Common European Framework of Reference for languages (CEFR) by using Rasch analysis. Data was collected with the help of various instruments in 2010: (1) listening, speaking, reading and writing tasks arranged in 21 booklets each comprising 20 tests (including anchor tests); (2) short questionnaires on the tests for pupils and (3) their teachers; (4) a questionnaire filled in by the teacher on pupils' background data; and (5) teachers were also invited to comment on each task. The paper discusses how the tests worked by analysing how pupils performed on them and how difficult the tasks were with a special focus on listening comprehension and reading comprehension tasks. Patterns of difficulty were somewhat different for the two receptive skills, but they tended to fall in line with estimated levels. In the last section we outline various explanations of the findings and areas where further research is necessary.

Introduction

In this paper first we outline the literature on assessing young language learners by starting with the construct of young learners' foreign language proficiency; then, we discuss recent developments in diagnostic assessment and how they are related to language frameworks. In the next section we draw the background to our study: readers are given insights into the most important characteristics of the Hungarian educational context and what is known about young learners' classrooms, proficiency, and testing. In the empirical part we present the aims of the large-scale project in which the study is embedded and the research questions, participants and the measuring instruments we used to collect data. After detailing the procedures we analyse data on listening comprehension and reading comprehension tests in order to answer the research questions. In the last section we suggest ways of further analyses and research.

Recent research on assessing young language learners

The construct of young learners' foreign language proficiency

The spread of early language programmes has brought about increased interest in testing young learners' (YLs') progress and proficiency: how children develop in their new language and what they can do (McKay 2006). The main issue in assessing YLs concerns the construct. According to Inbar-Lourie and Shohamy (2009), early programmes vary to a great extent from awareness raising to language focus programmes, and from content-based curricula to immersion. They argued that testing must be in line with 'the assessment constructs along with the language-content program continuum, particularly within the current integrated or embedded models in YL classrooms given its current status and use in diverse contexts' and they demonstrated how the reflective process they applied to various tests and exams illustrated 'the dynamics of testing construction and validation which need to be constantly re-thought and revised' (2009:93–94).

Once the construct is clear, test developers face many challenges when designing tests for YLs: they need to define and describe low proficiency levels along a continuum in small steps in order to allow test users to assess and document children's relatively slow development (Nikolov and Mihaljević Djigunović 2006). This is crucial for teachers, parents, and YLs so that they feel that they are making progress. Also, tests must be age appropriate. The earlier instruction starts, the more probable it is that YLs are at the early stages of literacy development in their first language; thus, what is typical for older learners is not directly applicable to YLs in the four skills (Nikolov and Mihaljević Djigunović 2011). Test developers must bear in mind that YLs are different from older ones not only in their interests and background knowledge of the world, level of literacy and other aspects, but assessment may impact children's attitudes, motivation and anxiety in different ways than in the case of older learners. In addition to these points, assessment should also be in line with how children develop not only in the target language but also in their first language. Recent research has shown that aptitude, including inductive reasoning, language learning motivation, anxiety and the learners' first language interact in complex ways (for overviews see Nikolov 2009a, Nikolov and Mihaljević Djigunović 2011). Thus, focusing on diagnostic assessment, assessment for learning besides assessment of learning is a must (e.g. Black and William 1998, McKay 2006, Nikolov and Szabó 2011, Teasdale and Leung 2000).

Various documents have been published in recent years quantifying what children can do. In Europe efforts have focused on adapting Common European Framework of Reference for languages (CEFR) descriptors (Council of Europe 2001) (e.g. Figueras and Noijons 2009, Jones and Saville 2009, Little 2007, Nikolov 2011) to young learners' needs and examinations (e.g. Hasselgreen 2005, Papp and Salamoura 2009, Pižorn 2009), but this process is far from accomplished and challenges are numerous (Bachman 2011). International exams are also available to provide YLs and their parents with a certificate on children's proficiency in English; indeed, four exam boards are widely known to offer such exams (Pearson Test of English Young Learners, *Cambridge English: Young Learners*, Integrated Skills in English, and City and Guilds ESOL for Young Learners). A detailed analysis is beyond our scope of inquiry, but a few features of these exams are important to consider (for a more detailed overview see Nikolov and Mihaljević Djigunović 2011). The constructs are placed more towards the middle of the language–content continuum: the typical topics focused on are supposed to be in line with the ones YLs are expected to be familiar with. The levels, as the official websites of these exams claim, cover A1 and A2 in the CEFR (Council of Europe 2001); however, there is no evidence in the literature that they actually do so. Published research is not available on how exams impact YLs' motivation, anxiety and further development, but in-house publications document how *Cambridge English: Young Learners* was developed and validated (e.g. Barker and Shaw 2007, Rixon 2007), whereas no similar information is shared with the public on the other exams.

In many educational contexts early language learning is now part of the national curriculum and in most countries a similar construct is used when educational authorities publish their achievement targets, implement research projects and introduce national exams for an increasingly younger age group. In Switzerland, for example, a three-year longitudinal study was conducted on YLs' development (Haenni Hoti, Heinzmann and Müller 2009), whereas in Slovenia research into what YLs can do resulted in validated national tests for sixth graders (Pižorn 2009). The present study aims to provide insights into what has been accomplished in Hungary.

Diagnostic assessment

Recent research into educational assessment has emphasised how dynamic testing may contribute to learning potential (Nisbett 2009, Sternberg and Grigorenko 2002) and many experts argue for assessment for learning or diagnostic assessment: how students benefit from classroom testing and feedback from teachers (Alderson 2005, Black and William 1998, Davison and Leung 2009, Leung and Scott 2009, McKay 2006, Teasdale and Leung 2000). McNamara and Roever (2006:251–252) suggested that assessment should be sensitive to readiness to develop and called for more research on learners' ability to benefit from instruction and interaction. In published studies on YLs classroom interaction takes place between teachers and YLs, as well as between peers (e.g. Nikolov 1999, Peng and Zhang 2009a, 2009b, Pinter 2007); however, more studies are necessary in this area, with a special focus on oral tests. The prioritisation of oral tests is due to the under-researched nature of this skill largely due to the time and resource demands to conduct such studies and also because oral skills are of primary interest in the YL age group.

Little is known about the ways teachers assess their young learners in their classrooms. Butler (2009) gave an overview of studies on teacher-based assessment in three Asian countries. She found that Korean and Taiwanese teachers faced a number of difficulties similar to what teachers had to cope with in other contexts: they had to manage large classes and lacked knowledge about teacher-based assessment, sufficient time to administer tests, and information on how to use the data they gained in assessment. In Japan, although teachers were not required to test children, they used self-assessment. An exploratory study conducted in Hungary, which was part of the larger project discussed later, found that teachers applied two typical techniques in their classroom assessment: (1) they rewarded best performances on all tasks and rewards were cumulative: good performers earned small rewards on a regular basis, whereas their less successful peers did not. This practice meant that more able and motivated learners got a lot of positive feedback, whereas the lack of reward meant negative feedback for less successful children; (2) the other type of assessment teachers applied involved achievements on classroom tests, most frequently in reading and writing. This dual practice reflected what teachers considered the aim of assessment: motivation, on the one hand, and feedback on actual achievement in English literacy rather than aural/oral skills, on the other (Hild and Nikolov 2010).

Some experts advocate the use of portfolios, especially in Europe, as portfolios and self-assessment are expected to contribute to autonomy and better learning. Hasselgreen (2005) analysed what the CEFR (2001) and the European Language Portfolio offered to YLs in Norway. However, Little (2007) warned that portfolio assessment was often perceived by teachers and learners as extra work. Overall, little is known about ways in which teachers and learners use portfolios in classrooms and how their uses impact learning.

As for self-assessment, two studies explored the topic in Korean elementary schools (Butler and Lee 2006, 2010). One examined the validity of students' self-assessments of their oral performance and the other study explored the effectiveness of self-assessment on a regular basis for a semester during English classes.

Discussions on diagnostic assessment should take into consideration teachers' knowledge and skills in this domain. The term 'diagnostic competence' was defined by Edelenbos and Kubanek-German (2004:260) as 'the ability to interpret students' FL growth, to skillfully deal with assessment material and to provide students with appropriate help in response to this diagnosis'. Teachers face many challenges: the emphasis on aural/oral skills requires teachers to work with children individually, in pairs or small groups rather than frontally in large classes and may not be in line with what they do more easily: administer reading or writing tests. Understanding and applying results of diagnostic assessment may also cause difficulties for many teachers.

The study

The educational context

In Hungarian schools Russian used to be mandatory for all learners for over four decades. All students started learning it at the age of nine in grade four, but the majority failed to achieve useful competencies by the time they graduated from secondary or tertiary education. Since the change of regime in 1989, Russian teachers have been retrained and many other teachers have graduated with a degree in English and German. Over the last two decades Hungarians' attitudes towards foreign language study have been extremely favourable, especially towards English as a lingua franca (Dörnyei, Csizér and Németh 2006). However, still few Hungarians speak foreign languages, though the trend is favourable: the ratio of young people with competences in English and German is on the rise.

Early foreign language education can be characterised by the following important trends:

- annually an increasing number of children start learning English before the mandatory fourth grade due to parental pressure
- a huge variety characterises foreign language programmes, as children may start in any year before grade four, the mandatory start, in one to five weekly classes; the quality of teaching also varies a lot, and there are no official achievement targets for the first three grades
- schools stream students into ability groups (the more able study in more intensive and earlier programmes)
- classes are divided for foreign language study

- large-scale research studies involving representative samples of learners have found a weak relationship between the number of years devoted to English and German and frequency of weekly classes and large differences in levels of proficiency
- the best predictor of proficiency over time is students' socio-economic status as reflected by their parents' level of education
- teachers often apply traditional classroom techniques: the most frequent task types are reading aloud, translation and grammar exercises
- teachers of young learners know how young children learn languages, but they often fail to apply principles of age-appropriate methodology
- assessment practices are often problematic and not in line with what young learners can be realistically expected to be able to do (for summaries see Nikolov 2009b, 2009c).

The background

As this short summary shows, there was a need to define what the aims of early language teaching are and to describe what young Hungarian language learners should be able to do at different levels of their development during their school years. Also, it was necessary to develop diagnostic tests to allow teachers to be able to find out where their students are in their development and to help them scaffold their learning based on the information they gain from diagnostic tests. These are the aims of a large-scale project designed and implemented at the Center for Research on Learning and Instruction, University of Szeged, with the support of The Social Renewal Operational Program (TÁMOP–3.1.9-08/01-2009-0001) for the first six grades of primary school. The project involved not only EFL but also mathematics, reading in the first language (Hungarian), science, and some cognitive and affective domains; however, in our study we focus on English. The overall aim was to design and to pilot diagnostic tests, to calibrate items for an item bank to be made available online at a later stage. The ultimate aim is to improve classroom practice over time.

The first phase of the English project aimed to explore classroom practice and to develop a framework for developing diagnostic tests. In the second phase tests were developed and piloted. The first results of this second phase are discussed in this paper. The framework (Nikolov 2011) consisted of two parts. The first one comprised an analysis of statistical data and published empirical studies, and defined the construct found in curricular requirements on the teaching of modern foreign languages to learners in grades one to six in Hungary (i.e., the ability to use a new language communicatively). The second part listed age-appropriate topics defined in the national curriculum, text and task types for the four basic skills and 'Can Do statements' in line with the construct and Hungarian learners' interlanguage development described in empirical studies, and CEFR (2001) levels (A1 and A2). This framework document served as a basis for developing tests by a team of trained item writers (further details on the process are given in the Procedure section).

Research questions

The research questions we seek to answer in this paper are the following:

1. In light of the statistical analyses, can the internal empirical validity of the tasks be demonstrated?
2. Was the difficulty of the listening and reading tasks in line with expectations? In other words, did task difficulty in the three sets of booklets increase sequentially?

Participants

A convenience sample of 2,173 students was involved in the project in 161 groups at 26 schools in various towns and villages around the country. Students attended grades two to seven and their age ranged between 7 and 13. Learners were at three estimated levels depending on the number of years and weekly hours of studying EFL. Despite the weak relationships found in empirical studies between years of language study and weekly classes (Nikolov 2009b, 2009c), these were the only reasonable indicators to rely on. Thus, we negotiated with teachers which of the three levels their learners were most probably at. The number of students filling in the 21 booklets ranged between 116 and 132. The number of students in the 161 groups ranged from four to 32, depending on the numbers of learners in various contexts.

Data collection instruments

A total of 21 booklets were used in the English project; each booklet comprised 20 tasks: five tasks for listening, speaking, reading and writing. As our analyses focus on the tests measuring the receptive skills, only listening and reading tests are described here. A total of 85 listening and 85 reading tests were piloted. The tests were arranged into seven booklets on three estimated difficulty levels, thus the total number of tests for each level was 28 plus one task used in all booklets. In order to allow us to compare the difficulty levels of every test, anchor tests were used: the very same listening and reading tests were used in all 21 booklets. The sequence, however, was different: the anchor task was the fifth on the lowest, third on the intermediate, and first on the most difficult estimated level.

The actual task types required multiple choice and multiple matching of visuals and short texts (a word, an expression or a short sentence); the number of items in all tests ranged between six and nine. All listening tests were recorded on a CD; texts were recorded twice, instructions were in English.

All 21 booklets had a teachers' book comprising a detailed description of the project, a question-and-answer section on how to use the tests in the classroom, a key to all listening, reading and some of the writing tasks and evaluation criteria for assessing some of the writing and speaking tasks. Teachers' booklets included the transcripts of listening texts.

After doing the actual tasks in English, students were asked to evaluate each test on a 4–1 scale (easy – difficult; familiar – unfamiliar; liked – disliked). For the sake of triangulation, teachers were also asked to fill in the same instrument, and also to write additional comments on the tests. In addition to these instruments, a questionnaire was filled in by the teachers on pupils' aptitude, motivation, parental support, and the time devoted to learning English (years and weekly classes).

Procedure

The whole project lasted 11 months between February 2010 and January 2011. First, an exploratory study was conducted on English teachers' assessment practices in order to find out what tests they used and how, which ones they found useful and why (Hild and Nikolov 2010). Then, teachers were asked to pilot sample tasks and to give feedback on how they worked. In the meantime the framework document on the main principles, levels, topics, task types, and detailed specifications was developed (Nikolov 2011) to be used by item writers preparing tests for large-scale piloting. Schools were recruited to allow their teachers and students to participate in the piloting in September 2010. All booklets were completed by the pupils in their regular English classes in November and December of 2011; data was entered into files centrally and analysed in January 2011.

In order to answer the research questions, the following analyses were performed. First, all tasks were evaluated using classical test analysis. This effectively meant examining tasks' reliability figures, descriptive statistics, score distribution data and item discrimination indices. Also, item response theory (IRT)-based fit statistics (WINSTEPS) were used to check item quality. IRT analyses, however, were performed for another reason as well. Since one aim of the project was to calibrate all items of each skill onto a common scale, it was inevitable to rely on a model going beyond Classical Test Theory. Accordingly, Rasch analyses were conducted in the following manner.

First, the anchor items' logit difficulty indices were estimated on the basis of all responses available. Since anchor items were included in all booklets for each skill, this meant that, theoretically, all students' responses to all anchor items would be available. Although in reality some of the students skipped some anchor tasks, the remaining population in each skill was sizeable enough (1,928 in the case of listening and 1,974 in the case of reading) to provide a solid basis for item difficulty estimates. Next, the person ability logits estimated in the course of determining anchor items' difficulty were used to estimate the difficulty of the rest of the items. Thus, eventually all items could be placed on a common difficulty continuum, making it possible to directly compare all of them with one another.

Results

The first stage was the classical analysis of the actual tasks. Table 1 provides an illustration of the type of information gained for all the 21 booklets.

As can be seen in Table 1, Booklet 12 comprised five listening tasks (numbered 11 to 15) and five reading tasks (numbered 21 to 25). All tasks appear to have an acceptable level of reliability, as shown by the alpha coefficients (Alderson, Clapham and Wall 1995, Bachman 2004), and descriptive statistics, distribution measures and mean item-total test correlation figures seem to indicate that the tasks performed relatively well. Results for the other 20 booklets were similar, and while occasional reliability and item discrimination problems did occur, the overwhelming majority of both listening and reading tasks were found to have worked in a satisfactory manner. IRT-based item fit statistics show a similar picture. While some items were found to be misfitting (most of which had discrimination problems), the tasks and the items therein were proven to have worked well in the light of the Rasch analyses as well.

Hence, with respect to the first research question, it appears to be reasonable to claim that, based on classical as well as Rasch analyses, the vast majority of the listening and reading tasks piloted performed appropriately and can be empirically demonstrated to be internally valid. Accordingly, most of the tasks seem suitable for measurement purposes, and after carefully checking the datasets item by item, most tasks appear to be of suitable quality to be placed in a future item bank.

However, an equally important issue is at what level they are to be applied. Indeed, as the main focus of the whole project was diagnostic testing, it is probably the single most important issue to deal with. As was discussed earlier, the research design made it possible to compare item difficulty figures of all items in all tasks directly. Let us then take a closer look at these actual comparisons, starting with listening tasks. Figure 1 presents a graphical representation of all listening items piloted.

Each dot in Figure 1 indicates one item; a total of 630 items were analysed. The sequence number of the item is an indication of which group of booklets included a particular item. Items with low sequence numbers were included in the booklets intended for the lowest level, while items with the highest sequence numbers were part of the booklets targeted at the highest level. As can be inferred from Figure 1, there appears to be a tendency for items to be more difficult as sequence numbers increase, even though there are some exceptions to this trend, such as the items marked with a circle.

More important than the impression, however, is whether such a tendency

Table 1 Listening and reading results of classical analyses for booklet 12

Booklet 12	N	N of items	Alpha	Mean	Median	Std. dev.	Min.	Max.	Skew	Kurtosis	SEM	Mean pent corr	Mean item-total
11	106	7	0.806	3.670	4.000	2.281	0.000	7.000	−0.034	−1.180	1.004	52	0.541
12	106	6	0.896	4.698	6.000	1.991	0.000	6.000	−1.444	0.751	0.644	78	0.723
13	106	9	0.883	5.189	6.000	2.822	0.000	8.000	−0.623	−0.973	0.966	58	0.682
14	106	8	0.799	4.160	4.000	2.496	0.000	8.000	−0.059	−1.004	1.120	52	0.508
15	106	7	0.876	4.255	5.000	2.537	0.000	7.000	−0.633	−1.047	0.893	61	0.660
21	106	7	0.826	5.160	6.000	1.585	0.000	7.000	−2.297	4.711	0.660	74	0.581
22	106	8	0.876	5.377	6.000	2.714	0.000	8.000	−0.712	−0.805	0.954	67	0.639
23	106	9	0.896	7.462	9.000	2.466	0.000	9.000	−1.853	2.569	0.797	83	0.669
24	106	7	0.890	5.038	6.000	2.418	0.000	7.000	−1.021	−0.337	0.801	72	0.691
25	106	8	0.884	6.594	8.000	2.235	0.000	8.000	−1.686	1.899	0.760	82	0.661

Figure 1 Distribution of all listening items (N=630)

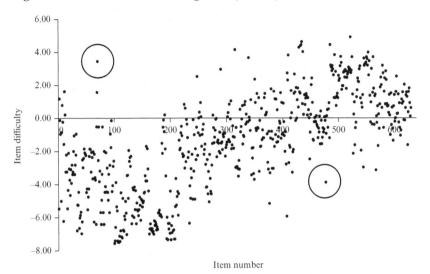

Item number

can in fact be verified, and whether the tasks in the different sets of booklets are significantly different in terms of difficulty. In order to answer this question, a one-way ANOVA was performed using SPSS 14.0. Since individual items all formed tasks, it seemed rational to analyse the relationship of the tasks rather than the individual items. The findings indicate that significant differences do exist, but the pattern of relationships is somewhat more complex than the three levels in which the booklets were arranged. Table 2 presents information about homogeneous subsets in the dataset.

As can be seen in Table 2, the first set of booklets aimed to be the least difficult (numbered 1 to 7) appear to form a more or less homogeneous subset. Similarly, the last set of booklets targeting the highest level (numbered 15 to 21) also appears to be relatively homogeneous. Admittedly, however, there are a number of overlaps, especially between the most difficult set of booklets and the 'intermediate-level' set. What this seems to indicate is that while the three targeted levels seem to emerge as genuinely different, the actual booklets aimed at these levels do not always clearly belong to one level or the other. Arguably, further analyses will need to be performed in order to find out whether it is particular tasks in certain booklets that were misclassified, or whether a more fundamental problem caused the overlaps.

The comparison of item and task difficulties followed a similar pattern in the case of reading as well. Figure 2 presents the distribution of the 598 reading items in the 84 tests. As can be seen in Figure 2, once again, there appears to be a tendency for the 598 items to become progressively more

Table 2 Homogeneous subsets in the listening tasks

		item_logit							
Scheffe									
Booklet	N	Subset for alpha = .05							
		1	2	3	4	5	6	7	8
4	31	−5.5252							
6	31	−5.0703							
7	31	−4.9055	−4.9055						
5	31	−4.7594	−4.7594						
2	34	−3.9400	−3.9400	−3.9400					
3	33	−3.1364	−3.1364	−3.1364	−3.1364				
1	32		−2.4288	−2.4288	−2.4288	−2.4288			
9	28			−2.1043	−2.1043	−2.1043			
8	29			−1.9293	−1.9293	−1.9293			
11	28				−.9993	−.9993	−.9993		
10	28				−.8961	−.8961	−.8961	−.8961	
13	29				−.8776	−.8776	−.8776	−.8776	
12	28				−.6371	−.6371	−.6371	−.6371	
16	31					−.5584	−.5584	−.5584	
14	29					−.3383	−.3383	−.3383	
21	29						.6731	.6731	.6731
20	28						1.0086	1.0086	1.0086
15	31						1.4184	1.4184	1.4184
18	29						1.4472	1.4472	1.4472
19	29							1.6197	1.6197
17	31								2.4974
Sig.		.113	.072	.467	.063	.372	.084	.058	.692

Notes:
Means for groups in homogeneous subsets are displayed.
a Uses harmonic mean sample size = 29.904.
b The group sizes are unequal. The harmonic mean of the group sizes is used. Type I error
levels are not guaranteed.

difficult as sequence numbers increase. However, this tendency seems less obvious than in the case of listening items, and there appears to be a much less emphatic difference between intermediate-level items and supposedly higher-difficulty ones. Also, there seems to be much more of a spread in terms of difficulty for supposedly low-level items. Once again, impressions can be tested through the ANOVA results, presented in Table 3.

As can be inferred from Table 3, the first seven booklets, targeting the lowest level, appear to form quite a homogeneous subset, even though there is considerable overlap with the next set of booklets (numbered 8 to 14), targeting the intermediate level. Also, it seems that the highest-level booklets (numbered 15 to 21) and the intermediate-level booklets tend to be quite similar in terms of difficulty, at least at the level of mean difficulty of tasks. Why this appears to be the case is once again to be investigated through further analyses. One potential explanation, again, is the inappropriate classification of

Figure 2 Distribution of all reading items (N=598)

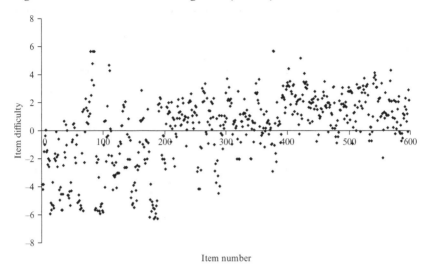

particular tasks. Alternatively, the response validity of candidates might be called into question.

In response to the second research question, then, it seems that listening tasks performed mostly in line with expectations, even though the differentiation between the intermediate and the highest level is not always quite clear. As for reading, it seems the uncertainty is somewhat greater in that low and intermediate-level tasks, although they appear to be different, are not always clearly recognisable, whereas intermediate and high-level tasks do not appear to be very different. It is important to clarify, on the other hand, that these findings should not be seen as final, as further analyses will need to clarify the causes of some unexpected results, which may or may not support the conclusions drawn above.

Further analyses need to establish how each individual listening and reading item and task worked. Data from children's and teachers' feedback on task familiarity and difficulty may throw light on the findings. Another avenue for further analyses should take into consideration how different task types, text types and whether or not tasks included only visuals, visuals and texts or only texts may have impacted results. Yet another perspective for further investigations has been launched: learners were invited to take tasks in different booklets and data was collected with think-aloud protocols to gain insights into how they went about solving the tasks, what strategies they applied and what caused difficulties – this is work in progress. Previous research showed (Nikolov 2006) that qualitative enquiries may provide useful information on tests and complement statistical analyses in important ways.

Table 3 Homogeneous subsets in the reading tasks

		item_logit				
Scheffe						
Booklet	N	Subset for alpha = .05				
		1	2	3	4	5
7	28	−2.7421				
1	28	−2.7086				
2	30	−2.5587	−2.5587			
4	29	−2.3162	−2.3162			
6	30	−1.9887	−1.9887	−1.9887		
5	29	−1.4197	−1.4197	−1.4197	−1.4197	
3	28	−.0479	−.0479	−.0479	−.0479	−.0479
9	30		.2300	.2300	.2300	.2300
12	30		.2497	.2497	.2497	.2497
10	28		.3679	.3679	.3679	.3679
8	28			.7971	.7971	.7971
11	29			.8155	.8155	.8155
13	27			.8315	.8315	.8315
21	28				.9557	.9557
17	28				1.2975	1.2975
14	30					1.5397
16	29					1.6214
20	26					1.6373
18	28					1.7789
19	27					2.0533
15	28					2.3736
Sig.		.145	.051	.085	.133	.361

Notes:
Means for groups in homogeneous subsets are displayed.
a Uses harmonic mean sample size = 28.434.
*b The group sizes are unequal. The harmonic mean of the group sizes is used. Type I error
levels are not guaranteed.*

It is also possible that results on the reading comprehension tests are different from those on listening comprehension tests not only because the actual tasks were different, but also because the underlying cognitive and first language reading comprehension skills interact differently with reading in EFL from listening comprehension in English. In further analyses it would be interesting to compare relationships between listening tasks and reading tasks to see how the amount and type of text and other characteristics of tests interacted with results.

Summary and the way forward

In this study our aim was to find out how well listening and reading tasks worked and to what extent they were of suitable quality to assess the target population: young learners of English. The other aim was to examine if the difficulty of the listening and reading tasks was in line with expectations: if the difficulty of the tasks included in the three sets of booklets increased sequentially. As has been shown, despite the fact that a few items did not seem to discriminate well, most of the tests worked well and after checking each and every item and changing or deleting the problem ones, the majority of the tests are eligible to become part of an item bank. Tests with problem items need to be scrutinised; problem items need to be changed or deleted and tests have to be piloted again.

As for the difficulty level of the tests, the predicted levels and the actual levels of difficulty seem to be in line with one another. Thus, the overall outcomes of the project are positive. However, as a next step further detailed analyses are necessary on the tests before they can be calibrated and placed in an item bank. In addition to this, although the tasks are claimed to be in line with CEFR levels, further enquiries should examine how the tests correspond to the A1 and A2 levels in the framework.

Useful data is available in the feedback collected from teachers and students on task familiarity, how easy and how motivating they found the tests. This should also be taken into consideration when individual tests are analysed. In addition to these points, if tests are going to be available on the internet, certain changes need to be made in formatting.

A next stage in the larger project should involve training teachers. It is not enough to develop and make good-quality diagnostic tests available to teachers; they need a certain level of diagnostic competence to be able to benefit from using the calibrated tests for diagnostic purposes with their pupils. This new stage will certainly mean new challenges.

References

Alderson, J C (2005) *Diagnosing Foreign Language Proficiency: the Interface Between Learning and Assessment*, London: Continuum.

Alderson, J C, Clapham, C and Wall, D (1995) *Language Test Construction and Evaluation*, Cambridge: Cambridge University Press.

Bachman, L (2004) *Statistical Analyses for Language Assessment*, Cambridge: Cambridge University Press.

Bachman, L (2011) *How do different language frameworks impact language assessment practice?,* paper presented at the ALTE 4th International Conference, 7–9 July 2011.

Barker, F and Shaw, S (2007) Linking language proficiency assessments for younger learners across proficiency levels (Phase 1), *Research Notes* 28, 14–18.

Black, P and William, D (1998) Assessment and classroom learning, *Assessment in Education* 5, 7–1.

Butler, Y G (2009) Issues in the assessment and evaluation of English language education at the elementary school level: Implications for policies in South Korea, Taiwan, and Japan, *The Journal of Asia TEFL* 6 (2), 1–31.

Butler, Y G and Lee, J (2006) On-task versus off-task self-assessment among Korean elementary school students studying English, *The Modern Language Journal* 90, 506–518.

Butler, Y G and Lee, J (2010) The effects of self-assessment among young learners of English, *Language Testing* 27, 5–31.

Council of Europe (2001) *Common European Framework of Reference for Languages: Learning, Teaching, Assessment*, Cambridge: Cambridge University Press.

Davison, C and Leung, C (2009) Current issues in English language teacher-based assessment, *TESOL Quarterly* 43, 393–415.

Dörnyei, Z, Csizér, K and Németh, N (2006) *Motivational Dynamics, Language Attitudes and Language Globalization: A Hungarian Perspective*, Clevedon, Avon: Multilingual Matters.

Edelenbos, P and Kubanek-German, A (2004) Teacher assessment: The concept of 'diagnostic competence', *Language Testing* 21, 259–283.

Figueras, N and Noijons, J (Eds) (2009) *Linking to the CEFR Levels: Research Perspectives*, Arnhem: Cito, EALTA.

Haenni Hoti, A, Heinzmann, S and Müller, M (2009) "I can you help?" Assessing speaking skills and interaction strategies of young learners, in Nikolov, M (Ed.) *The Age Factor and Early Language Learning*, Berlin: Mouton de Gruyter, 119–140.

Hasselgreen, A (2005) Assessing the language of young learners, *Language Testing* 22, 337–354.

Hild, G and Nikolov M (2010) Teachers' views on tasks that work with primary school EFL learners, in Lehmann, M, Lugossy, R and Horváth, J (Eds) *UPRT 2010: Empirical Studies in English Applied Linguistics*, Pécs: Lingua Franca Csoport, 47–62.

Inbar-Lourie, O and Shohamy, E (2009) Assessing young language learners: What is the construct? in Nikolov, M (Ed.) *The Age Factor and Early Language Learning*, Berlin: Mouton de Gruyter, 83–96.

Jones, N and Saville, N (2009) European language policy: Assessment, learning and the CEFR, *Annual Review of Applied Linguistics* 29, 51–63.

Leung, C and Scott, C (2009) Formative assessment in language education policies: emerging lessons from Wales and Scotland, *Annual Review of Applied Linguistics* 29, 64–79.

Little, D (2007) The common European framework of reference for languages: Perspectives on the making of supranational language education policy, *The Modern Language Journal* 91, 645–653.

McKay, P (2006) *Assessing Young Language Learners*, Cambridge: Cambridge University Press.

McNamara, T and Roever, C (2006) *Language Testing: The Social Dimension*, Oxford: Blackwell Publishing.

Nikolov, M (1999) "Natural born speakers of English": Code switching in pair- and group-work in Hungarian primary schools, in Rixon, S (Ed.) *Young Learners of English: Some Research Perspectives*, London: Longman, 72–88.

Nikolov, M (2006) Test-taking strategies of 12–13-year-old Hungarian learners of EFL: Why whales have migraine, *Language Learning* 57 (1), 1–51.

Nikolov, M (2008) 'Az általános iskola, az módszertan!' Alsó tagozatos angolórák empirikus vizsgálata [Primary school means methodology! An empirical study of lower-primary EFL classes], *Modern Nyelvoktatás* 10 (1–2), 3–19.

Nikolov, M (2009a) The age factor in context, in Nikolov, M (Ed.) *The Age Factor and Early Language Learning*, Berlin and New York: Mouton de Gruyter, 1–38.

Nikolov, M (2009b) Early modern foreign language programmes and outcomes: Factors contributing to Hungarian learners' proficiency, in Nikolov, M (Ed.) *Early Learning of Modern Foreign Languages: Processes and Outcomes*, Clevedon, Avon: Multilingual Matters, 90–107.

Nikolov, M (2009c) The dream and the reality of early programmes in Hungary, in Enever, J, Moon, J and Raman, U (Eds) *Young Learner English Language Policy and Implementation: International Perspectives*, Reading, UK: Garnet Education/IATEFL, 121–130.

Nikolov M (2011) Az angol nyelvtudás fejlesztésének és értékelésének keretei az általános iskola első hat évfolyamán [A framework for developing and assessing English language proficiency in the first six grades of primary school], *Modern Nyelvoktatás* XVII (1), 9–31.

Nikolov, M and Mihaljević Djigunović, J (2006) Recent research on age, second language acquisition, and early foreign language learning, *Annual Review of Applied Linguistics* 26, 234–260.

Nikolov, M and Mihaljević Djigunović, J (2011) All shades of every color: An overview of early teaching and learning of foreign languages, *Annual Review of Applied Linguistics* 31, 1– 25.

Nikolov M and Szabó G (2011) Az angol nyelvtudás diagnosztikus mérésének és fejlesztésének lehetőségei az általános iskola 1–6. évfolyamán [Diagnostic assessment and development of English language knowledge in grades 1 to 6 in the primary school], in Csapó, B and Zsolnai, A (Eds) *A kognitív és affektív fejlődés diagnosztikus mérése az iskola kezdő szakaszában*, Budapest: Nemzeti Tankönyvkiadó, 13–40.

Nisbett, R E (2009) *Intelligence and How To Get It: Why Schools and Cultures Count*, New York: W W Norton and Company.

Papp, S and Salamoura, A (2009) An exploratory study into linking young learners' examinations to the CEFR, *Research Notes* 37, 15–22.

Peng, J and Zhang, L (2009a) An eye on target language use in elementary English classrooms in China, in Nikolov, M (Ed.) *Early Learning of Modern Foreign Languages*, Bristol: Multilingual Matters, 212–228.

Peng, J and Zhang, L (2009b) Chinese primary school students' use of communication strategies in EFL classrooms, in Nikolov, M (Ed.) *The Age Factor and Early Language Learning*, Berlin: Mouton de Gruyter, 337–350.

Pinter, A (2007) Benefits of peer–peer interaction: 10-year-old children practising with a communication task, *Language Teaching Research* 11, 189–207.

Pižorn, K (2009) Designing proficiency levels for English for primary and secondary school students and the impact of the CEFR, in Figueras, N and Noijons J (Eds) *Linking to the CEFR Levels: Research Perspectives*, Arnhem: Cito, EALTA, 87–102.

Rixon, S (2007) Cambridge ESOL YLE tests and children's first steps in reading and writing in English, *Research Notes* 28, 7–14.

Sternberg, R J and Grigorenko, E L (2002) *Dynamic Testing: The Nature and Measurement of Learning Potential*, Cambridge: Cambridge University Press.

Teasdale, A and Leung, C (2000) Teacher assessment and psychometric theory: a case of paradigm crossing, *Language Testing* 17, 163–184.

19 A study of differential item functioning in the TestDaF Reading and Listening sections

Thomas Eckes

TestDaF Institute, Bochum, Germany

Abstract

Investigating test items for differential item functioning (DIF) plays a key role in frameworks on test fairness and test validity (Kunnan 2004, 2008, McNamara and Roever 2006, Xi 2010). The basic requirement is that items should measure the ability of interest without being affected by construct-irrelevant variance introduced through examinee background factors. To the extent that background factors have an impact on examinees' responses to test items, a given group of examinees will be advantaged or disadvantaged relative to other groups. In the present study, DIF was investigated in the context of the Reading and Listening sections of the *Test Deutsch als Fremdsprache* (TestDaF) – the *Test of German as a Foreign Language*. Drawing on two live TestDaF exams administered in April 2010 (N=2,859) and November 2010 (N=2,214), DIF was studied regarding gender groups as well as groups from different language backgrounds, with a focus on Chinese and Western European native speakers. DIF analyses were performed using four different approaches: the Mantel–Haenszel procedure, binary logistic regression, and two Rasch-based methods. Results are discussed in terms of substantive and methodological issues. The paper concludes with a brief outline of perspectives for future research.

Differential item functioning, item bias, and test validation

Differential item functioning (DIF) is present when examinees from different groups have differing probabilities of success on an item after they have been matched on the attribute being measured (Camilli and Shepard 1994, Clauser and Mazor 1998, Osterlind and Everson 2009). Within the context of language tests, the attribute being measured refers to language ability, or some aspect of that ability like grammar, vocabulary, or reading comprehension.

According to Ferne and Rupp (2007), the majority of language testing studies examined DIF for groups differing in terms of (a) language background, (b) gender, or (c) ethnicity. Typically, two groups are compared, one of which is called the *reference group*, providing the basis for comparison (e.g., males), and the other one the *focal group*, forming the focus of analysis (e.g., females). From a statistical point of view, which group is designated as reference and which as focal, is not relevant. In general, the grouping refers to a classification of examinees used to define the specific hypothesis studied. The hypothesis could be, for example, that males outperformed females on a particular reading comprehension item because males were more likely than females to answer the item correctly using specific background knowledge irrelevant to the construct being measured.

DIF can be examined for items scored dichotomously, as when responses to items are scored either correct or incorrect, and for items scored polytomously, as when responses to items are scored using a rating scale with three or more ordered categories (Osterlind and Everson 2009, Penfield and Camilli 2007). When considering dichotomously scored items, the null hypothesis of no DIF says that the probability of a correct response is identical for examinees belonging to different groups, but sharing the same level of ability. In other words, in the absence of DIF, the probability of an examinee's response to an item is independent of the examinee's group membership. If, on the other hand, performance on an item differs between groups after controlling for the level of examinee ability, the group having the lower probability of responding correctly to the item is at a disadvantage on that item.

Two forms of DIF are commonly distinguished: *uniform* DIF and *non-uniform* DIF (Clauser and Mazor 1998, Penfield and Camilli 2007). An item shows uniform DIF when the item provides a constant, or nearly constant, relative advantage for one and the same group, regardless of the ability level. That is, one group is advantaged over another group across the entire ability scale, and that advantage remains about the same across the scale. By contrast, an item shows non-uniform DIF when one group has an advantage at one section of the ability scale (e.g., at lower ability levels), but that advantage increases, decreases, or reverses at other scale sections (e.g., at higher ability levels). When the advantage is reversing, the item is said to exhibit *crossing* non-uniform DIF. This form of DIF is particularly problematic because it is not so easy to detect (in fact, only a few methods are suited to detect it at all, such as binary logistic regression, discussed later), and is even harder to account for when shown to be present.

It is important to note that the presence of DIF is a necessary but not sufficient condition for item bias (Clauser and Mazor 1998, McNamara and Roever 2006). When an item shows DIF, this is no more than statistical information that something unexpected has happened, something that needs to be explained. Such an explanation may suggest the impact of a *construct-relevant* factor, in which case the item could still be said to be fair or unbiased. Alternatively, the explanation may refer to an unintended, *construct-irrelevant* factor, in which case the item would be said to be unfair or biased.

Chen and Henning (1985) provided an example of a construct-relevant influence. In a DIF analysis of an English as a Foreign Language (EFL) test, the authors identified four vocabulary recognition items favouring Spanish over Chinese native speakers. Yet, Chen and Henning were able to explain these group-dependent performance differences by considering the DIF items' relation to cognates of the target language vocabulary in the first language (L1) of the Spanish examinees. Hence, the observed group differences were real differences in the underlying ability being measured by the test. Generally, real ability differences manifesting themselves in examinee performance on an item are called *item impact*.

When, however, DIF can be shown to be due to an unintended factor, that is, a secondary dimension that is not part of the test construct, the item is classified as unfair or biased. In other words, the term *item bias* refers to DIF accounted for by the specific influence that a construct-irrelevant factor has on the way examinees belonging to a particular group respond to an item. Identifying such a factor in the case of an item showing DIF usually is a difficult task posing a real challenge to content experts looking for an explanation. At a minimum, the experts need to carefully review item content, item format, and the overall test design, drawing on their knowledge of possibly relevant differences in examinees' educational, cultural, or language background in order to come up with a reasonable hypothesis as to why DIF occurred.

The analysis of DIF has an important role to play in more general frameworks on test fairness and test validity. As a prominent example, one of the fairness standards of the 1999 *Standards for Educational and Psychological Testing* (American Educational Research Association, American Psychological Association and National Council on Measurement in Education 1999) explicitly required that appropriate DIF studies be performed (Standard 7.3; see also Camilli 2006, Linn 2006). In a similar vein, Kunnan (2004, 2008) emphasised *absence of bias* as a test quality that along with validity and some other qualities establishes test fairness, and argued that one way of reducing or eliminating bias would be through DIF studies. McNamara and Roever (2006) adopted a broad perspective on test fairness and stressed the social dimensions of language testing as evident in the presence of DIF and item bias, respectively.

More recently, Xi (2010) linked the study of test fairness directly to test validation, viewing fairness as comparable validity for all relevant groups. Kane (2010) pointed out that validity and fairness are indeed closely connected, with validity theory focusing more 'on the accuracy and appropriateness of score-based interpretations and decisions about all of the individuals in the population of interest' (2010:181), and fairness analysis focusing more 'on group differences and on differences in the accuracy and appropriateness of interpretations and decisions across groups, which are defined in terms of race/ethnicity, gender, age, and so on' (2010:181).

Clearly, then, studies of DIF are an integral part of any test validation process. Within the context of the present study, DIF was analysed with respect to the *Test Deutsch als Fremdsprache* (TestDaF), or 'Test of German as a Foreign Language'. What follows is a detailed report on DIF analyses of the Reading and Listening sections of the TestDaF, thus adding to the already existing validity evidence on that test reported previously (e.g., Eckes 2005, 2008, 2010, Kecker and Eckes 2010).

Research questions

This research had two major objectives. The first objective was to perform DIF analyses of Reading and Listening items included in two live TestDaF exams administered in April 2010 and November 2010, respectively. The second objective was to apply four commonly used DIF detection methods and to compare the results produced by each of these methods, in particular with respect to DIF detection rates.

TestDaF Reading and Listening items

With each language skill, two different groupings of examinees were considered: the first grouping was based on examinee gender, the second grouping on examinee language background. As to the second grouping, the focus was on comparing Chinese and Western European native speakers. This particular language group comparison was deemed important for the following reasons: Chinese native speakers have been among the largest groups of TestDaF examinees; Western European languages, though not as widely spoken among TestDaF examinees as Slavic languages like Russian, Ukrainian, or Bulgarian, represent the target language family and culture. The languages included in the Western European sample were English, French, and Spanish. Additional DIF analyses also addressed groups of Korean and Slavic native speakers.

The research questions concerning the first objective were as follows:

- To what extent are TestDaF exams subject to gender-based DIF?
- To what extent are TestDaF exams subject to DIF related to language background?
- Is one group of examinees in each comparison consistently put at a disadvantage?

- Are there differences in DIF effects between Reading and Listening sections?
- Are there differences in DIF effects between the two exams?

DIF detection methods

Most applied studies of DIF have used a single method of DIF detection. Yet, referring to the findings of psychometric studies aiming at a comparison of two or more methods, Ferne and Rupp (2007:133) concluded that 'the utilization of a single method is undesirable and might represent an oversimplification due to a method effect, because different statistical methods typically yield conflicting results, at least for some items'.

In this study, four commonly used methods of DIF detection were employed. Hence, any DIF effects present in the data could be evaluated on a firm basis; moreover, the methods could be compared regarding their DIF detection across different data sets. The methods were: (a) the Mantel–Haenszel (MH) procedure (Mantel and Haenszel 1959), (b) binary logistic regression (Swaminathan and Rogers 1990, Zumbo 1999), (c) the DIF contrast method (Linacre 2011), and (d) the likelihood ratio test (du Toit 2003, Thissen, Steinberg and Wainer 1993).

Building on taxonomies proposed by Potenza and Dorans (1995) and Mapuranga, Dorans and Middleton (2008), Table 1 presents a classification of these methods according to three statistical features (a detailed discussion of each of these methods is beyond the scope of the present paper; the interested reader is referred to Holland and Wainer 1993, Osterlind and Everson 2009, Penfield and Camilli 2007). The distinguishing features refer to the approach used to estimating DIF effects (parametric, nonparametric), the kind of matching variable (observed score, latent variable), and the form of DIF that can be studied (uniform, non-uniform).

As can be seen, the MH procedure is the only method that employs a nonparametric approach to the estimation of DIF effects; that is, the MH procedure does not invoke a statistical model specifying a functional form for the relation between item score and the matching variable (i.e., the variable used to match examinee ability levels). The other methods either estimate regression parameters (binary logistic regression) or utilise the Rasch model (Bond and Fox 2007, Wright and Stone 1979) in order to estimate item difficulty parameters and log-likelihood statistics, respectively. A common feature of the MH procedure and binary logistic regression is to use observed scores as the matching variable; by contrast, the Rasch-based methods use estimates of the latent ability level. As the third feature shows, binary logistic regression is the only method among the methods studied here that tests for both uniform and non-uniform DIF (though the DIF

Table 1 Classification of DIF detection methods according to statistical features

Method	DIF estimation		Matching variable		DIF type	
	Parametric	Nonparam.	Observed score	Latent variable	Uniform	Non-uniform
Mantel–Haenszel		X	X		X	
Logistic regression	X		X		X	X
Rasch DIF contrast	X[a]			X	X	(X)
Likelihood ratio test	X[b]			X	X	

Notes:
Each X indicates that a given method has the statistical feature shown in the particular column.
[a] *The Rasch DIF contrast method uses joint maximum likelihood (JML) estimation.*
[b] *The likelihood ratio test uses marginal maximum likelihood (MML) estimation. The X in parentheses (last column) indicates that the Rasch DIF contrast method is suited to studying non-uniform DIF after inclusion of an appropriate person classification variable.*

contrast method, after inclusion of an appropriate examinee classification variable, can be used to study non-uniform DIF as well (Aryadoust, Goh and Kim 2011, Linacre 2011).

The two Rasch-based methods differ from one another in at least two ways. First, the DIF contrast method as implemented in the Rasch analysis software WINSTEPS (Linacre 2011) employs a joint maximum likelihood approach to estimating model parameters, where the DIF contrast measure (in logits) is defined as the difference between the item difficulty estimates obtained separately for the reference and focal groups; the likelihood ratio test as implemented in BILOG-MG (du Toit 2003) employs a marginal maximum likelihood approach to parameter estimation. Second, the likelihood ratio test procedure involves a comparison between two models based on log-likelihood statistics: the first statistic gives the model fit of a compact model representing the null hypothesis of no DIF in a set of items, and the second statistic gives the model fit of an augmented model representing the alternative hypothesis that DIF effects are present. No such model comparison based on global fit statistics is implemented in WINSTEPS.

The research questions concerning the second objective were as follows:

- To what extent do the four DIF detection methods yield congruent, incongruent, or even conflicting results?

- What is the nature of possible differences between methods when applied to the same set of data?

Method

Participants

The participants were from two separate samples of TestDaF examinees. The first sample comprised 2,859 examinees taking the TestDaF in April 2010 (1,855 females, 1,004 males), the second sample comprised 2,214 examinees taking the TestDaF in November 2010 (1,429 females, 785 males). All examinees were foreign students applying for entry to an institution for higher education in Germany.

In the April 2010 exam, there were 262 test centres involved (130 centres in Germany, 132 centres across 61 other countries). In terms of country of origin, the greatest numbers of participants in the April exam were from Russia, the People's Republic of China, Ukraine, Bulgaria, and the Republic of Korea. In the November 2010 exam, there were 279 test centres involved (133 centres in Germany, 146 centres across 60 other countries). The same set of countries of origin as in the April exam ranked highest in this exam (with Ukraine and Bulgaria changing places).

Instrument

The TestDaF is designed for foreign students applying for entry to an institution of higher education in Germany. The test measures the four language skills in separate sections (Reading, Listening, Writing, and Speaking). Examinee performance in each section is related to one of three levels of language proficiency, TDN 3, TDN 4, and TDN 5 (*TestDaF-Niveaustufen*, 'TestDaF levels'). The TDNs cover the Council of Europe's (2001) Lower Vantage Level (B2.1) to Higher Effective Operational Proficiency (C1.2); that is, the test measures German language proficiency at an intermediate to high level (see Eckes 2008, Kecker and Eckes 2010).

The TestDaF is officially recognised as a language entry exam for students from abroad. Examinees who have achieved at least TDN 4 in each section are eligible for admission to a German institution of higher education (see Eckes, Ellis, Kalnberzina, Pižorn, Springer, Szollás and Tsagari 2005). In the present samples, 36.8% of the participants sitting the April exam and 35.5% of the participants sitting the November exam proved to be eligible for admission, with 19.9% of the April examinees and 23.2% of the November examinees failing the respective exam (i.e., these examinees did not achieve TDN 3 in at least one section); the remaining examinees (43.4% in the April exam, 41.3% in the November exam) achieved at least TDN 3 in each section but failed to achieve at least TDN 4 in each section.

TestDaF Reading

The Reading section (duration: 60 mins.) measures the examinee's ability to understand, and respond adequately to, texts relevant to academic life presented in writing. Various types of tasks and items are used, including a matching task, multiple-choice questions, and forced-choice items of the type 'yes/no/no relevant information in the text'. There are three reading texts at increasing levels of difficulty: short texts on everyday life at university, newspaper or magazine articles, and articles from academic journals. The total number of items is 30. Examinee responses to items are scored either correct or incorrect.

TestDaF Listening

The Listening section (duration: 40 mins.) measures the examinee's ability to understand, and respond adequately to, spoken texts relevant to academic life. Various types of tasks and items are used, including short-answer and true/false questions. There are three listening texts at increasing levels of difficulty: a dialogue typical of everyday life at university, a radio interview with three or four speakers, and a short lecture or an interview with an expert. The tasks require comprehension of context and detail as well as implicit information. The total number of items is 25. Examinee responses to items are scored either correct or incorrect.

Analysis

The overall design of analysis was as follows: 2 (exams) × 2 (language skills) × 2 (gender groups; language groups) × 4 (DIF detection methods); that is, there were eight different data sets (e.g., April exam, Reading section, females). First, descriptive group statistics were computed for each data set. Then, the data was analysed using standard and specialised computer software to implement each of the four DIF detection methods.

DIF analysis software

IBM SPSS Statistics 19 was used to compute descriptive group statistics as well as to perform the binary logistic regression procedure along the lines laid out by Zumbo (1999) (see also Osterlind and Everson 2009). WINSTEPS (Linacre 2011) (see also Bond and Fox 2007) was used to implement the DIF contrast method as well as the MH procedure. Note that the MH and the Rasch-based DIF contrast approaches to testing the null hypothesis of no DIF are formally equivalent if the following conditions hold: (a) the data fits the Rasch model, (b) no item shows DIF except the studied item that may show DIF, (c) the matching variable is the number-correct score that includes the studied item, and (c) the samples of examinees compared are random samples from the respective reference and focal groups (Holland and Thayer 1988, Linacre and

Wright 1987). If any of these conditions is not met the procedures will yield different results, especially when sample size is small. The likelihood ratio test was performed using the BILOG-MG software (du Toit 2003).

DIF classification criteria

Each DIF detection method comes with a specific set of criteria for classifying items into a number of DIF categories or for distinguishing between DIF items and non-DIF items. In principle, a decision as to the DIF status of a given item could be reached based on statistical significance tests (i.e., testing the null hypothesis of no DIF). However, such tests are highly dependent on sample size, tending to flag items in large samples that in fact show only negligibly small DIF effects (due to very high statistical power), and possibly leaving undetected big DIF effects in small samples (due to very low statistical power). Therefore, commonly applied decision rules for classifying items usually rest not only on the results of significance tests but also on measures of the size of DIF effects.

A decision rule often used with the MH procedure was introduced by the Educational Testing Service (ETS) (Zieky 1993). The ETS system classifies items into one of three broad categories: small or negligible DIF (A-level), moderate DIF (B-level), and large DIF (C-level). Let $\hat{\lambda}$ be the DIF effect size estimator for the MH procedure; then the DIF categories can be defined as follows (Penfield and Camilli 2007):

- A_{MH}: $\hat{\lambda}$ is not significantly different from zero, or $|\hat{\lambda}| < 0.43$
- B_{MH}: $\hat{\lambda}$ is significantly different from zero and $|\hat{\lambda}| \geq 0.43$, and either: (a) $|\hat{\lambda}| < 0.64$, or (b) $|\hat{\lambda}|$ is not significantly greater than 0.43
- C_{MH}: $|\hat{\lambda}|$ is significantly greater than 0.43 and $|\hat{\lambda}| \geq 0.64$.

Within the logistic regression approach, where ΔR^2 serves as a measure of uniform or non-uniform DIF effect size, the following definitions of DIF categories have been proposed (Jodoin and Gierl 2001):

- A_{LR}: $\Delta R^2 < 0.035$
- B_{LR}: Null hypothesis is rejected and $0.035 \leq \Delta R^2 < 0.070$
- C_{LR}: Null hypothesis is rejected and $\Delta R^2 \geq 0.070$.

The DIF contrast and the likelihood ratio approaches each classify items into one of two DIF categories: (a) DIF is present, or (b) DIF is not present. As to the DIF contrast approach, let $\hat{\beta}_{DIF}$ be the estimate of the DIF contrast (in logits). Then, these two categories are defined as follows (Linacre 2011):

- DIF is not present: null hypothesis is not rejected or $|\hat{\beta}_{DIF}| < 0.50$
- DIF is present: null hypothesis is rejected and $|\hat{\beta}_{DIF}| \geq 0.50$.

That is, within this approach an item is flagged only if the logit measure is significantly different from zero and the (absolute) value of the DIF contrast is 0.50 or greater. As suggested by Zenisky, Hambleton and Robin (2003), in the present analysis, a two-stage purification process was employed to avoid contamination of the matching variable due to inclusion of items being flagged as DIF. That is, in the first stage a standard DIF contrast analysis was carried out and items were classified as DIF or non-DIF items according to the decision rule above; in the second stage, the items flagged for DIF were given a weight of zero, and the data was reanalysed to show the (purified) DIF contrast measures.

As mentioned previously, the likelihood ratio test described in the BILOG-MG software manual (du Toit 2003:638–651) utilises a somewhat different strategy. In particular, the likelihood obtained using the compact model is compared to the likelihood obtained using the augmented model by means of a likelihood ratio test statistic. If the likelihood for the augmented model (the DIF model) is significantly smaller than the likelihood for the compact model (the non-DIF model), that is, if the data fits the augmented model significantly better, DIF effects are said to be present. In that case, the differences in item difficulty estimates for the two groups (denoted by $\hat{\beta}_{LRT}$) are computed to identify which items showed DIF. It should be noted that this version of the likelihood ratio test differs from the procedure originally proposed by Thissen et al (1993), and implemented in MULTILOG (du Toit 2003:770–772): In the Thissen et al approach, the augmented model refers to a particular item examined for DIF, that is, one or more parameters of the studied item are free to vary between the reference and focal groups (for an illustrative example, see Kim 2001). In the version used here, and implemented in BILOG-MG (du Toit 2003:638–651), the augmented model refers to a set of items examined for the presence of any DIF effects (e.g., Geranpayeh 2008, Geranpayeh and Kunnan 2007). The decision rule for flagging items as used in the analysis was as follows:

- DIF is not present: likelihood ratio test statistic (for a given set of items) is not significant
- DIF is present: likelihood ratio test statistic (for a given set of items) is significant; null hypothesis of no DIF for a given item is rejected and $|\hat{\beta}_{LRT}| \geq 0.50$.

Finally, the MH, DIF contrast, and likelihood ratio procedures involve multiple significance tests at the item level. Therefore, critical significance levels should be adjusted to guard against falsely rejecting the null hypothesis of no DIF present in an item. To this purpose, a Bonferroni adjustment of the .05 level of significance was employed (e.g., Myers and Well 2003). Note that, by default, BILOG-MG (du Toit 2003) randomly reduces the sample of examinees to N=1,000, considering the proportions of examinees in the reference and focal groups. Yet, this reduction in sample size does not resolve the basic sample size dependence of statistical significance testing.

Results

Females versus males

Descriptive statistics

Table 2 presents means and standard deviations for females versus males in the Reading and Listening sections administered in the April and November exams, respectively. On each section and each exam, females outperformed males. The largest difference in mean performance (1.71 score points) was observed for the Listening section on the November exam.

Table 2 Summary statistics for females and males in the TestDaF Reading and Listening sections

Group	Reading			Listening		
	N	M	SD	N	M	SD
			April exam			
Females	1,855	21.54	4.89	1,855	18.40	4.37
Males	1,004	20.74	5.22	1,004	16.72	4.85
Total	2,859	21.26	5.02	2,859	17.81	4.62
			November exam			
Females	1,429	21.52	5.07	1,424	15.71	5.31
Males	785	20.51	5.22	784	14.00	5.44
Total	2,214	21.16	5.14	2,208	15.10	5.42

Note: The Reading section contained 30 items; the Listening section contained 25 items. For each section and each exam date, means for females and males differ significantly ($p < .001$).

DIF results

Table 3 presents the results of the MH and logistic regression DIF analyses. As can be seen, in the April exam there was not a single item showing DIF. In the November exam, there was only one item on the Reading section and one item on the Listening section showing DIF. In both cases, this was B-level DIF favouring females.

The results of the DIF contrast and likelihood ratio procedures are shown in Table 4. One item was flagged by the likelihood ratio test in the Reading section, April exam (favouring males); one Reading item, in fact the very same item, was flagged by both procedures in the November exam (favouring females).

To summarise, across exams, language skills, and methods of DIF detection, the overall level of gender DIF was extremely low. There was not any evidence of C-level DIF (MH, logistic regression). The Reading item that was consistently flagged in the MH, DIF contrast, and likelihood ratio analyses

Table 3 Results of the gender-based DIF analysis using Mantel–Haenszel and logistic regression procedures

Method	DIF level		
	A	**B**	**C**
	April exam		
Mantel–Haenszel			
Reading	30	0	0
Listening	25	0	0
Logistic regression			
Reading	30	0	0
Listening	25	0	0
	November exam		
Mantel–Haenszel			
Reading	29	1 F	0
Listening	24	1 F	0
Logistic regression			
Reading	30	0	0
Listening	25	0	0

Note: The Reading section contained 30 items; the Listening section contained 25 items. Entries in columns A, B, and C give the number of items at a particular DIF level and the group favoured (e.g., '1 F' in the B column, Mantel–Haenszel analysis, Reading section, November exam, means that one reading item showed B-level DIF favouring females).

Table 4 Results of the gender-based DIF analysis using DIF contrast and likelihood ratio procedures

Method	Not flagged	Flagged
	April exam	
DIF contrast		
Reading	30	0
Listening	25	0
Likelihood ratio test		
Reading	29	1 M
Listening	25	0
	November exam	
DIF contrast		
Reading	29	1 F
Listening	25	0
Likelihood ratio test		
Reading	29	1 F
Listening	25	0

Note: The Reading section contained 30 items; the Listening section contained 25 items. Entries in the 'Flagged' column give the number of DIF items and the group favoured (e.g., '1 M' in the likelihood ratio analysis of the Reading section, April exam, means that one item showed DIF favouring males).

turned out to be the easiest item on this section, and it was still easier for females than for males. Yet, expert review of item content did not succeed at suggesting any reasonable explanation for this particular DIF effect.

Chinese versus Western European native speakers

Descriptive statistics

Table 5 presents means and standard deviations for Chinese versus Western European native speakers in the Reading and Listening sections administered in the April and November exams, respectively. On each section and each exam, Western European native speakers outperformed Chinese native speakers. The largest difference in mean performance (5.60 score points) was observed for the Listening section on the November exam.

Table 5 Summary statistics for Chinese and Western European native speakers in the TestDaF Reading and Listening sections

Group	Reading			Listening		
	N	*M*	*SD*	*N*	*M*	*SD*
			April exam			
Chinese	275	18.87	4.92	275	14.18	4.64
W. Europ.	372	22.63	4.58	372	18.49	4.28
			November exam			
Chinese	221	20.00	4.27	221	10.15	4.30
W. Europ.	281	21.02	5.03	280	15.75	5.08

Note: The Reading section contained 30 items; the Listening section contained 25 items. For each section and each exam date, means for Chinese and Western European native speakers differ significantly ($p < .05$).

DIF results

Table 6 presents the results of the MH and logistic regression DIF analyses. As shown in the last column, the percentage of items exhibiting DIF when collapsing across levels B and C in the April exam, ranged from 13.3% (logistic regression, Reading section) to 40.0% (MH, Listening section). In the November exam, the overall level of DIF proved to be lower, reaching its maximum percentage of 20.0% in the Reading section (MH and logistic regression).

The results of the DIF contrast and likelihood ratio procedures are shown in Table 7. As revealed by the DIF% values, the proportion of items flagged for DIF by each of these methods was particularly high in the April exam (detailed results of the DIF contrast method for these two language groups are presented later).

Table 6   Results of the Chinese–Western European language group DIF analysis using Mantel–Haenszel and logistic regression procedures

Method	DIF level			DIF%
	A	B	C	
		April exam		
Mantel–Haenszel				
Reading	22	3 Ch / 2 WE	1 Ch / 2 WE	26.7
Listening	15	2 Ch / 4 WE	2 Ch / 2 WE	40.0
Logistic regression				
Reading	26	1 Ch / 0 WE	1 Ch / 2 WE	13.3
Listening	17	1 Ch / 4 WE	3 Ch / 0 WE	32.0
		November exam		
Mantel–Haenszel				
Reading	24	3 Ch / 3 WE	0 Ch / 0 WE	20.0
Listening	23	0 Ch / 1 WE	1 Ch / 0 WE	8.0
Logistic regression				
Reading	24	3 Ch / 2 WE	0 Ch / 1 WE	20.0
Listening	24	0 Ch / 0 WE	1 Ch / 0 WE	4.0

Note: DIF% gives the percentage of items at DIF levels B and C. The Reading section contained 30 items; the Listening section contained 25 items. Ch = Chinese L1 speakers. WE = Western European L1 speakers. Entries in columns A, B, and C give the number of items at a particular DIF level and the group favoured (e.g., '3 Ch' in the B column, Mantel–Haenszel analysis, Reading section, April exam, means that three reading items showed B-level DIF favouring Chinese L1 speakers).

Table 7   Results of the Chinese–Western European language group DIF analysis using DIF contrast and likelihood ratio procedures

Method	Not flagged	Flagged	DIF%
		April exam	
DIF contrast			
Reading	19	6 Ch / 5 WE	36.7
Listening	14	6 Ch / 5 WE	44.0
Likelihood ratio test			
Reading	19	6 Ch / 5 WE	36.7
Listening	14	6 Ch / 5 WE	44.0
		November exam	
DIF contrast			
Reading	26	1 Ch / 3 WE	13.3
Listening	18	4 Ch / 3 WE	28.0
Likelihood ratio test			
Reading	25	2 Ch / 3 WE	16.7
Listening	18	4 Ch / 3 WE	28.0

Note: DIF% gives the percentage of flagged items. The Reading section contained 30 items; the Listening section contained 25 items. Ch = Chinese L1 speakers. WE = Western European L1 speakers. Entries in the 'Flagged' column give the number of DIF items and the group favoured (e.g., '6 Ch' in the DIF contrast analysis of the Reading section, April exam, means that six items showed DIF favouring Chinese L1 speakers).

To summarise, across exams, language skills, and methods of DIF detection, there was a considerable proportion of items functioning differently in the language groups studied. The highest numbers of DIF items were identified by Rasch-based methods (36.7% in the April Reading exam, 44.0% in the April Listening exam). The November exam had substantially lower numbers of DIF items than the April exam. With one exception (Reading section, November exam), by far the least number of DIF items was identified by the logistic regression procedure. In each of the DIF analyses, the number of DIF items favouring one group over the other was about equal; that is, there was no evidence that the Reading and Listening sections, respectively, consistently put one language group at a disadvantage over the other group.

Asian versus European native speakers

Descriptive statistics

Table 8 presents means and standard deviations for Asian versus European native speakers in the Reading and Listening sections administered in the April and November exams, respectively. Regarding the group of Asian native speakers (i.e., Chinese versus Korean), there was only one statistically significant difference in mean performance: Korean speakers performed somewhat better on the Listening section of the November exam (i.e., 1.56 score points). Differences at a similarly low but statistically significant level were observed within the group of European native speakers (i.e., Western European versus Slavic) for three out of the four comparisons. By contrast,

Table 8 Summary statistics for Asian and European native speakers in the TestDaF Reading and Listening sections

Group	Reading			Listening		
	N	M	SD	N	M	SD
			April exam			
Chinese	275	18.87	4.92	275	14.18	4.64
Korean	105	18.51	4.72	105	14.21	4.56
W. Europ.	372	22.63	4.58	372	18.49	4.28
Slavic	929	22.07	4.48	929	18.93	4.05
			November exam			
Chinese	221	20.00	4.27	221	10.15	4.30
Korean	107	19.59	4.25	107	11.71	4.72
W. Europ.	281	21.02	5.03	280	15.75	5.08
Slavic	652	22.90	4.38	650	17.24	4.58

Note: The Reading section contained 30 items; the Listening section contained 25 items. Within each column, means not sharing a superscript differ significantly from one another (p < .05).

each and every comparison between Asian and European language groups yielded large and highly significant differences in mean performance. For example, on the Listening section of the November exam Slavic native speakers performed on average 7.09 score points higher than Chinese native speakers; that is, the Slavic group got on average 28% more Listening items correct than the Chinese group.

Detailed results of the DIF contrast analysis

To gain deeper insight into the pattern of DIF results for each of the four relevant language group comparisons (i.e., Chinese versus Western European, Chinese versus Korean, Chinese versus Slavic, Western European versus Slavic), Tables A1 through A4 in the Appendix present for each item on the Reading section (i.e., R01 to R30) and for each item on the Listening section (i.e., L01 to L25) whether DIF was present and which group was favoured. In order not to complicate the presentation of results, the analyses were performed using the DIF contrast method only. This method was chosen, because in the DIF analyses reported above it yielded the highest detection rates overall.

The pattern emerging from these analyses is contained in Table 9. Two points are particularly worth noting: First, *within-Asian* comparisons (i.e., Chinese versus Korean) and *within-European* comparisons (i.e., Western European versus Slavic) each yielded relatively small proportions of DIF items. Second, much greater proportions of DIF items were found when comparisons were *between* Asian and European language groups; that is, Chinese versus Western European, and Chinese versus Slavic native speakers, respectively.

Table 9 Number of DIF items as a function of the type of language group comparison

Language	Reading		Listening	
	N	%	N	%
	Within-Asian and within-European languages			
Chinese vs. Korean	2	3.3	2	4.0
Western European vs. Slavic	7	11.7	5	10.0
	Between Asian and European languages			
Chinese vs. Western European	15	25.0	18	36.0
Chinese vs. Slavic	22	36.7	24	48.0

Note: Number of DIF items per cell was computed across April and November exams (i.e., based on 60 Reading items and 50 Listening items, respectively). Results obtained using a DIF contrast analysis (with two-stage purification).

In addition to this clear-cut pattern, in the Chinese versus European comparisons, Listening items were more likely to show DIF than Reading items. Moreover, as noted before, the number of DIF items favouring one group over the other was about equal in each analysis (see the aggregate numbers in the last row of Tables A1 through A4).

Overall summary and conclusions

Substantive issues

Throughout the analyses, gender-based DIF was negligibly small or non-existent. The proportion of items showing DIF related to language background was similarly small for within-Asian and within-European language group comparisons. By contrast, DIF related to language background was considerably larger for comparisons between Asian and European language groups.

In cases where a non-negligible amount of DIF was observed, DIF effects cancelled each other out and, thus, had no substantial impact at the scale level (see also Li and Zumbo 2009, Roznowski and Reith 1999). For example, in the April Reading exam (see Table A1 in the Appendix), six items favoured Chinese native speakers and five items favoured Western European native speakers; similarly, six items favoured Chinese native speakers and six items favoured Slavic native speakers. The amount of imbalance reached a maximum of three items for the comparison between Chinese and Slavic native speakers in the November Listening exam, yet this difference in the number of items favouring one group over the other is still much too small to be considered problematic. Moreover, across test sections and exam dates, binary logistic regression did not indicate the presence of non-uniform DIF.

Due to the relatively large proportions of DIF items observed for the language group comparisons, language testing experts reviewed flagged items in order to find an explanation for the observed group-dependent differences in item functioning. Though for some items it was tempting to speculate about the possible influence of between-group differences in language learning experiences and typical instructional programmes, the experts failed to provide any conclusive answer pinpointing an unintended factor, or a set of unintended factors, that could be held responsible for the DIF effects revealed in this study. Future item reviewing work will focus on examinee responses to items on the Listening section that follow the short-answer format. These responses might give more reliable clues to the possible impact of some unintended factor.

The language group DIF studies yielded some evidence that the Listening section comprised a higher proportion of DIF items than the Reading section, irrespective of the exam date; this was particularly pronounced for the comparisons between Asian and European language groups. One reason for this may be that the Listening section requires online processing of spoken language, which poses a distinct challenge to Asian examinees. Regarding differences in DIF detection rates between exam dates, the analyses revealed a higher proportion of DIF items in the April exam than in the November exam; this was particularly pronounced for the Reading section. As usually, both TestDaF exams had no items in common, yet the Reading and Listening sections, respectively, had been equated across administrations using an external anchor test (see Eckes 2008). Hence, the presence of between-exam differences in the proportion of DIF items cautions that DIF studies be performed on a regular basis after each live exam.

Methodological issues

Overall, there was a high amount of congruence between the four DIF detection methods used in this study. There was not any evidence of contradictory results; that is, when one method showed DIF to be present in an item favouring a particular group, this advantage was confirmed in the majority of cases when a different method was used; reversals in the direction of DIF were not observed. When a given method, in particular the DIF contrast method, flagged more items than another method (e.g., MH procedure), the set of DIF items identified by the statistically more conservative, or less sensitive, method was a proper subset of the less conservative, or more sensitive, method.

Specifically, the DIF contrast and likelihood ratio procedures showed higher DIF detection rates than the MH procedure or logistic regression, respectively. This was in line with results of a simulation study comparing the MH procedure and a Rasch DIF model, as formulated in a marginal maximum likelihood estimation context (Paek and Wilson 2011). In that study, the Rasch DIF model approach showed higher detection rates than the MH procedure for sample sizes of 100 to 300 per group and test lengths of 4 to 39. Differences in detection rates were particularly pronounced in small samples and short tests (see also Schulz, Perlman, Rice and Wright 1996).

The likelihood ratio test statistic was significant in each and every comparison between compact and augmented models, indicating the presence of DIF effects even when the analysis at the level of individual items failed to show any DIF. An example of this divergence was provided by the gender-based DIF analysis of the Listening section: neither the April nor the November exam showed significant item-level DIF, though the likelihood ratio test statistic signalled that the augmented model fitted the data significantly better than the compact model. This illustrates a general problem associated with statistics of global model fit: given enough data, any model can be shown to be false, because psychometric models are always idealisations of empirical observations. This should be kept in mind when considering results of the likelihood ratio test.

Another issue concerns the circularity problem inherent in any DIF analysis where a measure of ability is used for matching examinees from reference and focal groups that is internal to the test itself (also called the ipsitivity problem; Penfield and Camilli 2007). If a test contains many items that are suspected of DIF, total test scores or measures of ability computed on the basis of all test items, that is, including the DIF items, are likely to be distorted to some extent. A possible solution of this problem is using some kind of purification approach (Clauser and Mazor 1998, Osterlind and Everson 2009). In the present study, a two-stage purification approach (Zenisky et al 2003) was adopted in the analyses using the DIF contrast procedure (this approach is readily implemented in WINSTEPS; see Linacre 2011). For the present data, differences between the items being flagged as DIF in Stage 1 (where all items were included in the analysis) and Stage 2 (items showing DIF in Stage 1 were excluded from defining the matching variable used in Stage 2) were negligible. For example, in each of the four DIF analyses for Chinese versus Western European native speakers, only one item changed its DIF status: in the April exam, one Reading item and one Listening item changed from non-DIF to DIF, as did one Listening item in the November exam; one Reading item in the November exam changed from DIF to non-DIF.

Problematic issues

A pervasive problem of most DIF studies is a serious lack of research and theorising into the possible causes of DIF. Examining test items for DIF is a challenge that may be met by any of the methods studied here or discussed extensively in the literature, explaining why DIF has been shown to be present in a particular item is an entirely different matter. One likely reason for the difficulties of finding clear explanations is that grouping variables like gender, language background, etc. are 'generally rather coarse proxies of those sets of variables that may actually help to account for the occurrence of DIF' (Ferne and Rupp 2007:128).

Of course, failing to account for the occurrence of DIF leaves an important question unanswered: is there an unintended factor causing DIF, and, therefore, should the item studied be considered biased or unfair? In fact, 'the only link we currently have between DIF and item bias is expert judgment specifying properties of items that can be predicted to yield biased test scores' (Penfield and Camilli 2007:162).

An example of this state of affairs is provided by a study of Ryan and Bachman (1992), which examined DIF on two tests of EFL proficiency, i.e. the Test of English as a Foreign Language (TOEFL) and the *First Certificate*

Table 10 Number of DIF items on two EFL tests as a function of group comparison in the Ryan and Bachman (1992) study

Test	DIF level			DIF%
	A	**B**	**C**	
	Gender group comparison			
TOEFL	140	6	0	4.1
FCE	38	2	0	5.0
	Language group comparison (IE vs. NIE)			
TOEFL	81	26	39	44.5
FCE	15	14	11	62.5

Note: DIF% gives the percentage of items at DIF levels B and C. TOEFL = Test of English as a Foreign Language (containing 146 items). FCE = First Certificate in English (containing 40 items). IE = Indoeuropean languages (e.g., French, German, Spanish). NIE = Non-Indoeuropean languages (e.g., Chinese, Japanese, Thai). For DIF detection, Ryan and Bachman (1992) used the Mantel–Haenszel method; in that study, DIF levels were defined according to the classification criteria proposed by Zwick and Ercikan (1989).

in English (FCE). Looking at two kinds of groupings highly similar to those studied in the present research, that is, gender and language background (Indoeuropean versus non-Indoeuropean languages), Ryan and Bachman reported the DIF results summarised in Table 10.

Whereas gender-based DIF was negligibly small, the grouping based on language background yielded substantial proportions of DIF items – a pattern much like the one borne out in Tables 3 and 4, and Tables 6 and 7, respectively. However, ratings of item content provided by experienced EFL teachers and applied linguists failed to yield consistent explanations for DIF in these tests. The researchers concluded that 'native language . . . is most likely a surrogate for a complex of cultural, societal and educational differences' (Ryan and Bachman 1992:22). Disentangling this complex set of factors is certainly one of the most challenging tasks of future research.

Among the more promising research methods aiming at this objective may be the following: (a) analysis of item content, in particular the analysis of item difficulty factors, possibly by means of explanatory IRT models (Wilson and de Boeck 2004), (b) analysis of cognitive processes involved in answering test items (e.g., using think-aloud protocols; see Jang and Roussos 2009), (c) analysis of instructional factors, including differential learning or test-taking strategies, and (d) analysis of the level of examinee proficiency as a moderating variable (e.g., DIF based on language background may be more pronounced at lower levels of language proficiency; see Ryan and Bachman 1992). To be sure, this list is far from being complete; yet, conducting research along these lines may eventually get us closer to the desired goal.

Acknowledgements

I would like to thank my colleagues at the TestDaF Institute for many stimulating discussions on various issues concerning the analysis and interpretation of group differences in foreign language proficiency. Special thanks go to Frank Weiss-Motz and Stefanie Whelan-Mostofizadeh for preparing the extensive data base for purposes of the present study and carrying out part of the analyses.

References

American Educational Research Association, American Psychological Association and National Council on Measurement in Education (1999) *Standards for Educational and Psychological Testing*, Washington, DC: American Educational Research Association.

Aryadoust, V, Goh, C C M and Kim, L O (2011) An investigation of differential item functioning in the MELAB listening test, *Language Assessment Quarterly* 8, 361–385.

Bond, T G and Fox, C M (2007) *Applying the Rasch model: Fundamental Measurement in the Human Sciences*, Mahwah, NJ: Erlbaum, 2nd edn.

Camilli, G (2006) Test fairness, in Brennan, R L (Ed.), *Educational Measurement*, Westport, CT: American Council on Education/Praeger, 4th edn., 221–256.

Camilli, G and Shepard, L A (1994) *Methods for Identifying Biased Test Items*, Thousand Oaks, CA: Sage.

Chen, Z and Henning, G (1985) Linguistic and cultural bias in language proficiency tests, *Language Testing* 2, 155–163.

Clauser, B E and Mazor, K M (1998) Using statistical procedures to identify differentially functioning test items, *Educational Measurement: Issues and Practice* 17, 31–44.

du Toit, M (Ed.) (2003) *IRT from SSI: BILOG-MG, MULTILOG, PARSCALE, TESTFACT*, Lincolnwood, IL: Scientific Software International.

Eckes, T (2005) Examining rater effects in TestDaF writing and speaking performance assessments: A many-facet Rasch analysis, *Language Assessment Quarterly* 2, 197–221.

Eckes, T (2008) Assuring the quality of TestDaF examinations: A psychometric modeling approach, in Taylor, L and Weir, C J (Eds), *Multilingualism and Assessment: Achieving Transparency, Assuring Quality, Sustaining Diversity – Proceedings of the ALTE Berlin Conference May 2005*, Studies in Language Testing volume 27, Cambridge: UCLES Cambridge University Press, 157–78.

Eckes, T (2010) The TestDaF implementation of the SOPI: Design, analysis, and evaluation of a semi-direct speaking test, in Araújo, L (Ed.), *Computer-Based Assessment (CBA) of Foreign Language Speaking Skills*, Luxembourg: Publications Office of the European Union, 63–83.

Eckes, T, Ellis, M, Kalnberzina, V, Pižorn, K, Springer, C, Szollás, K and Tsagari, C (2005) Progress and problems in reforming public language examinations in Europe: Cameos from the Baltic States, Greece, Hungary, Poland, Slovenia, France, and Germany, *Language Testing* 22, 355–377.

Ferne, T and Rupp, A (2007) A synthesis of 15 years of research on DIF in language testing: Methodological advances, challenges, and recommendations, *Language Assessment Quarterly* 4, 113–148.

Geranpayeh, A (2008) Using DIF to explore item difficulty in CAE listening, *Research Notes* 32, 16–23.

Geranpayeh, A and Kunnan, A J (2007) Differential item functioning in terms of age in the Certificate in Advanced English examination, *Language Assessment Quarterly* 4, 190–222.

Holland, P W and Thayer, D T (1988) Differential item performance and the Mantel–Haenszel procedure, in Wainer, H and Braunm H I (Eds), *Test validity*, Hillsdale, NJ: Erlbaum, 129–145.

Holland, P W and Wainer, H (Eds) (1993) *Differential Item Functioning*, Hillsdale, NJ: Erlbaum.

Jang, E E and Roussos, L (2009) Integrative analytic approach to detecting and interpreting L2 vocabulary DIF, *International Journal of Testing* 9, 238–259.

Jodoin, M G and Gierl, M J (2001) Evaluating Type I error and power rates using an effect size measure with the logistic regression procedure for DIF detection, *Applied Measurement in Education* 14, 329–349.

Kane, M (2010) Validity and fairness, *Language Testing* 27, 177–182.

Kecker, G and Eckes, T (2010) Putting the Manual to the test: The TestDaF–CEFR linking project, in Martyniuk, W (Ed.), *Aligning Tests With the CEFR: Reflections on Using the Council of Europe's Draft Manual*, Studies in Language Testing volume 33, Cambridge: UCLES Cambridge University Press, 50–79.

Kim, M (2001) Detecting DIF across the different language groups in a speaking test, *Language Testing* 18, 89–114.

Kunnan, A J (2004) Test fairness, in Milanovic, M and Weir, C J (Eds) *European Language Testing in a Global Context: Proceedings of the ALTE Barcelona Conference July 2001*, Studies in Language Testing volume 18, Cambridge: UCLES/Cambridge University Press, 27–48.

Kunnan, A J (2008) Towards a model of test evaluation: Using the test fairness and the test context frameworks, in Taylor, L and Weir, C J (Eds) *Multilingualism and Assessment: Achieving Transparency, Assuring Quality, Sustaining Diversity – Proceedings of the ALTE Berlin Conference May 2005*, Studies in Language Testing volume 27, Cambridge: UCLES/Cambridge University Press, 229–251.

Li, Z and Zumbo, B D (2009) Impact of differential item functioning on subsequent statistical conclusions based on observed test score data, *Psicológica* 30, 343–370.

Linacre, J M (2011) *A user's guide to WINSTEPS: Rasch-model computer programs*, Chicago: Winsteps.com.

Linacre, J M and Wright, B D (1987) *Item Bias: Mantel–Haenszel and the Rasch Model*, Memorandum No. 39, Chicago: University of Chicago, MESA Psychometric Laboratory.

Linn, R L (2006) The Standards for educational and psychological testing: guidance in test development, in Downing, S M and Haladyna, T M (Eds), *Handbook of Test Development*, Mahwah, NJ: Erlbaum, 27–38.

Mantel, N and Haenszel, W (1959) Statistical aspects of the analysis of data from retrospective studies of disease, *Journal of the National Cancer Institute* 22, 719–748.

Mapuranga, R, Dorans, N J and Middleton, K (2008) *A Review of Recent Developments in Differential Item Functioning*, Research Report RR-08-43, Princeton, NJ: Educational Testing Service.

McNamara, T F and Roever, C (2006) *Language Testing: The Social Dimension*, Malden, MA: Blackwell.

Myers, J L and Well, A D (2003) *Research Design and Statistical Analysis*, 2nd edn., Mahwah, NJ: Erlbaum.

Osterlind, S J and Everson, H T (2009) *Differential Item Functioning*, 2nd edn., Los Angeles, CA: Sage.

Paek, I and Wilson, M (2011) Formulating the Rasch differential item functioning model under the marginal maximum likelihood estimation context and its comparison with Mantel–Haenszel procedure in short test and small sample conditions, *Educational and Psychological Measurement* 71, 1,023–1,046.

Penfield, R D and Camilli, G (2007) Differential item functioning and item bias, in Rao, C R and Sinharay, S (Eds), *Handbook of Statistics: Psychometrics, Volume 26*, 125–167, Amsterdam: Elsevier.

Potenza, M T and Dorans, N J (1995) DIF assessment for polytomously scored items: a framework for classification and evaluation, *Applied Psychological Measurement* 19, 23–37.

Roznowski, M and Reith, J (1999) Examining the measurement quality of tests containing differentially functioning items: Do biased items result in poor measurement?, *Educational and Psychological Measurement* 59, 248–269.

Ryan, K E and Bachman, L F (1992) Differential item functioning on two tests of EFL proficiency, *Language Testing* 9, 12–29.

Schulz, E M, Perlman, C, Rice, W K and Wright, B D (1996) An empirical comparison of Rasch and Mantel–Haenszel procedures for assessing differential item functioning, in Engelhard, G and Wilson, M (Eds), *Objective Measurement: Theory into Practice Volume 3*, Norwood, NJ: Ablex, 65–82.

Swaminathan, H and Rogers, H J (1990) Detecting differential item functioning using logistic regression procedures, *Journal of Educational Measurement* 27, 361–370.

Thissen, D, Steinberg, L and Wainer, H (1993) Detection of differential item functioning using the parameters of item response models, in Holland, P W and Wainer, H (Eds), *Differential Item Functioning*, Hillsdale, NJ: Erlbaum, 67–113.

Wilson, M and de Boeck, P (2004) Descriptive and explanatory item response models, in de Boeck, P and Wilson, M (Eds), *Explanatory Item Response Models: A Generalized Linear and Nonlinear Approach*, New York: Springer, 43–64.

Wright, B D and Stone, M H (1979) *Best Test Design*, Chicago: MESA Press.

Xi, X (2010) How do we go about investigating test fairness? *Language Testing* 27, 147–170.

Zenisky, A L, Hambleton, R K and Robin, F (2003) Detection of differential item functioning in large-scale state assessments: A study evaluating a two-stage approach, *Educational and Psychological Measurement* 63, 51–64.

Zieky, M (1993) Practical questions in the use of DIF statistics in test development, in Holland, P W and Wainer, H (Eds), *Differential Item Functioning*, Hillsdale, NJ: Erlbaum, 337–347.

Zumbo, B (1999) *A Handbook on the Theory and Methods of Differential Item Functioning (DIF): Logistic Regression Modeling as a Unitary Framework for Binary and Likert-type (Ordinal) Item Scores*, Ottawa, Canada: Directorate of Human Resources Research and Evaluation, National Defense Headquarters.

Zwick, R and Ercikan, K (1989) Analysis of differential item functioning in the NAEP history assessment, *Journal of Educational Measurement* 26, 55–66.

Appendix

Table A1 Detailed DIF results for language group comparisons (Reading, April exam)

Item	Chin. / WE	Chin. / Korean	Chin. / Slavic	WE / Slavic
R01				
R02				
R03				
R04			Sl	
R05				
R06				
R07				
R08				
R09	WE			
R10	WE			
R11	WE		Sl	
R12	Ch		Ch	Sl
R13	Ch		Ch	
R14	Ch		Ch	
R15			Sl	Sl
R16				
R17			Sl	
R18	WE		Sl	WE
R19				
R20			Ch	
R21				
R22	Ch			
R23	Ch		Ch	
R24				
R25				
R26				
R27	WE	Ko		WE
R28				Sl
R29	Ch		Ch	
R30			Sl	
Total	6 Ch / 5 WE	0 Ch / 1 Ko	6 Ch / 6 Sl	2 WE / 3 Sl

Note: Ch = Chinese L1 speakers. WE = Western European L1 speakers. Ko = Korean L1 speakers. Sl = Slavic L1 speakers. Entries indicate the group favoured (e.g., 'WE' in row R09, column 2, means that Reading item 9 favoured Western European L1 speakers). Results obtained using a DIF contrast analysis (with two-stage purification).

385

Table A2 Detailed DIF results for language group comparisons (Listening, April exam)

Item	Chin. / WE	Chin. / Korean	Chin. / Slavic	WE / Slavic
L01				
L02				
L03	Ch			Sl
L04			Ch	WE
L05				
L06	WE		Sl	
L07				
L08				
L09	Ch			
L10	WE			
L11	Ch		Ch	
L12			Ch	
L13	Ch		Ch	
L14	Ch		Ch	
L15	Ch		Ch	
L16				
L17				
L18				
L19				
L20				
L21				
L22	WE		Sl	
L23			Sl	Sl
L24	WE		Sl	
L25	WE		Sl	
Total	6 Ch / 5 WE	0 Ch / 0 Ko	6 Ch / 5 Sl	1 WE / 2 Sl

Note: Ch = Chinese L1 speakers. WE = Western European L1 speakers. Ko = Korean L1 speakers. Sl = Slavic L1 speakers. Entries indicate the group favoured (e.g., 'Ch' in row L03, column 2, means that Listening item 3 favoured Chinese L1 speakers). Results obtained using a DIF contrast analysis (with two-stage purification).

Table A3 Detailed DIF results for language group comparisons (Reading, November exam)

Item	Chin. / WE	Chin. / Korean	Chin. / Slavic	WE / Slavic
R01		Ch		
R02				
R03				
R04				
R05				
R06				
R07			Sl	Sl
R08				
R09				
R10				Sl
R11				
R12				
R13			Ch	
R14				
R15				
R16				
R17	WE		Sl	
R18				
R19				
R20				
R21	WE		Sl	
R22				
R23				
R24			Ch	
R25			Sl	
R26			Ch	
R27				
R28	WE		Sl	
R29			Sl	
R30	Ch		Ch	
Total	1 Ch / 3 WE	1 Ch / 0 Ko	4 Ch / 6 Sl	0 WE / 2 Sl

Note: Ch = Chinese L1 speakers. WE = Western European L1 speakers. Ko = Korean L1 speakers. Sl = Slavic L1 speakers. Entries indicate the group favoured (e.g., 'Ch' in row R01, column 3, means that Reading item 1 favoured Chinese L1 speakers). Results obtained using a DIF contrast analysis (with two-stage purification).

Table A4 Detailed DIF results for language group comparisons (Listening, November exam)

Item	Chin. / WE	Chin. / Korean	Chin. / Slavic	WE / Slavic
L01				
L02				
L03				
L04			Ch	WE
L05	WE		Sl	
L06			Sl	
L07	Ch	Ch		Sl
L08				
L09			Ch	
L10				
L11	WE		Sl	
L12	Ch		Ch	
L13			Ch	
L14				
L15				
L16			Ch	
L17	Ch		Ch	
L18	Ch		Ch	
L19				
L20		Ko	Sl	
L21				
L22				
L23				
L24			Ch	
L25	WE		Sl	
Total	4 Ch / 3 WE	1 Ch / 1 Ko	8 Ch / 5 Sl	1 WE / 1 Sl

Note: Ch = Chinese L1 speakers. WE = Western European L1 speakers. Ko = Korean L1 speakers. Sl = Slavic L1 speakers. Entries indicate the group favoured (e.g., 'WE' in row L05, column 2, means that Listening item 5 favoured Western-European L1 speakers). Results obtained using a DIF contrast analysis (with two-stage purification).

20 Do gender, age and first language predict the results in the Deutsch-Test für Zuwanderer (DTZ)?

Gudrun Klein

The European Language Certificates GmbH, Germany

Abstract

The Deutsch-Test für Zuwanderer (DTZ) assesses immigrants' German language skills at the Common European Framework of Reference for languages (CEFR) (Council of Europe 2001) Levels A2 and B1, with B1 being a precondition for gaining German citizenship. This study aims to investigate whether and to which extent gender, age and first language (L1) and/or specific combinations of these variables, predict individuals' DTZ outcomes. Information on participants' gender, age and L1, as well as DTZ results are available from the total population of test takers in 2010. To have an outcome measure that is more sensitive to interindividual differences than the CEFR levels, the percentage of points gained in the Listening/Reading Comprehension, Writing and Speaking subtests are averaged, yielding 'mean percentage points'. Main and interaction effects of gender, age and L1 on this outcome measure are tested in multivariate regression analyses. To compare the unique contribution of the three predictor variables in explaining variance in the DTZ outcome, R^2-change resulting from removing single predictors out of the multivariate models is employed. L1 proves to be the most important predictor, accounting for 12% of the variance in mean percentage points, followed by age (7.5%). In contrast, the importance of gender in predicting the DTZ outcome seems to be negligible (0.3%). While there is no evidence for an interaction between gender and age, the effects of age and, respectively, of gender on mean percentage points are found to be dependent on participants' L1. More specifically, DTZ appears to constitute a particular challenge for (a) participants with L1 Turkish (especially if they are female), Italian and Arabic, (b) candidates of advanced age (particularly if they belong to L1 groups Italian, Chinese or Turkish), and (c) male participants with L1 Russian or Polish. It might be advisable to offer these individuals intensified support in exam preparation.

Background

In recent years, more and more European countries have introduced proof of language competency as a necessary requirement for migrants wishing to obtain a visa (Extramiana and Van Avermaet 2011); this concerns migrants aiming to study or work in the country as well as those wishing to immigrate for family reasons. Equally, language certificates are required from people applying for citizenship in an increasing number of countries (Extramiana and Van Avermaet 2011). In most cases, language requirements for migration purposes are specified with reference to the Common European Framework of Reference for languages (CEFR) (Council of Europe 2001). In Germany, for example, residence regulations require an A1 certificate from immigrants applying for a visa to be able to join their partner living in Germany; and those seeking to obtain German citizenship need to reach CEFR Level B1 in a standardised German language test for migrants, the Deutsch-Test für Zuwanderer (DTZ) (Perlmann-Balme, Plassmann and Zeidler 2009).

In addition to claims that CEFR-based language examinations for migrants must be fair and fit their high-stake purposes (see, for example, Balch, Corrigan, Gysen, Kuijper, Perlmann-Balme, Roppe, Rübeling, Steiner, Van Avermaet, and Zeidler (2008)), it appears crucial that sufficient and suitable support in exam preparation be provided for as many migrants as possible. In Germany, language courses comprising 600 to 900 lessons, which form the major parts of general integration courses and which prepare for the DTZ, are accessible to migrants free of charge. The curriculum of the integration course and, accordingly, the contents of the DTZ are geared to the needs of the target group (for more detailed information on the contents of the language course as part of the general integration course see www.bamf.de/EN/Willkommen/DeutschLernen/Integrationskurse/InhaltAblauf/inhaltablauf-node.html). Furthermore, different types of integration courses are offered for specific subgroups of migrants (e.g. young adults, parents, and women). But with regard to the high heterogeneity of migrants from all over the world (Kluzer, Ferrari and Centeno 2011), there might still be room for improvement in adapting exam preparation to the individual needs of DTZ participants. I am not aware of any empirical evidence published in the academic literature regarding the performance of different subgroups of migrants in a standardised German language test. Hence, to begin filling this important knowledge gap, the present study investigates whether and to which extent participants' gender, age, and first language (L1), as well as specific combinations of these characteristics, are predictive for DTZ outcome. We will thus gain knowledge as to which DTZ test takers are less likely to pass the examination than others, given the existing system of language courses preparing for the examination. It will provide useful insights for preparation courses and exam content.

Method

The original development, implementation, and test structure of the DTZ

In 2009, the DTZ was implemented as the final test of integration courses for migrants, which aim at Level B1 of the CEFR. The DTZ was commissioned by the Federal Ministry of the Interior and developed by the Goethe-Institut and telc GmbH in cooperation. DTZ has a dual level format to test German language proficiency at CEFR Levels A2 and B1.

The DTZ follows the communicative approach and consists of a written and an oral part. The written part measures an individual's language competency in listening/reading comprehension and in writing, and lasts about 100 minutes in total. In the oral exam, two candidates are usually tested together. It focuses on speaking skills and takes about 10 minutes per candidate. An overview of the structure of the test with information on the nature and type of the items and tasks is provided in Table 1.

A participant's performance in each of the three test parts is assessed separately. For the Listening/Reading part, assignment to CEFR levels 'below A2', 'A2' or 'B1' is accomplished according to the number of points gained. For Writing and Speaking, in contrast, assignment to CEFR levels is based on criteria-based ratings. For determination of the final overall CEFR level, summarising the candidate's performance in the total test, the following general rule is applied: B1 may be obtained by a participant who has reached Level B1 in the speaking part and in at least one of the written parts (listening/reading comprehension or writing). The same applies for the A2 level. Thus, there is a focus on an individual's speaking competency.

Study population and procedure

DTZ examinations are conducted at examination centres of the Federal Office for Migration and Refugees (*Bundesamt für Migration und Flüchtlinge* (BAMF)), all over Germany. Administration and scoring is accomplished centrally at the telc Head Office in Frankfurt. Hence, we have access to the outcome data of all test takers. The present analyses were conducted using anonymised data from the total population of test takers in 2010 aged 16–80 years. A sample description with regard to socio-demographic characteristics is presented in Table 2.

Data for variables employed as predictors in the present regression

Table 1 Structure of the Deutsch-Test für Zuwanderer (DTZ)

Subtest	Aim	Number and type of items/tasks	Time
1 Receptive Skills		**45 items**	**70 min.**
1.1 Listening		**20 items**	**25 min.**
Part 1	Understanding voice mail messages, understanding short public announcements	4 multiple-choice items	
Part 2	Understanding statements in the media	5 multiple-choice items	
Part 3	Understanding everyday conversations	4 true/false and 4 multiple-choice items	
Part 4	Understanding different opinions about a topic	3 matching items	
1.2 Reading		**25 items**	**45 min.**
Part 1	Understanding lists of information in catalogues, on the internet, etc.	5 multiple-choice items	
Part 2	Understanding general and specific information in advertisements	5 matching items	
Part 3	Understanding information and opinions in press releases and formal announcements	3 true/false and 3 multiple-choice items	
Part 4	Understanding informational brochures	3 true/false items	
Part 5	Completing a letter	6 multiple-choice items	
2 Writing	Writing formal and semi-formal emails	**1 writing task** (out of 2)	**30 min.**
3 Speaking		**3 tasks**	about
Part 1A	Talking about yourself	Task sheet with key words	**10 min./** participant
Part 1B	Answering follow-up questions	Examiner questions	
Part 2A	Talking about experiences	Task sheet with pictures	
Part 2B	Answering follow-up questions	Examiner questions	
Part 3	Planning something together	Task sheet with guiding points	

analyses (i. e. socio-demographic and language-background variables) are routinely gathered on the first page of the answer sheet at the beginning of the examination procedure. The computation of the outcome variable (see 'Measures' section below) used as a criterion in the regression models is also entirely based on routine data.

Measures

For the present analyses, an outcome measure sensitive to even small differences in individuals' overall performance in the DTZ was needed. The

Table 2 Sample description with respect to socio-demographic characteristics

	%
Gender	
Male	65.6
Female	34.4
Age	
Mean (years)	74.4
SD	10.4
First language	
Russian	30.7
Turkish	27.0
Arabic	16.0
Polish	7.8
Spanish	4.8
English	4.1
Portuguese	2.6
French	2.2
Chinese	2.0
Italian	1.4
German*	0.8
Hungarian	0.6
Czech	0.26

Notes: Proportion of participants with missing values was 1.4% for gender, 0.3% for age, 36.9% for L1.

SD = standard deviation

* The majority of DTZ participants indicating German as their first language are most certainly Ethnic German resettlers ('Spätaussiedler'). This term denotes a legal status which applies to people from the successor states of the former Soviet Union and from other East European states who – while being citizens of another state – have German ethnicity ('deutsche Volkszugehörigkeit'), or whose parents had it. The criteria are: German ancestors, the ability to have a simple conversation in German, and either a general adherence to German culture or a status as 'German national' in the country of origin (which was possible in the former Soviet Union). By means of a special acceptance process, Ethnic German resettlers are entitled to live in Germany. Between 1950 and 2005, 4.5 million Ethnic German resettlers came to the Federal Republic of Germany. Thus, it is not a small group of people. Nowadays, they compose only approximately 3,000 per year. Ethnic German resettlers arriving in Germany since 2005 are entitled to attend an integration course once free of charge. At the end of the course, they may take the DTZ exam.

CEFR-level variable (see above, last paragraph of the section 'The original development, implementation, and test structure of the DTZ') does not suit this purpose because it only differentiates between three different competence levels (below A2, A2, B1 or higher), thus constituting a rather rough measure of an individual's overall German language proficiency. Therefore, a new outcome measure had to be constructed. To this end, participants' percentage points in each of the three test parts were combined, using arithmetic averaging. The resulting variable 'mean percentage points', varying between 0 and 100, constitutes a metric outcome measure of participants' overall performance in the DTZ.

Data analyses

Multivariate multiple regression analyses were conducted to examine the relation of the three predictors gender, age and L1 to the DTZ outcome variable mean percentage points. Because initial univariate descriptive analyses indicated a potential, albeit only slight violation of the linear trend assumption for the association between age and mean percentage points, polynomial modelling was applied. This allowed analysing the pattern of the association between age and mean percentage points more deeply. Since adding second and third polynomials to the regression equation (thus modelling a u- and an s-shaped relationship, respectively) did not result in a meaningfully higher proportion of explained variance of the outcome measure (according to R^2-change), the linear trend assumption was not rejected. Therefore, only the first polynomial for age was used in subsequently conducted multivariate regression models predicting mean percentage points.

The relative importance of the three predictors (gender, age and L1) in explaining inter-individual differences in the DTZ outcome was assessed employing the hierarchical linear modelling approach. This means that the amount of variance in mean percentage points accounted for by the model that included each of the three predictors (full model) was compared with a model that did not account for either gender, age, or L1 (nested model). The resulting R^2-change was used as a measure for the amount of variance in mean percentage points attributable to the predictor that was left out in the respective nested model.

In further analyses, it was also investigated whether the associations between either of the predictor variables (e.g., gender) and the DTZ outcome depended on individuals' characteristics regarding the other predictors (e.g., age and L1, respectively). To this end, the interaction terms gender*age, age*L1 and L1*gender were tested one by one in multivariate regression models predicting mean percentage points, in addition to the main effect terms for each of the three predictors. All analyses were conducted using the software package Stata/MP 11.1.

Results

From the total population of DTZ test takers aged 16–80 in 2010, 12% were classified as 'below CEFR Level A2' with respect to the German language skills demonstrated in the DTZ, 38.2% were allocated to CEFR Level A2 and 49.8% to CEFR Level B1 or higher. On average, participants reached 68.8 mean percentage points across the three test parts of the DTZ (standard deviation (SD) = 21.5).

Main effects of gender, age and first language on the DTZ outcome

The results of a multivariate multiple regression analysis simultaneously modelling effects of gender, age and L1 (model B1) are given in Table 3. The unstandardised regression coefficients b (see fourth column of the table) and the associated significance levels p (see sixth column) reveal that female gender (b_{female} = 2.8, p <0.001) and younger age (b_{age} = −0.6, p <0.001) are significantly positively associated with the DTZ outcome. The interpretation of these statistics is as follows: when controlling for differences in age and L1, females score on average 2.8 mean percentage points more than males. Further, a decline of −0.6 mean percentage points for each one-year increase in age is predicted by model B1.

For interpretation of the b-coefficients for the L1 dummy variables (see L1-rows in the Table), it is necessary to keep in mind that they represent the predicted differences in L1 subgroup means compared to the L1 reference group 'Russian'. Interpretation is facilitated by Figure 1, which depicts the predicted mean percentage points for each L1 group when holding the covariate gender constant at the mode (female) and the covariate age at the median (36 years). The graph shows that, when accounting for differences in gender and age, participants with either of the L1s Russian, Polish, Spanish,

Table 3 Results from a multiple regression analysis predicting the DTZ outcome: model B1 accounting for main effects of gender, age and L1

Model	Dependent variable	Independent variables	b	SE	p	R^2
B1	mean pct points	female	2.8	0.16	<0.001	0.181
		age [years]	−0.6	0.01	<0.001	
		L1_Turkish	−18.1	0.21	<0.001	
		L1_Arabic	−7.1	0.25	<0.001	
		L1_Polish	0.0	0.31	0.921	
		L1_Spanish	0.1	0.38	0.829	
		L1_English	−0.7	0.41	0.079	
		L1_Portuguese	−3.4	0.51	<0.001	
		L1_French	−2.3	0.54	<0.001	
		L1_Chinese	−0.7	0.57	0.197	
		L1_Italian	−7.3	0.68	<0.001	
		L1_German	−0.5	0.90	0.596	
		L1_Hungarian	8.2	1.05	<0.001	
		L1_Czech	1.5	1.53	0.333	
		constant	92.4	0.44	<0.001	

Note: Female is a dummy variable for gender, with females coded as 1 and males coded as 0.
In the set of L1 dummies (L1_Turkish . . . L1_Czech), 'Russian' serves as reference category.
b = unstandardised regression weights
SE = standard error
pct = percentage

Figure 1 Main effects of L1 (prediction from model B1)

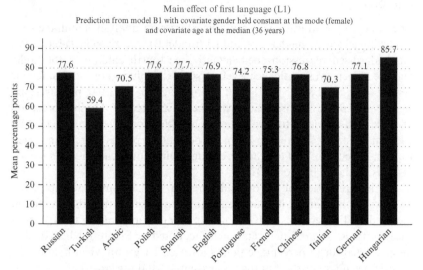

Main effect of first language (L1)
Prediction from model B1 with covariate gender held constant at the mode (female)
and covariate age at the median (36 years)

First language (in descending order of subgroup size)

English, Chinese and German achieve almost equal DTZ results, on average. It also becomes obvious that L1 Hungarian is associated with higher mean percentage scores on the DTZ, whereas some other L1s occur to have a negative effect on the DTZ outcome. This is especially true for Turkish, followed by Italian and Arabic. Small negative effects are found for L1 Portuguese and French.

In sum, the three predictor variables account for 18.1% (R^2-statistic, last column of Table 3) of the total variance of the DTZ outcome as measured by mean percentage points.

The findings of a series of comparisons of model B1 with some nested models allow assessment of the relative importance of each of the three predictor variables. The respective R^2-change statistics can be derived from Table 4. Using only age and L1 to predict individuals' DTZ results, model B2 is able to explain 17.8% of the variance in DTZ mean percentage points. The difference in R^2 to model B1 is 0.003. This means that the predictor gender only accounts for 0.3% of the variance in the DTZ outcome. Further nested model comparisons (see Table 4) show that 7.5% of the variance in mean percentage points can be attributed to differences in participants' age and that L1 explains 12% of the variance in DTZ outcome.

Table 4 Results from comparisons between regression model B1 and nested models arising from model B1 by deletion of single predictors

Model	Dependent variable	Independent variables	R^2	R^2-change compared to B1
B1	mean pct points	female age first language (L1)	0.181	---
B2	mean pct points	age first language (L1)	0.178	0.003
B3	mean pct points	female first language (L1)	0.106	0.075
B4	mean pct points	female age	0.061	0.120

Note: The R^2-change statistic allows comparison of the amount of variance explained in mean percentage points that can be attributed to each of the three predictors in B1.
pct = percentage

Interaction effects of gender, age and first language on the DTZ outcome

The results of three interaction analyses, which test the effects of specific combinations between pairs of predictor variables on the DTZ outcome, are given in detail in Table 5–Table 7 and visualised in Figure 2–Figure 4. They answer the question as to whether the effect of one predictor variable on the DTZ outcome is dependent on either of the other predictor variables.

The DTZ outcome and combinations of age*gender

Model C1 was conducted to analyse whether the effect of age on the DTZ outcome differs between male and female participants. When interpreting the regression coefficients in Table 5, it must be kept in mind that the b coefficient for age is, by itself, only applicable to the sub-group of male participants, which is the reference category of the gender variable 'female'. To have the effect of age on DTZ results in females, the b coefficient of age must be added to that of the gender*age-interaction term. This statistic thus indicates the difference in the change in mean percentage points with each one-year increase in age between males and females. It turns out to be very small (b=−0.02) and not statistically significant (see Table 5). This can also be seen in Figure 2, which shows that the effect of age on the DTZ outcome is roughly the same among males and females.

Table 5 Results from a multiple regression analysis predicting the DTZ outcome (model C1)

Model	Dependent variable	Independent variables	b	SE	p	R^2
C1	mean pct points	female	3.52	0.59	<0.001	0.181
		age (years)	−0.56	0.01	<0.001	
		female*age	−0.02	0.01	0.218	
		L1_Turkish	−18.14	0.21	<0.001	
		L1_Arabic	−7.06	0.25	<0.001	
		L1_Polish	0.03	0.31	0.913	
		L1_Spanish	0.09	0.38	0.809	
		L1_English	−0.72	0.41	0.081	
		L1_Portuguese	−3.35	0.51	<0.001	
		L1_French	−2.34	0.54	<0.001	
		L1_Chinese	−0.74	0.57	0.195	
		L1_Italian	−7.29	0.68	<0.001	
		L1_German	−0.47	0.90	0.605	
		L1_Hungarian	8.17	1.05	<0.001	
		L1_Czech	1.49	1.53	0.331	
		constant	94.75	0.51	<0.001	

Figure 2 Interaction effect of gender*age: prediction from model C1 with covariate first language held constant at the mode (Russian)

Note: The age variable was categorised only to ease readability of this graph. In the underlying regression analyses, the uncategorised variable age has been used.

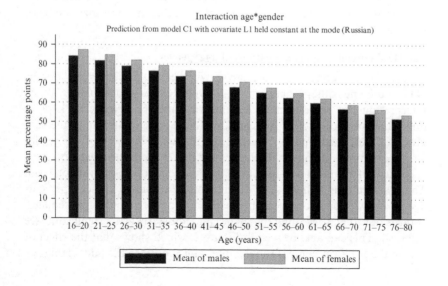

Table 6 Results from a multiple regression analysis predicting the DTZ outcome: model C2 testing the interaction effect of age*first language

Model	Dependent variable	Independent variables	b	SE	p	R^2
C2	mean pct points	female	2.96	0.16	<0.001	0.188
		L1_Turkish	−4.50	0.78	<0.001	
		[...]				
		L1_Czech	1.96	5.56	0.724	
		age (years)	−0.44	0.01	<0.001	
		age*L1_Turkish	−0.36	0.02	<0.001	
		age*L1_Arabic	−0.17	0.02	<0.001	
		age*L1_Polish	−0.14	0.03	<0.001	
		age*L1_Spanish	−0.12	0.04	0.004	
		age*L1_English	0.16	0.05	0.001	
		age*L1_Portuguese	−0.27	0.05	<0.001	
		age*L1_French	−0.10	0.06	0.106	
		age*L1_Chinese	−0.36	0.06	<0.001	
		age*L1_Italian	−0.58	0.06	<0.001	
		age*L1_German	0.44	0.08	<0.001	
		age*L1_Hungarian	0.18	0.10	0.071	
		age*L1_Czech	0.00	0.15	0.984	
		constant	87.02	0.57	<0.001	

The DTZ outcome and combinations of age*first language

According to the results of the above-reported regression analysis focusing on the main effects (model B1, see Table 3), age is generally negatively related to the DTZ outcome. Results from interaction analysis (model C2, see Table 6 and Figure 3) suggest that this association does to some degree differ depending on participants' L1. Note that the b coefficient for age is, by itself, only applicable to participants with L1 Russian, which is the L1 reference category. With each 1-year increase in age, test takers in this subgroup score on average 0.44 mean percentage points less. For subgroups of participants with any of the other L1s, the b coefficients of age and that of the respective age*L1 interaction coefficient need to be added up to be interpretable.

As can be seen in Figure 3, the negative effect of age on the mean percentage points is intensified in several L1 subgroups (Italian, Chinese and Turkish). At the other end of the scale, it is less pronounced in participants with L1 English and Hungarian and it is not at all present in participants with L1 German. In this subgroup, age does not seem to be associated with DTZ outcome at all.

The DTZ outcome and combinations of gender*first language

Gender*first language interaction analysis results (model C3, see Table 7 and Figure 4) show that the positive effect of female gender on the DTZ outcome found in the main effect analysis (model B1, see Table 3) does not apply to each of the L1 subgroups. Rather, the effect of gender on the mean percentage points appears to differ depending on participants' L1. Figure 4 reveals that

Figure 3 Interaction effect of age*first language: prediction from model C2 with covariate gender held constant at the mode (female)

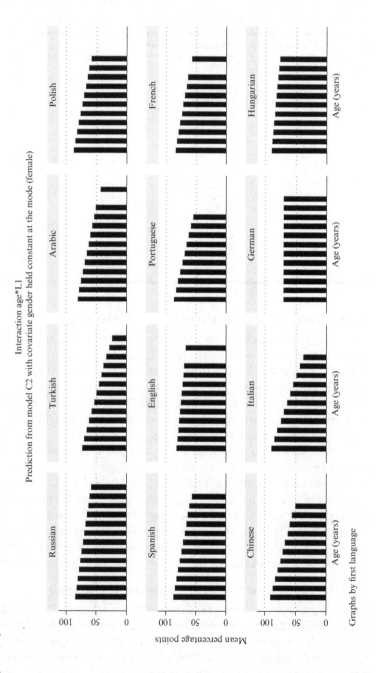

Table 7 Results from a multiple regression analysis predicting the DTZ outcome: model C3 testing the interaction effect of gender*first language

Model	Dependent variable	Independent variables	b	SE	p	R²
C3	mean pct points	age (years)	−0.56	0.01	<0.001	0.198
		L1_Turkish	4.66	0.74	<0.001	
		[...]				
		L1_Czech	1.89	8.75	0.829	
		female	9.76	0.29	<0.001	
		L1_Turkish*female	−13.72	0.43	<0.001	
		L1_Arabic*female	−10.10	0.48	<0.001	
		L1_Polish*female	0.02	0.70	0.973	
		L1_Spanish*female	−8.08	0.81	<0.001	
		L1_English*female	−8.51	0.82	<0.001	
		L1_Portuguese*female	−9.08	1.15	<0.001	
		L1_French*female	−12.68	1.10	<0.001	
		L1_Chinese*female	−2.71	1.47	0.066	
		L1_Italian*female	−7.04	1.36	<0.001	
		L1_German*female	−3.26	1.85	0.079	
		L1_Hungarian*female	−3.85	2.39	0.107	
		L1_Czech*female	−0.99	4.59	0.829	
		constant	80.40	0.60	<0.001	

the positive effect of gender on DTZ particularly applies to participants with L1 Russian and Polish and – albeit to a lesser degree – also to L1 Chinese, German and Italian. The differences between males and females are negligible in the L1 Spanish, English, Portuguese and Arabic group. In participants with L1 Turkish and, albeit only to a small extent, in the L1 French group, female gender appears to be associated with a lower scoring in the DTZ.

Conclusions

Even though a large majority of DTZ participants are known to attend an integration course consisting of 600 up to 900 training units preparatory to the examination, half of them (50.2% of test takers in 2010 aged 16 to 80 years) do not reach CEFR Level B1, which is required for naturalisation in Germany. In view of this, the present study examined the importance of gender, age and language background in terms of L1 in predicting participants' performance in the DTZ. The aim was to give some indication as to which subgroups of participants might have need of a more intensive exam preparation than others.

From the three predictor variables analysed, L1 was found to be the most important predictor of individuals' DTZ outcome. In comparison with a number of L1 groups that tend to get similar outcomes, test takers with L1 Arabic, Italian and, to some more extent, Turkish seem to perform worse. On the other hand, L1 Hungarian occurs to be associated with a higher scoring

Figure 4 Interaction effect of gender*first language: prediction from model C3 with covariate age held constant at the median (36 years)

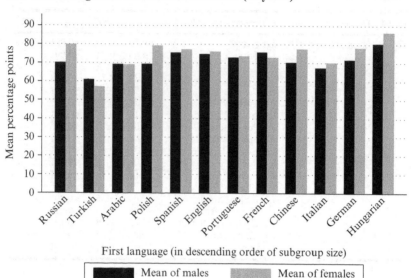

First language (in descending order of subgroup size)

■ Mean of males   ▨ Mean of females

on the DTZ. In addition, a negative effect of age on DTZ was detected. With increasing age, a lower scoring in the DTZ was predicted by the multivariate regression model. A slightly higher scoring of females compared to males notwithstanding, the gender effect appears to be negligible. As opposed to the main effects of L1 and age, gender only accounts for a very small proportion of the variance in the DTZ outcome.

While age seemed to be associated with the mean percentage points independent of the association between gender and DTZ outcome, subsequently conducted interaction analyses found that both the effect of gender and the effect of age on the mean percentage points differed depending on participants' L1. The age effect was particularly pronounced in test takers with L1 Italian, Turkish and Chinese (but only weakly present in L1 groups Hungarian and English) and not at all evident in participants with L1 German. The slight overall superiority of female compared to male participants does not equally apply to all L1 groups. While particularly pronounced in L1 groups Russian and Polish, it could not (or only very weakly) be confirmed for L1 groups Spanish, English, Arabic and Portuguese. Most notably, it was found to be the opposite among participants with L1 Turkish and, but only to a very small degree, in the L1 French group. In these two groups, males appear to outperform females.

There are some limitations to this study that must be considered when interpreting the findings summarised above. Firstly, when testing the predictive power of gender, age and L1 on the DTZ outcome, it was not possible to control for further covariates such as education and socio-economic status, which might just as well impact an individual's performance in a language test. As a consequence, it must be considered that, for example, the effect of L1 on the DTZ outcome established in this study might to some extent be attributable to differences between participants belonging to different L1 groups with respect to education or other confounders (and not to their L1 itself). Secondly, not unusual for population-based routine data, L1 subgroups in the current data set were highly unbalanced. This results in differences in statistical power when the effects of the different L1 on the DTZ outcome are tested. By far the smallest subgroup was the L1 Czech group (n=15). For that reason, interpreting regression analytic results with respect to effects of L1 Czech was not carried out. Thirdly, the high rate of missing values for L1 (36.9%) must be taken into account. Note that regression modelling can only be performed on data from participants who provide comprehensive data with regard to all predictor and criterion variables in the regression equation. Hence, the magnitude of the resulting bias that is to be expected depends on the extent that participants who do indicate their L1 on the DTZ answer sheet might be considered to differ in meaningful ways from those who do not.

In subsequent research, the effects of further potentially relevant predictors on the DTZ outcome should be evaluated. These might comprise, for example, participants' country of origin and for how long they have already been staying in Germany when taking the test (due to technical restriction in data acquisition, this was not yet possible when the present analyses were conducted). In addition to assessing the main effects of variables of that kind on the DTZ outcome, it might be illuminating to gain more insights as to their potential role as mediators or moderators in the above-evidenced relationships of L1 and, respectively, age with the DTZ outcome.

In conclusion, according to the current findings derived from the data of the population of DTZ test takers in 2010, the DTZ appears to constitute a particular challenge for (a) participants with L1 Turkish (especially if they are female), Italian and Arabic, (b) candidates of advanced age (especially if they belong to L1 groups Italian, Chinese or Turkish), as well as (c) male participants with L1 Russian or Polish. It might be fruitful to offer these subgroups of DTZ test takers more intensive support in exam preparation. This might imply an increase in the number of training lessons, an enhanced individualisation of learning contents to the specific needs of these candidates, or both.

References

Balch A, Corrigan M, Gysen S, Kuijper H, Perlmann-Balme M, Roppe S, Rübeling H, Steiner S, Van Avermaet P and Zeidler, B (2008) *Language tests for social cohesion and citizenship – an outline for policymakers*, thematic study prepared for the seminar Linguistic Integration of Adult Migrants, Strasbourg, June 2008.

Council of Europe (2001) *Common European Framework of Reference for Languages: Learning, Teaching, Assessment*, Cambridge: Cambridge University Press.

Extramiana, C and Van Avermaet, P (2011) *Language Requirements for Adult Migrants in Council of Europe Member States: Report on a Survey*, Strasbourg: Council of Europe.

Kluzer, S Ferrari, A and Centeno, C (2011) *Language Learning by Adult Migrants: Policy Challenges and ICT Responses. Policy Brief*, Luxembourg: Publications Office of the European Union.

Perlmann-Balme, M, Plassmann, S and Zeidler, B (2009) *Deutsch-Test für Zuwanderer A2–B1: Prüfungsziele, Testbeschreibung [German test for migrants: test description and examination objectives]*, Berlin: Cornelsen Verlag.

21 Exploring the relative merits of cognitive diagnostic models and confirmatory factor analysis for assessing listening comprehension

Vahid Aryadoust and Christine C M Goh
National Institute of Education, Nanyang Technological University, Singapore

Abstract

A number of scaling models – developed originally for psychological and educational studies – have been adapted into language assessment. Although their application has been promising, they have not yet been validated in language assessment contexts. This study discusses the relative merits of two such models in the context of second language (L2) listening comprehension tests: confirmatory factor analysis (CFA) and cognitive diagnostic models (CDMs). Both CFA and CDMs can model multidimensionality in assessment tools, whereas other models force the data to be statistically unidimensional. The two models were applied to the listening test of the Michigan English Language Assessment Battery (MELAB). CFA was found to impose more restrictions on the data than CDMs. It is suggested that CFA might not be suitable for modelling dichotomously scored data of L2 listening tests, whereas the CDM used in the study (the Fusion Model) appeared to successfully portray the listening sub-skills tapped by the MELAB listening test. The paper concludes with recommendations about how to use each of these models in modelling L2 listening.

Introduction

In testing and assessment, scaling models are used to examine the relationship between the theoretical assumptions underpinning an assessment's scoring procedures and the latent trait it hopes to test; to determine the internal relationships between test items (Wolfe and Smith 2007); and to 'condense' assigned test scores into an individual score which represents the target latent trait. To date, a number of scaling models have been developed, some of which have been applied to language assessment tools in general and listening tests in particular. Some of these models assume unidimensionality, implying that only a single ability is used to perform on the test items. These models (e.g., Rasch models) 'force the test data to be unidimensionally asymptotic, whereas research shows that language and educational assessment tools typically tap into an array of attributes or sub-skills, each of which could create a statistically separable dimension' (Aryadoust 2011:2). Buck (1994) argues that most language tests involve multiple sub-skills, and Kunina-Habenicht, Rupp and Wilhelm (2009:64) state that 'most constructs in educational assessment require multiple cognitive skills'. If the language ability under assessment is multidimensional in nature, forcing test items to be unidimensional will result in misfit, and some otherwise effective test items might be left out of the measurement process. Because multidimensional models of data analysis can provide fine-grained information about language test takers' performance on each sub-skill in a language test – if the design of such tests allows for modular diagnostic measurement of the targeted skills (Jang 2005, 2008) – language assessment experts have recently adopted a variety of these models.

Two main approaches have been attempted in multidimensional modelling of listening and reading comprehension: cognitive diagnostic models (CDMs) and confirmatory factor analysis (CFA). CDMs, which use information from field experts and test developers to describe the relationships between test takers' performances and postulated sub-skills (Sinharay and Almond 2009), were first developed to investigate criterion-referenced (CR) tests, but have been recently retrofitted to norm-referenced (NR) tests such as the Concept Assessment Tool for Statics (CATS) (Santiago-Román, Streveler and DiBello 2010), the National Assessment of Educational Progress (NAEP) (Xu and von Davier 2006, 2008), and the Test of English as a Foreign Language (TOEFL) (von Davier 2005). The major goal of this study is to compare the success of CDMs and CFA in creating multidimensional second language (L2) listening comprehension sub-skill profiles using a common data set. The paper also seeks to characterise the research problems for which these kinds of models are suitable.

We used data from a retired version of the Michigan English Language Assessment Battery (MELAB) listening test, an NR test, to a large group of international test takers. Our main research questions were as follows:

a) What listening sub-skills do the MELAB listening test items examined in the present study measure?

b) Which type of multidimensional modelling can more successfully model the L2 listening ability of test takers?

Multidimensionality of listening comprehension sub-skills

L2 listening comprehension is widely, but not universally, understood to be a multidimensional process (see Bodie, Worthington, Imhof and Cooper 2008). Multidimensionality implies that comprehension comprises multiple sub-skills that are *divisible* (Lee and Sawaki 2009). Alderson (2000:10) writes of lingering doubt 'whether separable comprehension sub-skills exist, and what such sub-skills might consist of and how they might be classified', echoed by Sawaki, Kim and Gentile (2009:207): 'No matter how sophisticated psychometric models become, it seems that the fundamental conceptual issue – the 'elusiveness' of the L2 comprehension constructs – will continue to be a major challenge that language testers have to grapple with'. However, in practice, 'it is commonplace for language teachers and language test developers to distinguish different comprehension sub-skills or levels of understanding of a given text as a basis for planning a syllabus, describing students' language competence, and developing test items in a mother tongue as well as in a foreign language' (Song 2008:436).

The applied linguistics literature proposes a number of taxonomies of listening comprehension sub-skills. Some of these taxonomies (e.g., Aitken 1978, Munby 1978, Oakeshott-Taylor 1977, Richards 1983) are speculative and concerned with 'higher-order' processing (Buck and Tatsuoka 1998). Aitken's (1978) taxonomy, for example, disaggregates listening comprehension into 'bottom-up' and 'top-down' processes. The problem with the speculative approach followed is that it fails to provide empirical evidence of the validity of the proposed taxonomies, or the separability of the proposed sub-skills.

Among research-based taxonomies, some originate from regression-based studies (Freedle and Kostin 1996, Nissan, DeVincenzi and Tang 1996), and others originate from studies using latent trait models such as the Rule Space Model (Buck and Tatsuoka 1998, Buck, Tatsuoka, Kostin and Phelps 1997) and CFA (Eom 2008, Goh and Aryadoust 2010, Wagner 2002, 2004). Wagner (2004) proposed two related listening comprehension sub-skills: comprehension of explicitly articulated information and comprehension of implicitly stated information. He posited that the two components were highly correlated yet distinct in nature, and that test items could distinguish test takers' ability level in each sub-skill.

Buck and his colleagues' work categorises test 'attributes', a more general term than 'sub-skill'. An attribute is 'anything that affects performance on a task: either a task characteristic, or any of the knowledge, skills or abilities necessary to complete the task' (Buck and Tatsuoka 1998:121). Buck and Tatsuoka identified 15 major listening attributes alongside 14 interactions, and categorised the identified major attributes into five groups, for example:

task identification, context, information location/processing, response construction and information attributes (e.g., the ability to process very fast text automatically).

Other scholars have taken a process-based approach to listening, in which listening is regarded as a set of decoding and meaning-building processes (Field 2008, forthcoming 2013). According to this approach, the listener decomposes larger elements into smaller ones and then reconstructs them into standard language, by using a variety of abilities, such as the ability to identify vowels or recognise vocabulary and syntax (Rost 1999, 2002).

As Sawaki et al (2009) indicate, a thoroughly validated L2 listening comprehension construct remains 'elusive' despite the many empirical studies conducted on the subject. Importantly, this inconclusiveness is partly a result of the different empirical methods of past studies: these methods, such as CFA and CDMs, have been employed in essentially different contexts, and have not yet been rigorously compared using common data sets. It seems quite possible that some listening comprehension taxonomies are in fact reliable, but have been evaluated by inappropriate tools.

Confirmatory factor analysis

CFA is a multivariate data analysis tool used to examine the relationships between latent variables and observable variables (assessment items). These relationships are established *a priori* according to an available theory, and assessment items are statistically regressed on the latent variables to determine whether the latter appear to explain the variation in the former.

CFA application to L2 reading, writing, and speaking tests has been relatively successful (Aryadoust 2010, Bae and Bachman 1998). However, it has failed to provide supporting evidence of validity in a number of the research studies that have adopted it (Bodie, Worthington and Fitch-Hauser 2011, Goh and Aryadoust 2010, Liao 2007). This failure has two possible explanations in a given study: a) that the postulated model simply fits the data poorly because of a poor theoretical underpinning (Bodie et al 2011); or b) that the postulated latent variables are excessively highly correlated with one another, rendering them inappropriate (Goh and Aryadoust 2010, Liao 2007). An examination of the literature shows that where CFA has failed to fit the data or discriminate among listening sub-skills, the test data has been dichotomous (i.e., the responses are either right or wrong). CFA has been quite successful in other contexts. For example, Bodie et al (2011) investigated the constituent structure of a listening test with dichotomous data and reported that the test structure did not emerge as multi-factor, which contradicts claims about the test structure in the literature. By contrast, a comparative study of CDMs and CFA in the context of *polytomous* data suggests that the two models function similarly well, though only CDMs can provide granular diagnostic information about test takers' ability levels (Kunina-Habenicht et al 2009).

Cognitive diagnostic models

Cognitive diagnostic assessment was developed from item response theory (IRT) models, which require unidimensionality. CDMs partition the IRT difficulty parameter into a number of discrete sub-skill-based difficulty indices to depict each test taker's ability. Sub-skill-based partitioning portrays the content of test items in detail, and generates an overall model of the test's underlying structure that registers each sub-skill required to answer each test item.

A number of CDMs regard sub-skills as binary – *mastered* or *non-mastered* by test takers, who are assigned either a 0 or a 1 indicating their mastery (notated as α_j). If the test assesses N sub-skills, there are $N \times \alpha_j$ mastery score indices ($\alpha_1, \alpha_2, \alpha_3 \ldots, \alpha_k$). CDMs are 'confirmatory': researchers specify the relationships between observable variables and latent variables (sub-skills), and associate observables to latent variables on the basis of an *a priori* theoretical specification (Fu and Li 2007).

We used a multidimensional IRT model called the Fusion Model (FM) (DiBello, Roussos and Stout 2007, Hartz 2002 and Hartz, Roussos and Stout 2002). The psychometric features of the FM have been shown to be reliable in language datasets, and the information it provides to the researcher in dichotomous response data is quite useful (DiBello et al 2007).

CDM has been used only once in listening assessment (Jang 2009) and makes no reference to speaking and writing skills, since the models currently available cannot handle rater severity and leniency, which must be controlled for in production tests. Alderson (2010) finds that CDMs have generally failed to establish that the list of sub-skills provided by test developers actually produces real diagnostic information (Lee and Sawaki 2009, Sawaki et al 2009). CDMs modelling in L2 tests – as actually practised – has also often ignored the relationships (if any) between the specified sub-skills. By failing to investigate the correlations between sub-skills, this research cannot assess their empirical divisibility.

Method

Data source

The data used in the study was provided by the English Language Institute at the University of Michigan, now CAMLA. The data set comprised 852 test takers, 425 female (49.9%) and 427 male (50.1%), from 76 countries who took Version FF of a retired version of the MELAB test.

Materials

The MELAB listening test data used here had two parts: 20 short conversation items and 15 radio interview items. These were the second and third sections of the test; the first section (15 questions) seemed to have a less communicative structure, which could affect the modelling (Goh and Aryadoust 2010). The listening test is entirely multiple choice, and audio stimuli are played only once. In each section, correct responses are scored one, and incorrect or unanswered items zero; all sections weigh equally towards the composite listening score. Examples of test items are available at: www.cambridgemichigan.org

Item analysis and modelling the test structure

Researchers may use three methods to match sub-skills to test items: consulting pertinent literature, expert judgement, and verbal protocol analysis (VPA), a qualitative research method that elicits verbal reports from test participants (Alderson 2010, Jang 2009). Because the test items are still in use and secure, undertaking VPA was impossible for this study, leaving expert judgement the only feasible option. The absence of VPA data can limit content analysis, given that expert judgement is conducted by people whose proficiency level is beyond that of the test takers (Alderson 2010). However, Buck and Tatsuoka's (1998) research has shown that careful examination of test items can yield reliable content specification.

The summary in the *MELAB Technical Manual* of the principal aims of the test (Johnson 2003:34) is an important resource for identifying the listening comprehension abilities that the MELAB listening test measures. A summary of the competencies listed in the manual is as follows:

- ability to use one's schemata to interpret meaning
- ability to use components of one's linguistic system (e.g., grammar, vocabulary, etc.) to construct understanding
- ability to use a range of comprehension skills and strategies
- ability to make inferences and draw conclusions.

Excluding the perception and recognition sub-skills facilitating comprehension (see Dunkel, Henning and Chaudron 1993), we posit a model centring around major or complex sub-skills that are 'conceptually distinguishable'; are identified in 'a minimal number of items'; and agree with the item design descriptions (Kim and Jang 2009:839).

We controlled the inter-rater reliability of the codings to the extent possible, by repeatedly discussing our individual findings in an iterative content analysis consisting of multiple meetings. This investigation yielded a number of proposed sub-skills, some of which we deleted because they were defined very similarly to others, or because we concluded that they facilitated but were not part of comprehension.

Here, we provide a brief account of the coding process. (We cannot use secure MELAB items.) Table 1 presents a few examples which are adapted from Wagner (2004:9). The first row includes an item that taps Wagner's sub-skill of understanding explicitly articulated information. The short text where the answer is located states that *skunks are mammals*, which is the correct answer. The second row presents an example which requires para-phrasing the oral language to arrive at the answer. The correct option is *b*, but the text does not include the exact wording of the answer.

Table 1 Finalised sub-skills and examples (adapted from Wagner 2004)

Listening sub-skill	Example from Wagner (2004)
1. Ability to understand explicitly articulated or detailed information	*The striped skunk is the most common type of skunk found in North America. Skunks are omnivorous mammals, about 2 feet in length. Q: A skunk is a type of _____. a. bird b. insect c. reptile d. mammal* (2004:8).*
2. Ability to make paraphrases	*And humans have also benefited from the presence of skunks, because skunks eat bugs like grasshoppers and insect larvae that often eat human agricultural crops. Q: Grasshoppers and larvae are examples of _____. a. different types of skunk b. agricultural pests that skunks eat* c. chemicals that cause a skunk's odor d. predators that sometimes eat skunks (2004:9)*
3. Ability to make propositional inferences	*There are probably more skunks alive today than there were a thousand years ago. This is mostly because human development usually involves clearing the land of tree cover. This is fortunate for skunks, because they like to live in open areas. Q: According to the speaker, skunks have_____. a. been raised by humans as pets b. evolved in the last thousand years c. benefitted from the presence of humans* d. almost gone extinct because of human development (2004:10)*
4. Ability to make enabling inferences	*A skunk's odor works as a very good defence against predators. Skunks spray their musk at predators, causing a really bad smell. Q. Why is the skunk's smell a good defence against predators? a. The predators can smell the skunks. b. Skunks use their odor to blend in to their environment. c. Skunks do not taste very good to predators because their odor is so bad. d. The predators know that if they attack the skunks, they will end up smelling very bad.* (2004:10)*

A number of items engaging propositional and enabling inferences were further identified (Hildyard and Olson 1978). Propositional inferences are syllogisms or logical arguments which do not explicitly state conclusions and require the comprehender to make inferences about the conclusion. For example, if given *A is bigger than B*, the listener might conclude that *B is smaller than A*, which is the conclusion proposition. Item 3 in Table 1 engages this sub-skill; the listener must draw an inference from two separate statements: *human development usually involves clearing the land of tree cover* and *they like to live in open areas*, which together imply that skunks benefit from human deforestation activities.

By contrast, enabling inferences require that listeners connect ideas to their knowledge base. Hildyard and Olson (1978:95) define enabling inferences as 'inferences that must be drawn to make discourse coherent and, therefore, comprehensible'. There are two important pieces of information in the fourth example in Table 1 that must be understood to draw the inference: *Skunks spray their musk as predators* and *causing a really bad smell.*

Confirmatory factor analysis

We tested our four-factor model of listening comprehension using a two-stage CFA conducted through the LISREL statistical program, Version 8.8 (Jöreskog and Sörbom 2006). To undertake the CFA, we developed a matrix of polychoric correlations and an asymptotic covariance matrix for the ordinal data (Du Toit and Du Toit 2001). We initially postulated a four-factor baseline model based on the hypothesis that the MELAB listening test measures four related sub-skills, although it was modified into three- and two-factor models.

For example, Figure 1 presents a CFA model with three latent variables. For space reasons, only a few test items are displayed. There are three latent variables, represented as circles. Each latent trait is assessed by three test

Figure 1 Illustration of a CFA model with three latent variables

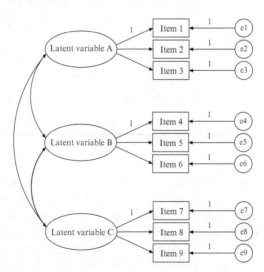

items, represented as squares. It is postulated that the observed variance in each item is mainly accounted for by the posited latent variables. The unexplained variance is attributed to random errors which are represented as small circles with arrows heading to the items. Regression paths are indicated as unidirectional arrows and correlations are indicted as bidirectional arrows.

Following Kline (1998) and Schumacker and Lomax (2004), we calculated a range of fit statistics for each of the models we developed, as follows:

- normed chi-square test (χ^2/df), an index that shows the difference between the observed and implied covariance matrices (Hair, Black, Babin and Anderson 2010)
- RMSEA (Root Mean Square Error of Approximation), a measure that represents the fit of a model to the population
- NNFI (Non-Normed Fit Index), used to compare the postulated model and the baseline model
- CFI (Comparative Fit Index), an incremental index to evaluate the fit of a model relative to a baseline model.

In addition, we examined the correlation coefficients of the postulated sub-skills to ascertain the plausibility and validity of the models they comprised. Excessively high coefficients violate discriminate validity, because measures of theoretically different latent traits cannot be empirically discriminated. Excessively low coefficients violate convergent validity, because measures of theoretically related latent traits are not empirically related. We opted for a correlation range between .50 and .80 as a secure range where both classes of statistical validity are actualised (Schumacker and Lomax 2004). Coefficients which exceed unity ('offending' estimates), render the model inadmissible. Offending estimates can have several statistical causes (Brown 2006), but generally indicate that the input matrix cannot be inverted due to the linear dependency of some variables, errors in keying in the data, large amounts of missing data, or lack of variation.

Fusion modelling and Q-matrix

We developed a Q-matrix to model the findings of the item analysis, and then subjected the Q-matrix to FM analysis, using Arpeggio Suite for Windows, Version 3.1.001 (DiBello and Stout 2008a).

Three FM parameters were computed: p_i, r_{ik}^*, and c_i. Together, these indices provide rich diagnostic information about each test taker and item, and about the features of the Q-matrix and the misspecifications observed. The p_i parameter is the probability that a test taker will answer a given test item correctly, given that the test taker has mastered all sub-skills required by the item. Higher p_i indices are desirable, as they indicate that masters have a higher probability of successfully executing the sub-skills required by that item. An ideal matrix would produce r^*_{ik} estimates below .90, suggesting that the test item *discriminates* well between masters and non-masters; sub-skills with values below .50 on a test item are regarded as necessary to answer that item correctly (Roussos, Xueli and Stout 2003). The parameter c_i ranges from 0 to 3 and approaches 3 if the Q-matrix fully specifies the sub-skills required to successfully answer the item, and 0 if the Q-matrix does not specify the relevant sub-skills (DiBello and Stout 2008a).

Following DiBello and Stout (2008b), we designated test takers who had at least a .60 probability of answering an item correctly as masters of the relevant sub-skill, and test takers with less than .40 probability non-masters. The area between these two probabilities is the 'indifference' region.

We developed a Q-matrix informed by the item analysis; calibrated the test items; examined model fit estimates and sub-skills mastery profiles; and calculated the mean differences in proportion-correct values between masters and non-masters of the sub-skills required to answer each test item. We also investigated the correlations between sub-skills. Fusion modelling provides no explicit estimate of these correlations, but we obtained estimates through the following procedure: the tetrachoric correlations between sub-skills are estimated during each time step of the MCMC parameter estimation algorithm used in FM by calculating the mean of the correlation values in each time series; the average index is the precise estimate of the tetrachoric correlation between sub-skills (DiBello, personal communication May 6 2011).

Results

Descriptive statistics and reliability analysis

All items possess skewness and kurtosis coefficients between -2 and $+2$ and the Cronbach's alpha coefficients for the hypothesised sub-skills are: detailed (explicit) information: .45 (6 items); close paraphrase: .60 (13 items); propositional inference: .50 (9 items); and enabling inference: 0.42 (7 items).

Selection, fit, and interpretation of CFA

As Table 2 demonstrates, the four-factor model fits the data well ($\chi^2 = 773.42$; $\chi^2/df = 1.39$; NNFI = 0.96; CFI = 0.96; GFI = 0.95; RMSEA = 0.021). However, the presence of an offending correlation index of 1.11 between the *detailed information* and *close paraphrase* latent variables precluded accepting the model. In an endeavour to produce a model with plausible latent variable correlations, we collapsed these two latent variables into a general 'explicit information' latent variable. This model fits satisfactorily ($\chi^2 = 784.62$; $\chi^2/df = 1.40$; NNFI = 0.96; CFI = 0.96; GFI = 0.93; RMSEA = 0.021), but the offending correlation indices persist between the explicit information variable and the ability to make both propositional and enabling inferences (1.06 and 1.10, respectively). This finding led us to collapse propositional and enabling inferences into an 'inference making' variable, for a two-factor model along with 'explicit information'. This model also fits satisfactorily ($\chi^2 = 794.56$; $\chi^2/df = 1.42$; NNFI = 0.96; CFI = 0.96; GFI = 0.95; RMSEA = 0.021), but with an offending correlation index (1.02).

Table 2 CFA models to confirm the underlying structure of the test

Model	χ^2	df	χ^2/df	NNFI	CFI	GFI	RMSEA	RMSEA 90% confidence interval
4-Factor model	773.42**	554	1.39	0.96	0.96	0.95	0.021	0.018 to 0.024
3-Factor model	784.62**	557	1.40	0.96	0.96	0.93	0.021	0.018 to 0.025
2-Factor model	794.56**	558	1.42	0.96	0.96	0.95	0.021	0.018 to 0.025
Constraint tenable	Non-sign.	—	< 3	0.95	0.95	0.95	< 0.08	Narrow interval

*Note: **p< 0.001. NNFI: Non-Normed Fit Index. CFI: Comparative Fit Index. GFI: Goodness of Fit Index. RMSEA: Root Mean Square Error of Approximation. df: degree of freedom.*

All models have similar fit properties, and item loading coefficients are almost the same in all models and significant at $\alpha = 0.01$. This was expected, since all three models are similar in preserving the theoretical assumption that listening comprehension consists of the ability to understand both explicitly and implicitly stated information, though the more parsimonious models did not distinguish subclasses of these major sub-skills.

Fusion modelling

The mean difference in proportion-correct values between masters and non-masters across all items is .640, indicating that the MELAB listening test has fairly good diagnostic capability in this sample.

Figure 2 displays the distribution of masters and non-masters for each test item. The proportion of test takers who fall within the indifference area increases slightly throughout the test. For example, item 1 has 690 identified masters, 114 non-masters, and 110 unclassified test takers, and item 35 has 655 masters, 122 non-masters, and 132 unclassified test takers. The number of non-masters also increases through the test, which matches theoretical expectations; item difficulty increases slightly through the test, though not

Figure 2 Proportion of masters and non-masters for each test item

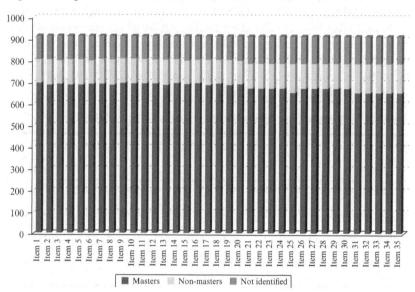

completely consistently (Goh and Aryadoust 2010). On average, test items discriminate between masters and non-masters 86.5% of the time, indicating fairly high diagnostic capacity.

The non-masters who possessed high listening ability (high non-masters) outnumbered the non-masters with low ability (low non-masters), indicating that the test items were relatively easy for this sample of test takers. More test takers had difficulty with the items engaging higher-level listening sub-skills such as inference-making, a finding that supports the content validity of the item coding.

Table 3 presents p_i, r^*_{ik}, and c_i parameters for all test items. All items but item 11 have high p_i indices, indicating that test takers who have mastered the pertinent sub-skills are highly likely to answer the items correctly. Item 11 has a fairly low p_i index, likely indicating that the sub-skill specification of this item in the Q-matrix could be extended to include further sub-skills. r^*_{ik} estimates for all test items except question 9 fall below .90, suggesting that the test items discriminated well between masters and non-masters. The r^*_{ik} values approaching 0.50 (items 2 and 12) indicate that the relevant listening sub-skill was highly necessary to answer the question correctly. Another column in Table 3 displays c_i indices, all of which are high (> 0.80), indicating that the Q-matrix accurately specifies the sub-skills required to successfully answer each test item. The c_i and p_i indices are significantly correlated (.606; $p <$ 0.01), which might be expected since both indices measure sub-skill mastery.

Table 3 Results of the application of the Fusion Model

Item	p_i^*	$r^* 1$	$r^* 2$	$r^* 3$	$r^* 4$	c_i
1	0.813	0	0	0.671	0	1.878
2	0.823	0.538	0	0	0	2.215
3	0.936	0	0.622	0	0	1.730
4	0.946	0.666	0	0	0	1.467
5	0.887	0	0	0	0.667	1.961
6	0.821	0	0.827	0	0	1.073
7	0.975	0	0.654	0	0	1.525
8	0.924	0	0	0	0.698	2.059
9	0.986	0	0	0.902	0	1.436
10	0.848	0	0	0.846	0	1.757
11	0.586	0	0.609	0	0	2.581
12	0.774	0	0	0.580	0	2.159
13	0.876	0	0	0.738	0	2.008
14	0.916	0	0	0.744	0	1.138
15	0.988	0.839	0	0	0	0.877
16	0.882	0	0	0.885	0	1.059
17	0.930	0	0	0	0.871	1.230
18	0.924	0	0.856	0	0	1.435
19	0.951	0	0	0	0.760	2.359
20	0.909	0	0.791	0	0	1.332
21	0.640	0	0.718	0	0	2.406
22	0.990	0	0.744	0	0	1.404
23	0.858	0.644	0	0	0	1.475
24	0.914	0	0.640	0	0	2.106
25	0.901	0.606	0	0	0	1.935
26	0.819	0	0.791	0	0	1.861
27	0.911	0	0.894	0	0	1.325
28	0.987	0.819	0	0	0	1.422
29	0.729	0	0.805	0	0	1.193
30	0.923	0	0.767	0	0	2.044
31	0.978	0	0	0.852	0	1.489
32	0.885	0	0	0	0.617	1.867
33	0.818	0.895	0	0	0	1.675
34	0.717	0	0.659	0	0	1.709
35	0.922	0	0.788	0	0	1.478

Figure 3 displays a scatterplot of observed and expected test scores. The correlation between the two sets of scores is .997, significant at $p < 0.01$, supporting the validity of the latent trait solution being tested.

Figure 4 presents tetrachoric correlations between sub-skills. The highest and lowest estimated correlation coefficients between the detailed information and close paraphrase sub-skills (the 'Sub2&1' line) were .70 and .49, respectively (mean .613; SD = .071). The average correlation of the detailed information and propositional inference sub-skills (the 'Sub3&1' line) was the lowest (mean .496; SD = .108), and the correlation between close paraphrase and enabling inferences the highest (mean .629; SD = .082) on average. This indicates that, unlike the CFA model, the FM has been successful in profiling the hypothesised listening sub-skills.

Figure 3 Comparison between observed and expected item difficulty distribution

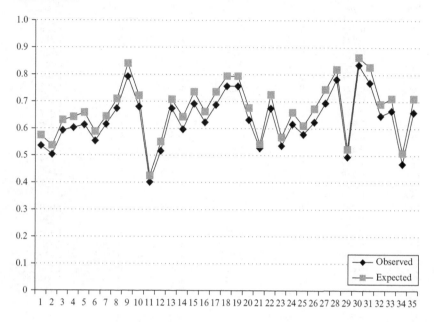

Figure 4 Tetrachoric correlations between sub-skills estimated during each time step of MCMC parameter estimation

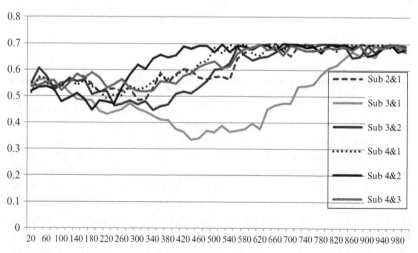

Finally, we developed sub-skill profiles for test takers on the basis of the proportion of identified and unidentified test takers. Two patterns were identified:

a) Almost all test takers' response patterns are classified accurately, indicating that the designation of latent classes was successful.

b) On average, 74% of the test takers had mastered all sub-skills; 12.5% were non-masters; and 13.5% fell in the indifference region. This shows that although the test was not very challenging for a number of test takers, it had some power to discriminate.

Discussion and conclusion

This study set out to investigate the relative merits of CFA and fusion modelling (a type of CDM) in language assessment. Our findings support the emerging body of opinion that CDMs can be retrofitted into high-stakes language tests (Jang 2005, 2008); we found that the FM conformed closely to the theoretical underpinnings of the test and furnished granular diagnostic information about test takers' sub-skill mastery. By contrast, CFA imposed more stringent constraints on the data, obliging us to collapse sub-skills into less precise representations of the latent traits required by test items. We briefly discussed our findings, and the issues surrounding the selection of a pertinent scaling model in language tests.

This study first investigated which listening comprehension sub-skills are tapped by the MELAB listening test. Our item coding revealed four principal sub-skills: understanding explicitly articulated information, making close paraphrases, making propositional inferences, and making enabling inferences. This taxonomy closely resembles the major L2 listening abilities specified in the *MELAB Technical Manual* (Johnson 2003). The agreement between the item coding and the test manual is evidence for the content validity of the taxonomy developed here, though it does not empirically support the divisibility of the sub-skills.

This study then examined the relative merits of CFA and the FM in empirically assessing the divisibility of the proposed listening sub-skills. CFA failed to explain the covariance structure of the data or profile the sub-skills, and yielded offending estimates and inappropriate sub-skill correlations that forced us to collapse our four latent variables (the four posited sub-skills) into two broader variables: understanding explicitly articulated information and making inferences. Even then, the correlation between the two variables was still high and inadmissible.

High and/or inadmissible correlations between latent variables in CFA have been observed in numerous previous studies of L2 listening tests that were scored *dichotomously* (e.g., Bodie et al 2011, Liao 2007), but not in studies where L2 listening comprehension was scaled polyto-mously (e.g., Song 2008; see also Bodie and Worthington 2010). Where data from Likert scale instruments has been used, the polychoric matrices of correlations used in CFA have functioned successfully (e.g., Muthén 1993), although when there are fewer than five response categories the fit and function of the polychoric-matrix CFA is endangered (Jöreskog and Sörbom 1981).

Bodie et al (2011:38) suggest that 'perhaps dichotomous scoring does not fully reflect listening ability, with the valid use of dichotomous scoring likely dependent on context'. This point is quite plausible, but it has not yet been well researched. In dichotomous (or binary) scoring scales, responses are considered either wrong or right; only the extreme responses are considered. Assigning a zero to a response indicates non-mastery of the ability tapped by the item, and a one indicates mastery. This can increase the inter-rater reliability of scoring, although very likely at the expense of validity because of the interplay between these two concepts (Bachman 1990). Dichotomous scoring is an instance of an 'absolute scale' with only two qualitatively distinct levels (Bachman 1990:344); Aryadoust (2012) underscores the compromise of validity when such scales are employed in L2 listening tests, and postulates that there may be multiple qualitatively different methods by which test takers answer listening test items. Likewise, Stöber, Dette and Musch (2002) report that continuous scoring can yield higher Cronbach's alphas and better convergent validity than dichotomous scoring when assessing student personality traits. Fundamentally, it seems likely either that CFA is inappropriate for dichotomous L2 listening tests, or the tests must use a polytomous scale to effectively represent test takers' ability levels.

The FM, however, functioned as we expected: it fit the data and distinguished among the postulated listening sub-skills. This may have a number of explanations. First, the FM was developed to model sub-skills as dichotomous using Q-matrices, whereas CFA was originally developed to investigate the underlying structure of polytomous scales. The FM does not model partial mastery of the ability tapped by a test item, which likely makes it appropriate for handling dichotomous data and parameter estimation in multidimensional data.

We conclude that it is not advisable to use CFA in dichotomous listening tests. Based on this conclusion, we suggest that the early factor analysis research into the structure of L2 listening tests that hinted at the indivisibility of listening sub-skills (e.g., Oller 1978, 1979, 1983, Oller and Hinofitis 1980, Scholz, Hendricks, Spurling, Johnson and Vandenburg 1980) is likely an artefact of methodology. We argue that it is possible to empirically separate primary L2 listening sub-skills, but two factors should be taken into consideration for successful psychometric modelling:

a) L2 listening sub-skills, although divisible, are an interwoven network and affect one another. This interconnection can create a kind of dependence and as a result high correlation among sub-skills. Because of this complex structure, factor analysis does not seem to be able to successfully model L2 comprehension. The psychometric model that researchers employ to portray this complex network must not fall prey to high (polychoric/tetrachoric/Pearson) intercorrelations and produce counterintuitive results that might be wrongly regarded as attenuating evidence of the model's fit. Therefore, the psychometric model itself must be initially validated in an L2 listening context prior to employing it for significant decision-making processes about the uses and interpretations of test scores.

b) The scoring scale of the test is an important element in choosing a psychometric model. Regrettably, the relevant literature does not give clear guidelines for making this decision, and we are often at the mercy of speculation or rituals. We recognise the richness of the language assessment literature and the utility of many scaling models used in the field, but also highlight the need for some guidelines for selecting psychometric models. The present article is a step in this direction, but obviously cannot address all issues surrounding the question.

Future research can further compare the results of CFA and fusion modelling (or other CDMs) in L2 listening and other language tests where different scoring scales are used. Research might also compare the results of test takers' performance on a test which has been scored once on a dichotomous scale, and another time on a polytomous scale: this research could fruitfully examine the potential effects of 'discretizing' (Kunina-Habenicht et al 2009) continuous performance scales.

Acknowledgement

The authors are greatly thankful to the Spaan Fellowship Program and the University of Michigan for the support received for this study.

References

Aitken, K G (1978) *Measuring Listening Comprehension in English as a Second Language*, TEAL Occasional Papers volume 2, Vancouver: British Columbia Association of Teachers of English as an Additional Language.

Alderson, J C (2000) *Assessing Reading*, Cambridge: Cambridge University Press.

Alderson, J C (2010) Cognitive diagnosis and Q-Matrices in language assessment: a commentary, *Language Assessment Quarterly* 7, 96–103.

Aryadoust, V (2010) Investigating writing sub-skills in testing English as a foreign language: A structural equation modelling study, *TESL-EJ* 13 (4), 1–20.

Aryadoust, V (2011) Cognitive diagnostic assessment as an alternative measurement model, *SHIKEN: The JALT Testing and Evaluation SIG Newsletter* 15 (1), 2–6, available online: http://jalt.org/test/PDF/Aryadoust1.pdf

Aryadoust, V (2012) Differential item functioning in while-listening performance tests: The case of the IELTS listening test, *International Journal of Listening* 26, 40–60.

Bachman, L F (1990) *Fundamental Considerations in Language Testing*, Oxford: Oxford University Press.

Bae, J and Bachman, L F (1998) A latent variable approach to listening and reading: testing factorial invariance across two groups of children in the Korean/English two-way immersion program, *Language Testing* 15 (3), 380–414.

Beall, M L, Gill-Rosier, J, Tate, J and Matten, A (2008) State of the context: listening in education, *The International Journal of Listening* 22 (2), 123–132.

Bodie, G (2009) Evaluating listening theory: development and illustration of five criteria, *The International Journal of Listening* 25, 81–103.

Bodie, G D and Fitch-Hauser, M (2010) Quantitative research in listening: explication and overview, in Wolvin, A D (Ed.) *Listening and Human Communication in the 21st Century*, Oxford: Blackwell, 46–93.

Bodie, G D and Worthington, D L (2010) Revisiting the listening styles profile (LSP-16): a confirmatory factor analytic approach to scale validation and reliability estimation, *The International Journal of Listening* 24 (2), 69–88.

Bodie, G D, Worthington, D L and Fitch-Hauser, M (2011) A Comparison of four measurement models for the Watson-Barker Listening Test (WBLT)-Form C, *Communication Research Reports* 28, 32–42.

Bodie, G D, Worthington, D L, Imhof, M and Cooper, L (2008) What would a unified field of listening look like? A proposal linking past perspectives and future endeavors, *International Journal of Listening* 22, 103–122.

Brown, T A (2006) *Confirmatory Factor Analysis for Applied Research*, New York: The Guilford Press.

Buck, G (1994) The appropriacy of psychometric measurement models for testing second language listening comprehension, *Language Testing* 11, 145–170.

Buck, G and Tatsuoka, K (1998) Application of the rule-space procedure to language testing: examining attributes of a free response listening test, *Language Testing* 15, 119–157.

Buck, G, Tatsuoka, K, Kostin, I and Phelps, M (1997) The sub-skills of listening: rule-space analysis of a multiple-choice test of second language listening comprehension, in Huhta, V A, Kurki-Suonio, L and Luoma, S (Eds) *Current Developments and Alternatives in Language Assessment: Proceedings of LTRC 96*, Jyvaskyla, Finland: University of Jyvaskyla and University of Tampere, 589–624.

Cooper, L O and Buchanan, T (2010) Listening competency on campus: a psychometric analysis of student listening, *The International Journal of Listening* 24 (3), 141–163.

Davis, J, Thompson, C R, Foley, A, Bond, C D and DeWitt, J (2008) An examination of listening concepts in the healthcare context: differences among nurses, physicians, and administrators, *The International Journal of Listening* 22, 152–167.

DiBello, L V, Roussos, L A and Stout, W (2007) Review of cognitive diagnostic assessment and a summary of psychometric models, in Rao, C R and

Sinharay, S (Eds) *Handbook of Statistics, Volume 26: Psychometrics*, Elsevier Science B V: The Netherlands, 45–79.

DiBello, L and Stout, W (2008a) *Arpeggio Documentation and Analyst Manual*, Chicago: Applied Informative Assessment Research Enterprises (AIARE) – LLC.

DiBello, L and Stout, W (2008b) *Arpeggio Suite, Version 3.1.001*, [Computer program], Chicago: Applied Informative Assessment Research Enterprises (AIARE) – LLC.

Du Toit, M and Du Toit, S (2001) *Interactive LISREL: User's Guide*, Lincolnwood, IL: Scientific Software International, Inc.

Dunkel, P, Henning, G and Chaudron, C (1993) The assessment of a listening comprehension construct: a tentative model for test specification and development, *Modern Language Journal* 77, 180–191.

Eom, M (2008) Underlying factors of MELAB listening construct, *Spaan Fellow Working Papers in Second or Foreign Language Assessment* 6, 77–94.

Field, J (2008) *Listening in the Language Classroom*, Cambridge: Cambridge University Press.

Field, J (forthcoming 2013) Cognitive validity, in Geranpayeh, A and Taylor, L (Eds) *Examining Listening: Research and Practice in Assessing Second Language Listening*, Studies in Language Testing volume 35, Cambridge: UCLES/ Cambridge University Press.

Flynn, J, Valikoski, T and Grau, J (2008) Listening in the business context: reviewing the state of research, *The International Journal of Listening* 22, 141–151.

Freedle, R and Kostin, I (1996) *The prediction of TOEFL listening comprehension item difficulty for mini-talk passages: implications for construct validity*, TOEFL research report RR 96–29, Princeton, NJ: Educational Testing Service.

Fu, J and Li, Y (2007) *Cognitively diagnostic psychometric models: an integrative review*, paper presented at the annual meeting of the National Council on Measurement in Education, Chicago, April 2007.

Goh, C C M (2005) Second language listening expertise, in Johnson, K (Ed.) *Expertise in Second Language Learning and Teaching*, UK: Palgrave Macmillan, 64–84.

Goh, C C M (2010) Listening as process: learning activities for self-appraisal and self-regulation, in Harwood, N (Ed.), *Materials in ELT: Theory and Practice*, Cambridge: Cambridge University Press, 179–206.

Goh, C C M and Aryadoust, V (2010) Investigating the construct validity of MELAB listening test through the Rasch analysis and correlated uniqueness modelling, *Spaan Fellowship Working Papers in Second or Foreign Language Assessment* 8, 31–68.

Hair, J F, Black, W C, Babin, B J and Anderson, R E (2010) *Multivariate Data Analysis*, New Jersey: Pearson Educational Product, 8th edn.

Hartz, S (2002) *A Bayesian framework for the Unified Model for assessing cognitive abilities: blending theory with practice*, unpublished doctoral thesis, University of Illinois at Urbana-Champain.

Hartz, S, Roussos, L and Stout, W (2002) *Skill diagnosis: theory and practice* [Computer software user manual for Arpeggio software], Princeton, NJ: ETS.

Hildyard, A and Olson, D (1978) Memory and inference in the comprehension of oral and written discourse, *Discourse Processes* 1, 91–107.

Jang, E E (2005) *A validity narrative: effects of reading skills diagnosis on teaching and learning in the context of NG TOEFL*, unpublished doctoral dissertation, University of Illinois at Urbana-Champaign.

Jang, E E (2008) A framework for cognitive diagnostic assessment, in Chapelle, C A, Chung, Y-R and Xu, J (Eds) *Towards Adaptive CALL: Natural Language Processing for Diagnostic Language Assessment*, Ames, IA: Iowa State University, 117–131.

Jang, E E (2009) Cognitive diagnostic assessment of L2 reading comprehension ability: validity arguments for applying Fusion Model to LanguEdge assessment, *Language Testing* 26, 31–73.

Johnson, J (2003) *MELAB Technical Manual*, Ann Arbor: English Language Institute, the University of Michigan.

Jöreskog, K G and Sörbom, D (1981) *LISREL: Analysis of Linear Structural Relationships by the Method of Maximum Likelihood* (version V), Chicago: National Educational Resources, Inc.

Jöreskog, K G and Sörbom, D (2001) *LISREL 8.8: User's reference guide*, Lincolnwood, IL: Scientific Software International, Inc.

Jöreskog, K G and Sörbom, D (2006) *LISREL 8.8 for Windows* [Computer software], Lincolnwood, IL: Scientific Software International, Inc.

Kim, Y-H and Jang, E E (2009) Differential functioning of reading subskills on the OSSLT for L1 and ELL students: A multidimensionality model-based DBF/DIF approach, *Language Learning* 59, 825–865.

Kline, R B (1998) *Principles and Practice of Structural Equation Modelling*, New York: Guilford Press.

Kunina-Habenicht, O, Rupp, A A and Wilhelm, O (2009) A practical illustration of multidimensional diagnostic skills profiling: Comparing results from confirmatory factor analysis and diagnostic classification models, *Studies in Educational Evaluation* 35, 64–70.

Lee, Y-W and Sawaki, Y (2009) Cognitive diagnostic approaches to language assessment: an overview, *Language Assessment Quarterly* 6, 172–189.

Liao, Y (2007) Investigating the construct validity of the listening section and grammar and vocabulary sections of the ECCE, *Spaan Fellow Working Papers in Second or Foreign Language Assessment* 5, 37–78.

Liu, X L and Goh, C (2006) Improving second language listening: awareness and involvement, in Farrell, T S C (Ed.) *Language Teacher Research in Asia*, Alexandria: TESOL, 91–106.

Marsh, H W and Hocevar, D (1988) A new, more powerful approach to multitrait-multimethod analyses: application of second-order confirmatory factor analysis, *Journal of Applied Psychology* 73, 107–117.

Munby, J (1978) *Communicative Syllabus Design*, Cambridge: Cambridge University Press.

Muthén, B O (1993) Goodness of fit with categorical and other nonnormal variables, in Bollen, K A and Long J S (Eds) *Testing Structural Equation Models*, Newbury Park, CA: Sage, 205–234.

Nissan, S, DeVincenzi, F and Tang, L (1996) *An analysis of factors affecting the difficulty of dialogue items in TOEFL listening comprehension*, TOEFL research report RR 95–37, Princeton, NJ: Educational Testing Service.

Oakeshott-Taylor, J (1977) Information redundancy and listening comprehension, in Dirven, R (Ed.) *Hörverständnis im Fremdsprachenunterricht* [*Listening Comprehension in foreign language Teaching*], Kronberg/Ts: Scriptor, 83–112.

Oller, J W, Jr (1978) How important is language proficiency to IQ and other educational tests, in Oller, J W Jr and Perkins, K (Eds) *Language in Education: Testing the Test*, Rowley, Massachusetts: Newbury House Publishers, 1–16.

Oller, J W, Jr (1979) *Language Tests at School*, London: Longman.

Oller, J W, Jr (1983) Evidence for a general proficiency factor: an expectancy grammar, in Oller, J W Jr (Ed.) *Issues in Language Testing Research*, Rowley, Massachusetts: Newbury House Publishers, 3–10.

Oller, J W, Jr and Hinofitis, F B (1980) Two manually exclusive hypotheses about second language ability: indivisible or partly divisible competence, in Oller, J W Jr, and Perkins, K (Eds) *Research in Language Testing*, Rowley, Massachusetts: Newbury House Publishers, 13–23.

Richards, J C (1983) Listening comprehension: approach, design, procedure, *TESOL Quarterly* 17, 219–39.

Rost, M (1999) *Introducing Listening*, Harmondsworth: Penguin.

Rost, M (2002) *Teaching and Researching Listening*, London: Longman.

Roussos, L, Xueli, X and Stout, W (2003) *Equating with the Fusion Model using Item Parameter Invariance*, unpublished manuscript, University of Illinois, Urbana-Champaign.

Santiago-Romàn, A I, Streveler, R A and DiBello, L (2010) *The development of estimated cognitive attribute profiles for the concept assessment tool for static*, proceedings of the 40th ASEE/IEEE Frontiers in Education Conference, October, Washington, DC.

Sawaki, Y, Kim, H-J and Gentile, C (2009) Q-Matrix construction: defining the link between constructs and test items in large-scale reading and listening comprehension assessments, *Language Assessment Quarterly* 6, 190–209.

Schnapp, D (2008) Listening in context: religion and spirituality, *The International Journal of Listening* 22 (2), 133–140.

Scholz, G, Hendricks, D, Spurling, R, Johnson, M and Vandenburg, L (1980) Is language ability divisible or unitary? A factor analysis of 22 English language proficiency tests, in Oller, J W Jr and Perkins, K (Eds) *Research in Language Testing*, Rowley, Massachusetts: Newbury House, 24–33.

Schumacker, R E and Lomax, R G (2004) *A Beginner's Guide to Structural Equation Modelling*, Mahwah, NJ: Lawrence Erlbaum.

Sinharay, S and Almond, R G (2009) Bayesian network models for local dependence among observable outcome variables, *Journal of Educational and Behavioral Statistics* 34, 491–521.

Song, M Y (2008) Do divisible subskills exist in second language (L2) comprehension? A structural equation modeling approach, *Language Testing* 25, 435–464.

Stöber, J, Dette, D E and Musch, J (2002) Comparing continuous and dichotomous scoring of the Balanced Inventory of Desirable Responding, *Journal of Personality Assessment* 78, 370–389.

Tatsuoka, K (1983) Rule space: an approach for dealing with misconceptions based on item response theory, *Journal of Educational Measurement* 20, 345–354.

von Davier, M (2005) *A general diagnostic model applied to language testing data*, ETS Research Rep. No. RR-05-16, Princeton, NJ: Educational Testing Service.

Wagner, E (2002) Video listening tests: a pilot study, *Working Papers in TESOL and Applied Linguistics, Teachers College, Columbia University*, 2/1.

Wagner, E (2004) A construct validation study of the extended listening sections of the ECPE and MELAB, *Spaan Fellow Working Papers in Second or Foreign Language Assessment* 2, 1–23.

Wolfe, E W and Smith, E V, Jr (2007) Instrument development tools and activities for measure validation using Rasch models: Part I – Instrument Development Tools, *Journal of Applied Measurement* 8, 97–123.

Xu, X and von Davier, M (2006) *General diagnosis for NAEP proficiency data*, ETS Research Report No. RR-06-08, Princeton, NJ: Educational Testing Service.

Xu, X and von Davier, M (2008) *Fitting the structural general diagnostic model to NAEP data*, ETS Research Report No. RR-08-27, Princeton, NJ: Educational Testing Service.

Notes on contributors

Vahid Aryadoust is a PhD candidate in Applied Linguistics at the National Institute of Education of Nanyang Technological University, Singapore. He has written books and articles on language and psychosociological assessment and teaching. His current research focuses on the application of unidimensional and multidimensional latent trait models and Adaptive Neuro-Fuzzy Inference Systems (ANFIS) to language assessment; G-theory; and neuroanatomy of comprehension processes.

Maria Brau is Unit Chief of the Language Testing and Assessment Unit (Language Services Section, Directorate of Intelligence, Federal Bureau of Investigation), member of the Intelligence Community Testing and Assessment Expert Group. As co-chair of the Interagency Language Roundtable (ILR) Translation and Interpretation Committee, she presided over the development of the ILR Skill Level Descriptions for Translation, Interpretation, and Audio Translation. She has presented papers on translation testing issues at various government fora and academic conferences, such as the International Association of Applied Linguistics (AILA) and the International Language Testing Association (ILTA).

Rachel L Brooks manages the Testing Standards Program in the Federal Bureau of Investigation's Language Testing and Assessment Unit. She oversees the speaking tester programme, test quality control, research and validation projects, and tester training. Her research and publications address government testing issues, including rater characteristics and forensic linguistics methods applied to testing.

Ágnes Dévény is an Associate Professor at Budapest Business School, Hungary. She is currently Deputy Head of the Language Department. She has been teaching and testing Language for Specific Purposes (LSP) for more than 20 years. She completed her PhD in the field of language assessment. Her research interests are in language teaching and language testing especially in measuring different language skills. She is a teacher trainer, author of textbooks, curricula and testing materials. She has several publications. She is currently responsible for heading the Language Department's research group.

Bart Deygers is a test validation officer at the Certificate of Dutch as a Foreign Language. He is responsible for the Business Dutch exam as well as for rating scale development and validation. His main research interests include rating scale design, Language for Specific Purposes (LSP) testing and task-based language testing.

Thomas Eckes is Head of the Psychometrics and Research Methodology Department at the TestDaF Institute, University of Bochum, Germany. Dr Eckes has extensive teaching experience in educational measurement and statistics. He has published numerous articles in edited volumes and peer-reviewed journals, including *Language Testing, Language Assessment Quarterly, Diagnostica, Journal of Classification,* and *Multivariate Behavioral Research.* Recently, he has authored a book entitled *Introduction to Many-Facet Rasch Measurement: Analyzing and Evaluating Rater-Mediated Assessments* (2011). His research interests include: rater effects in large-scale assessments; test fairness and validity; polytomous item response theory (IRT) models; validation of C-tests as measures of general language proficiency; standard-setting methods; computerised item-banking; and internet-delivered testing.

Christine C M Goh is Associate Professor of Applied Linguistics and Associate Dean (Higher Degrees) at the National Institute of Education, Nanyang Technological University, Singapore. She has published many peer-refereed international journal articles, book chapters and books on the topic of second language listening. Her latest book (with Larry Vandergrift) is *Teaching and Learning Second Language Listening: Metacognition in Action* (2012). She is interested in validity issues in national-level listening examinations and in exploring alternative forms of assessment for second language (L2) listening, particularly for young learners.

Giuliana Grego Bolli is Associate Professor of Glottology and Linguistics at Università per Stranieri Perugia (USP), Italy. She is currently Director of CVCL (Centro per la Valutazione e le Certificazioni, Centre for Evaluation and Certification). Her research interests are in language testing and language teaching. Professor Bolli worked on the development of the CELI (Certificati di Lingua Italiana) Examinations Suite and has been collaborating with the Association of Language Testers in Europe (ALTE) since 1990. She is a member of the SurveyLang Programme Board in the project for the definition of the European Indicator of Language Competences. She was the Italian co-ordinator of the Reference Level Descriptions (RLD) project in Italian. She is the author or co-author of several publications on the CVCL's Certification activities and projects involving CVCL's collaboration with the Council of Europe with regard to possible applications of the Common

European Framework of Reference for languages (CEFR), particularly in the field of language assessment.

Ursula Hehl has been working as a teacher of English and German as a Foreign Language for 20 years, both at universities and private institutions. Since October 2008 she has been employed as a co-ordinator for English courses at the Language Centre of the University of Bonn. Her responsibilities include teaching, designing courses including final tests, and management of the teaching staff. She is currently involved in developing a curriculum for language courses at the Language Centre. Her research interests focus on questions of learner autonomy and blended learning.

David Horner has worked in oral testing since the 1980s. He is currently head of the Language Department at École nationale de la statistique et de l'administration économique (ENSAE) ParisTech, and is also responsible for Cambridge ESOL Oral Examiners in France and Luxembourg. His book on oral testing, *Le CECRL et l'évaluation de l'oral*, was published by Belin in France in 2010.

Elzbieta (Ela) Jarosz is academic director at Bell Kraków school of English in Poland, chair of the Board of Inspectors of an accreditation body in Poland PASE (Polish Association for Standards in Language Education) and a member of an international accreditation body EAQUALS (Evaluation and Accreditation of Quality in Language Services). As a member of the EAQUALS Certification Project, she is involved in the practical implementation of the Common European Framework of Reference for languages (CEFR) in curricula, syllabuses and assessment systems as well as in the implementations of EAQUALS CEFR-based Certificates of Achievement for students.

Neil Jones holds a PhD in Applied Linguistics from the University of Edinburgh on the application of item response theory. He was Director of the first European Survey on Language Competences (ESLC), a project co-ordinated for the European Commission by University of Cambridge ESOL Examinations (Cambridge ESOL), which published its results in June 2012. Neil's interest in learning-orientated assessment developed from a first career in English language teaching in countries including Poland and Japan, where he set up departments and teaching programme at university level. Neil has worked for Cambridge ESOL since 1993 on innovative testing developments such as item-banking and computer-adaptive testing. He has worked on the construction and use of multilingual language proficiency frameworks such as the Common European Framework of Reference for languages (CEFR), and was Research Director for the multilingual Asset Languages scheme, developed for the UK government's national languages strategy.

Sien Joos is responsible for the societal exam suite at the Certificate of Dutch as a Foreign Language. Her main research interests include test fairness and test equity as well as Language for Specific Purposes (LSP) examinations.

Marylin Kies is currently Head of the English Department at Prolingua Language Centre, a provider of tailored language training for professionals in Luxembourg. She previously spent 20 years teaching EAP/ESP (English for Academic Purposes/English for Specific Purposes) and co-ordinating the EFL certification programme at the University of Siena, Italy. She has conducted research on attitudes and motivation in relation to language certification, and since completing her MRes in Educational and Social Research with the University of London's Institute of Education has analysed the structure and content of language certification exams and has attempted to make them more transparent for professional and academic test users. Her most recent publication is 'A framework for analysing and comparing CEFR-linked certification exams' in issue 42 of the University of Cambridge ESOL Examinations journal *Research Notes* (2010).

Gudrun Klein is a psychologist and is employed as a test statistician in the test development team at telc in Frankfurt, Germany. From her former positions at several research institutions she possesses broad experience in statistical analyses and test construction methods. Currently, she is concerned with the development of a Mathematics test as part of a university admission examination aimed at applicants without formal education. Another main focus of her work is to investigate the quality of language tests both in the initial test development phase and in quality monitoring of tests in use.

Nicole Kruczek joined the University of Göttingen, Germany in 2010. Currently, she is responsible for the language test centre within the language centre. She has previously worked at Ruhr-Universität Bochum and University of Bonn, both in Germany. Her research interests are applied linguistics, the role of assessment in academic contexts and particularly teacher training. She is a member of the UNIcert® committee (German network for university language testing) and has experience in test development and teacher training in some European countries.

Lucia Luyten has been working at the Centre for Language and Education, Katholieke Universiteit Leuven (KU Leuven) since 2002. She is responsible for the academic exam suite at the Certificate of Dutch as a Foreign Language. The projects she has been focusing on are mainly situated in adult education, in particular in literacy and language testing. Her main research interests include validity, reliability, objectivity and standardisation in language testing.

Beth Mackey is a Language Testing Program Manager for the United States Department of Defense. She holds an MA in Teaching English as a Second Language and an MA in Russian and East European Studies. Her research interests are in the field of testing listening. She has served as co-chair of the Interagency Language Roundtable Testing Committee since 2003.

Waldemar Martyniuk is Assistant Professor of Applied Linguistics at the Jagiellonian University in Kraków, Poland. He is a teacher trainer, author of textbooks, curricula, and testing materials for Polish as a foreign language, visiting professor and lecturer at universities in Germany (Bochum, Giessen, Göttingen, Mainz, Münster), Switzerland (Basel), and in the United States (Stanford University). He is translator of the Common European Framework of Reference for languages into Polish (2003); and since October 2008, Executive Director at the European Centre for Modern Languages of the Council of Europe based in Graz, Austria.

Masashi Negishi is Professor of Applied Linguistics at Tokyo University of Foreign Studies (TUFS), Japan. He has participated in a number of research projects, including national education surveys and the development of English proficiency tests in Japan. He has also published several authorised English high school textbooks. His current interests focus on the application of the Common European Framework of Reference for languages (CEFR) to English language teaching in Japan, and the analysis of criterial features across the CEFR levels. He is a member of the CEFR-J Project, and is at present a member of the Japanese Ministry of Education Committee on Foreign Language Education Policy.

Marianne Nikolov is a Professor at the Department of English Applied Linguistics at the University of Pécs, Hungary; at the time the study was implemented she was a fellow at the Center for the Advanced Study in the Behavioral Sciences at Stanford University. Her research focuses on early language learning and teaching, individual differences in language learning, language testing, language policy and teacher education. Her studies have been published in *Annual Review of Applied Linguistics*, *Language Learning*, *Language Teaching Research* and various journals in Hungary. She is the author of edited volumes, many empirical studies and a monograph.

Brian North is Head of Academic Development at Eurocentres, the Swiss-based foundation with language schools in countries where the languages concerned are spoken, and is also currently Vice-Chair of the international accreditation body EAQUALS (Evaluation and Accreditation of Quality in Language Services). Both EAQUALS and Eurocentres are NGO consultants to the Council of Europe Language Policy Division. Brian has specialised in curriculum development, language testing and the formulation of language proficiency descriptors and educational quality standards. He is co-author of the Common European Framework of Reference for languages (CEFR), co-author of the Swiss and EAQUALS/ALTE European Language Portfolios, developer of the CEFR descriptor scales (his PhD) and co-ordinator of the 'CEFR Manual' team. He has led the EAQUALS Special Interest Projects (SIPs) in the areas of Curriculum and Assessment since 2007. At the time of writing he is leading an EAQUALS SIP to develop classroom CEFR-based assessment tasks for English and French.

Michaela Perlmann-Balme has been the representative of the Goethe-Institut in the Association of Language Testers in Europe (ALTE) since 1994. She currently holds the chair of the Standing Committee and has conducted seminars on benchmarking of spoken samples according to the levels of the Common European Framework of Reference for languages (CEFR). She has been involved in developing tests for migration and integration, and has been director of the project *Deutsch-Test für Zuwanderer* ('German Test for Immigrants') which began its implementation in Germany nationwide in July 2009. Currently, she is responsible for the German test items in SurveyLang, a European project on foreign language competences of school learners.

Enrica Piccardo is Assistant Professor at the Ontario Institute for Studies in Education of the University of Toronto. She has a large and international experience in language teaching and testing. Her publications in different languages (French, English, Italian and German) focus on three main domains of research: the role of creativity in second/foreign language learning, assessment and its role in the curriculum, and language teacher education. She is a specialist of the CEFR and of its impact on language education and the co-ordinator of an international project funded by the Council of Europe, *Encouraging the Culture of Evaluation among Professionals* (ECEP). She has given several talks, presentations and seminars in different countries and has published articles and book chapters in the fields of language education and teacher development. She is also editor-in-chief of the academic journal *Synergies Europe.*

Paweł Poszytek is the co-founder of the Institute for Quality in Education (IQE) which serves as the National Institute for Languages in Poland. Previously, from 1998 to 2010, he was the co-ordinator of the Lingua programme and European Language Label, then member of the managing board and the director of the Polish Socrates and LLP National Agency. He also contributed to the participation of Polish schools in the eTwinning programme. He is a former member of several advisory boards for languages at national and European level, the national co-ordinator of the Council of Europe's project *Country Profile*, a former member of the national committee for the European Language Portfolio (ELP) and a former member of the executive committee of the European Association of Language Testing and Assessment (EALTA). He is also an author of a book on language testing and a number of articles on language education. He is currently involved in the Language Rich Europe project and the social campaign, 'Language is the key. Learn Languages'.

Lorenzo Rocca is a Consultant to the Centro per la Valutazione e le Certificazioni Linguistiche (CVCL) at the University for Foreigners in Perugia. He has a degree in Classics and a postgraduate degree in the Teaching of Italian as a Foreign Language. After having been a teacher of Italian as Foreign Language and a tutor in the Master's course in the Teaching of Italian as a Foreign Language at the University for Foreigners in Perugia, he has worked in CVCL since 2004. His professional duties include marking, oral examining, item writing and presenting seminars on assessment literacy, among others. Since 2006, he has been co-ordinator of a research project concerned with the development and construction of language tests for migrants and an impact study on the link between teaching and evaluation in migration contexts. He has published both the *Specifications of the CELI (Certificati di Lingua Italiana) Exams for Migrants* and a *Knowledge of Society* book for A2 learners.

Gábor Szabó is an Assistant Professor at the Department of English Applied Linguistics, University of Pécs, Hungary. He has been involved in various national and international testing projects, including co-operation with the European Consortium for the Certificate of Attainment in Modern Languages (ECL) and the European Center for Modern Languages (ECML). Currently he is also member of the Hungarian Accreditation Board for Foreign Language Examinations. His main field of interest is the application of item response theory (IRT) in language assessment, especially applying IRT in item bank building.

Tomoko Takada is Associate Professor of English Language Pedagogy at Meikai University, Japan. She previously taught at the secondary school level, and is now a teacher trainer. Her current research interests include the implementation of the portfolio-oriented approach, and learners' attitudes and beliefs relating to foreign language learning. As a member of Professor Yukio Tono's project team, she has participated in the development of the modified version of the Common European Framework of Reference, the

CEFR-J. She has contributed to *TESOL Matters*, *JALT Journal* and *Annual Review of English Language Education in Japan*.

Yukio Tono is Professor of Corpus Linguistics at Tokyo University of Foreign Studies (TUFS), Japan. His current research interests include corpus applications in language syllabus and materials design, corpus-based analysis of learner language, second language (L2) vocabulary acquisition, and L2 lexicography. He is the author and editor of several books, including *Research on Dictionary Use* (2001), *Corpus-Based Language Studies* (2004) with Tony McEnery and Richard Xiao, *ACE CROWN English-Japanese Dictionary* (2009), *Developmental and Crosslinguistic Perspectives in Learner Corpus Research* (2012) and *Frequency Dictionary of Japanese* (forthcoming). He also directed a government-funded project for implementing a modified version of the Common European Framework of Reference (CEFR-J) into Japan.

Piet Van Avermaet is Director of the Centre for Diversity and Learning at the University of Ghent, Belgium, where he also teaches Multicultural Studies. His expertise and research interests are: diversity and social inequality in education, educational linguistics, multilingual and multicultural education, language and integration of immigrants, sociolinguistics and language testing. He worked for many years at the Centre for Language and Education at the University of Leuven, where he was co-ordinator of the Certificate Dutch as a Foreign Language (CNaVT).

Koen Van Gorp has been working at the Centre for Language and Education, Katholieke Universiteit Leuven (KU Leuven), since 1991. He specialised in second language learning, teaching and assessment. He received his PhD in Linguistics at the KU Leuven on a study of second language development and knowledge construction (April 2010). Development of teaching materials, teacher training, and project management have been part of his functions at the centre. Currently he is co-ordinator of preschool, primary and secondary education at the Centre for Language and Education. Since September 2010 he is project leader of the Certificate Dutch as a Foreign Language (CNaVT).

Katrin Wisniewski is a research assistant at the Institute of Romance Studies of the Technical University in Dresden. Her research interests are validity aspects of language testing and the linguistic analysis of learner language as used in tests, with a particular focus on spoken language (Italian and German). She is currently working on a PhD about the empirical validity of the Common European Framework of Reference for languages (CEFR) scales for fluency and vocabulary in language tests of Italian and German.

She has published studies about rating variability in the interpretation of CEFR scales, about CEFR scale validity, and about pragmatic aspects of learner language produced in tests.

Presentations at the ALTE Conference Kraków, 2011

Mohammad Alavi, Fatemeh Danesh
University of Tehran, Iran
Examining the construct validity of TOEF L-iBT reading comprehension test type using a verbal protocol approach

Vahid Aryadoust, Christine Goh
National Institute of Education, Singapore
Exploring the relative merits of cognitive diagnostic assessment models and confirmatory factor analysis

Karen Ashton
University of Cambridge ESOL Examinations, United Kingdom
The European Survey on Language Competences: comparing language learning and proficiency across Europe

Simona Catrinel Avarvarei
Ion Ionescu de la Brad University of Agricultural Sciences and Veterinary Medicine, Romania
Escaping peripherality – about language learning at university level

Professor Lyle F Bachman
University of California, Los Angeles (UCLA), United States
How do different language frameworks impact language assessment practice?

Jungok Bae, Yae-Sheik Lee, Incheol Choi, Jonathan Jordahl, Daria Soon-Young Suk
Kyungpook National University, Republic of Korea
Language and creativity

Purya Baghaei
Islamic Azad University, Department of English, Mashhad Branch, Iran
Multidimensional Rasch model for language tests with multiple subtests: an approach to improve measurement precision

Cristina Banfi, Silvia Rettaroli, Silvia Prati
Ministry of Education – City of Buenos Aires, Argentina
FL curriculum and assessment: a fruitful relationship in Buenos Aires

Khaled Barkaoui
Faculty of Education, York University, Canada
Ibtissem Knouzi
University of Toronto, Canada
Rating scales as frameworks for assessing L2 writing: examining their impact on rater performance

Lyan Bekkers, Judith Janssen
Cito, Netherlands
Rating of speaking exams: random assignment of raters to candidates and tasks

Catherine Blons-Pierre
University of Fribourg/Language Centre, Switzerland
L'impact du CECR sur le fonctionnement d'un centre de langues dans une université bilingue Suisse

Adriana Boffi Cánepa
Universidad Nacional de La Plata, Argentina
The users of the CEFR

Inmaculada Borrego Ledesma
Cursos Internacionales, Universidad de Salamanca, Spain
SURVEYLANG : un proyecto de evaluación en cinco idiomas

Maria Brau, Rachel Brooks
Federal Bureau of Investigation, United States
ILR-based translation tests

Tineke Brunfaut, Andrea Révész
Lancaster University, United Kingdom
The effect of linguistic complexity on listening test performance related to different levels of proficiency

Heidi Byrnes
Georgetown University, United States
When the frameworks don't fit: removing the glass ceiling for collegiate L2 learning

Nicola Carty
University of Glasgow, United Kingdom
A Scottish Gaelic language learning framework: values and implications

Dominique Casanova, Alexandra Crendal
Chambre de commerce et d'Industrie de Paris (DRI/E-CCIP), France
Marc Demeuse
INAS – UMONS, Belgium
Aligning the TEF (*Test d'évaluation de français*) with different language frameworks

Lucy Chambers, Chris Hubbard
University of Cambridge ESOL Examinations,United Kingdom
Online speaking examiner training: a key element in a framework of quality assurance

Xueling Chen
Shanghai Lixin University of Commerce, China
The impact of the ALTE Can-Do statements on College English teaching in China

Deshini Chetty, Ardeshir Geranpayeh
University of Cambridge ESOL Examinations, United Kingdom
Benchmarking language proficiency for the workplace

Monika Ciesielkiewicz
Messiah College, United States
El portfolio electrónico de las lenguas como herramienta didactica y de evaluación

Alina Cirlanescu
Jagiellonian University Language Centre, Poland
The Blogosphere: a new frontier in teaching and learning

Michael Corrigan
ALTE Validation Unit, United Kingdom
Linking tests to the CEFR: exploring the horizontal dimension

Michael Corrigan
ALTE Validation Unit, United Kingdom
Francesca Parizzi
CVCL, Università per Stranieri di Perugia, Italy
Measuring language competence better: perfecting grading – the CELI exams of Italian

Michael Corrigan
ALTE Validation Unit, United Kingdom
Michaela Perlmann-Balme
Goethe-Institut, Germany
Roberta Rondoni
CVCL, Università per Stranieri di Perugia, Italy
Enhancing rater performance: case studies in the implementation of enhanced systems of rater monitoring

Renato Corsetti
University of Rome 'La Sapienza', Italy
Ilona Koutny
Adam Mickiewicz University, Poland
The impact of the European Language Framework on the teaching and assessment of Esperanto

Maria Cuquejo, Xoán Rivas Cid
Xunta de Galicia, Spain
Los Certificados en Lengua Gallega (CELGA): anàlisis del sistema y desafíos

Clara de Vega, Marta Garcia
Cursos Internacionales Universidad de Salamanca, Spain
CER TIUNI: Accreditation of language levels in the Spanish university sector

Ágnes Dévény
Budapest Business School, Faculty of Commerce, Catering and Tourism, Hungary
Foreign language mediation task in a criterion-referenced proficiency examination

Thomas Eckes, Frank Weiss-Motz, Stefanie Whelan-Mostofizadeh
TestDaF Institute, Germany
A study of differential item functioning in the TestDaF Reading and Listening sections

Robert Edwards
Université de Sherbrooke, Canada
The development of a test of academic writing ability
in French as a second language

Melanie Ellis
Instytut Badań Edukacyjnych, Poland
Borderlines: a data-driven description of the limits of A2 spoken performance

Ina Ferbežar, Marko Stabej
Univerza v Ljubljani, Slovenia
Slovene or not Slovene? Testing speakers of closely related languages

Johann Fischer
Georg-August-Universität Göttingen, Germany
Stefania Dugovičová
Comenius University, Slovakia
Catherine Chouissa
Université de Strasbourg, France
Guidelines for task-based university LSP testing

Vincent Folny, Sébastien Georges
Centre international d'études pedagogiques (CIEP), France
Analyse du jugement des panelistes ayant participé au Standard Setting du Test de Connaissance du Français (TCF)

Jenö Fonyódi
ITK, Hungary
The Hungarian Junior Exam

Jon-Simon Gartzia
Basque Government, Spain
Ética y fiabilidad en la corección de la producción escrita o Redacción

Tatjana Gochkova- Stojanovska, Iskra Panovska-Dimkova
'Blazhe Koneski' Faculty of Philology, 'SS. Cyril and Methodius' University, The Former Yugoslav Republic of Macedonia
Setting standards in teaching and assessmentof Macedonian as a foreign language

Anthony Green
University of Bedfordshire, United Kingdom
The impact of the CEFR on the content of a test of grammar and vocabulary

Giuliana Grego Bolli
Università per Stranieri, Perugia, Italy
Migration policies in Italy in relation to language requirements. The project 'Italiano, lingua nostra': impact and limitations

Maria José Grosso, Catarina Isabel, Sousa Gaspar
Centro de Avaliação de Português Língua Estrangeira (CAPLE), Universidade de Lisboa, Portugal
Previous knowledge of communicative language ability and its consequences in foreign language assessment

Rachida Guelzim
British Council, Morocco
The CEFR – an instrument for coordinating language learning, language teaching and assessment in the world

Bertil Geurts
Cito, Netherlands
CEFR and vocabulary

Susan Hackett
National Qualifications Authority of Ireland – Accreditation & Coordination of English Language Services, Ireland
The relationship and impact of the Irish National Framework of Qualifications on assessment in ELT: an exploration

Baocheng Han
Beijing Foreign Studies University, China
Hongjiang Li, Wenlong Shi
Beijing Education Examinations Authority, China
Developing the national English proficiency scales to improve English education in China

Baocheng Han
Beijing Foreign Studies University, China
Hongjiang Li, Wenlong Shi
Beijing Education Examinations Authority, China
Revising the oral exam (BOEC) and linking it to the new Chinese EFL proficiency scales

Anthony Harvey
University of Cambridge ESOL Examinations, France
David Horner
ENSAE ParisTech, France
International certification in French state schools: the first three years of the project

Ursula Hehl
University of Bonn, Germany
Nicole Kruczek
ZESS – Georg-August- Universität Göttingen, Germany
The impact of the CEFR on teaching and assessment at university language centres

Sahbi Hidri
Higher Institute of Languages in Tunis, Tunisia
A theoretical framework of validating the test task characteristics of listening comprehension tests: impacts on learning, teaching and assessment

Laura van Hofwegen, Henk Kuijper
Cito, Netherlands
Relating examinations to the CEFR: checks and balances

Piotr Horbatowski
Jagiellonian University, Poland
Wpływ egzaminów certyfikatowych na proces nauczania, na podstawie egzaminówz języka polskiegoprzeprowadzonych w Tokio

David Horner
ENSAE ParisTech, France
Towards a new phonological control grid

Eunice Jang
Ontario Institute for Studies in Education, Canada
Democratic validation of the Steps to English Proficiency assessment framework

Neil Jones
University of Cambridge ESOL Examinations, United Kingdom
Defining an inclusive framework for languages

Neil Jones, Karen Ashton
University of Cambridge ESOL Examinations, United Kingdom
SurveyLang and the European Survey on Language Competences

Piotr Kajak
Polonicum, University of Warsaw, Poland
Kultura popularna w Europejskim Systemie Opisu Kształcenia Językowego

Anne Katz
The New School, San Francisco, United States
Margo Gottlieb
World-Class Instructional Design & Assessment Consortium, United States
The evolution of standards-referenced language frameworks: implications for instruction and assessment of young language learners

Marylin Kies
Prolingua Luxembourg, Luxumbourg
How frameworks can help test users choose appropriate certification exams for their needs

Gudrun Klein
telc GmbH, Germany
Do gender, age and first language predict the results in the 'Deutschtest für Zuwanderer' (DTZ)?

Wassilios Klein
telc GmbH, Germany
Audiovisuelle Rezeption (Hör-Sehverstehen) im GER und Ansätze für eine Umsetzung in Online-Tests

Miyoko Kobayashi
Kumamoto University, Japan
Hiroshi Moritani
Tokiwa University, Japan
Examining language frameworks: a qualitative analysis of two Japanese language tests

Henk Kuijper
Cito, Netherlands
Dittany Rose
University of Cambridge ESOL Examinations, United Kingdom
A framework for quality management: the ALTE audit approach

Galina Kurteva, Desislava Dimitrova
New Bulgarian University, Bulgaria
The CEFR and Bulgarian as a foreign language: some methodological questions about teaching and assessment

Gisella Langé
Ministry of Education – Lombardy Education Authority, Italy
The impact of different frameworks and of CLIL mainstreaming in the Italian school system

Michel Laurier
University of Montreal, Canada
Different frameworks for different needs

Bozena Lechowska
Universidad Industrial de Santander, Colombia
Bilingual Colombia and the Common European Framework of Reference for Languages: an analysis of language policy from Colombia

Constant Leung
King's College, United Kingdom
Jo Lewkowicz
Lingwistyczna Szkoła Wyższa, Poland
Assessing communicative competence – focusing on participatory engagement

Tziona Levi
Tel-Aviv University, Israel
The effect of Dynamic Assessment on learners' performance in EFL oral proficiency tests

Gad Lim, Angela ffrench
University of Cambridge ESOL Examinations, United Kingdom
The function of providing coherence: a framework applied to writing assessment

Ling-Ying Lin, Pei-Jiun Lan
Steering Committee for the Test Of Proficiency-Huayu, Taiwan
Cut-off scores of the new Chinese proficiency test based on the Angoff Standard Setting Method

Ling-Ying Lin, Pei-Jiun Lan
Steering Committee for the Test Of Proficiency-Huayu, Taiwan
Li-Ping Chang
National Taiwan Normal University, Taiwan
The Chinese Profile Project

Denise Lussier
McGill University, Canada
Planning curriculum and testing in intercultural communicative competence

Beth Mackey
US Department of Defense, United States
Rachel Brooks
Federal Bureau of Investigation, United States
Who, what, where, WENS? The native speaker in the ILR Skill Level Descriptions

Margaret Malone
Center for Applied Linguistics, United States
Understanding language testing frameworks: efforts to improve applications for assessment in the United States

Waldemar Martyniuk
Jagiellonian University, Poland
The plurilingual and intercultural approach of the Council of Europe and its implications for evaluation and assessment in language education

Liz McIlvanney, Joëlle Crowle
Bologna University, Italy
Lexical features of reading tasks in Italian university 'CEF -indexed' proficiency and placement tests

Bruno Mègre, Sébastien Georges
Centre international d'etudes pédagogiques (CIEP), France
L'évaluation de la production écrite: le cas du TCF

Branislav Meszaros
Université Paris Descartes, France
Mesurer l'impact du CECR via les Référentiels sur les supports textuels en francais langue étrangère

Iwona Misztal
Jagiellonian University Medical College, Poland
Testing English for Specific Purposes in Science

Martina Mollering
Macquarie University, Australia
Testing language, testing culture: citizenship testing and linguistic integration in Germany and Australia

Machteld Moonen, Rick de Graaff
Utrecht University, Netherlands
Alessandra Corda
Leiden University, ICLON, Netherlands
Implementing the CEFR in Dutch secondary education: impact on language teachers' educational and assessment practice

Steve Morris
Swansea University – Academi Hywel Teifi, United Kingdom
Developing a core vocabulary for A1/A2 in a lesser-used language: a case study in Welsh

Abel Murcia Soriano, Fernando López Murcia
Instituto Cervantes Cracovia, Poland
Implicaciones de la aparición del MCRE en la red de Centros del Instituto Cervantes. El ejemplo del Instituto Cervantes de Cracovia

Masashi Negishi, Yukio Tono
Tokyo University of Foreign Studies, Japan
Tomoko Takada
Meikai University, Japan
A progress report on the development of the CEFR –J

Marianne Nikolov
University of Pecs, Hungary
Developing diagnostic tests for young learners of English as a foreign language in grades 1 to 6

Brian North
EAQUALS, Switzerland
Elżbieta Jarosz
EAQUALS/Bell Kraków, Poland
Implementing the CEFR in teacher-based assessment at a language school: approaches and challenges

Sabina Nowak
Państwowa Wyższa Szkoła Zawodowa w Tarnowie, Poland
The need for content and language integrated learning (CLIL) development

Tony O'Brien
British Council, Poland
Paweł Poszytek
Fundacja Instytut Jakoœci w Edukacji, Poland
The construct of the Index of European Language Policy and Practices

Ana Larissa Oliveira
UFMG, Brazil
Critical English teaching in Brazil: is it time for a more inclusive approach to assessment?

Szilvia Papp
University of Cambridge ESOL Examinations, United Kingdom
Shelagh Rixon
Warwick University, United Kingdom
The link between teaching, learning and assessment of young learners of English worldwide: survey results

José Pascoal
University of Lisbon, Portugal
The CEFR and curriculum standards versus language proficiency: a two-sided story?

Dr Michaela Perlmann-Balme
Goethe-Institut, Germany
The comparability of the A1-level across five European languages based on the experience of the European Survey of Language Competences

Olena Petrashchuk
National Aviation University, Aviation English Assessment and Testing Centre, Ukraine
Measurability of oral speech samples

Enrica Piccardo
OISE University of Toronto, Canada
'Assessment recollected in tranquility': the ECEP project and the key concepts of the CEFR

Sibylle Plassmann
telc GmbH, Germany
A framework for the family language – learning Turkish at German schools

Paweł Poszytek
Fundacja Instytut Jakoœci w Edukacji, Poland
The impact of the CEFR on language policy in Poland

Laura Puigdoménech Farell
General Directorate of Language Policy, Generalitat de Catalunya, Spain
Developing a new C2 certificate from scratch: the Catalan approach

Paz Rabanal García
Cursos Internacionales, Universidad de Salamanca, Spain
El nuevo examen DELE de nivel C1 y su adaptación al Marco Común Europeo
Romualda Raguotiene
Vilnius Psychological Pedagogical Service, Lithuania
Reading competence, linguistic and social contexts of the students

Angeliki Salamoura
University of Cambridge ESOL Examinations, United Kingdom
Annette Capel
Cambridge University Press, United Kingdom
Building the English Vocabulary Profile for the CEFR: implications for learning, teaching and assessment

Nick Saville
University of Cambridge ESOL Examinations, United Kingdom
Language testing and access – a framework for considering the issues

Anna Seretny
Jagiellonian University, Poland
Standaryzacja wymagań leksykalnych – znajomość słownictwa jako parametr oceny stopnia biegłości językowej w polskich egzaminach certyfikatowych

Joseph Sheils
Formerly Head of the Language Policy Division, Council of Europe
Council of Europe core values and language policies for migration

Professor Elana Shohamy
Tel-Aviv University, Israel
An engagement with the CEFR: a critical view and time for change

Poorvadevi Sreekanthan
Ebek Language Laboratories, India
From A to B to C: exhibiting differential levels of language competence

Magdalena Szpotowicz
Instytut Badań Edukacyjnych, Poland
Challenges of measuring young learners' language development during their school education

Julia Todorinova, Mardik Andonyan,, Aspazia Borisova
Sofia University, Department for Language Teaching, Bulgaria
The impact of language frameworks on teaching and assessment in Bulgarian as a foreign language

Geoff Tranter, Martin Beck
MONDIALE-Testing GmbH, Switzerland
Developing online tests for technical English –needs and provisions

Erwin Tschirner
University of Leipzig, Germany
Elvira Swender
ACTFL, United States
The impact of the ACTFL Proficiency Guidelines on teaching foreign languages in the US

Paul Tucker
University of Bedfordshire, United Kingdom
Identifying and measuring diagnostic profiles of lexical proficiency at the Intermediate/Advanced Threshold

Przemyslaw Turek
Jagiellonian University, Poland
The certification of Slavic languages according to European standards and the special case of Macedonian

Aylin Unaldi
Bogazici University, Turkey
Revisiting the assessment of academic reading

Piet Van Avermaet
Ghent University, Belgium
Language testing for integration – access through closed gates?

Koen Van Gorp, Sien Joos, Bart Deygers
CNaVT, KULeuven, Belgium
The influence of the CEFR on rating scale design: a case study of the CNaVT

Koen Van Gorp, Lucia Luyten
CNaVT, KULeuven, Belgium
Quantitative test analysis for lesser taught languages: pitfalls and strategies

Rafael Santiago Vidal Uribe
Centro Nacional de Evaluacíon para la Educacíon Superior (Ceneval AC), Mexico
El Centro Nacional de Evaluación para la Educación superior (Ceneval) y el desarrollo del ECELE

Dina Vîlcu, Ioana Sonea
Babeş-Bolyai University, Romania
The CEFR: an instrument for standardisation or a procrustean solution? The case of Romanian as a Foreign Language

Katerina Vlasáková, Katerina Hlínová
Charles University in Prague, Czech Republic
The impact of the CEFR on language courses and examinations at ILPS CU: challenges

Dianne Wall, Cathy Taylor
Trinity College London, United Kingdom
Barry O'Sullivan
Roehampton University, United Kingdom
Using a framework to establishing evidence of construct: a case study

Daniel Waller
University of Central Lancashire, School of Languages and International Studies, United Kingdom
Metadiscourse markers in timed essay writing at levels B2 and C1 of the CEFR

Cyril Weir
University of Bedfordshire, United Kingdom
The big picture – a historical frame of reference

Katrin Wisniewski
Technical University of Dresden, Germany
Assessing L2 oral fluency with the CEFR

Sha Wu
National Education Examination Authority, China
Profile of Advanced Competence in English (PACE) – a new ESP exam system in China

Yoriko Yamada-Bochynek
OJAE (Oral Japanese Assessment Europe), Germany
Michiko Takagi
ICHEC, Brussels Management School, Belgium
OJAE (Oral Japanese Assessment Europe) CEFR – orientated: report, DVD with benchmarked video samples, problems, and perspectives

Sakiko Yoneda
Hokuriku Gakuin University, Japan
Jason Hughes
Hokuriku Gakuin Junior College, Japan
CEFR – aligned Cambridge testing outcomes in Japan and challenges to adopting a global evaluation standard

Ewa Zajdler
University of Warsaw, Faculty of Oriental Studies, Department of Chinese Studies, Poland
Optimizing the process of basic modern Chinese teaching and proficiency tests for adults in sinological glottodidactics in the Polish language environment

Beate Zeidler
telc GmbH, Germany
Aspects of item difficulty in the receptive skills

Boris Zhigalev
Nizhniy Novgorod State Linguistics University, Russian Federation
Writing as the aim and means in teaching a foreign language: problems of assessment